Writing Western History

Writing Western History

ESSAYS ON MAJOR WESTERN HISTORIANS

Edited by
Richard W. Etulain

Published in cooperation with the
UNM Center for the American West

University of New Mexico Press: ALBUQUERQUE

Library of Congress Cataloging-in-Publication Data

Writing western history : essays on major western historians / edited by
Richard W. Etulain. — 1st ed.
      p.   cm.
   "Published in cooperation with the UNM Center for the American
West."
   Includes bibliographical references.
   ISBN 0–8263–1288–8 (hardback). — ISBN 0–8263–1289–6 (pbk.)
   1. West (U.S.)—Historiography. 2. Historians—West (U.S.)
I. Etulain, Richard W. II. University of New Mexico. Center for
the American West.
F591.W88   1991
978'.0072--dc20   91-15290
                                                           CIP

Design: Susan Gutnik

© 1991 by the University of New Mexico Press
First edition.

For my colleague
Gerald D. Nash,
historiographical pioneer

Contents

III
RECENT WESTERN HISTORIANS

Acknowledgments

The contributors to this volume would like to thank the following institutions for permission to quote manuscript materials from their collections: the Huntington Library, the State Historical Society of Wisconsin, the Bentley Historical Library of the University of Michigan, and the Barker Texas History Center of the University of Texas.

In addition, the editor is indebted to the Research Allocations Committee at the University of New Mexico for supporting his research. He also wishes to thank Earl Pomeroy, Martin Ridge, Gerald D. Nash, and Walter Nugent for their helpful suggestions in planning the volume. Pat Devejian typed several sections of the manuscript, and she and Thomas Jaehn also proofread various versions of the volume. Most of all, the editor is grateful to the group of busy scholars who prepared these essays.

Introduction

The Rise of
Western Historiography

RICHARD W. ETULAIN

$\mathcal{B}$ETWEEN 1880 AND THE
mid-1920s, western American historiography emerged, flowered, and
became a major ingredient in American historical writing. In the first
two decades of this nearly half-century, historians such as Francis Parkman, H. H. Bancroft, and Justin Winsor were completing their long
careers or publishing their best-known works, while others like Josiah
Royce, Theodore Roosevelt, and Frederick Jackson Turner were finishing
their first work on the frontier or American West. Although many
writers had discussed the frontier from the moment they landed on
the shores of the New World and although a variety of historians continued to discuss the new country to the west during the seventeenth,
eighteenth, and early nineteenth centuries, it was not until the 1880s
and 1890s that a notable group of academic and lay historians took the
moving frontier or regional West as their major focus. Later, in the first
two or three decades of the twentieth century, other historians built
primarily on these earlier interpretations, established an organization
and major journal for "western" history, and embedded the frontier
and West as a central theme in American historiography.[1]

Before viewing a nascent western historiography of the 1880s and
1890s through the eyes of Frederick Jackson Turner, however, one needs
at least a sketchy introduction to what writers were saying about the
American West in the earlier decades of the nineteenth century. Two
strains characterize these pioneer historiographical efforts: one emerges
from the accounts of explorers and travelers in the first half of the cen-

1

tury, and the other springs from Wild West literature so popular after midcentury.

In the opening decades of the nineteenth century such explorers as Meriwether Lewis and William Clark, Zebulon Pike, and Stephen H. Long (Long's account was written by Edwin James) produced factual records of their expeditions into the West, emphasizing first of all what they saw and did. Rather than providing imaginative reshapings of their experiences, these writers stressed the flora and fauna they encountered, described the terrain they crossed, and furnished rather straightforward descriptions of western Indian groups. Although nearly two-thirds of the Lewis and Clark journals were excised by the prudish Philadelphia lawyer Nicholas Biddle before they were published and much of their freshness was emasculated, and even though James's account of Long's expedition misled many Americans for nearly a half-century into thinking the central and lower plains were a Great American Desert, these accounts were much less romanticized and exaggerated than the works of the Wild West tradition.[2]

Three other well-known eastern literary figures—James Fenimore Cooper, Washington Irving, and Francis Parkman—published notable works about the West in the generation stretching from the 1820s to the 1840s. A man of country-gentry backgrounds who never traveled west of his native New York, Cooper created the most notable frontier hero of the nineteenth century, Natty Bumppo, or the Deerslayer, in his five-volume Leatherstocking Saga. Obviously drawn to his hero and the wilderness he inhabited, Cooper nonetheless betrayed an ambivalence about Natty's uncivilized and sometimes boorish actions. As English writer and critic D. H. Lawrence explained, Cooper loved Natty and his wilderness but seemed afraid that he would belch at dinner.

The historical volumes of Irving and Parkman, who both made short visits to the West, also contain these conceptual ambiguities. During a month-long stay in present-day Oklahoma, Irving took copious factual notes and later read widely in appropriate historical works for his writings on the West, but when he prepared such works as *A Tour of the Prairies* (1835), *Astoria* (1836), and *The Adventures of Captain Bonneville* (1837) for publication, he "shaped" his notes, separating the uncivilized West from the cultured East, romanticizing the wilderness through which his explorers trudged, and making explicit the social distinctions between his unpolished frontiersmen and their sophisticated eastern companions. Boston Brahmin Francis Parkman likewise followed this pattern of love for the primitive and pristine wilderness but snobbish distaste for many of those who inhabited this Eden. From his earliest years Parkman cultivated a "cult of masculinity," much as three other easterners—Theodore Roosevelt, Owen Wister, and Frederic Remington—would do at the end of the century. Yet once in the wilderness with Indians and frontiersmen—"the society of savages and men little better than savages"—Parkman produced his classic account of *The Oregon Trail* (1849), as much an illustration of the ethnocentricism of a Proper Bostonian as a factual account of the frontier in the late 1840s.[3]

Richard Dana and Susan Shelby Magoffin—two other sophisticated nonwesterners—also illustrate this ambivalent attitude toward the West. A New Englander and Harvard student, Dana shipped before the mast and visited Mexican California in the 1830s. From this voyage and a stay on the West Coast came his popular book *Two Years Before the Mast* (1840) in which Dana provided telling descriptions of California coastal life; but his narrative, filtered through his puritanical predilections, depicted the Californios as lazy, illiterate, and unprogressive. As a young, well-educated bride on her way in 1846 from Kentucky to Mexico, and as one of the first Anglo women to travel the Santa Fe Trail, Magoffin praised the politeness of New Mexicans and drew appealing word-pictures of their food and dances but was even more repulsed by other actions. "The women slap about with their arms and necks bare, perhaps their bosoms exposed (and they are none of the prettiest or whitest)," she wrote in *Down the Santa Fe Trail and into Mexico*; and when they crossed a creek, she added, "they pull their dresses . . . up above their knees and paddle through the water like ducks. . . . I am constrained to keep my veil drawn closely over my face all the time to protect my blushes." Still other visitors to the Southwest complained of the cigarillos Mexicanas smoked and the low-necked dresses they wore.[4]

By the outbreak of the Civil War, historical writings about the West had fallen into recognizable patterns. Some travelers had written factual records of what they had seen and done; other narratives, like those by Irving, Parkman, and Magoffin, were as much revelations of the writer's biases as historical narratives. All these books were by outsiders: the West as viewed through eastern eyes. Although these writings failed to exhibit a single viewpoint, they often revealed an ambivalence that cherished the open landscape and freedom of the West on the one hand but hesitated to embrace frontier characters and sociocultural life on the other.

Meanwhile, images of the frontier and American West as Wild West had gradually emerged before 1800. New England Puritans, for instance, spoke of the frontier as a howling wilderness, infested with a dark Devil and his minions and barbaric Indians. Forced because of economic circumstances to move onto that evil frontier, Puritans and other early Americans structured captivity narratives and stories of military or hunter heroes like Daniel Boone to dramatize "civilization" overcoming remote regions inhabited by "savage" Indians.[5]

These varied images colored the visions of persons visiting or writing about the West in the nineteenth century. Despite their variety, however, these myths about the West had a unifying core: since the West was less advanced than the East, it needed civilizing agents, and progress dictated that less advanced people and ideologies must give way to higher laws of progress and civilization. The West was truly wild—in need of giant doses of society and culture, which the East alone could provide.

This Wild West ideology powered much thinking and planning about the West in the nineteenth century. Religious and educational leaders such as Lyman Beecher and his daughter Catharine pointed to the frontier as a vital part of the country's future, but as a territory that needed to be "saved" through an infusion of ministers and teachers. Political and economic spokesmen reiterated this need to win the West from lesser peoples and to preserve it for worthy Americans. Given this rather widespread consensus about the West, it is not surprising that much of the writing about the region in the nineteenth century portrayed it as a wild and unsettled section.

In the decades after the Civil War, these depictions of a Wild West took two forms. One was the treatment of historical figures as larger-than-life characters in history, biography, and fiction; the other was the creation of legendary figures, based usually on oral traditions, who figured prominently in folklore and literature. Biographers and historians often used historical figures such as Billy the Kid, Calamity Jane, Wild Bill Hickok, and Kit Carson to create the sensational heroes and heroines needed to capture a Wild West. In these romantic accounts Billy the Kid kills a bad man for each of his twenty-one years, Calamity Jane rides and shoots like a hellcat, Wild Bill is flashingly quick with his fists and guns, and the small, wiry Kit Carson becomes a ring-tailed roarer, a gigantic Samson. Since for these writers the West was a wild, forbidding place, only historical persons depicted as strong-armed demigods could be victorious and thus pave the way for western settlement.[6]

The most significant of the historical figures who became legends in their own time was William Frederick "Buffalo Bill" Cody. A former Pony Express rider, buffalo hunter, scout, and Indian fighter, Cody also fathered the Wild West show, which probably did more than any other attraction to popularize the West as a wild frontier. An experienced pioneer, a compelling dramatist of his exploits, and a perceptive judge of Americans' instincts, Cody opened a Wild West exhibition in 1883, which dramatized one frenetic appearance after another: stagecoach holdups, trick riding and shooting, Indian fights, and appearances by Annie Oakley ("little sure shot"), Buck Taylor ("King of the Cowboys"), and Chief Sitting Bull. So successful was the Wild West show that it toured the United States for many years and even made appearances in several European cities. It also inspired several competitors. Others, seeing the popularity of Buffalo Bill's extravaganzas, copied his program, and together they began a tradition of such frontier exhibitions that lasted well into the 1930s. If audiences had questions about the nature of the American West, Cody and his Wild West and other such blowouts assured them that it was indeed a land of riders, ropers, and renegades—superheroes of the sagebrush. Conversely, there were no places for farmers and city citizens.

In the fertile twilight zone between fact and imagination, legendary frontier heroes took root late in the nineteenth and early in the twentieth centuries. In the northern West, the gigantic lumberjack Paul Bunyan and his enormous companion Babe the Blue Ox stalked through forests and lumber camps like a whirlwind armed with sharp axes. When Paul mistakenly dragged his spiked pole he gouged the Grand Canyon. Together, Paul and Babe hollowed out Puget Sound—Paul used a glacier for a scoop—so they would have a place to store their logs. Following in Bunyan's seven-league strides were Pecos Bill, the supercowboy of the Southwest who rode a mountain lion with barbed-wire reins; or Febold Feboldson, the titanic Nebraska farmer who fashioned knots in the tails of tornadoes as they flashed over the plains. Here was a pantheon of manufactured gargantuan western heroes whose mien and deeds illustrate the fearless, mighty people needed to save and settle the West.

At the same time that popular histories, biographies, newspaper stories, and such events as the Wild West shows were launching the careers of several historical and legendary Wild West heroes and heroines, the dime-novel Western arose to provide a new outlet. The discovery of an inexpensive method of printing newspapers and books, especially nickel and dime novels produced on pulp paper, allowed publishing firms to turn out thousands of cheap novels for the tidal wave of new readers after the Civil War. More than half of these sensationalized novels dealt with the frontier or American West, thereby greatly increasing the possibilities for overly dramatic and sentimentalized depictions of the Wild West.

From the 1860s on, dozens of authors, nearly all of whom were easterners with little knowledge of the West, utilized such new heroes as Kit Carson, Billy the Kid, Calamity Jane, and Buffalo Bill for their dime novels. No matter that the lives of these protagonists were created without fear or research; eastern readers bought dime novels by the hundreds of thousands and evidently believed much of what they were reading about a region and society foreign to them. Not content with revising and tinkering with the lives of historical figures, other writers created fictional frontier figures such as Deadwood Dick, Rattlesnake Ned, and the Black Avenger. They too were endowed with the physical prowess, stamina, and derring-do that characterized their historical brothers and sisters. Authors of dime novels were more than happy to provide whatever kind of characters satisfied the wish-needs of their readers.[7]

But the pell-mell actions of these stereotyped characters who rode like the wind, killed several Indians with one hand, and also won the heroine's attention could become tiresome. By the 1890s sales of dime novels had fallen off rapidly—just as the cowboy, the newest and most romantic figure, galloped onto the scene. While some of the earliest literary and artistic depictions of the cowpuncher treated him as unruly and in need of a dose of refinement, by the time novelist Owen Wister and artist Frederic Remington became his champions in the 1890s they pictured him as a buoyant, romantic hero stripped of the excessive heroics of earlier Wild West characters but sufficiently vivacious and charming to gain large audiences for theirs and similar works dealing with the cowboy. The publication of Wister's cowboy stories in leading magazines of the 1890s—often accompanied by Remington illustrations— and the eventual appearance of his classic Western *The Virginian* (1902) prepared the way for a long line of popular Westerns stretching from the works of Zane Grey, Ernest Haycox, and Luke Short to the Westerns of the most popular writer of them all, Louis L'Amour. While these popular Westerns were more literary than the dime novels, they too capitulated before the hunger for a Wild West that arose well before 1900 and continues to the present time. Although the Wild West tradition did not exclusively dominate the literary and historiographical scene in the 1880s and 1890s, it did profoundly influence nearly everyone writing about the frontier and American west, including historians writing about those topics during that period.[8]

Of the first professional frontier historians, Frederick Jackson Turner pondered more deeply than the others *what* ought to be written about the frontier and *how* these writings should bear on what other historians of the time were writing about the American past. Indeed, a closer look than previous commentators have given to Turner's observations about historical methods and approaches during the 1890s supplies a useful introduction to the first stages of western historiography. Turner was profoundly interested in what he considered the best approaches to American history as well as intrigued with how new ways to study the frontier would reshape what his contemporaries thought about the American past. More than anything, Turner wanted to reorient the study of American history, which would include much more concentration on the large role the frontier had played in shaping the American past.[9]

Convinced that Atlantic Coast historians knew little about the trans-Appalachian frontier, Turner frequently argued that this oversight led to a skewed vision of the American past. Even before he had published his first substantive essays, he wrote to his mentor William Allen at the University of Wisconsin to criticize the graduate offerings in American history at Johns Hopkins University, where he was enrolled for his doctorate. "The great lack of it all," he told Allen, "is in getting any proper conception of the Great West. Not a man here that I know of is either studying, or hardly aware of the country beyond the Alleghenies. . . ."[10] Moreover, as he revealed to one of his students, Carl Becker, years later, his pathbreaking essay on the importance of the American frontier "was pretty much a *reaction*" to what he considered the mistaken notions of his Hopkins mentor, Herbert Baxter Adams, who insisted to his students "that American institutional history had been well *done*. That we would better turn next to European institutions!" "Due to my indignation," Turner added to Becker, he determined to show others the significance of the frontier.[11]

If easterners were overlooking the palpable influences of the Great West, how could their mistaken ways be mended? Turner would show them—by admonition and by example. When he came to write his dissertation and his first essays, Turner practiced what he preached, treating the Indian trade in Wisconsin in broad perspective and noting frontier topics that merited attention. In his published dissertation, a revision and expansion of his master's thesis, Turner endeavored, among other things, to show how western events both illuminated and influenced national and international happenings. Centering on trade with Indians in Wisconsin, Turner moved on from this local topic to show that strong competition for trade among the French, English, and Americans markedly influenced international diplomatic rivalries and national political and economic policies. Without saying so, Turner was demonstrating how western affairs were of central importance for understanding economic, political, and diplomatic affairs of the seventeenth, eighteenth, and early nineteenth centuries.[12]

One year later, in his provocative essay "Problems in American History," Turner sounded a familiar note. Using the writings of Hermann von Holst as example, Turner asserted that von Holst and other historians of his persuasion were too tied to the issues of slavery and the Civil War and had "lost sight of the fundamental, dominating fact of United States history, the expansion of the United States from the Alleghenies to the Pacific." "The real lines of American development, the forces dominating our character," Turner continued, "are to be studied in the history of westward expansion."[13] If easterners, as well as other American historians, would trace the geographical, institutional, and constitutional impact of Indians on American policy and plot the wave-after-wave movements of immigrants into the trans-Allegheny areas, they would be able to show the largest influences of the frontier on American history.

Seen as a continuation of this line of thinking, Turner's best-known essay, "The Significance of the Frontier in American History," becomes part of his quarrel with eastern historians for continuing to overlook the power of the frontier. Turner makes that point clear early on by boldly stating, "The true point of view of the history of this nation is not the Atlantic coast, it is the Great West." Indeed, he might have retitled his notable article "Research Opportunities in Frontier History," for, as he wrote, the essay was intended "to call attention to the frontier as a fertile field for investigation, and to suggest some of the problems which arise in connection with it."[14] Beginning with the "Indian Trader's Frontier," Turner moved through successive groups coming to the frontier and asked his listeners and readers to consider carefully the large impact these experiences had made on American history and character. Together, these three writings, his dissertation and two early essays, furnish one of Turner's illuminating convictions about American historiography in the early 1890s: it was badly in need of reorientation with a refocusing by eastern historians, especially, on the Great West and its major influence on the American past.

These early writings by Turner—as well as many of his later ones—calling for a new perspective on the frontier contained a good deal of regional chauvinism, although Turner undoubtedly would not have thought so. Repeatedly, he called attention to the history and peoples between the Appalachians and Mississippi as the locus of so much that was of benefit to America, its democracy, its corporate nationality, and its individualism. And for his own Wisconsin and its state university Turner served as an ideal drummer, selling to others what he considered the reformist, go-ahead, democratic spirit of the state and its educational system.[15]

Turner was also elated, for example, when the American Historical Association chose Cleveland as its meeting site for 1897. Writing to another colleague about the convention agenda, he urged more emphasis on the West: "I wish we might have a full representation of Western history on the program. We ought to try to secure papers from Western men in the Pacific Coast, the Prairie West, the Southwest, and Old Northwest and the Old Southwest. With our more central location, it would be well to make a particular effort to give a national aspect to our program." He admitted that he might "be over zealous" in his efforts in behalf of his region, but "more attention should be paid" to its history; and so he "rejoiced in the selection of Cleveland partly because of the stimulus it will give to Western history work."[16] If some of these comments smacked of regional defensiveness, the spirit remained strong in western historiography and in other western intellectual efforts well into the twentieth century. Later westerners such as Walter Prescott Webb and Bernard DeVoto frequently bragged of western virtues and achievements while they concurrently denounced the colonialism they felt the East had thrust upon the West and the South. Not until after World War II did most of this defensive spirit disappear from western historical writings.[17]

But Turner did not expend all of his critical darts on eastern historians; he saved some of his sharpest barbs for earlier and contemporary interpreters of the West. If writers like von Holst and James Ford Rhodes were too caught up in writing about sectional conflicts between the North and South and thereby overlooked the West, too many of the writers treating the West had fallen victim to romantic narration, stultifying antiquarianism, and overemphasized detail. If the West were to be treated truthfully, these historiographical pitfalls also must be avoided.

Who were these misguided historians of the West, and what were specific evidences of their mistakes? Here, Turner was less ready to name names and to point a finger. But his later private correspondence and some of his early reviews clarify his general discontent with previous interpreters of the West. In 1922, Turner succinctly summarized in a letter to Constance Skinner what was being written about the frontier when his career was launched:

> *I began my publication when [Theodore] Roosevelt and [Justin]*
> *Winsor were active, and my colleague, [Reuben Gold] Thwaites*
> *soon took up his editorial work. Roosevelt, though with a breadth*
> *of interests, was more concerned with* men *than with*
> *institutions, and especially with the strenuous life, and more*
> *particularly, the fighting frontier. Winsor approached the West*
> *as a cartographer and librarian. Thwaites' instincts were toward*
> *the romantic side, and toward editorial publication.*[18]

Turner's reviews of these three men's major works, as well as those of Francis Parkman, are generally positive, but he also clearly expresses his dissatisfactions. Although saluting the pathbreaking, literary, and lively qualities of Roosevelt's multivolume *Winning of the West*, Turner thinks the author should be more interested in institutional development in the West, that region's influence on the East, and the "later history of events in the areas across which the waves of pioneers have passed." Granted, Roosevelt moves beyond previous local historians in working in several American archives and in embedding his narrative in broader international perspectives than they had considered, but he is not "disposed . . . to devote as much attention to social and economic aspects of the [westward] movement as the student of the period would like to have him give." Moreover, Roosevelt's work leans "to the romantic side" of his subject, with sometimes too much emphasis on the heroic, derring-do of individual frontier leaders.[19]

Turner has much less to say about Winsor, the librarian, cartographer, and historian of Harvard. In reviewing Winsor's *Westward Movement* (1898), Turner praises the author's thoroughness and breadth as well as his factualness. If Roosevelt is intrigued with the picturesque, vivacious leaders, and stirring campaigns, Winsor is more interested in exhaustively detailing his stories. "He knew the uses of the card catalogue," Turner writes, and "loved an abundance of facts." Still, he lacks the "artistic instinct" and the "historical imagination" to give framework and meaning to his mountains of "classified cards." In short,

Westward Movement is a "thesaurus of events for the student, rather than a history for the general reader."[20] Missing here, Turner seems to conclude, is the interpretive design that would suffuse Winsor's indefatigable labors with the power and larger meanings that frontier history needed.

For Thwaites, his Wisconsin colleague, and for Francis Parkman, one of his schoolboy favorites, Turner has much less criticism. He commends Thwaites's tireless and immensely successful editorial work and his large contributions to the study of the West, although he seems to admit that Thwaites might make even more significant contributions if he were less romantic and less tied to stories of exploration.[21] In reviewing a new edition of Parkman's works in 1898, Turner applauds the Boston historian's "correct scholarship, fidelity, graphic power, and literary beauty," but, he adds, Parkman is "not so skilful in exposition of the development of institutions," thus causing some of his volumes to be less "satisfactory to the critical historian." Since Parkman loves the romantic, dramatic, and picturesque, he tends to skip over less lively details, indicating that he might be less "preeminent in other fields of historical research" dealing with less theatrical topics. In the end, Turner concludes that Parkman's "work will live because he was even greater as an artist than as a historian."[22]

So if American historians such as Rhodes and von Holst erred badly in overemphasizing slavery and overlooking the signal importance of the frontier and West in American history, several writers who had turned their attention to the frontier had not yet provided satisfactory models for others wishing to specialize in the West. Some like Roosevelt and Parkman tended to be too romantic, and others such as Winsor were too fact-ridden and bordered on antiquarianism. And all failed to ask the questions concerning "significance" that interested Turner so deeply. He had tried, he wrote to Miss Skinner, "to see it [the West] as a whole,—on its institutional, social, economic, and political side, its effects upon the nation as a whole, and . . . [its] persistent pervasive influence in American life."[23]

Here, then, was Turner's idealistic, prescriptive agenda. Not only would he push historians away from what he considered excessive emphases on sectionalism and slavery; he would urge on them and on others an increased stress on the frontier as process, which demanded comprehension of its political, social, and economic ingredients. And he would try to persuade these western specialists to abandon their provincial, antiquarian studies and to avoid seeing the frontier as only a dramatic theater for Indian fights, exploration, and other lively happenings.[24]

This snapshot portrait of young Turner as ambitious theorist and practitioner in the 1890s foreshadows many of the controversies swirling around historical writing about the West in the twentieth century. The reorientations in western historiography that Turner so enthusiastically called for a century ago continue to be debated in the pages of many western history journals and contested vociferously in annual roundups of western historians. Should western historiography center on frontier experiences, told in dramatic fashion? or should western historians be more interpretive, searching primarily for the significance of their research in large conceptions or paradigms?

Ironically, Turner and his followers may have been more successful in converting American historians to newer and more searching understandings of the frontier's shaping influences on American history than they were in saving their western brethren from antiquarian and romantic excesses. Soon after the turn of the century—and most certainly by 1920—Turner's frontier gospel had won over most students of American history. Indeed, in that year a collection of Turner's essays, *The Frontier in American History*, won near-unanimous praise from professional historians and hosts of general readers and was awarded a Pulitzer Prize. Meanwhile, Turner had succeeded to the coveted presidency of the American Historical Association in 1910, the same year he was elevated to a prestigious chair of history at Harvard. And Turner's emphases were further illustrated when several of his "western men" helped establish the Mississippi Valley Historical Association in 1907 and its journal, the *Mississippi Valley Historical Review*, in 1913 as outlets for the expanding number of western specialists. With the publication of *The Spanish Borderlands* in 1921 by Turner's former student Herbert Eugene Bolton and his successor at Wisconsin Frederic Logan Paxson's Pulitzer Prize–winning *History of the American Frontier 1763–1893* in 1924, both owing a good deal to Turner's preachments on the importance of the frontier, Turner seemed to have captured the scene. Indeed, by the mid-1920s frontier historical studies were well established, not only as a separate scholarly field but also as an important focus in American historiography. But to push the story farther is to duplicate material in the following essays.[25]

In preparing their essays, writers were asked to treat the life, professional career, and major works of their subject. (The exceptions were the two essays on Turner, one to deal with frontier, the other to treat section/region.) They were also requested to evaluate that historian's impact on the field of western history. Together, these essays, along with the volume editor's appended overview of new trends in western historical writing since 1970, serve as an introduction to the main currents of a full century of western historiography. In this way, this volume complements the earlier historiographical collections edited by Michael P. Malone and Roger L. Nichols, which follow topical organization; and the even more recent volume compiled by John R. Wunder, which is arranged alphabetically and contains briefer treatments of fifty-seven historians. Had the editor been able to follow his original, idealistic table of contents, this volume would have been twice as long with additional essays on Francis Parkman, Theodore Roosevelt, Bernard DeVoto, Frederick Merk, John D. Hicks, Oscar O. Winther, John Caughey, Paul Gates, J. Frank Dobie, and Wallace Stegner.

The editor would like to thank the contributors for their willingness to take part in this project and for their patience as the volume proceeded step by step. Their careful and probing essays should serve as major contributions to the ongoing reevaluation of western historiography.

NOTES

1. A history of western historiography is lacking, but two recent volumes approach the subject topically: Michael P. Malone, ed., *Historians and the American West* (Lincoln: University of Nebraska Press, 1983); Roger L. Nichols, ed., *American Frontier and Western Issues: A Historiographical Review* (Westport, Conn.: Greenwood Press, 1986). For a very helpful collection of historiographical essays dealing with fifty-seven individual historians, arranged alphabetically, see John R. Wunder, ed., *Historians of the American Frontier: A Bio-Bibliographical Sourcebook* (Westport, Conn.: Greenwood Press, 1988). The most recent brief overview, organized topically, is Brian Dippie, "American Wests: Historiographical Perspectives," *American Studies International* 27 (October 1989):3–25. As this volume goes to press, Gerald D. Nash has completed a sweeping overview of western historiography in his forthcoming *Creating the West: Historical Interpretations, 1890–1990* (Albuquerque: University of New Mexico Press, 1991).

2. No study of nineteenth-century western historiography has been written, although Henry Nash Smith deals glancingly with the topic in his classic study *Virgin Land: The American West as Symbol and Myth* (Cambridge: Harvard University Press, 1950). Also useful is the brief overview of Cooper, Irving, and Parkman in G. Edward White, *The Eastern Establishment and the Western Exper-*

ience: The West of Frederic Remington, Theodore Roosevelt, and Owen Wister (New Haven: Yale University Press, 1968; Austin: University of Texas Press, 1989), 31–51. See, also, Lee Clark Mitchell, *Witnesses to a Vanishing America: The Nineteenth-Century Response* (Princeton, N.J.: Princeton University Press, 1981).

3. Following the point of view of Bernard DeVoto, Robert Edson Lee argues, in *From West to East: Studies in the Literature of the American West* (Urbana: University of Illinois Press, 1966), that the East misread the West, thereby bequeathing a distorted image of the region and its history to other Americans.

4. Stella M. Drumm, ed., *Down the Santa Fe Trail and Into Mexico: The Diary of Susan Shelby Magoffin 1846–1847* (New Haven, Conn.: Yale University Press, 1926), 95. Few women's diaries were published in the nineteenth century, so their reactions to the West and westering did not become clear until well into the twentieth century. On this subject, see, for example, Annette Kolodny, *The Land Before Her: Fantasy and Experience of the American Frontiers, 1630–1860* (Chapel Hill: University of North Carolina Press, 1984).

5. For a thorough discussion of the mythologizing of the American frontier, see Richard Slotkin, *Regeneration Through Violence: The Myth of the American Frontier, 1600–1860* (Middletown, Conn.: Wesleyan University Press, 1973).

6. Kent L. Steckmesser's *The Western Hero in History and Legend* (Norman: University of Oklahoma Press, 1965) remains a very useful introduction to these topics. For lively discussions of visual images of the American frontier and West, see William H. Goetzmann and William N. Goetzmann, *The West of the Imagination* (New York: W. W. Norton, 1986).

7. In addition to the pathbreaking chapters on the dime novel in Smith, *Virgin Land*, consult Christine Bold, *Selling the Wild West: Popular Western Fiction, 1860–1960* (Bloomington: Indiana University Press, 1987).

8. Robert Hine's smoothly written overview of frontier and western history contains several useful sections on these topics: *The American West: An Interpretive History*, 2d ed. (Boston: Little, Brown, 1984). Also very helpful are the lively chapters in Ray A. Billington, *Land of Savagery/Land of Promise: The European Image of the American Frontier* (New York: W. W. Norton, 1981).

9. As are all writers on Frederick Jackson Turner, I am much indebted to Ray Billington's magisterial biography, *Frederick Jackson Turner: Historian, Scholar, Teacher* (New York: Oxford University Press, 1973).

10. Frederick Jackson Turner to William Allen, October 31, 1888, Box 1, Turner Papers, Henry E. Huntington Library (hereafter cited as HEH), quoted in Wilbur R. Jacobs, ed., *The Historical World of Frederick Jackson Turner: With Selections From His Correspondence* (New Haven: Yale University Press, 1968), 77.

11. Turner to Carl Becker, December 16, 1925, quoted in Billington, *The Genesis of the Frontier Thesis: A Study in Historical Creativity* (San Marino, Calif.: Huntington Library, 1971), 234. Billington disagrees with the interpretation given here in *Genesis*, 27–29.

12. Turner's dissertation was reprinted in Turner, *The Early Writings of Frederick Jackson Turner* (Madison: University of Wisconsin Press, 1938), 87–181. More

recently, the dissertation is again reprinted with a stimulating introduction that discusses climates of historiographical opinion that surrounded Turner; see Turner, *The Character and Influence of the Indian Trade in Wisconsin: A Study of the Trading Post as an Institution*, ed. David Harry Miller and William W. Savage, Jr. (Norman: University of Oklahoma Press, 1977), vii–xxxiv.

13. Turner, "Problems in American History," *The Aegis*, November 4, 1892, repr. in *Early Writings*, 71–83; the quote is on 72.

14. "The Significance of the Frontier in American History," *Proceedings of the Forty-First Annual Meeting of the State Historical Society of Wisconsin* (Madison, Wisc., 1894), 79–112; repr. in *Early Writings*, 185–229; quotes on 187, 188.

15. For one sample of Turner's regional chauvinism, see Jacobs, *Historical World*, 81–82.

16. Turner to Henry E. Bourne, January 20, 1897, Box 2, Turner Papers, HEH.

17. Colonialism in early twentieth-century western thought and historiography is traced in Gene M. Gressley, "Colonialism: A Western Complaint," *Pacific Northwest Quarterly* 54 (January 1963):1–8; and Richard W. Etulain, "A New Historiographical Frontier: The Twentieth-Century West," in *The Twentieth-Century West: Historical Interpretations*, ed. Gerald D. Nash and Richard W. Etulain (Albuquerque: University of New Mexico Press, 1989), 1–31.

18. Turner to Constance L. Skinner, March 15, 1922, Box 31, Turner Papers, HEH, as quoted in Billington, *Genesis*, 214. Although he did not mention here the works of Josiah Royce or H. H. Bancroft and seems not to have reviewed their writings, Turner did use Bancroft's multivolume works in several of his essays and books. As early as 1910, he was also citing the writings of Josiah Royce. Turner cited Royce's ideas on "provincialism" in his Phi Beta Kappa address in Ann Arbor, Michigan, on May 14, 1910; see Turner Papers, Folder 23, Box 55, HEH.

19. Turner reviewed volumes in Roosevelt's *Winning of the West* in several scattered reviews: *The Dial* 10 (August 1889):71–73; *The Nation* 50 (March 28, 1895):240–42; 43 (October 8, 1896):277; *American Historical Review* 2 (October 1896):171–76; quotes from *AHR*, 171; *Nation*, 241. Martin Ridge supplies an excellent summary of Turner's book reviews, including comments on all the reviews mentioned here. See his "A More Jealous Mistress: Frederick Jackson Turner as Book Reviewer," *Pacific Historical Review* 55 (February 1986):49–63.

20. Turner, review of Justin Winsor, *The Westward Movement*, in *American Historical Review* 3 (April 1898):556–61; quotes on 557.

21. Turner, review of Reuben Gold Thwaites, *Early Western Travels*, in *The Dial* 37 (November 16, 1904):298–302; 41 (July 1, 1906):6–10.

22. Turner, "Francis Parkman and His Work," *The Dial* 25 (December 16, 1898):451–53; quotes on 451, 452, 453.

23. Turner to Skinner, in Billington, *Genesis*, 214.

24. Turner presented several research opportunities in his "The West as a Field for Historical Study," in *Annual Report of the American Historical Association for 1896* (Washington, D.C., 1897), I:281–96. In his most famous essay, Turner

urged that the frontier not be seen "from the point of view of border warfare and the chase, but as a field for the serious study of the economist and the historian," Turner, *Early Writings*, 157.

25. Interestingly, Peter Novick does not deal with these developments in western historiography—in fact, with few subjects in regional historical writing—in his otherwise lengthy, thorough, and provocative study of American historiography: *That Noble Dream: The "Objectivity Question" and the American Historical Profession* (Cambridge: Cambridge University Press, 1988).

I

Precursors to Frederick Jackson Turner

1

Josiah Royce: The West as Community

ROBERT V. HINE

*J*OSIAH ROYCE WAS ANXIOUS to go, to leave the West, his native California.[1] The young philosopher wrote to William James, who had instigated his move to Harvard, that he considered "an egg in Cambridge as worth more than a brood of chickens" in Berkeley. The "chickens" of California were now providing no intellectual sustenance for him. "Californians generally, and on the whole with very good reason, regard one another with profound suspicion and contempt," he wrote. "I have now a little son, three weeks old. . . . I shall be overjoyed at the thought of bringing him up in an Eastern atmosphere."[2] Within three years this jaundiced observer of his homeland penned one of the sharpest interpretations of his state ever written, a pithy volume of insight and foresight that has been read with profit and has provoked controversy for over a century.

A year after Royce's arrival at Harvard, an acquaintance in San Francisco, William W. Crane, died. Crane had signed with Houghton Mifflin of Boston to write a history of California, and his death caused the publishers to seek out Royce, now across the river in Cambridge, for the project. Royce, with no historical training and little knowledge of the subject beyond his own Californian background, undertook the book, which he foresaw as the first history of California written by a native son. He called it "a side-work, an amusement of idle hours," but he admitted that such amusements can be "pretty serious things." To another friend he acknowledged being tempted by the money, "by the affection that I should feel for the task," and by the good that might

19

be accomplished in examining "the moral and general significance" of California history.[3]

This incipient western historian was born in 1855 in perhaps the most thriving of the Mother Lode towns, Grass Valley. Quartz mining underlay Grass Valley's prosperity; while other towns had dwindled as placer gravels gave out, Grass Valley survived because very early it had required capital for deeper hard-rock operations. One-mule-and-a-pan, independent prospectors either drifted through or knuckled under as hired laborers. Royce's father, Josiah, Sr., was almost as itinerant as the pocket hunters, but he was a grocery merchant looking for the right market that he never seemed to find. He had brought his wife and baby daughter alone across the plains in 1849. On that journey Sarah Bayliss Royce, Josiah's mother, transcended dangers and loneliness through a mystical communion with her God. In the mines, while her husband was often away, she maintained her spirit, bore, raised, and educated her children (including two other daughters and Josiah, the last child), and actively supported the religious and educational life of the town.

Mother Sarah educated her only son Josiah until he was eleven, when the family moved to San Francisco. After grammar and high school in the city, Josiah enrolled in the University of California in Oakland, joining a tiny student body that soon moved to the new campus in Berkeley. A bachelor's degree in classics led to a year's study of philosophy in Germany and a doctorate at Johns Hopkins (1878). His first job returned him to Berkeley as an assistant in the Department of English. He was there for another four chafing years before William James, who had recognized his talents at Johns Hopkins, called him east.

For thirty-four years Royce championed the cause of philosophy at Harvard, molding a department and professionalizing a discipline during the golden age of American philosophy. Few would doubt his role in that work nor his status as the prime defender of Idealism and Absolutism in a period that leaned more and more toward Pragmatism. William James, his close friend, felt that his own conclusions would have been weaker, perhaps impossible, without the frequent interchanges with Royce. The two vitally affected American thought in the twentieth century.

But in the summer of 1884 none of this was suspected. The new Harvard instructor threw himself into the job of writing a history of California. Mercifully for Royce, Hubert Howe Bancroft and his crew of writers, then in the midst of their monumental labors on the West and publishing the first of their California volumes, allowed him free access to their documents. In their rooms on Valencia, near Mission Street, in San Francisco, Royce pored through collections like those of Thomas Oliver Larkin and Mariano Vallejo. He tried valiantly to be his own researcher, but in the end admitted that "without Mr. Bancroft's documents" he would have been "unable to find my [Royce's] way out of the labyrinth." In another situation he confessed, "His [Bancroft's] library is the truly original source here, and my research. . . is at this one most important place but a following of his already beaten trail."[4] Royce befriended Bancroft and one of his writers, Henry Lebbeus Oak. Those relationships deeply influenced his work and stand in curious contrast to his failure in contacting another active contemporary writer of California history, the lawyer Theodore Hittell. The fault must have lain with Hittell, a far more private man than Bancroft. But even Bancroft may have been more chary of his raw material had not Royce's limited agenda seemed to him no competitive threat to his multivolume work.[5]

As Royce researched and wrote, his purposes expanded. Before he was through, he saw his history as nothing less than a revelation of the national character. Ultimately, it might "serve the true patriot's interest in a clear self-knowledge and in the formation of sensible ideals of national greatness." Inasmuch as there had been wrongdoing, his writing might be an atonement for his country's honor.[6]

He restricted his history to ten years, 1846 to 1856, a decade he saw as absolutely pivotal. He himself was born on the cusp-end of this period, so that the bridges into his own contemporary world lay rather close. When he described California's varied landscape he included his own Grass Valley childhood memories of "frowning higher mountains" and buttes "springing up like young giants." He may have been commenting on himself rather than the state when he noted a drawback in the healthful climate: it prompted "active people to work too steadily, to skip their holidays, and, by reason of their very enjoyment of life, to wear out their constitutions with overwork."[7]

It was the conquest of California that for Royce most exposed the American character. The nation here engaged in a morally if not politically indefensible act. The Bear Flag Revolt was incited by the false rumors of John Charles Frémont, who for Royce became the butt of the moral problem. Far from justifiable, Frémont's call to military action before the United States Navy arrived could have brought such anarchy to California that England might well have accepted overtures from the inhabitants for a protectorate. In any case, the institution of guerrilla warfare was not in the best interests of the United States either politically or morally; as Royce put it, therein "we can date the beginning of the degradation, the ruin, and the oppression of the Californian people by our own."[8]

The unprovoked violence, a consequence of Thomas Hart Benton's dispatches to Frémont in the Klamath forests, became "a violation of the laws of nations, under circumstances of peculiar atrocity."[9] Thomas O. Larkin, not Frémont, was pursuing the proper national course, the peaceful support of a local movement for independence from Mexico, presuming eventual annexation to the United States. In these acts and in the official military conquest that followed, Royce saw the nation as typically ambivalent in its desire to conquer but its unwillingness to assume the role of conqueror. Instead, it clothed its aggression, as Frémont himself had done, in the garb of peaceful intentions and conscientious duty. Royce's own generation, beginning to wrestle with overseas markets, acquisitions like Alaska, and Chinese exclusion, was addressed in an oft-quoted digression:

> It is to be hoped that this lesson, showing us as it does how much
> of conscience and even of personal sincerity can coexist with a
> minimum of effective morality in international undertakings,
> will some day be once more remembered; so that when our nation
> is another time about to serve the devil, it will do so with more
> frankness and will deceive itself less by half-conscious cant. For
> the rest, our mission in the cause of liberty is to be accomplished
> through a steadfast devotion to the cultivation of our own inner
> life, and not by going abroad as missionaries, as conquerors, or
> as marauders, among weaker peoples.[10]

Between the conquest and admission, California was destined to endure "a time of doubts, of problems, of complaints, and of weariness."[11] In such moments the American nature could be at its best— moderate, self-controlled, and astute in the design of new communities. But in the Gold Rush, California was "to be morally and socially tried as no other American community ever has been tried," and it would exhibit "both the true nobility and the true weakness of our national character."[12] The nobility was seen in a polyglot population that successfully dealt with North–South dissensions; in the activities of women who injected family and religious values into a raw society; and in the average American's "instinctive cleverness" at self-government.[13]

Royce cautioned, however, at exaggerating that "marvelous political talent."[14] It must be seen against two evidences of weakness: civic irresponsibility and a local manifestation of our diseased national feeling toward foreigners. Both of these tendencies allowed orderly, friendly life to degenerate into serious, violent disorder. Although miners in a spirit of compromise and good humor bound themselves into "little republics," their camps were so devoid of broader civic responsibility that they endured difficult years of disorder and violence.

The social fabric needed considerable mending. Royce bitterly described the cruelty, irresponsibility, and ineffectiveness of lynch law in the mines and pointed out the inconsistency of contemporaries who whined about law and order but refused to be taxed for jails.[15] As for foreigners, Royce wrote, "You cannot build up a prosperous and peaceful community so long as you pass laws to oppress and torment a large resident class of the community."[16] Foreigners were kept by law and vigilantism in fear and misery.

Disorder served in the end to teach social responsibility. San Francisco's fearful fires of the early 1850s preceded sounder buildings, safer docks, more organized fire departments. Overexcitement, self-absorption, extravagance, and nervous strain were balanced in time by family life and church-oriented circles. The vigilance committees of 1851 and 1856 eventually rooted out the social apathy and public carelessness that surrounded them. This trip through the valley of despond also included the Land Act of 1851 (requiring all existing titles to be confirmed by a commission, expressing "our natural meanness and love of good order in one") and all of the new state politicians like John Bigler, David Broderick, and William Gwin ("too selfish to be wise").[17] In the end, however, the journey produced a living, dynamic community:

> *It is the State, the Social Order, that is divine. We are all but dust save as this social order gives us life. When we think it our instrument, . . . we call it sordid, degraded, corrupt, unspiritual, and ask how we may escape from it forever. But if we turn again and serve the social order, and not merely ourselves, we soon find that what we are serving is simply our own highest spiritual destiny in bodily form. It is never truly sordid or corrupt or unspiritual; it is only we that are so when we neglect our duty.*[18]

Seldom has a history led to such lofty conclusions. California's ten formative years were not just the germ of a future, not just a parable for the American character; they were lessons in the proper ordering of human society.

His history was hardly finished when in the summer of 1886 the young college professor wrote a novel. Royce thus joined many another young academic, past and present, in trying his hand at fiction. Even that same summer Henry Adams and Adolph Bandelier were so engaged. "I think it has something to do with earning my living," Royce wrote, and he must have been thinking of his ill wife pregnant with their second child. But social purposes, though less obvious than those of a Helen Hunt Jackson or an Ignatius Donnelly, were nevertheless involved, and he gave his story the same kind of philosophical base that he gave his history. He had learned that history "talks back," leaves documents that must be coped with, and never "stands still to be counted." Philosophy (and by implication its counterpart in literature) is "submissive and plastic." The novel gives the historian new freedom, inviting him to go beyond the document where nothing "talks back" but his own imagination.[19]

Royce had long embraced literature. As a junior at the fledgling University of California, he delivered a prize Charter Day oration on the modern novel, later printed in the *Berkeleyan*. The future historian, he said, will place few "influences that have molded our destiny" higher in importance than current fiction. His favorite novelist was the contemporary George Eliot, and her *Mill on the Floss*, because it exceeded *Adam Bede* and *Middlemarch* in its moral lesson, showed "the instructive influence a novel may exercise."[20]

Royce's own story is usually seen as a stepping-stone on his philosophical path—a study in the conflict between duty and desire, a "perspective on identity and morality."[21] It is far more. Royce here continued the exploration of his state's history; it became history and fiction combined for a philosophic message. The central problem of the novel comes straight out of his *California*—whether land should be held in the traditional, large rancho holdings or should be broken into smaller parcels. He considered the issue fundamental. The section in his history dealing with the Sacramento squatter riots of 1850 was the only portion of his book that he extracted and expanded for a separate article in the *Overland*, and he eventually used that essay for one of his *Studies of Good and Evil* (1898). Now it would be the centerpiece of his story. He turned down the publisher's suggestions of a more literary title and chose one closer to the geography and the history: *The Feud of Oakfield Creek: A Novel of California Life*.[22]

The land in question, located between Mount Diablo and the Contra Costa hills, was claimed by small squatters, including a bohemian college professor, Alf Escott (whose idealism was patterned after the leader of the Sacramento squatters), and a magnate living in a Nob Hill mansion, Alonzo Eldon. They were both old Californians and had fought the Paiutes together. But they clashed over Eldon's desire to build a Medici fortune rather than be concerned, like Escott, with the common people who made such affluence possible. Ironically, the robber baron Eldon assuaged his conscience with a closet attachment to the teachings of Henry George, yearning for a society in which opulence like his own would be impossible.

The plot is complicated and need not detain us here. The characters are a varicolored group, including the idealistic and loyal Escott; his loving but unrealistic daughter; the shrewd but unprincipled Eldon; his careless son; a complicated woman, Margaret; a wandering widower; and a flamboyant, corrupt newspaper editor. The action includes the Brotherhood of the Noble Rangers, squatters defending their rights under a higher law in the pattern of the Sacramento Settlers' Association or the San Francisco vigilance committees. In the end, forty settlers resist the approach of Eldon and his men, and in the consequent shooting, old Escott, Eldon's son, and four others die. The final scene is a virtual replay of the events in Sacramento in 1850, and they are reminiscent, too, of the Mussell Slough incident (May 11, 1880), which Frank Norris recreated in *The Octopus* (1901). For Norris, characters were victims in naturalistic traps—the surging growth of the wheat; the uncontrollable energy of the railroad—surrounded by values at flux in the surge of evolution. For Royce, characters stood in moral dilemmas, facing conflicting loyalties between higher law or immediate needs, between family or communal attachments, but the ultimate values were unshakable, and they had to include loyalty to a cause beyond the self. Royce, as well as Norris, found that a California novel, like California history, was an effective tool for a moral purpose.

The debut of Royce as California historian and novelist was anything but bright. Reviewers of both *California* and *The Feud* hit hard his wordiness and moralizing. Even an age accustomed to rhetorical excess rejected the style and the manner, and little perspective could be expected on the ideas of a freshman historian and a first novelist.

California took the brunt of the attack. An unsigned review in the *Overland Monthly*, for which Royce had written during his days in Berkeley and for which he held real attachment, was vicious. The book was described as "contract work, done under pressure," without unity "except in its uniformity of sermonizing reproof of Americans." Sprinkled through the review were words like *immaturity, flippancy, diffuseness,* and *unidiomatic English,* and it concluded with a patronizing nod: "defects like this . . . will naturally disappear with longer experience in writing history; and we advert to them for Professor Royce's good." The anonymous reviewer found the censure of Frémont and California frontiersmen excessive and unproved. And in the end "both as literature and as history, it is, on the whole, a failure."[23]

Shortly before, in the *Nation,* Royce had unfavorably compared Theodore Hittell's new history with Bancroft's emerging work, and now the author mistakenly assumed that the *Overland* reviewer was the incensed Hittell. Royce revealed little resentment, however, at least in a letter to his friend and the journal's editor, Milicent Shinn. Henry Oak, in the next month's issue of the *Overland,* firmly supported Royce's position on Frémont and affirmed the book "both as literature and as history" to be "a very perfect piece of work," superior to anything yet done. William A. Dunning, in the *Political Science Quarterly,* was more guarded: "If only the excellence of the author's literary style were at all proportionate to the captiousness of his criticism, his book would easily take rank as a classic."[24]

Royce's interest in history was now too deep to be easily deflected. The rebukes he suffered from reviewers led to more activity, not less. He corrected a minor detail in the *California* by a letter to the editor of the *Overland.* He contributed a series of biographies on figures in California history to *Appleton's Cyclopaedia.* He edited lengthy documents and letters by George H. Fitch, William Coleman, William Tecumseh Sherman, John B. Montgomery, George Bancroft, and James Buchanan in a series of contributions to *Century.* At the same time, he wrote five lengthy reviews of the emerging Bancroft and Hittell volumes. In these, he championed Bancroft's sound documentary evidence and Hittell's readability, while castigating Bancroft's failure to credit his coauthors and Hittell's failure to profit from Bancroft's documentary leadership.[25]

Royce was a fighter. His writings in this period took on the nature of an extended rebuttal to his critics, clarifying questions, and adding proofs. Frémont died in July 1890, and Royce in an *Atlantic* article was quick to assess the general's life and work. Royce pronounced Frémont a "faithful knight and hero" with "winning eyes and gentle voice," one who "possessed all the qualities of genius except ability." He was "a creature escaped from a book, wandering about in a real world when he was made for dreamland." Royce again charged Frémont with refusal to take the ordered and more desirable course of neutrality, conciliation, and ultimate annexation with less fighting and with fewer resentments. "General Frémont was simply not the conqueror of California. All that he did . . . was of no effect except to alienate its people."[26]

Although Frémont's death might have dashed the hope that the general would disclose anything more on the California conquest, a twelve-page, double-columned article appeared in the April 1891 *Century*, "edited" by Jessie Benton Frémont from the notes of her deceased husband. Here, Frémont's military actions were justified by the threat of the British occupation of California. Further, the article contended that Frémont was given the power to act in his secret instructions for the 1845 scientific expedition. When Lt. Archibald Gillespie found him on the Oregon border, the messages showed that conciliation was "no longer practicable" and in any case would have been "in conflict with our own instructions." Frémont dismissed one part of Gillespie's dispatches (Buchanan's orders to Larkin) and concentrated on the other (the packet from Benton), "a trumpet," which "made me know distinctly that at last the time had come when England must not get a foothold; that we *must be first*. I was to *act*, discreetly but positively."[27] To support his position, Frémont submitted an 1886 memorandum from George Bancroft, now retired in Rhode Island. In it, Bancroft denied that there had been much fear of England, but he admitted that, if he had been in Frémont's place, he would have felt bound to do what he could to promote the purpose of the president, the possession of California.

In the same issue following the Frémont article, the *Century* printed Secretary of State Buchanan's letter to Larkin (the Gillespie dispatch) with an editorial note by Royce. Royce pointed to this as the *only* official dispatch received by Frémont. Buchanan had indicated that, although the government wished no foreign control over California, still "this government has no ambitions to gratify and no desire to extend our federal system over more territory than we already possess, unless by the free and spontaneous wish of the independent people of adjoining territories."

The *Century* readers were wearying of the California controversy, so Royce was forced to turn to the *Nation*, where in May 1891 (while completing a book on philosophy, contemplating six articles on Goethe, and considering an offer to move from Harvard to Stanford) he offered his final words on the subject. He protested that George Bancroft's comments did not change the picture; that every agent of the United States had orders to conciliate the Mexicans; that cooperation was thwarted by Frémont's false reports and irregular warfare; and that the retired Bancroft's letter was sprinkled with errors in memory. For further evidence Royce quoted verbatim the dispatch of Bancroft to Commodore Sloat, once more ordering conciliation. The truth was that Frémont "lawlessly thwarted [orders] for his own glory." "I should myself never think of attacking the Frémont legend so often, were it not so unsubstantially immortal. I shall rejoice if ever the pale ghost ceases to walk in broad daylight. The twilight regions of our historical consciousness in this country will probably never be rid of it."[28] And with these words he closed his public comment on John Charles Frémont and the history of California.

Royce's preoccupation with the role of Frémont in the conquest had lasted for six years. In his letters during the period he vacillated between giving Frémont the benefit of the doubt and, at the other extreme, applying the "thumb-screws" to "the deceiver."[29] Something inexplicable seems to have motivated Royce in his unwillingness at least to assume Frémont's good intentions, even if thoroughly mistaken. Why did he not understand, to use his own later words, "the art of honoring your opponent's loyalty."[30] Andrew Rolle has suggested that we may be observing the psychological overreaction of one strong will to the authoritarianism of an equally strong will. If so, it must be added that Royce throughout his life loved to explore differences and heartily championed the clash of minds. Even in his childhood he enjoyed frequent philosophical wranglings with his sister. And his later life would see gargantuan debates with his colleagues at Harvard, Francis Abbott and William James.[31]

In spite of its cool welcome, *California* has in its first century been reprinted twice. In 1948, during the Gold Rush centennial, Alfred Knopf commissioned Robert Glass Cleland for an introduction, kept the new edition in print until 1961, and sold three thousand copies (about average among its historical reissues of that day).[32] The reviewers this time were far more positive than the first ones had been. True, George R. Stewart and Joseph Henry Jackson cautiously reiterated the concern over balance. But Rodman Paul praised the excellence of the research and the way Royce probed ultimate significance, and Charles Barker complimented the book on its condemnation of Frémont, the respect for Larkin, the technological insights, and the influence of place on law and religion.[33]

In 1970 Gibbs M. Smith chose Royce's *California* as one of the first four books to be published by his new Peregrine Press in Santa Barbara.

Since he considered it "the most insightful history of California ever written," he was disappointed that it sold only three thousand copies and went out of print long before one of the companion volumes, *The Shirley Letters*. This time Earl Pomeroy wrote the introduction, a splendid assessment of Royce as a historian. Reviewers unanimously praised Pomeroy's contribution, and the book was generally accepted as a classic in the Zamorano 80 tradition.[34]

Judged by the standards of his day or by the basic canons of scholarship, Royce as a historian of California comes off rather well. For errors of detail his *California* is occasionally vulnerable, especially in the introduction on pre-American California, the section with which he was little concerned and for which he claimed no scholarship. In it, he underestimated Indian uprisings against the missions, underplayed the Monterey stay of Commodore ap Catesby Jones in 1846, and had the Donner Party's Reed banished on foot rather than horseback. He also confused the number and nature of the prisoners taken by the Bear Flaggers.[35] And he wholeheartedly accepted J. Tyrwhitt Brooks ("a perfectly trustworthy observer") as a prime source for life in the mines. We now know that Brooks's journal was a hoax, revealed fifty years afterward by its author (Henry Vizetelly), but, of course, the entire historical profession believed Brooks in Royce's day.[36]

Against these details must be placed the body of the work. Over and over, Royce's reverence for documentation shone clearly. "The purpose has been throughout to write from the sources,"[37] and by sources he meant a range of newspapers, letters, and diaries. The importance of detail even led him to construct a statistical table for the members of the Constitutional Convention of 1849 showing nativity, length of residence, occupation, and age, a table still useful to scholars. He called his historical bent "my respect for thoroughness," and it lay behind his enthusiasm for Bancroft's work.[38] Like Bancroft, Royce also realized the significance of oral testimony in corroborating detail. Hence his decision to take oral histories from John and Jessie Frémont. He conducted the interviews in a highly professional manner, allowing the subjects a chance to amend, read the proofs, and offer their rebuttal.[39] As he was writing his *California* he expressed to Henry Oak the anguish of the careful documentary historian: "It is fearfully hard to tell the truth in these things. Again and again I write what I think I have just learned from a document or book, and, looking again at my source, have to tear up my MS. in disgust."[40]

As for style, he dreamed of brevity, but, alas, often sank into verbosity. The year before his death, looking backward, he bemoaned his own profuseness by extolling a friend's "finished self-control and brevity of style."[41] The lament was astute self-criticism. In both the history and the novel, Royce wrote countless sentences of twelve to fifteen lines, many of which would be infinitely clearer were they shorter. His paragraphs were sometimes interminable. Wordiness occasionally veered into pedantry; a few times he even described the provenance of a source in the text.[42] He was sarcastic: "Providence, again, is known to be opposed to every form of oppression; and grabbing eleven leagues of land is a great oppression. And so the worthlessness of Mexican land-titles is evident."[43] He argued from analogy: "If we desired to steal our neighbor's fine horse, why should we first coax him into confinement and then scourge him with whips in his stall, to make him break his bones?"[44] His metaphors were sometimes overdrawn: "The devil's instrument it actually proved to be, . . . and we have got our full share of the devil's wages for our use of it [the Land Act of 1851]."[45] He editorialized and personalized his arguments in ways the modern historian might envy but would never dream of doing.[46]

Yet the final stylistic impact is one of grandness, of an exciting mind caught up in the joy of intellectual pursuit. His phrasing betrays that exhilaration: "April and May are the spendthrift months of wealthy nature." The year 1849 is "the boyish year of California." Speculative investors "will be destroyed like flies in the autumn."[47] Sometimes overdrawn, his similes were more often apt: "California would have been ready to drop into our basket like a mellow apple."[48] His literary allusions revealed a thoughtful breadth. The Bible was ever ready. From it he viewed the Mexican War through the Old Testament story of Ahab coveting Naboth's vineyard. Again, the population "was full of Jonahs, . . . fleeing over seas and deserts." Elsewhere were scattered wild grapes and manna and ravens in the wilderness. Thucydides and Aristotle were also there. And so were Jonathan Swift and Lewis Carroll (no less than the Boojum from *The Hunting of the Snark*). In all, Royce was a writer of literary merit. He was, as the Princeton critic Vincent Buranelli has written, "an artist capable of rising into great prose."[49]

Royce holds a curious place in western American historiography, coming as he did after Parkman, coincidental with Bancroft, and before Turner. One critic would place Royce's *California* close on the shelf with *The Oregon Trail* and Prescott's *The Conquest of Mexico*.[50] Yet there is no evidence that Royce ever read either Parkman or Prescott. He wrote in their tradition of preprofessional history (not academically trained or in the academy), but, then, so did Bancroft. Royce, Bancroft, and Turner were all concerned with a professional use of sources, with Royce even engaging along with Bancroft in sophisticated oral history. In western history, however, it was Turner who marked the shift to the academic, though his writing maintained much of breathtaking sweep. Bancroft and Royce continued to write in the grand scale of Parkman and Prescott; to that grandness Royce added an extra measure of literary allusion and an even greater portion of philosophy.

Royce, however, deduced a momentous moral from a short compass, which was the reverse of Bancroft—little morality from an enormous canvas. The historian is engaged in a dialogue, Dominick LaCapra has suggested, between two identities: the scholar (the judge pronouncing balanced appraisals of the documentary evidence) and the intellectual (the philosopher dissecting and analyzing the argument).[51] Bancroft's identity was with the scholar, more in a tradition that would produce Reuben Gold Thwaites and Henry Wagner; Royce was the intellectual and, in this sense, more the precursor of Turner. Turner, although he wrote some detailed documentary appraisals, will be remembered far more for his theory, and in the same way Royce's stature will depend on his analytical acumen.

Bancroft saw the frontier as significant and proved his belief by telling its story in great detail. But Royce prefigured Turner in seeing those details as far more grandly significant, illuminating nothing less than a national and humanistic frame. Turner's frontier would be a far more deterministic force; the frontier, for example, determined the participatory nature of our democracy and our peculiar obsession with individualism. If there was any determinism in Royce, on the other hand, it was negative: the frontier had produced, though not necessarily, an irresponsible society broken by violence and special interests; like life itself, it was "restless, capricious, and therefore tragic."[52] Only when individuals chose to exert their wills could a dialectic be set in motion to redirect that irresponsibility into order, and that was only possible when individuals were engaged in a cause that transcended their selfishness. Turner realized the values of cooperation, but he did not, as Royce did, find the loner a tragic figure. Turner's frontier contained all the power of gravity; Royce's frontier embodied all the dangers of a centrifuge.

Royce relied on Bancroft, as we have seen, and in turn Turner used Royce. Turner was intrigued with Royce's analysis of provincialism and quoted him in lectures and in both *The Frontier* and *Sections*. He built on and championed Royce's definition of provincialism. He agreed with Royce's worries over conformity (a "remorseless mechanism—vast, irrational") and the passions of the mob. And he also found an antidote in "the promise of what that wise and lamented philosopher, Josiah Royce called, 'the beloved community.' In the spirit of the pioneer's 'house raising' lies the salvation of the Republic."[53]

When Turner came to Harvard in 1910, Royce had already been there twenty-eight years. The two men sat beside one another at a dinner party one evening in 1912, and Turner found Royce "very bright and interesting," especially since Royce was exulting that night over the election of Wilson, who was dear to Turner's heart.[54] These two men, chatting over their soup and wine, had each in his way seen far beyond the details of western history and into "the twilight regions of our historical consciousness."[55] That was a phrase Royce had written long before, about the time Turner was conceiving his famous essay on the frontier. Royce had indeed embarked on that twilight road almost a decade before Turner more dramatically lit the trail.

Still, a hundred years have passed, and we should ask whether Royce, beyond what he meant to his own time, speaks to us now? How does he relate to more recent currents of intellectual inquiry? To begin with, his stated purpose sounds surprisingly like a dictum from the new social history: "The social condition has been throughout of more interest than the individual men, and the men themselves of more interest than their fortunes. . . ."[56] Thus he wrote no biography of Frémont but a critique of how Frémont's actions muddied future racial relations; he related little of the life of James King, the martyred editor, but explored at length how King's death changed the reform consciousness of San Francisco.

In another respect, Royce was an ecologist in that he conceived of life as interacting with an environment. In an address to the National Geographic Society in 1898, "A Psychological Study of the Relations of Climate and Civilization," he continued an interest, first explored in his *California*, in "how the physical features of the Pacific Coast may be expected to mould our national type." In part, he said, the mild climate leads to an intimacy with nature and ultimately to a habit of personal independence.[57] It was the land and its resources, not simply political decisions, that determined patterns of legal title and settlement. Land was the base of his article on the Sacramento squatter riots and it lay at the heart of *The Feud*. But land for Royce went beyond a question of possession; it should lead ultimately to a developed sense of place. Thus geography fed psychology. True, in his own life he abandoned his place, his West, for the East, like Bernard DeVoto later, rather than addressing the East from a base in the West, like Charles Shinn or Vernon Louis Parrington. But, as Kevin Starr has observed, Royce, whatever his personal hegira, always understood the fundamental importance of place and rootedness in a well-ordered community.[58]

As a sociologist Royce recognized racial issues. His sympathetic treatment of Mexican society is not unlike that in Leonard Pitt's *Decline of the Californios* (although when Royce described that society as free, careless, and charming, he sounded more like the generation of Robert Glass Cleland). In the description of the Mexican lineage of Tom in *The Feud*, Royce pursued his racial generalization into a strain of elitism that also emerged in his history, as when he called "the better families" of the community "superior to the average Mexicans."[59] But enlightened attitudes on race were reflected later in his life when, against a tide of national nativism, he publicly supported free immigration.[60]

"Every man looked out for himself in those days," wrote Royce about the mining camps, voicing his refrain on the kind of individualism that had proved so destructive to society.[61] Given the importance of individuality, how could one hope for community? The problem was intrinsically American, having first been formulated by Tocqueville a half-century before. Royce like Tocqueville worried about the leveling "tendency to crush the individual."[62] This intricate tension between the individual and the group would intrigue Royce for the remainder of his life, flowering at the turn of the century in *The World and the Individual*. But always for him the universal came first, like the child beginning with an undifferentiated world and then only slowly recognizing the specifics of individualized milk and mother. Ultimately, however, the individual must return to the realization that he is grounded in the universal, in the one reality.[63] For example, Royce saw the mining camps, at that milk-and-mother stage, as composed of atomized individuals who must someday grope for social cohesion. Such a concept thus foreshadowed his ultimate philosophy.

He likewise understood, like Robert Bellah in our day, how tricky is the concept of individualism, how important it is to isolate its elements. Bellah recognizes two aspects, the expressive and the utilitarian. Royce saw a moral and an immoral side to individualism, depending on whether it led to a strengthening or a weakening of the society.[64] He could embrace some forms of individualism while remaining devoted

to the ultimate community. The values and joys of individualism produced a tension, but finally there should come a release from that tension, a release to be found in social cohesion. Later in his life he claimed
to be a pragmatist while refusing to give up the antithetical position of
absolutism. It was as if he accepted, even courted, ambiguity as a proper
ingredient in human affairs, and so he would not worry about appearing to be both individualistic and communitarian.

Knowing both a dominant mother and a talented wife, Royce was
never ambiguous about the importance of women. In *The Feud* he created a woman of great strength, Margaret, whose complexity went far
beyond any narrowly Victorian concept of womankind. She was falli-
ble, struggling with moral problems such as the love for a married man,
and she earned her goodness, unlike the men of the story for whom
moral dilemmas were given and clear cut. Margaret questioned the stereotype of women as creatures of feeling and concluded, "men are the
least rational beings on earth." In the history Royce clearly saw women—
the catalysts of family, church, school, and local interest—as a strong
counterweight to social disruption and mob disorder.[65]

In the process of examining domestic life, marital relations, and the
behavior of women, Royce thought to ask his own mother, Sarah Bayliss
Royce, to write her memoirs. She responded in a book-length account
of her months on the trail in 1849 and her years in Weaverville, Sacramento, and San Francisco. The manuscript illustrated for Royce how a
religious steadfastness could be intensified on the plains journey, how
a few lonesome families could forge a community, and how vital a role
religion played in early San Francisco life.[66] Royce, who owed so much
to her, gratefully dedicated his history "To my mother, a California pioneer of 1849."

A major strain of modern sociological history is built on Max Weber's
work on collective consciousness (the collective mores of Protestant-
ism, for example, support the presuppositions of capitalism)—what
the more recent historian calls "mentalities." In such thinking, biography is eschewed in favor of a more all-embracing social entity, and
Royce was on an early version of that track. He saw the struggle for
order transcending the conflicting and confused voices of individuals.
Vigilante justice was more than meetings and hangings; it was no less
than "the confession of the past sin of the whole community,"[67] and
as such it held communal meaning. In *The Feud* it was the collective
cause, the fight of Escott's neighbors in the land dispute, that finally
brought changes in individual consciousness.

Like the modern cultural anthropologist, Royce was concerned with the sources of order and disorder. Perhaps his emphasis on social order is not surprising, since he came to maturity in the 1880s, the period in which the modern historian Robert Wiebe found America's self-directed communities faltering before centralized government and the tendency to separate by occupation rather than by community. In Royce's mind, early Californians were creating the very forms that Royce's own society was losing, and he might in consequence have championed the founders of community in California more than he did the perpetuators of self-reliance. The builders of the commonwealth for Royce were not the entrepreneurs and businessmen, as important as they were to him, but the men and women who were bringing traditional forms to a raw, unkempt life. The new society Royce championed was a renewal, not a denial, of the old; ontogeny recapitulated phylogeny. And that society of close-knit community had been undermined by the frontier and was now under attack again by the modern marketplace, factory, and city.

This is not to say that Royce accepted uncritically all forms of traditional community. Groups like individuals could act immorally. The vigilance committee of 1856, for example, for all of its beneficial social effects, was itself no more than a "Business Man's Revolution," a group of entrepreneurs furthering its own economic interests. This hard-headed concept of the vigilance committee has taken a firm hold on subsequent historical interpretation.[68]

As a part of culture, religion was for Royce a keystone. In the 1850s San Francisco, through the eyes of his mother, included "a very goodly array of pioneer churches, supported by active and not poverty-stricken societies." In so balancing the stereotype of the wild and licentious society, he foreshadowed the later writings of John Caughey and Kevin Starr, to name only two.[69] Religion was not just social cement; it was society's affirmation of the universal, the door through which individuals exercise expressive differences while conforming to the unity of tradition.

And, worthy of the recent French *Annales* school of historians, Royce foresaw the modern carryover from technology to culture, notably in underlining the social effects of mining techniques. The shovel and the pan allowed pure individualism; they precluded "secure progress in the organized life of the camps." The cradle was an agent of social change, creating "a collection of mutually more or less independent, but inwardly united bands." Later mining techniques "acted indirectly on society, as a check to the confusion and disorder . . . ," finally bringing men together in companies and more complex social relations. The sluice thus became the "basis for the social life of a civilized community."[70]

Politics as politicians and parties did not much interest Royce, unlike Bancroft and Turner. Royce confined that kind of California activity to a scant six pages at the end of his history. Instead, he frequently delved into political theory as, for example, in extolling the political bent of the typical American or evaluating the forces at the constitutional convention.[71] In his interpretive stance, however, he did not embrace the theoretical radicalism of his own time. He was aware of it, had once in a lecture appeared as an idealistic socialist, and in his history threw side glances at Henry George and the Populists (though never at Karl Marx). The ideas of his fellow Californian, Henry George, certainly lay behind his concerns for "the unfortunate concentration of the land in a comparatively few hands," and it is hardly accidental that Escott in *The Feud* was a closet follower of *Progress and Poverty*.[72]

In the arena of the newer intellectual history Royce today might face the largest number of raised eyebrows. Royce wrote in the history-of-ideas tradition best exemplified by Perry Miller in his monumental efforts to evoke the New England mind. It is the lumping together of such aggregates that most bothers the recent intellectual historian. He is leary of treatises on the national mind or even on the regional mind, preferring to examine groups like the genteel or particular phenomena like the Edenic image, regeneration, or "the hegemonic function of the jeremiad." Historians now typically use individuals in their work as avenues to concepts like antimodernism rather than as insights into something as amorphous as the national character. As a consequence, the new history tends to fragment the past, dissecting classes and separating currents of ideas, which Royce did only on the path to synthesis. Modernists are often more concerned with conflict, as between elites and the common man; when they synthesize, they walk closer to Royce's footsteps. But he attempted more than a simple synthesis; rather, he searched for the essential consensus at the heart of all experience.

Perhaps one best grasps larger national dimensions from a marginal locus. Turner did so from his Middle West; Royce, from California. Neither were then centers of power, but Americans in action there may have come closer to essentially American traits than the people of Washington or New York. Royce understood the importance of the local as an avenue to the universal. The idea would flower in his *Philosophy of Loyalty* (1908): "if you want a great people to be strong, you must depend upon provincial loyalties to mediate between the people and their nation."[73] Thus diversity could embrace unity; California could prefigure the nation.

Josiah Royce loved his native California for what its story said about American values. Physically he had to leave it; intellectually he embraced its message throughout his life. How could a homeland he was so anxious to leave become so soon extolled and revered? It can be argued that Royce had to transcend California in order to become an intellectual, that he was in no sense a California philosopher, but rather a German Idealist, and that all of his significant ideas germinated elsewhere.[74] Such a view can at best be defined as narrow. Any life is the intersection between the direction it faces and the experiences that intersect that bearing. Royce's course was determined in California; the rest was elaboration, though admittedly extensive. All great men must intellectually outgrow the society in which they were born. Royce's birthplace gave him an experience with a very young, immature community, an experience which he both focused and expanded in his history and his novel. Before he died, he came to think that the rest of his life was a resonance from those beginnings.

As a budding philosopher, Royce saw history and literature on a grand scale. Beyond his facts lay an overarching world of meaning. Even his obsession with Frémont's role in the conquest was, in the end, a matter of authority and damaged race relations; the Gold Rush society was an early study in the search for what he would later call the beloved community. Still, through his philosophy emerged remarkable premonitions of a social-science history whose canons would not capture most historians for generations. He saw mining camps as societies wrestling with technological change. He realized the importance of a sense of place, of technology as a factor in social change, of collective consciousness, of the limitations on individualism. "I have learned, as I have toiled for a while over the sources, to see in these days a process of divinely moral significance," he wrote.[75] Divine or otherwise, the significance he saw still speaks to those who yearn for community.

NOTES

1. Major portions of this essay appear with the permission of the editors of *California History*.

2. Josiah Royce, *Letters*, ed. John Clendenning (Chicago: University of Chicago Press, 1970), 112–13.

3. Ibid., 129, 128.

4. Josiah Royce, *California, from the Conquest in 1846 to the Second Vigilance Committee in San Francisco: A Study of American Character* (Santa Barbara: Peregrine Press, 1970), 106, 111. This essay will use throughout the 1970 edition (with introduction by Earl Pomeroy). Except for the front matter, the pagination in the 1970 edition is identical with the original 1886 edition, as it is with the 1948 edition (with introduction by Robert Glass Cleland).

5. Royce, *California*, 92–93.

6. Ibid., 40.

7. Ibid., 6–8.

8. Ibid., 88.

9. Ibid., 106.

10. Ibid., 123.

11. Ibid., 156.

12. Ibid., 175.

13. Ibid., 201.

14. Ibid., 217.

15. Ibid., 255.

16. Ibid., 283.

17. Ibid., 369, 380.

18. Ibid., 394.

19. Royce, *Letters*, 202, 178.

20. *Berkeleyan* 1 (April 1874):10–11.

21. Thomas F. Powell, *Josiah Royce* (New York: Twayne, 1967), 188. John Clendenning, in his introduction to *The Feud of Oakfield Creek* (p. xvii), finds Escott at the philosophic heart of the novel. John O. King III, in *The Iron of Melancholy* (Middletown, Conn.: Wesleyan University Press, 1983), emphasizes the character of Margaret (pp. 210–12).

22. Royce, "The Squatter Riot of '50 in Sacramento: Its Causes and Significance," *Overland Monthly* 6 (September 1885):225–46. Royce, *Letters*, 204.

23. *Overland Monthly* 8 (August 1886):222–23.

24. 1 (1886):492; the Oak reply, *Overland Monthly* 8 (September 1886):330.

25. *Overland Monthly* 8 (August 1886):216. *Appleton's Cyclopaedia* (New York 1887–89), articles on Alvarado, Arce, Bryant, Brannon [?], Coleman [?]. *Century* 18 (1890):775–94; 21 (1891–92):133–50, 296–309; 19 (1891):780–83, 928–29. *Nation* 42 (March 11, 1886):220–22; 43 (July 29, 1886):99–101; 44 (January 13, 1887):39–40; 48 (February 14, 1889):140–42, 164–65.

26. Royce, "Frémont," *Atlantic* 66 (October 1890):557, 548, 550, 555.

27. Royce, "The Conquest of California," *Century* 19 (April 1891):923.

28. Royce, "The Frémont Legend," *Nation* 52 (May 21, 1891):425.

29. Royce, *Letters*, 157–65, 170–74.

30. Royce, *Philosophy of Loyalty* (New York: Macmillan, 1908), 287.

31. Royce, *Basic Writings*, ed. John L. McDermott (Chicago: University of Chicago Press, 1969), I:32. Andrew Rolle, "Exploring an Explorer: Psychohis-

tory and John Charles Frémont," *Pacific Historical Review* 51 (May 1982):135–63.

32. Ashbel Green to Robert V. Hine, March 7, 1986.

33. Stewart, New York *Times*, September 12, 1948; Jackson, San Francisco *Chronicle*, September 20, 1948; Paul, *Mississippi Valley Historical Review* 35 (1948–49):711–12; Barker, *American Historical Review* 54 (April 1949):705–6.

34. Gibbs M. Smith to Robert V. Hine, February 11, 1986; Kenneth Johnson, *Journal of the West* 10 (October 1971):751; *Zamorano 80* [catalogue of an exhibition] (San Marino, Calif.: Huntington Library, 1986), no. 66. The Zamorano Club—historians, librarians, collectors—in 1945 chose the eighty most important books on California.

35. Royce, *California*, 59, 61, 40–50.

36. Ibid., 228.

37. Ibid., xvii.

38. Royce, *Letters*, 178. Donald C. Biggs, *Conquer and Colonize* (San Rafael, Calif.: Presidio Press, 1977):183, uses Royce's table.

39. Ibid., 174; Royce, *California*, 324–25.

40. Royce, *Letters*, 178.

41. Royce to John W. Buckham, June 15, 1915, Clifford L. Barrett Collection, Box 1, Huntington Library.

42. Royce, *California*, 79.

43. Ibid., 371.

44. Ibid., 110; see also the comparison of vigilantes to coyote packs, 267.

45. Ibid., 369.

46. Ibid., 164, 171.

47. Ibid., 8, 242, 333.

48. Ibid., 130.

49. Ibid., 41–42, 62, 216, 267; Vincent Buranelli, *Josiah Royce* (New York: Twayne, 1964), 24.

50. Buranelli, *Royce*, 147.

51. Dominick LaCapra, *Rethinking Intellectual History* (Ithaca, N.Y.: Cornell University Press, 1983), 16–17.

52. Royce, *Spirit of Modern Philosophy* (New York: Dover, 1983), 264.

53. Frederick Jackson Turner, *The Significance of Sections in American History* (New York: Holt, 1932), 45; *The Frontier in American History* (New York: Holt, 1920), 157–58, 358.

54. Turner to Mae Turner, November 16, 1912, Box H, Turner Papers, Huntington Library.

55. Royce, "The Frémont Legend," *Nation* 52 (May 21, 1891):425.

56. Royce, *California*, xvii.

57. Royce, *Basic Writings*, 1:182, 195–97; Royce, *Race Questions, Provincialism, and other American Problems* (New York: Macmillan, 1908), 170.

58. Kevin Starr, *Americans and the California Dream* (New York: Oxford University Press, 1973), 143–45.

59. Royce, *California*, 25.

60. Mercedes M. Randall, ed., *Beyond Nationalism: The Social Thought of Emily Greene Balch* (New York: Twayne, 1972), 51; Martha Winnacker to Robert V. Hine, October 7, 1986.

61. Royce, *California*, 232.

62. Royce, *Race Questions*, 75.

63. Royce, *Letters*, 342; Bruce Kuklick, *Josiah Royce: An Intellectual Biography* (Indianapolis: Bobbs-Merrill, 1972), 110.

64. Robert Bellah, et al., *Habits of the Heart* (New York: Harper and Row, 1985), 32–35.

65. Royce, *The Feud of Oakfield Creek* (New York: Johnson Reprint, 1970), 29; except for front matter, this reprint is paged identically with the 1887 edition. Royce, *California*, 295.

66. Sarah Bayliss Royce, *A Frontier Lady* (New Haven: Yale University Press, 1932).

67. Royce, *California*, 332.

68. Ibid., 346; the most impressive recent reflection is Peter R. Decker, *Fortunes and Failures* (Cambridge: Harvard University Press, 1978), 139–41.

69. Royce, *California*, 311. John Caughey, *Gold is the Cornerstone* (Berkeley: University of California Press, 1948), 272–74; Starr, *Americans*, 69–86.

70. Royce, *California*, 225, 227, 244, 245.

71. Royce was wrong in assessing the southern forces at the convention; Walton Bean and James Rawls, *California: An Interpretive History* (New York: McGraw-Hill, 1983), 102; it is interesting to note, however, how closely in other connections Bean and Rawls follow Royce: for example, see pp. 77–78.

72. Royce, *California*, 386; Royce, *Feud*, 357–58.

73. Royce, *Philosophy of Loyalty*, 248.

74. Robert Whittemore, *Makers of the American Mind* (New York: William Morrow, 1964), 380.

75. Royce, *California*, 394.

BIBLIOGRAPHY

WRITINGS BY JOSIAH ROYCE

Basic Writings. Ed. John J. McDermott, with annotated bibliography by Ignas Skrupskelis. 2 vols. Chicago: University of Chicago Press, 1969.

California, from the Conquest in 1846 to the Second Vigilance Committee in San Francisco: A Study of American Character. Boston: Houghton Mifflin, 1886; with introduction by Robert Glass Cleland, New York: Knopf, 1948; with introduction by Earl Pomeroy, Santa Barbara, Calif.: Peregrine, 1970.

The Feud of Oakfield Creek: A Novel of California Life. Boston: Houghton Mifflin, 1887; with introduction by John Clendenning, New York: Johnson, 1970.

Letters. Ed. John Clendenning. Chicago: University of Chicago Press, 1970.

WRITINGS ABOUT JOSIAH ROYCE

Clendenning, John. *The Life and Thought of Josiah Royce*. Madison: University of Wisconsin Press, 1985.

Conser, Walter, Jr. "The Reassessment of Josiah Royce." *American Studies* 27 (Fall 1986):54–60.

Hine, Robert V. "The American West as Metaphysics: A Perspective on Josiah Royce," *Pacific Historical Review* 58 (August 1989):267–91.

———. "A Centennial for Josiah Royce," *California History* 66 (June 1987):82–93, 153.

———. *Community on the American Frontier: Separate but Not Alone*. Norman: University of Oklahoma Press, 1980.

———. *Grass Valley to Harvard: Josiah Royce and the American West*. Norman: University of Oklahoma Press, 1991.

Kuklick, Bruce. *Josiah Royce: An Intellectual Biography*. Indianapolis: Bobbs-Merrill, 1972.

Oppenheim, Frank M. "Josiah Royce's Intellectual Development: An Hypothesis." *Idealistic Studies* 6 (January 1976):85–104.

———. "Some New Documents on Royce's Early Experiences of Communities." *Journal of the History of Philosophy* 6 (1968):381–85.

Paul, Rodman W. "Sarah Eleanor Bayliss Royce." *Notable American Women*, vol. 3 (Cambridge: Harvard University Press, 1971), 205–6.

Perry, Ralph Barton. "Josiah Royce." *Dictionary of American Biography,* vol. 8 (New York: Scribner's, 1936), 205–11.

Pomeroy, Earl. "Josiah Royce, Historian in Quest of Community." *Pacific Historical Review* 40 (February 1971):1–20.

Royce, Sarah Eleanor Bayliss. *A Frontier Lady: Recollections of the Gold Rush and Early California*. Ed. Ralph H. Gabriel. New Haven: Yale University Press, 1932.

Starr, Kevin. *Americans and the California Dream, 1850–1915*. New York: Oxford University Press, 1975.

2

Hubert Howe Bancroft: First Western Regionalist

CHARLES S. PETERSON

*H*UBERT HOWE BANCROFT WAS and remains a perplexing figure among western historians. He sold books successfully in nineteenth-century San Francisco, accumulated a modest fortune, collected a vast library of California and other Pacific Slope materials, produced assembly-line history under his name, published the thirty-nine volumes of Bancroft's *Works*, and made it pay. He was also beleaguered with challenges rising from the ethics of his production methods and questions about his emphases on narrative history and exhaustive detail. Perhaps more significantly, he established a great history collection, now the Bancroft Library at the University of California, Berkeley, and before others had marked the way, he laid out the boundaries and proportions of regional history in the western part of North America. Productive, resourceful, controversial; any of the three might have given him lasting fame. Yet personal qualities joined with his commercial approach to flaw his reputation, even while his approach to a region's history was widely emulated by others.

Bancroft has been an enigma to historians. During his life some were enthusiastic about his work. A handful classed him as great. Others found much to condemn. Some were put off by how business management impacted upon historical method, while others were offended by his prejudices. Although hundreds of westerners—collectors and regional writers—shared his passions, and, in measures less grand, followed in his footsteps, as well as used the books he had written, he belonged to no school of history from which to take discipline, and he had few protégés to sing his praise.

With their attention running to Frederick Jackson Turner, Herbert Eugene Bolton, or Walter Prescott Webb, modern historiographers, too, have paid Bancroft scant attention, and in a few cases they have denounced him outright. Even in praise they have maintained a certain distance. A case in point is David Weber who in articles on provincialism and borderlands history gives him only a passing nod.[1] To some degree, this is even true of Bancroft's major biographer John W. Caughey, in *Hubert Howe Bancroft: Historian of the West* (1946). In what is clearly a labor of love, Caughey offers a sympathetic appraisal of Bancroft and analyzes each of the thirty-nine volumes of his *Works* appreciatively. But in his approach, Caughey stops short of the close embrace that a Van Wyck Brooks might reserve for a William Prescott in *The Flowering of New England*.

If there is reserve in Caughey's treatment, Harry Clark's *A Venture in History: The Production, Publication, and Sale of the Works of Hubert Howe Bancroft* (1973) manages an almost clinical distance in an insightful and otherwise fairhanded study that emphasizes Bancroft's undertaking as a business operation. And Kevin Starr, who is happy enough to use Bancroft to establish several early points in his superb *Americans and the California Dream, 1850–1915* (1973), lapses into what might be termed outright Bancroft-bashing when he sees "hatred" and "inarticulate fury" in his discussion of Spanish architecture.[2]

Western historians have nevertheless depended heavily upon Bancroft's contributions. For generations regionalists were influenced by the patterns and proportions set in his *Works*, a phenomenon that led Caughey to conclude that Bancroft was more influential than ever in 1946. As late as the 1960s, in an article that ranked Bancroft with the great Frederick Jackson Turner, historian Earl Pomeroy recognized a continuing need for Pacific Coast scholars to look beyond Bancroft's anachronisms to his strengths and called for an enlarged use of his works.[3]

My purpose in this essay will be to consider again where Bancroft stands in a field of history for which his *Works* provided a foundation but in which he has never been fully accepted. My assumptions are that Bancroft left an enduring legacy both as collector and as historian. He was a man of his times. His response to the past was the product of those times. The success of his response helped project the influence of those times into the regionalist historiography of the West until at least 1950. In the decades since, as regional studies have suffered, changed and, at least at times, declined, Bancroft and the continental drift of popular tastes in history that he reflected are still forces to be reckoned with.

The West "fastened itself upon" Hubert Howe Bancroft by entirely typical means.[4] He was born to a westering family in 1832 at Granville, Ohio, in "an atmosphere of pungent and invigorating puritanism."[5] Of "sturdy New England stock," Bancroft's father was driven by a "spirit of unrest," arriving in Granville after two moves with his parents in 1814. Later he moved to New Madrid, Missouri, "the land of puckering persimmons," as Bancroft called it, only to return after "three years of ague and earthquakes agitation."[6] With the Gold Rush, the elder Bancroft followed his oldest son, Curtis, to California although he was twice the age of most argonauts. Soon Hubert himself and several other Bancrofts joined the rush to the west.

Although proud of the "stern rectitudes" of Granville's puritanism, young Hubert's roots were sufficiently shaken by the move to Missouri and other elements of his early life that they did not sink deep in the Midwest.[7] At sixteen he abandoned formal schooling forever when a sister's marriage to book dealer George Derby opened a beginning-slot opportunity in Buffalo, New York. After fumbling badly as an odd-jobs boy, he returned to Ohio with a consignment of books that he peddled to good advantage, demonstrating as much initiative when working on his own as he had displayed ineptitude under his brother-in-law's critical eye. A longer period at the Buffalo shop followed during which Bancroft strutted away his leisure but blossomed as a clerk. His sense that the region of his youth was a good place to grow up but a bad place to spend a lifetime began to assert itself at this time.[8]

His apprenticeship now filled, he was off to California in 1852. With a supply of books and close friend George L. Kenny, a fellow clerk, he made an exciting passage via Havana, Nicaragua, and Panama. This first of many Isthmian trips suggests that there may well have been an autobiographical dimension to the regional form he later gave to his *Works*. After landing briefly at San Diego and Monterey, he arrived during March 1852 in San Francisco, well ahead of the books he was to sell. First determining that Sacramento would be the most promising market for his books, he proceeded to the mining camps. For six months he worked in his brother's Rich Bar store and skinned mules with his father, experiencing the mining boom at the diggings level, before returning to Sacramento and learning of George Derby's untimely death. The books were disposed of at a nice profit in a deal that left Bancroft unemployed. In experiencing another dimension of the Gold Rush, he hunted work fruitlessly in San Francisco for six months before moving to Crescent City. Hard work and a clerkship with privileges to merchandize his own stationery line enabled him to net six thousand dollars, which he invested in a commercial building. He also observed mining camp justice in its rawest form before returning to the East late in 1855 via the Panama route.[9]

Homecoming was first joyous and then disappointing, and Bancroft's thoughts turned again to the opportunities and freedoms of the Pacific Coast. In the West, "all was new, all was to be done"; in the East "beginnings were pretty well over."[10] In 1856 he was off with a new bride and a head full of plans. Bank-rolled by his sister, George Derby's widow, and with loans finagled on that panic-period's tight money markets, he took a well-chosen stock of books and paper supplies with him. Friend George Kenny became his partner, and with a growing staff of able and loyal men, H. H. Bancroft Company was established in rented San Francisco quarters.[11]

His business quickly expanded into a full line of book and publishing-related services. Included in its operation were wholesale and retail branches, printing and binding operations, and book and paper supplies in law, business, school, and music as well as general literary materials. Joined by younger brother A. L., who became a key management figure, Bancroft was a basic supplier for regions extending from Mexico to Alaska and the Rocky Mountains. Conforming generally to the region his history defined, Bancroft Company's book and paper supply trade became the largest in the West. By 1870 it may even have been "one of the most extensive in the world," as he later opined without undue modesty.[12] The Civil War particularly was a time of profits and advance. The 1869 construction of a large new building on Market Street far beyond the heart of town was a gamble, but it proved to be an astute move as the town grew in that direction. Hard times, due to changes in the competition caused by the transcontinental railroad, challenged Bancroft's business acumen, as did organizational and promotional problems incident to his growing love for regional history.[13]

By his early thirties Bancroft could well be numbered among what he later called the builders of the western commonwealth. Accumulating a modest fortune he was able to maintain it in spite of disastrous fires, bitter family and business struggles, historiographic challenge, and some truly ingenious entrepreneurial experimentation. This wealth became his first step in an accumulative process by which westerners, individuals and society alike, tended to collect first "riches" then "parlor bric-a-brac," and finally "local history, all," as historian Earl Pomeroy explained, "uncritically and in excessive quantities."[14]

Bancroft epitomized many of the motives and tendencies of this regional pattern. Indeed, his financial success was only tentatively established when his mind turned to historical collection in 1859. Even in this first modest endeavor there was an instinctive impulse to make history serve both business and the cause of regional identity. Bancroft Company's nascent publication program included a California almanac for which information had to be checked. To this end, all the books relating to California history that could be found around the business were shelved near the editor's desk. From this initial assemblage of fewer than seventy-five books, Bancroft's collection grew quickly to a thousand volumes by 1862 as he exhausted the holdings of rare book dealers on the West and East coasts.[15]

A growing appreciation of the Hispanic role in California and trips abroad led him to look for materials in England and Europe. About this time, he also determined to make his in-gathering truly comprehensive, which meant that he not only looked for everything on an event or person but that he also extended his search across class lines and international borders as he followed Spanish penetration, exploration, and course of empire, everyday life, and the fur trade into Pacific Slope regions extending from Panama to Alaska. He also increased his efforts to gather materials that reflected the lives of common people. Papers regarded as junk by others became rare finds as he indulged his interest in ordinary doings. To facilitate this broadened strategy and now beginning to write, he placed his California business increasingly under the competent direction of his brother A. L. He also hired European agents and bibliographers and personally searched unnumbered book stalls, antiquarian warehouses, and catalogs. Within a year or two he had "rifled America and ransacked Europe."[16]

About this time European auctions attracted his attention, signaling yet another advance in his strategy. Although he was selective in his buying he invested boldly when necessary, acquiring entire collections on some occasions. Among the most important was the 1868 purchase of three thousand items from the renowned collections carried out of Mexico by Maximilianist exile José María Andrade. Never, thought Bancroft, had such a loss "fallen on the country" since Zumárraga set torch to irreplaceable Aztec manuscripts.[17] Only a little less spectacular was the 1876 purchase from the E. G. Squier collection of some six hundred volumes emphasizing Central America and including items from Alexander von Humboldt's library. Another coup was the Ramírez Mexicana purchase that cost Bancroft thirty thousand dollars, a staggering sum that made him think his own collection was "worth at least a million dollars by 1880."[18]

With his library holding more than sixteen thousand volumes, and headed for a total of sixty thousand, Bancroft's always keen fear of fire was sharpened by a blaze late in 1872 that by good fortune did not reach his library on the fifth floor of his Market Street building.[19] He lived with this threat for upwards of a decade when business pressures combined with this consuming fear to convince him that his library had to have a new home. Finding a promising site on Valencia Street, he built a highly functional building for the Bancroft Library, which he hoped would be not merely a "depository of learning but a society for the promotion of knowledge."[20]

After the famous auction purchases, Bancroft moved into a phase directly connected with the writing and sale of his *Works* during the later 1870s and 1880s. At no time in his European and earlier Hispanic American collecting had he paid much attention to the great public and church archives either in the New World or in Spain or Portugal. Nor did he now appear to be fully aware of their significance, but pressed by the demands of writing he turned to various public and quasipublic archives located mainly in the United States but, in some degree, in Mexico as well. He also recognized that collecting private papers could be a boon to sales. High-powered salesmen, including Bancroft himself, flocked across the West and Mexico, presenting the now-in-full process *Works* as a public service to the various subregions that would be enhanced by personal dictations from prospective buyers. The vanity pitch also encouraged prospects to donate private papers and collections, thus becoming collaborators in what Bancroft argued was the only truly cooperative history.[21]

Perhaps the prime example of this was General Mariano Guadalupe Vallejo, "the noblest Spaniard of all," in Bancroft's eyes, to whom master pitchman Enrique Cerruti "laid seige." Vallejo was "the very embodiment of history" but "wary." Cerruti was "wily" but ready to take what he could get if he could not get what he wanted. Ultimately, Cerruti won Vallejo's affection as well as his historical collection, scoring what Caughey terms the greatest coup of Bancroft's entire collecting career.[22] Another case involved Mormon–Utah collections that Bancroft himself nurtured with periodic visits, flattery, honest sympathy, and the work of a battery of dictation-taking salesmen. Meanwhile, a corps of copyists and abstractors transcribed and abstracted the holdings of various public and government archives, especially in California. Newspapers, "bad masters but good and indispensable servants," were sought for their usefulness to history and came in at the rate of fifty thousand per year.[23]

In all, it was a colossal undertaking and successful beyond Bancroft's dreams. A region's form was embodied in the historical sources it brought together. Strong for the entire stretch of the Pacific Coast and western slope of the continent, it was comprehensive in its coverage of California.[24] Beginning with the earliest Spanish approach, issues of chronology and social development including the ebb and flow of Hispanic influence and the political and economic conquest of the Yankees had produced a scattered but extensive regional record. Almost the first American collector in the field, Bancroft recognized that the harvest was ripe and effectively gathered it. By the 1870s he possessed a growing collection that by its very existence gave perspective to a region that was primarily American yet reached beyond the bounds of any single set of cultural or political influences. He now set out to apply his collection to history with the same businesslike practicality that had initially led him to utilize a handful of books on California to improve the early almanac.[25]

As the 1870s progressed, Bancroft was increasingly moved to write and publish. An early plan was a proposed historical encyclopedia of California. At that stage he neither understood how his library would be used or what role he personally would play as a writer. It is clear, however, that some interest was shown in the encyclopedia as a cooperative effort and that, among others, John S. Hittell, the author of a handbook on California resources, had placed his considerable prestige behind it. Yet problems persisted, including some related to Bancroft's own determination to write and questions of how the rapidly growing collection could be utilized, as well as the inherent problems of business organization. As the encyclopedia project foundered Bancroft lost interest, but he returned from a trip to the East late in 1871 more than ever determined to write and resolved to meet the challenges of business and data management.[26]

At this point, a word should be interjected about Bancroft and history. As one contemplates his autobiographical writings and his career, as well as what later historians have said, it is clear that he was sensitive to a large number of impulses that were more or less historically related. Indeed, he was an extraordinarily complex individual within whom the sensibilities of his times met in various degrees of impact.

Never really worked into a systematic order in his mind, this array of consciousness contributed to the great versatility of his personality but complicated his career, making it difficult to assess his contributions.

Among the forces that moved him were continuing influences from the romantic movement. Although an increasingly industrialized and urbanized East was moving into an era when the literature of realism would be more appreciated, the influence of New England's romantic historians was still large. National as well as regional tastes were still willing to accept romantic and narrative conventions, particularly in their application to western themes. The influence of George Bancroft's romantic nationalism and the narrative claims of both William Prescott and Francis Parkman were widely appreciated. Although there are significant differences between Bancroft and the romantic nationalists, important parallels exist, especially where Prescott and Parkman are concerned, including an affinity for narrative history, an interest in Hispanic and frontiering themes, and a dependence on subscription marketing to reach the public.[27]

Yet, California and San Francisco, rather than Boston and the eastern shore, lay at the heart of Bancroft's historical world. To him, California represented an almost sublime consummation. In it was epitomized the march of the American people westward, fulfilling a larger destiny that had rolled forth from the first migrations of classical times. Now, at last, the human tide, enlightened by the contributions of science, morality, and the attributes of freedom, played out a final chapter as civilization came full circle. As Bancroft put it, "there was on this coast the ringing-up of universal intelligence for a final display of what man can do at his best, with all the powers of the past united, and surrounded by conditions such as had never before fallen to the lot of man."[28] Nostalgia and national pride have seldom swelled stronger. No further Wests existed. By the 1870s sentiment filled Bancroft's heart. His were mythic ideas, to be sure, and romantically poetic in expression, but widely shared, they formed the backbone for what struck Bancroft as a once-in-all-time opportunity and a transcending responsibility.

The West's stage of development played an important part in the shape that Bancroft's interest in history took, giving romanticism a sharp regional turn. In the national destiny, empire's course had been east to west. The record of the eastern shore had been collected and its story told. California by contrast was unstoried, and there Bancroft and his small cohort of literary workmen traversed unmarked terrain. Advancing beyond its first beginnings California had tempered, and now a summing up seemed possible. Yet it was far from old; many of its first generation survived, eye witnesses to culminating global events in a heretofore repeated process of westering that mankind could never relive again.[29]

If, for many, the continental perspective progressed from east to west, there was a south-to-north bias for Bancroft. His initial approach had been south to north, and so it remained as trade territory, and finally collection and writing firmed up his regional perspectives. Not only did he regard the Yankee tide coming to lodge against his last coast with nostalgia, but he incorporated the Spanish conquest and the broader maritime struggles for empire as grand epochs in the best romantic tradition. Such awareness gave a different bent to his geographical perspectives, if indeed they did not totally free him from the westering biases of Manifest Destiny. History, for him, was the definition of a region with California as center and culmination, extending south to north, transcending national boundaries as if drawn by the sea, and articulating inland to the Pacific Slope states. In Indian relations, exploration, and fur trade, his *Works* extended eastward from the Pacific Slope, but in not much else. In the main, he drew his region's eastward boundary with states that lay along the Continental Divide. Such a geography allowed him to tell a story of local enthusiasm and regional pride in all the comprehensive and colored detail that his situation as a participant prepared him for emotionally.

Ultimately, however, full treatment and chronology dominated his mind. The full story guided him as he wrestled with the problems of organization, composition, and publication in the same way that comprehensive coverage had guided the collection of data. The seven-and-a-half feet of Bancroft's *Works* indelibly attest that history is the full story in exhaustive detail.[30] Although chronological limits might have simplified his task, full narrative demanded that history start at the beginning and proceed chronologically.[31] This Bancroft learned in the early 1870s as he turned out his first awkward chapters on Spanish beginnings in Central America and Mexico. Recognizing that everywhere he touched the Spanish story Indians were there earlier, he paused to initiate the five volumes of the *Native Races* in the middle 1870s. As volumes multiplied during the early 1880s the stories of Central America, Mexico, and California also unfolded chronologically. Thereafter, volumes were issued on a state-by-state basis, with each repeating a familiar chronology as the entirety of Bancroft's *Works* was completed by 1890.

The full narrative also "dealt in facts"; facts of which there were too few in "current history"; facts "gathered from new fields and conveniently arranged." In that form, he hoped his histories would be "the raw material for students in the branches of science, and for philosophers in their generalizations." Theories at this stage of the game seemed premature, indeed, "worse than thrown away."[32] At an early point he declared the presentation of facts was the noblest work; "the more we penetrate into fact, the more will our nature be quickened, enriched, and exalted."[33] Thus he was freed from the "trammels" that advancing tastes in history might have placed on him.[34] He was left to mine his sources and, in lengthening recitation, to present the facts.

If he was not deeply interested in historical judgements, Bancroft still arrived at strong opinions from the sources. Indeed, he viewed some individuals and events by standards that for his time were both advanced and courageous. Examples might include the critical light in which he cast the role of the United States in the Mexican War and his adverse portrayal of John C. Frémont in the Bear Flag Revolution for which he was read out of the California Historical Society in 1893.[35] Yet another example was his sympathetic treatment of the Mormons, establishing them firmly in the context of regional history and in effect leading the changing spirit by which they were accepted into full national fellowship after 1890.[36] Yet even in making such concessions to his judgmental capacities, the critical process was less important to Bancroft than the story, comprehensive in its totality yet measured in its relative importance by its regional relationships to California, by romantic interest, and by market considerations.[37]

Conceived as raw material and comprehensive recitation, Bancroft's published account drew on almost interminably. Running to millions of words and thirty-nine, eight-hundred-page-volumes, the *Works* have been likened to reference or research sources more than history. In 1884 a reviewer accurately called one of his books "an historical library condensed," and yearned for appropriate generalizations as he moaned that "we are drowned in details and gasp for breath." In 1886 Lord James Bryce commented cryptically on Bancroft's effort to catalog "every bullock whose hide was ever exported from Mexican California." Another Englishman observed that Alaska had no history and that Bancroft had written it in 750 pages. With piercing insight and tongue only partly in cheek, Earl Pomeroy has written that to copy from him is hardly plagiarism.[38] In this light, the essential likeness of Bancroft's *Works* to the editorial feats of Reuben Gold Thwaites and other great western editors down to the time of LeRoy Hafen, Donald Jackson, and Mary Lee Spence may be recognized.

It is also clear that certain cultural predispositions and biases colored Bancroft's view of history. Progress was of the natural order. Social Darwinism and ideas of racial superiority often lay behind his assumptions about human events and the relations of peoples.[39] Neoclassical influences show strongly in his sense of antiquity's worth, as they do in his prose, which is liberally sprinkled, if not crowded, with Latin phrases and allusions to classical events and figures.[40] Typical was his confession that while it would clearly be beyond him, his dream was to be to the Pacific Coast as Homer had been to Greece.[41]

Perhaps an even stronger force was the business ethic, the moral and organizational superiority of which he stoutly defended. Wealth was both attainable and indispensable. With it, intellect could be ransomed, for one not to prosper in California was inexcusable. Equally apparent in his writing are Puritan and Victorian values, including his ideas about work, thrift, success, and antifeminist biases that, however, did not keep him from being a loving and even submissive husband.[42]

Not surprisingly, Jacksonian elements also abound in Bancroft's values. He repeatedly stated his faith in the common man's ability to perform any function. Writing the history of the Pacific Coast was as immense an undertaking as building the transcontinental railroad had been. But small men with no special preparation built a railroad, and a small man, even an untutored one, could write great history.[43] In important aspects, this point of view was a matter of self-confidence. But it was also a social view that contributed to the exhaustive detail of his history as well as to the organization that he set up to write it. One dimension of this view is illustrated in his introduction to the *History of Central America,* written very early as something of a preface to his entire work. There, he acknowledged his interest in the deeds of great men and heroic traditions, but then added, "as for rulers and generals, we discover in them the creatures, not the creators of civilization." Without resolving contradictions between his admiration of success and the importance of the rank and file, he concluded that he sought "the man," the art, the culture, and the custom "even down to dress, or the lack of it," for these were "the man and the man is the nation."[44]

Another suggestion of Jacksonian influence may be seen in the limited role formal education played in his own life and in his attitudes toward higher education. Statements that nearly reject advanced education run through his biographical writings. He thought a college education for a son would be a liability except in training for specific professions. Having made this concession, he expressed outright distrust of those for whom higher education was necessary. Moreover, he saw little evidence that college men made contributions of real consequence. In his experience it was not they who conducted "the great affairs of life." Genius, he granted, was incomplete without cultivation, but even acknowledging this, few were "educated into greatness." Few also were the great men, "who made primary use of education in building their ladder to fame."[45] While this attitude may reflect a sense of inferiority, Bancroft rarely admitted to any personal deficiency connected with his own truncated schooling. His faith in the common man and his disdain for advanced education may turn attention again to the way he organized his work force to mass-produce history.

By the early 1870s the initial experiments had been made. The encyclopedia project had been tried and dropped. A gifted librarian had been found in Henry L. Oak, and the library had been moved to the fifth floor of Bancroft's Market Street building. There, Bancroft began to establish what he called a literary workshop and to work out the "division of labor" necessary to write and market history.[46]

Bancroft's collections assembled the best "products of 10,000 minds."[47] Yet in writing history he did not surround himself with the best historical and literary minds in the land. He thought, rather, that common sense and willingness to work were more essential, and he proceeded by trial and error to put his research and writing force together. Gradually, a core of loyal and capable workers was organized. Some were journalists, a few had publishing or editorial experience, several were accomplished linguists, and many had commercial, consular, and military experience. Of the inner group, most were foreign born. With one or two possible exceptions, they had no very clear institutional connections. Although they were widely traveled and cosmopolitan, Bancroft's comment that one of them was "of no very pronounced parts" seems applicable to the entire group.[48] Yet, under his direction, they were capable of prodigious achievement. That he molded a productive staff was an accomplishment that paralleled the brilliant work of John Wesley Powell in bringing together the geological and artistic talents necessary to unlock the natural history of the West. During the two decades that Bancroft's *Works* were in progress, some six hundred employees passed through his literary workshop. Of these, no more than one hundred stayed long, with perhaps fifty working at a given time. As few as a score proved to be really proficient, and ten or twelve became truly indispensable.[49]

Chief assistant was Henry L. Oak, an intelligent, industrious man. Born in Garland, Maine, in 1844, he was one of the few Yankees in Bancroft's literary workshop, and he was also an exception in his formal education, having graduated from Dartmouth. He taught in the East for a time, then moved to California, where he clerked, taught again, and edited a Presbyterian journal before joining Bancroft. He was expert in Spanish and French, a tireless worker, an effective administrator, and had "a talent for . . . clear, effective writing." He was indispensable in the library and actually wrote more of Bancroft's *Works* than any other person.[50]

Also important was William Nemos. Born to a noble Swedish family in 1848, Nemos's formal schooling included stints at St. Petersburg and the Stockholm gymnasium. However, family reverses interfered with plans for university training and forced him into a succession of clerkships in London. There, he perfected his English, traveled widely on the Continent, and read extensively in philosophy. In 1870 he went to the Australian gold fields and from there to Hawaii, San Francisco, Oregon, and back to Bancroft's workshop. Lingual gifts, administrative experience, a flare for writing, and an ingratiating personality enabled him to "become Bancroft's right-hand man in the training of workers and planning of procedure." He later claimed that his duties included much of the hiring for the literary staff and the supervision of even his foremost peers.[51]

Another key contributor was regionalist Frances Fuller Victor. The only woman in the top assistants, she was born in New York in 1826. She early showed an affinity for writing and had published poetry and fiction before moving to San Francisco with her husband in 1863. There, she wrote for the *San Francisco Bulletin* under the pen name Florence Fane, before moving to Oregon where she had written two fine examples of what would later be called regional history, *River of the West* (1870) and *All Over Oregon and Washington* (1872). An exception in that she was a well-established writer when she joined Bancroft in 1878, she overcame his determined bias that women lacked the sustained energy to produce effectively. For years she gave unstinting and faithful service. Among Bancroft's assistants, only she enjoyed a historical reputation independent of his *Works*. That reputation, like her work for Bancroft, was clearly in the regional mold.[52]

Of New England parentage was Central American specialist Thomas

Savage. He was born in Havana in 1823, and grew up there and in Central America, speaking Spanish as his first language but acquiring full skills in English and French. He had a distinguished career in commerce and the consular service in Cuba before and during the Civil War. Contributing further to his immense personal knowledge of Latin America were editorial, commercial, and diplomatic experiences in El Salvador and Guatemala before he moved to San Francisco and joined Bancroft.[53]

Much appreciated for his rare promotional gifts, including his ability to feed Bancroft's ego, was Italian Enrique Cerruti, who claimed noble heritage and involvement in an amazing list of Central American intrigues. Possessed of an "irresistible tendency to rise above the truth," he also had an "unerring perception" of when to flatter and when to "be matter of fact." These qualities, plus his success in placing promotional articles in Italian, French, and Spanish journals and his great success as a collector, made Ceruti Bancroft's favorite. After his 1876 suicide, an affection that transcended the realities of Cerruti's considerable contributions was apparent in Bancroft's lament, "Alas, Cerruti! . . . I could have better lost a better man!"[54]

Only less important were several others, mostly of European background. Walter M. Fisher and T. Arundel Harcourt were Englishmen who joined the group in 1872. They were widely read, fascinated with California, and aspired to literary careers. After a relatively short time, they left Bancroft's shop, with his blessing, to take over the editorship of the *Overland Monthly*, previously edited by Bret Harte, where the good support they gave to their former employer speaks well for the professional boost he provided them. Returning to England, Fisher criticized much about California in his book *The Californians* (1876), but he was "most cordial" in his references to Bancroft, whose personal copy he inscribed "to the greatest Californian of them all."[55]

J. J. Peatfield and Alfred Bates were also British. They arrived in San Francisco by way of mining, commercial, and editorial experiences in Canada, New Zealand, and the American West. Like Oak, Peatfield was a college man with a degree from Cambridge. Bates had assisted historian John S. Hittell and was recommended to Bancroft by him as was New Yorker Edward P. Newkirk, a veteran of the Civil War and military service in California and Alaska. All three gave good service but appear to have been little advanced by their stint with Bancroft.[56]

Although the list of Bancroft assistants included many individuals of Hispanic background as well as others from America and Europe, our list here may be rounded out by reference to Ivan Petroff. Schooled in St. Petersburg he had spent years in Paris and New York and had served in the Union army. After the war he worked for the Russian American Company in Alaska, and he was said to have even sustained a wound from an encounter with Shoshone Indians while en route to that employment. Returning to San Francisco in 1870, he became Bancroft's expert on the Russian language and a prime figure in collecting and writing the Alaska and Washington histories.[57]

These ten assistants and a few others stand out as people who actually shared in the authorship of Bancroft's *Works*.[58] Whatever else can be said for them, they joined Bancroft for varying periods in an intellectual undertaking that was maintained from 1870 to about 1890. It involved conceptual planning, intensive research, writing against a tight schedule, and sustained effort. In the beginning, at least, it was an exhilarating experience. For Bancroft himself it was an escape from tedious commercial work and an intellectual consummation. There can be no doubt that his passion for history and his vision of the *Works'* mission were transmitted to his assistants. Many of them shared his enthusiasm, especially in the early years. Writing primarily of Fisher and Harcourt but also of other close associates, Bancroft gave a sincere if flowery sense of their experience when he declared: "Oh, the grand days we had, warm with hope and strong with endurance! If no man says it, I dare to say it, there have been lesser heroes than we, up on that fifth floor in a San Francisco bookshop, fighting against the smiles of the children of mammon and of Belial, fighting alone, modest and silent."[59]

As the 1870s progressed, Bancroft and key assistants launched his work. By trial and error, they first indexed his collection to put it at the disposal of researchers and writers, and then with indexing taking form as an industrial procedure, they began to write. As with all writing, getting started was difficult. Experimenting toward a technique that was essentially a process of compressing data, their early drafts misfired and were abandoned.

Bancroft did not "fancy" Indian history, but an impasse on Spanish beginnings was not resolved until they decided that the subject of native races would have to be treated first.[60] This decision itself raised challenges of immense proportions. Anthropology and archaeology were in their infancy. Bancroft apparently had some question about the popularity of Indian history and may have worried about how it would sell. Nevertheless, he hoped to avoid negative views and was determined to represent Indians as "they stood . . . before the withering hand of civilization was laid upon them."[61] Planning a volume on wild tribes and one on civilized peoples (Aztecs and Mayas), his workshop moved ahead, with writers more or less keeping pace with reductionists who indexed, organized, and placed the material before them. The data was good, the biases of the writers were not retrogressive for the time, and devices used for organization were innovative and intelligent. Classifications working from north to south were devised, and lingual distinctions and architectural attainments were described. Yet the five volumes that *Native Races* finally filled failed to work out scientific methods that would have significant impact.

As the first volume approached publication in 1874, Bancroft made a decision that led ultimately to bitter recrimination among his top collaborators and to lasting criticism from historians. It had been his plan that the refinement of data would flow smoothly from the library's vast reservoirs through a succession of assistants to an ultimate step in which he actually wrote his histories.[62] Although he wrote untiringly with a wordy fluency, this plan did not work. In practice, it was necessary to have others do much of the writing, although Bancroft maintained full conceptual responsibility and to some degree appears to have edited almost everything that came out under his name. Also, for purposes of promotion and sales, it was much easier to establish reputation and eye appeal for a single writer than for a team. Thus, a history organized for business purposes but extending into scholarly functions was jointly written but attributed to Bancroft alone.[63]

As a key step toward establishing his reputation, Bancroft took a prepublication copy of the first volume of *Native Races* east on a barnstorming tour during which he laid his "scrivenings . . . on the lap of the gods."[64] He was already far enough into the review process to be keenly aware of prejudice against "scholarly writing by men of the market place," and he knew well that many easterners believed no scholarly good could come from California. Consequently, he had traveled eastward with great trepidation.[65] Fortified by letters of introduction and guides picked up along the way, he described his assembly-line methods of research and promoted *Native Races* to an amazing list of literary notables. Among scores, he visited Asa Gray, John Greenleaf Whittier, Ralph Waldo Emerson, Henry Wadsworth Longfellow, George Bancroft, and William H. Prescott. Key contacts were Francis Parkman and Clarence King, both of whom wrote favorable reviews. Bancroft lined up D. Appleton and Company as publishers for *Native Races* and talked with editors, including T. W. Higginson of *Scribner's*, E. L. Godkin of the *Nation*, and William Dean Howells of the *Atlantic*. He also sent copies to Herbert Spencer, Thomas Huxley, and Charles Darwin, among other English greats.[66]

This campaign was apparently limited to private meetings and review solicitation. In the published record, there is no evidence that Bancroft lectured before learned societies, universities, or the public, nor does it appear that he did so later in his career. Why lectures do not appear on his eastern agenda is difficult to know, but it seems consistent with his misgivings about higher education and the trepidation his entire career manifested for the learned. However, the eastern tour produced a rich harvest of endorsements, and when the first volume of *Native Races* appeared it was often favorably reviewed. Bancroft enthusiastically wrote that "never" was "a book so generously reviewed" and "never an author so suddenly brought to attention."[67]

By 1874 Bancroft had established a flourishing subscription department under the direction of Nathan J. Stone, a "hard working . . . New Englander" with book-selling experience in Japan.[68] Sometime after the initial contract with D. Appleton Company for *Native Races* ran out, Bancroft shifted publication to his own shop. Aggressive sales techniques were applied, including the scheduled publication of a new volume every three months, installment-plan buying, and the assurance that the *Works* would be sold only as a set. Potential buyers were also encouraged to see their subscriptions as an essential part of a public work that would be "a lasting benefit" to their part of the country.[69] Canvassers covered the entire West, ultimately selling six thousand or more orders for one or the other of the numerous forms in which the set was offered. This number, of course, fell far short of best-seller classification, but it did total about one-quarter of a million books and probably represented a saturation of the market for an expensive item of its kind. Both of Bancroft's biographers concluded that the *Works* more than paid their own way.[70]

A major effort was made to aid sales by establishing a continuing flow of books. Proceeding in approximate chronological order, the set also progressed more or less from south to north. Volumes are numbered through the five volumes of *Native Races*; to the three volumes for the *History of Central America*; six volumes for the *History of Mexico*; two volumes for the *History of the North Mexican States and Texas*; seven volumes for the *History of California*; plus four volumes on special California topics, including *Popular Tribunals*, a superb, if loosely attributed, work; and nine volumes for neighboring states of which the *History of Oregon* and the *History of the Northwest Coast* each comprise two volumes. The *History of Utah*, the *History of British Columbia*, and the *History of Alaska* each receive a single volume; and multiple-state volumes treat the *History of Arizona and New Mexico*, the *History of Nevada, Colorado, and Wyoming*, and the *History of Washington, Idaho, and Montana*. The autobiographical *Literary Industries* and a miscellaneous collection of essays completed the thirty-nine volumes of Bancroft's *Works*.

Scholars have concluded that Bancroft himself wrote only about nine volumes.[71] Several of these have been termed "essays" and lack the intensive footnoting that characterizes much of the rest of the set. It must also be admitted that they lack the discipline and order that works by some of the other writers achieved, although for strength of presentation and spontaneity the special California volumes, including *Popular Tribunals*, which he wrote, made lasting contributions. As the *Works* were published, only a general effort was made to maintain numerical order. Books came out as they were finished, with the last of them appearing in 1890.

After 1886 evidences of mounting strains may be seen. In that year the Market Street building burned. Bancroft was crippled emotionally by the blow, although much of the literary work was by this time carried on at the library on Valencia Street. Nathan Stone, Oak, and others moved copy forward in the production process, thus maintaining the publication schedule. A. L. Bancroft, who had long since emerged as chief business manager, quickly took advantage of proffered credit and widespread sympathy to get the broader business moving again before fundamental policy disagreements split the two brothers as a team and left them battling in the courts and as inveterate personal enemies. With A. L. now in competition, Hubert advanced a nephew, William Bancroft, with whom he also had a major falling out by the early 1890s.[72]

Meanwhile, the sales campaign and production of the histories came on hard times. Subscribers first complained as the tide of costly volumes ran beyond their interest, then revolted as they learned they had signed ironclad contracts. Reviews became increasingly caustic as the procedures by which Bancroft had managed publicity deteriorated. In Montana, a sense that vanity had been unethically manipulated as a sales ploy flared into an embarrassing and injurious incident. This was doubly untimely since Bancroft was moving into an even more patent application of vanity publication. Unblushingly called the "Chronicle of the Kings" initially, but later reined back to become *Builders of the Commonwealth*, this series aimed at a thousand westerners of note who were to pay by the page for biographical sketches and pictures. Although only about one hundred subscribed, the project was carried profitably for a time but led to further recrimination about the vanity aspects of Bancroft's *Works* and to yet another bitter fight, this time between Bancroft and Nathan Stone whose capable management of the sales division had been an important part of the *Works'* success.[73]

Worst of all, personal relations broke down in the literary workshop. Fire, law suits, and personal acrimony between Bancroft and the management team played on tensions that had never been entirely absent. Published in 1890, *Literary Industries* proved unequivocally that Bancroft did not intend to credit collaborators in any way for their writing. Ceruti was dead, and Fisher and Harcourt, who contributed so vitally to the euphoric spirit of the first years, were long gone. For those who remained, the strain of unremitting effort was strong, and amid a mounting sense of injury Henry L. Oak, William Nemos, and Francis Fuller Victor took their leave.

Within a few years, each of them challenged Bancroft's claim to sole authorship of the *Works*. In an Oregon exhibit at the 1893 Chicago World's Fair, Victor displayed four volumes under her name. The same year, Henry L. Oak published his embittered *"Literary Industries" in a New Light*. Defending the success of the *Works* as annals although acknowledging their shortcomings as history and admitting that Bancroft was the "best writer of the entire staff," Oak insisted that he and other collaborators were actual authors.[74] For himself Oak claimed about ten volumes, to Nemos and Victor he attributed about five each, and to others varying smaller contributions. Although his attack has been called mean-spirited and inept, Oak's count has been pretty much accepted.[75] Back in Sweden, Nemos's claims were more private in character but extended to rather broad conceptual and administrative credits as well as to writing. A further examination of who wrote what was the 1903 work of Oregon historian William Morris, who, in a spirited defense of Francis Fuller Victor, carefully analyzed the relative contributions of all parties, including Bancroft, for the *Quarterly of the Oregon Historical Society*.

It was a rough decade, but Bancroft survived the 1890s with some wealth and a considerable portion of his self-esteem. Still abounding in energy, he stepped up his tempo in the vanity field, publishing about twenty volumes that can probably be best described under that rubric, and wrote an expansionist work on the Spanish American War. As he moved toward retirement, nothing did more to stabilize and extend his reputation than the arrangement whereby his library was transfered to the University of California in 1905. Questions about its worth were silenced by an appraisal at 300,000 dollars by Reuben Gold Thwaites, the widely acknowledged editor and regionalist from Wisconsin. At length, Bancroft was paid 150,000 dollars and credited with a 100,000-dollar donation to the university. During the next ten or twelve years Bancroft continued a vigorous although largely unsung career as a writer turning out at least a half-dozen books on San Francisco, Mexico, and related topics. If he was little praised, at least criticism died down. A certain diffidence in public situations continued to characterize his life, but in his intimate family he enjoyed good relations and much happiness. In 1918 Bancroft's long life ended a few days after what had appeared to be a minor accident involving a streetcar.[76]

More than seven decades later, Hubert Howe Bancroft continues to pose certain enigmas for western history. Fundamentally, questions about him seem to relate to his position between the romantic past and the scientific future, a stance that was itself complicated by the way his personality and career placed him at a point of tension and misunderstanding between enterprise and letters. It is significant that his collections are still widely hailed. The interests of thousands of bibliophiles in business, public life, and local history have continued to reflect the Bancroft Library's content, although not much is made of the connection between Bancroft and the emergence of the Borderlands field of western history under Herbert Eugene Bolton, who after 1911 was curator of the Bancroft Library as well as professor of history at the University of California. Because of their vastness and a half-life as business achievement as well as their unconventional authorship, Bancroft's *Works* remain difficult to assess. In person he is no less an enigma since merging currents from earlier values, contemporary forces, personal qualities, and a hybrid career confound efforts to understand him.

Thus, the reader is still dependent upon biographers and historiographers who have addressed Bancroft in one way or the other. One may long for the effusive praise of a Vernon Parrington, but a realistic sampling of Bancroft's *Works*, perhaps *Literary Industries*, and one or two other volumes in their entirety and extensive reading in a dozen others, would confirm that the reserved sympathy with which John

W. Caughey and Harry Clark approached him is, after all, the greater service. Indeed, one wonders if a spirit of biographical sympathy may not have carried Caughey too far when he repeatedly credited partial volume treatments for Colorado, Wyoming, or Washington as being in proper proportion to Bancroft's overall story. On the other hand, one tends to read with appreciation when Californian Caughey generously concludes that "the aggregate knowledge of California history, . . . derives less from . . . [all] modern [pre-1946] scholars than from Bancroft."[77] Yet a further venture is needed into questions involved in the way Bancroft embodied the tensions between enterprise and letters, on the one hand, and, on the other hand, stood on the fault line between the continental drift of society's general tastes in history and the surface action of professional or scientific history.[78]

One also takes satisfaction from Caughey's comparative analysis. Comparison is especially striking when Caughey places Bancroft's treatment of Cortez in Mexico ahead of William Prescott's *The Conquest of Mexico* in access to facts and in an attitude responsive to the Aztec situation, and only somewhat behind it in readibility.[79] Also interesting is Caughey's suggestion that as a history of the North American fur trade, the two-volume *History of the Northwest Coast*, of which Bancroft was the primary author, "might well be put" ahead of Hiram Chittenden's famed *The Early American Fur Trade in the Far West*.[80] Caughey might have added that there is organizational strength in Bancroft's foray into larger Wests that provides both continental and national symmetry for a regionalism that hinges at California and swings along the Pacific Coast and Rocky Mountains. Certainly, it was a symmetry that was not lost upon Bernard DeVoto as he wrote *The Course of Empire* (1952), or as he defined a "continental dynamic" in *The Year of Decision* (1943); undertakings that branded DeVoto as a romantic, and led him to write in 1943 that he had "found you had better not decide that Bancroft was wrong until you have rigorously tested what you think you know."[81] Together with his sense for California as summation, Bancroft's fascination with Cortez and his appreciation for the continental sweep of the fur trade marked him as one in whom regionalism and romanticism came together. It was a union of mood and theme into which not only DeVoto but many other regionalists and indeed an entire region's society followed him.

With business as the primary focus of his study, Harry Clark's conclusions highlight other aspects of the Bancroftian dilemma. In keeping with others, Clark grants that "comprehensive acquisition" made Bancroft's library significant in its time.[82] Thereafter, analysis from the point of business explains some of the tension lines between enterprise and letters. To produce history, Bancroft compressed his holdings and presented them to the public by means of subscription sales. His method required capital, enormous resources of information, and competent writers content with anonymity, plus a means of rebuilding depleted capital. In his use of eyewitness accounts and newspapers Bancroft was ahead of most of his contemporaries. His use of assistants to process his data was logical and defensible to a point. Clark further explains that scheduled production and the custom of offering large volumes in subscription marketing (matters of size and speed) led to the use of "aimless ramblings" when filler became necessary and overdependence on footnotes in small print to cram wordy manuscripts into allocated pages.[83] Even worse, subscription history left little time for analysis or synthesis, realities that Bancroft defended by arguing that the historian's highest purpose was the presentation of facts.

Clark's Bancroft was more "impresario" than historian.[84] He had a genius for improvising, but lacked a capacity for deliberate planning. He possessed boundless energy that under control kept him at his task for twenty years, but running loose broke his business to pieces and alienated his associates. He created a business technique that, for a time, maintained a market but was too specialized to create a lasting trend. He was aware of the scientist's insistence on facts but failed to follow the scientific method into the formulation and testing of principles. Rather than finished history, his *Works* were a comprehensive source "shaped in large part by the manner of [their] production, publication, and sale." Although Clark concludes that Bancroft's *Works* were a dead end both as a business procedure and as a historical method, he agrees with Caughey that as a comprehensive record they have a continued relevancy.[85]

Clark's insights are profound but provide only a limited view of the man. Caughey's treatment is much fuller. Similar in spirit is Pomeroy's important article pairing Bancroft with Turner as the primary promoters of an "absorption" with the West as nostalgia and consummation. Both historians sold, according to Pomeroy, "the one as idea, the other as mass, as shelf space—to a public" of whom they were a reflection.[86] Pomeroy was bold in pairing Bancroft with Turner, but perhaps he failed to go far enough. Bancroft's nostalgia in the face of a closing frontier preceded Turner's by nearly forty years. And ultimately, it well may be that his reticence about the scholarly community, his nostalgic affinity for comprehensive treatment, and his romantic elaboration more accurately reflected broadly held popular tastes in history than did Turner's penchant for theories and interpretation, although it must be admitted that in his poetry, romance, and nationalism Turner, as well, reflected popular tastes that go far to explain the lasting power of his work.

In conclusion, Bancroft may be viewed as fully consistent with his times. He partook of influences that were both forward-looking and timeworn. He had the entrepreneur's will to experiment boldly, the romantic's love for drama and sweeping action, and the scientist's instinct for fact. As an American he understood that more is better. As a businessman he entered a supporting rather than central industry and then worked himself into history, a business so specialized, as Clark says, that it could not establish a trend, and a literary pursuit so businesslike that historians ever since have distrusted him. He brought romantic and Jacksonian views to history at a time when scientific analysis and specialization were displacing romanticism and the common man. In the sense that he never trained anyone to do better what he had done, he had no direct disciples to proclaim his name. He manipulated the review process to sell books rather than to refine or enlarge his views. He made history serve vanity. He only partially attributed writing others had done. And he gave little thought to theory and interpretation.

In all this, it is clear that he responded directly to broad undercurrents in American culture. Faithful to these influences, his systemization was along regional lines, factual content, and romantic view. He conceived of a different regionalism for America. He handled it to incorporate cultural and geographical considerations as well as nationalism's spirit. It was a course of development by which he made significant contributions to the patterns in which western history has since been treated. If he failed to bring scientific testing to history, he brought respect for sources and honesty as he contemplated the record. He was courageous in stating his positions, and as DeVoto pointed out, many of his biases can be explained.[87] And finally he was the primary force in conceiving, organizing, and writing one of the greatest works on western history.

In all, it was a notable achievement, one that places him alongside such contemporaries as Reuben Gold Thwaites and Frederick Jackson Turner. He was a worker in the field of western history upon whom historians and westerners continue to depend.

NOTES

1. David J. Weber, "Mexico's Far Northern Frontier, 1821–1854: Historiography Askew," *Western Historical Quarterly* 7 (July 1976):279–94; and "Turner, the Boltonians, and the Borderlands," *American Historical Review* 91 (February 1986):66–81. Articles in which Bancroft's historical methods are given more or less attention include William Alfred Morris, "The Origin and Authorship of the Bancroft Pacific States Publications: A History of A History," *Quarterly of the Oregon Historical Society* 4 (December 1903):287–364; William A. Dunning, "A Generation of American Historiography," American Historical Association, *Annual Report* (1917):347–54; John R. McCarthy, "Wholesale Historian: Hubert Howe Bancroft," *American Heritage* 1 (Spring 1950):17–19; Hazel Emery Mills, "The Emergence of Frances Fuller Victor—Historian," *Oregon Historical Quarterly* 62 (December 1961):309–36; John H. Krenkel, "Bancroft's Assembly Line Histories," *American History Illustrated* 1 (February 1967):44–49.

2. Kevin Starr, *Americans and the California Dream 1850–1915* (New York: Oxford University Press, 1973), 395–96.

3. John W. Caughey, "Hubert Howe Bancroft, Historian of Western America," *American Historical Review* 50 (April 1945):461–70; Earl Pomeroy, "Old Lamps for New: The Cultural Lag in Pacific Coast Historiography," *Arizona and the West* 2 (Summer 1969):107–26.

4. Hubert Howe Bancroft, *Literary Industries*, 29, *The Works of Hubert Howe Bancroft* (San Francisco: History Company, Publishers, 1890), 143.

5. *Literary Industries*, 63.

6. *Literary Industries*, 77–78; John W. Caughey, *Hubert Howe Bancroft: Historian of the West* (Berkeley: University of California Press, 1946), 3. Caughey follows the biographical format of *Literary Industries* fairly and in some detail as he presents Bancroft's life.

7. *Literary Industries*, 63–109.

8. *Literary Industries*, 109–20.

9. *Literary Industries*, 120–65; Bancroft, *California Inter Pocula*, 35, *The Works of Hubert Howe Bancroft* (San Francisco: History Company Publishers, 1888), chaps. 5–7; and Caughey, *Hubert Howe Bancroft*, 27.

10. *Literary Industries*, 143–44; Caughey, *Hubert Howe Bancroft*, 41–42; Harry Clark, *A Venture in History: The Production, Publication, and Sale of the Works of Hubert Howe Bancroft*. (Berkeley: University of California Press, 1973), 6.

11. *Literary Industries*, 147–67.

12. *Literary Industries*, 162.

13. *Literary Industries*, 156, 164.

14. Pomeroy, "Old Lamps for New," 118.

15. *Literary Industries*, 173–75.

16. *Literary Industries*, 177–85.

17. *Literary Industries*, 189.

18. *Literary Industries*, 185–96; and Caughey, *Hubert Howe Bancroft*, 74–77.

19. *Literary Industries*, 578.
20. *Literary Industries*, 201.
21. *Literary Industries*, 764–68; and Caughey, *Hubert Howe Bancroft*, 272.
22. Caughey, *Hubert Howe Bancroft*, 111.
23. *Literary Industries*, 33, 575.
24. Caughey, *Hubert Howe Bancroft*, 190.
25. Caughey, *Hubert Howe Bancroft*, 85.
26. *Literary Industries*, 229.
27. Both Caughey and Clark see parallels in Bancroft's and Prescott's interests. Certainly, Bancroft sought support from them. *Literary Industries*, 287, 338; Caughey, *Hubert Howe Bancroft*, 118, 149, 170; and Clark, *Venture in History*, 39–42, 45–47.
28. *Literary Industries*, 2.
29. *Literary Industries*, 3–17, 278.
30. *Literary Industries*, 601.
31. *Literary Industries*, 288.
32. *Literary Industries*, 32; Bancroft, *Central America*, 1:ix, 113.
33. *Central America*, 1:xiv.
34. *Literary Industries*, 343.
35. Caughey, *Hubert Howe Bancroft*, 341–46.
36. *Literary Industries*, 631–40, 759–61.
37. Both John Caughey and Harry Clark address these questions at length, Caughey in a general consideration and Clark with a focus tending strongly to market questions.
38. Arthur R. Roper, *English Historical Review* 3 (January 1888):182–83; *Nation*, March 11, 1886, 220; *English Historical Review* 1 (July 1886):591. All as quoted in Pomeroy, "Old Lamps for New," 110–11.
39. The immutability of progress is never consistently developed but appears repeatedly in *Literary Industries* and guides his assumptions about race and conquest in his *Works* generally. See p. 785 for a glaring example of how far his mind ran on this issue.
40. Although a specialist was hired to help lace the *Works* with allusions to mythology, ancient history, and the classicists of more recent time, *Literary Industries* fairly bristles with them, and one assumes Bancroft himself was adept at their use. Point after point is thus introduced. Examples can be found on pp. 76, 77, 79, 87, 95, 103, 107, 164, 587, 607, and 609, among others.
41. *Literary Industries*, 278.
42. *Literary Industries*, 101–11, on business especially, but throughout; for Bancroft's feminist point of view, see *Literary Industries*, 235–36.
43. *Literary Industries*, 286, 230–306; also Caughey, *Hubert Howe Bancroft*, 99–101.
44. *Central America*, 1:xxii.
45. *Literary Industries*, 150, 676.
46. *Literary Industries*, 579.

47. *Literary Industries*, 232.

48. *Literary Industries*, 264; for general descriptions of his method, see *Literary Industries*, 230–306; and Caughey, *Hubert Howe Bancroft*, 99–102.

49. Caughey, *Hubert Howe Bancroft*, 102.

50. *Literary Industries*, 219–24, 246–51; Caughey, *Hubert Howe Bancroft*, 104–5; Henry L. Oak, *"Literary Industries" in a New Light: A Statement on the Authorship of Bancroft's Native Races and History of the Pacific States, with Comments on These Works and the System by Which They Were Written* (San Francisco: Bacon Printing Co., 1893); and William A. Morris, "Authorship of the Bancroft Pacific States Publications."

51. *Literary Industries*, 251–55; Caughey, *Hubert Howe Bancroft*, 106–7; William A. Morris, "Authorship of the Bancroft Pacific States Publications"; and Harry Clark, *Venture in History*, adds considerable information not found elsewhere, 22–32.

52. *Literary Industries*, 259–61; William A. Morris, "Authorship of the Bancroft Pacific States Publications," 314–18; Mills, "The Emergence of Frances Fuller Victor—Historian," 309–36; and Caughey, *Hubert Howe Bancroft*, 108–9.

53. *Literary Industries*, 255–59; and Caughey, *Hubert Howe Bancroft*, 107.

54. *Literary Industries*, 365–76, 383–445; and Caughey, *Hubert Howe Bancroft*, 110–11.

55. *Literary Industries*, 261–63; and Caughey, *Hubert Howe Bancroft*, 112–13.

56. *Literary Industries*, 265–69; and Caughey, *Hubert Howe Bancroft*, 113.

57. Ibid.

58. In addition to these, Caughey credits Albert Goldschmidt,[?] Kuhn, G. B. Griffin, and A. Bowman with writing fragments up to one-half a volume. *Hubert Howe Bancroft*, 262–63.

59. *Literary Industries*, 263.

60. *Literary Industries*, 295–97.

61. Ibid.

62. *Literary Industries*, 230–306, 245–46.

63. John Caughey describes this decision as the gravest mistake of Bancroft's life. See Caughey, "Hubert Howe Bancroft, Historian of Western America," 467; and Caughey, *Hubert Howe Bancroft*, 268.

64. Caughey, *Hubert Howe Bancroft*, 114.

65. *Literary Industries*, 310–11.

66. *Literary Industries*, 355.

67. *Literary Industries*, 361, Caughey, *Hubert Howe Bancroft*, 156.

68. Clark, *Venture in History*, 61.

69. *Literary Industries*, 791–93.

70. Caughey, *Hubert Howe Bancroft*, 300; and Clark, *Venture in History*, 164.

71. Caughey, *Hubert Howe Bancroft*, 262–63.

72. By all odds, the best treatment of difficulties after 1886 is in Clark, *Venture in History*, 143–53.

73. Clark, *Venture in History*, 145–47.

74. Oak, *"Literary Industries" in a New Light*, 35; and Caughey, *Hubert Howe Bancroft*, 332–38.

75. Clark, *Venture in History*, 26; and Caughey, *Hubert Howe Bancroft*, 336.

76. Caughey, *Hubert Howe Bancroft*, 391–408.

77. Vernon L. Parrington, *The Romantic Revolution in America 1800–1860*, vol. 2, *Main Currents in American Thought* (New York: Harcourt, Brace and Company, 1927), 427–31; Caughey, *Hubert Howe Bancroft*, 200.

78. Caughey, *Hubert Howe Bancroft*, 197–98.

79. Caughey, *Hubert Howe Bancroft*, 118, 132, 170.

80. Caughey, *Hubert Howe Bancroft*, 219–20.

81. Bernard DeVoto, *The Year of Decision, 1846* (Boston: Houghton Mifflin Company, 1943), 525.

82. Clark, *Venture in History*, 155.

83. Clark, *Venture in History*, 165.

84. Clark, *Venture in History*, 161.

85. Clark, *Venture in History*, 166.

86. Pomeroy, "Old Lamps for New," 117–19.

BIBLIOGRAPHY

BOOKS BY HUBERT HOWE BANCROFT

Achievements of Civilization: The Book of Wealth. 10 vols. New York: Bancroft Co., 1896–1908.

The Book of the Fair. 2 vols. Chicago and San Francisco: Bancroft Co., 1893–1894.

The Chronicles of the Builders of the Commonwealth. 7 vols. San Francisco: History Co., 1891–1892.

The Native Races of the Pacific States of North America. 5 vols. New York: D. Appleton, 1874–1876. Reissued as *Native Races*.

The New Pacific. New York: Bancroft Co., 1900.

A Popular History of the Mexican People. San Francisco: History Co., 1887.

Retrospection. New York: Bancroft Co., 1912.

Vida de Porfirio Díaz: Reseña Histórica y Social Pasado y presente de México. San Francisco: History Co., 1887.

The Works of Hubert Howe Bancroft. 39 vols. San Francisco: A. L. Bancroft and Company, 1882–1890.

WORKS ABOUT HUBERT HOWE BANCROFT

Bloom, Jo Tice, "Hubert Howe Bancroft." In John R. Wunder, ed., *Historians of the American Frontier: A Bio-Bibliographical Sourcebook*. Westport, Conn.: Greenwood Press, 1988, 56–64.

Caughey, John W., "Hubert Howe Bancroft, Historian of Western America." *American Historical Review* 50 (April 1945):461–70.

———. *Hubert Howe Bancroft: Historian of the West*. Berkeley and Los Angeles: University of California Press, 1946.

Clark, Harry. *A Venture in History: The Production, Publication, and Sale of the Works of Hubert Howe Bancroft*. Berkeley and Los Angeles: University of California Press, 1973.

Cutter, Donald C. "A Dedication to the Memory of Hubert Howe Bancroft, 1832–1918." *Arizona and the West* 2 (Summer 1960):105–6.

Dunning, William A. "A Generation of American Historiography." In American Historical Association, *Annual Report* (1917):347–54.

Krenkel, John H., "Bancroft's Assembly Line Histories." *American History Illustrated* 1 (February 1967):44–49.

McCarthy, J. R. "Wholesale Historian: Hubert Howe Bancroft." *American Heritage* 1 (Spring 1950):17–19.

Morris, William A. "The Origin and Authorship of the Bancroft Pacific States Publications: A History of a History." *Oregon Historical Quarterly* 4 (December 1903):34–74.

Oak, Henry Lebbeus. *"Literary Industries" in a New Light*. San Francisco: Bacon Printing Co., 1893.

Pomeroy, Earl "Hubert Howe Bancroft." In Howard R. Lamar, ed., *Reader's Encyclopedia of the American West*. New York: Thomas Y. Crowell Co., 1977.

———. "Old Lamps for New: The Cultural Lag in Pacific Coast Historiography." *Arizona and the West* 2 (Summer 1960):107–26.

II

*Frederick Jackson Turner
and Classic Western Historians*

3

Turner's First Stand:
The Significance of Significance
in American History

WILLIAM CRONON

𝒜T THE BEGINNING OF THE last decade of the nineteenth century, a young historian from the University of Wisconsin rose before a gathering of his peers to deliver a lecture that would announce to the world a new way of thinking about American history. Not yet thirty years old, he spoke with a scholar's quiet passion about a revolution then taking place in studies of the past, a new scientific approach that would supersede the old-fashioned histories of an earlier generation. To understand the United States, he argued, historians should move beyond biographies of heroic leaders and narratives of great political events to discover the deeper forces that had shaped the nation and its citizens. "The story of the peopling of America," he declared, "has not yet been written. We do not understand ourselves."[1]

It was a watershed in the development of history as an academic discipline.[2] The young historian was of course Frederick Jackson Turner, but the year was not 1893 and the speech was not "The Significance of the Frontier in American History."[3] Turner was speaking on a sultry August evening in 1890 to a group of public schoolteachers who had gathered in Madison, Wisconsin, for a meeting of the Southwestern Wisconsin Teachers' Association.[4] His topic was much broader than the one that would make him famous: he was urging upon his listeners not the significance of the frontier, but of history itself. His arguments revealed the enthusiasms of a recently minted Ph.D. for the German scholarship he had read in graduate school, but they were also one of the earliest systematic statements of a progressive approach to the American past that would soon dominate history as a discipline. Without understanding what Turner said about "The Significance of History" that August evening, one cannot understand how and why he approached "the frontier" as he did.

Turner began by noting that the great American historians of an earlier time had seen their work primarily as a form of literature, a great narrative about the political events that had shaped the United States as a nation. Whatever the merits of such an approach, he argued, it was now being supplemented if not replaced by the new analytical methods that American scholars were learning from Germany. The initial object of the new techniques had been to get as close as possible to past politics through a precise examination of original documents. But the new methods were also opening up nonpolitical approaches that could considerably broaden the canvas on which historians worked. Economic history, in particular, seemed to hold out the promise of getting beneath politics to root causes, showing that "property, the distribution of wealth, the social conditions of the people, are the underlying and determining factors" of history.[5] If only one could get at such factors, one could transform history from literature into science.

Exploring past economics instead of past politics not only brought one closer to the deeper causes of past change; it also brought one closer to "the great mass of the people," to a truly democratic history. Instead of "the brilliant annals of the few," American historians should seek to uncover the ordinary lives of the many. "Far ofter than has yet been shown," Turner said, "have these underlying economic facts affecting the breadwinners of the nation been the secret of the nation's rise or fall, by the side of which much that has passed as history is the merest frippery."[6] In the years since the Civil War, economic questions— about currency, about factories, about labor and capital—had all emerged as the new storm centers of American political life because of their profound effects on the farmers and workers who were the vast majority of American citizens. To understand these modern controversies, one had to trace their stories backward in time. "Viewed from this position," the young scholar declared, "the past is filled with new meaning."[7]

New meaning was what Turner sought, and it led him to the most radical argument he offered to the Wisconsin schoolteachers that evening. History, he said, was not a subject about which one could ever reach a final and definite conclusion. It would ever remain in a state of flux, reshaped by the questions that people now living asked about themselves and the past from which they came. Antiquarians might cherish the "dead past"; historians must seek in their subject "the living present."[8] Despite their passion first and foremost for discovering the truth about earlier eras, they were inevitably partisans of their own time. There was no objective Archimedean point upon which a scholar could stand to gain an unbiased view of history, and so "no historian can say the ultimate word."[9] It would be foolish even to try. The power of good history derived not from the past, but from the ongoing encounter between past and present that occurred when people sought to discover the meaning of their lives so as to plot their best course into an unknown future. "Today," Turner said, "is so much a product of yesterday that yesterday can only be understood as it is explained by today."[10]

One wonders what the schoolteachers made of all this. The German immigrants among them—and those who knew their Emerson—could perhaps recognize the philosophical idealism that underpinned Turner's arguments, but they surely also experienced some tension between what he was saying and the rote history they taught from their textbooks.[11] It was an extraordinarily relativist and presentist message for a nineteenth-century audience to hear, but it pointed the way toward the pragmatic epistemological stance that would so characterize American progressive thought. Turner was nothing if not a progressive. The specific historical agenda he urged on his listeners had all the earmarks of an early, optimistic progressivism—just as his own argument predicted it would.

Reading that agenda today, it is impossible not to see in it the seeds of the frontier thesis.[12] But because Turner framed "The Significance of History" even more broadly than he did his better-known later works, one can also discover in it the intellectual commitments that led Turner to think the frontier so important. One was a belief that history must draw from all other intellectual disciplines: it was not just past politics or economics or literature or religion—it was all these things together. Its traces were everywhere, so that one must cast one's research net well beyond the library to do the subject justice: "wherever there remains a chipped flint, a spearhead, a piece of pottery, a pyramid, a picture, a poem, a coliseum, or a coin," Turner said, "there is history."[13] The story one pieced together from such fragments was ultimately about evolution, a progressive narrative about the sequential stages of social growth that mimicked what Darwin had discovered in biology. If this was true, then the history of every time and place, no matter how seemingly trivial or insignificant, partook of the great epic that was life itself.

If one could recapture local history from the antiquarians, one would find in it a meaning that could stand proudly even next to the famed histories of Greece or Rome. "Each age," Turner said, "must be studied in the light of all the past; local history must be viewed in the light of world history."[14]

Here was a powerful new source of significance for the American past. To locate it, American historians had only to trace the evolution of the United States and its people back to their European roots. America was a land of immigrants. Wherever its restless inhabitants went, they carried with them the hopes, legacies, and burdens of a thousand other places, a thousand other times. Their encounter between the world they had left behind and the world that had become their new home was the central drama of the American past, from which all other meanings derived. American history was world history. Here, Turner neared the climax of his sermon. "Consider," he said,

> *how our vast Western domain has been settled. Louis XIV devastates the Palatinate, and soon hundreds of its inhabitants are hewing down the forests of Pennsylvania. The bishop of Salzburg persecutes his Protestant subjects, and the woods of Georgia sound to the crack of Teutonic rifles. Presbyterians are oppressed in Ireland, and soon in Tennessee and Kentucky the fires of pioneers gleam. . . . These men have come to us historical products, they have brought to us not merely so much bone and sinew, not merely so much money, not merely so much manual skill, they have brought with them deeply inrooted customs and ideas. . . . Our destiny is interwoven with theirs; how shall we understand American history without understanding European history?[15]*

How indeed? The Yankees, Germans, Swedes, Irish, and other Wisconsinites who sat in the hall that evening could instantly recognize the pasts that had just received Turner's most exuberant rhetorical flourish. The significance of history was the significance of their own lives.

The young man who spoke so eloquently that evening had come to the lecture podium by a fairly direct path. Born of old New England stock on November 14, 1861, Frederick Jackson Turner had spent the first eighteen years of his life in the small Wisconsin town of Portage.[16] Few midwestern sites had an older European heritage. It was on this marshy strip of land between the Fox and Wisconsin rivers that Jacques

Marquette and Louis Jolliet had crossed from the watershed of the Great Lakes into that of the Mississippi on their journey of discovery nearly two hundred years before Turner's birth. A key link in the fur trade, Portage by the mid-nineteenth century had emerged as a thriving agricultural and lumbering center as well, with nearly three thousand inhabitants the year before Fred Turner was born. Its prosperous wood-framed houses and brick commercial structures marked it as one of the more promising towns in Wisconsin, as did its flour mill, grain elevator, iron furnace, chair factory, and two breweries.[17] Portage was already nearing the end of what Turner would call its "frontier phase," but the signs of its recent transformation were everywhere. Like other Wisconsin communities, its inhabitants were a polyglot jumble. "It was," Turner remembered, "a town with a real collection of types from all the world, Yankees from Maine & Vermont, New York Yankees, Dutchmen from the Mohawk, braw curlers from the Highlands, Southerners—all kinds." In the countryside around it, Norwegian, Swiss, Scottish, and Welsh communities clustered in little farming hamlets that seemed straight out of Europe.[18]

Fred's father, Andrew Jackson Turner, was the editor of the local newspaper and a prominent figure in town politics. Jack Turner had an editor's knack for speaking to the diverse constituencies of his town and "helped to shepherd a very composite flock" in a way that taught his son the social realities at the foundation of American party politics.[19] Just as importantly, he was an avid sportsman who regularly took his son on fishing expeditions to various wild sections of the state. Some of Fred's most vivid childhood memories were of the forests, lakes, and marshes he saw on those trips and of the occasional Menominee Indians who reminded him that his own people were hardly the first to have occupied this land. "The frontier in that sense, you see," wrote a much older Turner, "was real to me, and when I studied history I did not keep my personal experiences in a watertight compartment away from my studies."[20]

The other great legacy of Turner's childhood was a fascination for oratory. His studies at Portage High School exposed him to the typical subjects of a nineteenth-century secondary education: algebra, geography, history, and, not least, Latin and rhetoric. He earned consistently high marks in all. By the age of fifteen, he had offered his first public speech, a declamation at the local Young Men's Lyceum to honor the Civil War dead on Memorial Day. As a newspaperman's son, he had a special interest in language, written and spoken. He read widely among the great writers, philosophers, and orators of his century. He filled scrapbooks with the passages that most impressed him and even for a time published many of them in a regular column in his father's paper. His great favorite was Ralph Waldo Emerson, from whom he learned not only the exuberant idealism and broad patriotism that would later characterize his historical essays, but also the high style of one of America's great writers and speakers.[21] By the time he left school, his rhetorical skills were polished enough to win him first prize—a copy of Macaulay's *History of England*—in the orations that seniors were required to give as part of graduation.[22]

It is thus not surprising that upon his arrival in Madison to attend the University of Wisconsin young Fred quickly gravitated to activities where his skills as a writer and speaker could be displayed to best advantage. He gained fame as an orator in fraternity celebrations, served as an editor for the new campus newspaper, and helped found a new literary society whose members participated in campus-wide debates and oratorical competitions. By his junior year, he had won the university's highest rhetorical prize for a speech entitled "The Poet of the Future." He worked on it for months, filling his commonplace book with the drafts and extracts he would use in it, and poured into it his own youthful idealism as well. The future poet, Turner announced from the podium,

> *will find beauty in the useful and the common. . . . In his ear humanity will whisper deep, inspiring words, and bid him give them voice. He will unite the logic of the present and the dream of the past, and his words will ring in the ears of generations yet unborn, telling them the grandeur of today which boils and surges with awakening life. He will reflect all the past and prophesy the future.*[23]

However much the speech may have reflected the Emersonian cadences and ideas that Turner had for so long been practicing in his notebooks, one can still detect in it the emerging voice and style of his mature essays. Perhaps even its prophecy is recognizable, reflecting both a young man's dreams for himself and the conviction he would urge on the Wisconsin schoolteachers in 1890 that a poet—or even a young historian—to live up to his calling must reflect and give voice to the age in which he lived.

Turner entered Wisconsin intending to take its Ancient Classical course and did in fact concentrate in Latin and Greek until his junior year. Then, in one of those accidental encounters that can without warning turn a person's life onto an unexpected path, he stumbled into the classroom of William Francis Allen. Allen was a gifted historian with far-reaching interests and an unusually catholic sense of his subject. Although his scholarly interests lay deep in the past, he was no less engaged with the modern world. Trained in Germany in Latin and ancient history, he had spent time in the post–Civil War South gathering the spirituals and work songs of ex-slaves before coming to Wisconsin in 1867.[24] There, he ranged across the entire sweep of European and American history, concentrating especially in the medieval period. What caught the attention of his young student from Portage, however, was less the subjects he taught than the way he taught them. Never content with mere narrative or dry textbook facts, Allen sought to discover the relevance of history for the present by thinking of it as a *problem* and relating it to the geographical, social, economic, and political forces that lay beneath its outward appearances. He approached his subject as a social science, arguing that no fact had value unless it shed light on human nature and broader historical phenomena. One sign of his intellectual commitments was the kind of writing he did. Most of his publications were reviews and articles on topics ranging from political economy to ornithology to history in national journals such as the *Nation*.[25]

Allen gave Turner a model of the engaged scholar who saw his main audience as the broader educated public. He showed his student that history could best be understood according to the insights of Darwinian evolution, as the broad progress of humanity from barbarism to civilization. At a time when history was taught almost entirely by rote from textbooks, he had his undergraduates explore unsolved scholarly problems by sending them to the archives to research primary documents. He set Turner to work on the social consequences of French land tenure systems in Wisconsin by having him research the Grignon grant in Portage.[26] For a young man who had barely heard of Marquette and Jolliet as a child, the discovery that his own home town could be the object of legitimate scholarship came as a kind of revelation.[27] Turner's commonplace books began to fill with sketches of future projects that would compare towns in Wisconsin to the life of European peasant villages, tracing the linkages between land tenure and social progress.[28] Throughout it all, Allen's example was a beacon. "He made me realize," Turner later wrote, "what scholarship meant; what loyalty to truth demanded. I never had, in Hopkins or elsewhere, his equal as a scholar and a simple sincere *acute* mind."[29]

Turner graduated from Wisconsin in 1884 without a clear idea of what he wanted to do with himself. Although he was offered an assistant instructorship in rhetoric and elocution at the university, he chose instead to follow his father into journalism, serving as the Madison correspondent for several papers. Then, in 1885, William Francis Allen turned him toward history once again. Allen had extracted a leave from the university for a research trip to Europe and suggested that Turner serve as his replacement while he was gone. The young man leapt at the chance. By the time Allen returned, any thought of journalism had vanished from Turner's mind. In order to stay on at the university, he agreed to accept the rhetoric appointment he had earlier rejected and was soon assisting Allen by teaching American history as well. At the same time, he embarked on a master's thesis under Allen's supervision that would begin to qualify him for a more permanent post.

During the next several years, Turner gathered and wove together the various themes that would preoccupy him for the rest of his scholarly career. He organized his American history classes around a narrative about the occupation of the continent. He followed Allen's lead in emphasizing broad social scientific processes and began to jot down in his notebooks endless ideas for possible research projects: the role of territorial expansion in American federalism, the responses of immigrant communities to their new homes, the linkages between ethnicity and party politics, the stages of social evolution in western settlement. More and more, he became convinced that the history of the region in which he had grown up was the great untapped subject that previous historians had ignored. "I do not talk anything now but Western history," he wrote his future wife, Caroline Mae Sherwood, in 1888. "I have taken a fever of enthusiasm about the possibilities of the study of the great west and of the magnificent scope of United States history in general."[30]

When Turner received his master's degree in June 1888, Allen advised him that he could not hope to pursue an academic career without obtaining the doctorate. The obvious place to acquire that degree was Johns Hopkins, then the leading center of graduate education in the United States. In September, Turner headed off, none too happily, for a year of study under the direction of Herbert Baxter Adams. Although he bridled a little at Adams's tendency to study American institutions solely in terms of their supposed origins in Teutonic folk customs, his time at Hopkins was a rich encounter with the finest social scientific thought of the day. Adams carried him even deeper than Allen had done into the rigorous German historical methods that might be applied to an American context and taught him to think of society in the organic terms that made it susceptible to Darwinian analysis. Richard Ely introduced him to the political economic implications of land rents and to the staged theories of socioeconomic evolution that German economists had been developing. Woodrow Wilson taught him politics and became a good friend on long walks in which southerner and westerner could rail against the biases that led eastern scholars to ignore the significance of their home regions.

Turner's doctoral dissertation, on *The Character and Influence of the Indian Trade in Wisconsin*, was a reworked version of his master's thesis that incorporated the new concepts and vocabulary he had picked up at Hopkins.[31] In it, he used a collection of French fur documents at the State Historical Society of Wisconsin to argue that the trading post had been a key institution in the evolution of the United States. By acting as the meetingplace where a "primitive" society encountered an "advanced" one, the fur trade became a "transforming force" in society. As such, it set in motion the staged evolutionary sequence that had repeatedly characterized different regions of the United States. After the Indians had come the colonizing hunters, and they in turn were followed by the explorers and traders. Then, "after the game decreased the hunter's clearing was occupied by the *cattle-raiser*, and his home, as settlement grew, became the property of the *cultivator of the soil*; the *manufacturing era* belongs to our own time." In this sense, the trader had been "the pathfinder for civilization," and many of America's greatest highways and cities could trace their origins back to Indian paths and fur posts.[32]

By the time Turner returned to Wisconsin in 1889 to begin teaching as an assistant professor of American history, he had already identified his life's work: applying the techniques of social science and German historical scholarship to the settlement and social evolution of the United States, particularly to the region beyond the Appalachians that he and his contemporaries called the Great West. Like Allen before him, Turner and the scholars with whom he worked at Johns Hopkins saw themselves recasting American history into a more scientific framework that would reach outward from the facts of past politics to generalize about the larger processes of social change. When he stood before the Wisconsin schoolteachers in 1890 to urge upon them "The Significance of History," he was defending an already coherent vision of scholarship that he had learned from Emerson, from Allen, and from his teachers at Hopkins. By declaring that *"each age writes the history of the past anew with reference to the conditions uppermost in its own time,"* he was throwing down a gauntlet to define an agenda for his generation of American historians.[33] If they followed his lead and the lead of his teachers, they would embrace the most exciting scientific paradigm of their day—Darwin's evolutionary theory—and extend it to society. They would think of society as an organism and study the general processes that shaped its development in time. They would move beyond great leaders to study races, mass populations, and ordinary people. They would encompass the nation as a whole, not just the elites of New England and Virginia. They would transform American history.

The vehicle for that transformation was of course the frontier thesis. Turner had been accumulating its elements for nearly a decade, but it finally crystallized in his mind in 1891–92.[34] When he rose before his colleagues to deliver "The Significance of the Frontier in American History" in July 1893, the argument was virtually complete and would change almost not at all for the rest of Turner's life. He was thirty-two years old.

Unsurprisingly, social evolution was at its core. Different parts of America had recapitulated the stages of civilization from hunter to trader to cattle raiser to farmer to city dweller as frontier processes swept over them. The encounter between Indians and pioneers had been a meeting of savagery with civilization and had had profound effects for both peoples. The Indians found themselves more and more tied into the web of European commerce and eventually discovered their game disappearing in a way that forced them to retreat before the waves of European settlement. Just as importantly, Europeans were forced to shed their own traditional practices as they moved out into unsettled areas. In so doing, they became Americans.

There were two great social forces at work in Turner's frontier process. One was the civil–savage encounter, which compelled European settlers to regress to an earlier developmental stage, thereby giving them a raw primitive energy that accounted for the special characteristics they began to acquire as a people. Social regression gave Americans the chance to start evolution over again and remake Europe. The other great force was "free land," which Turner used in the special technical sense of political economists like Richard T. Ely and the Italian scholar Achille Loria.[35] Such land was not free of *inhabitants*; it was free of *rents*. Whether because Indian hunter–gatherer and shifting agricultural modes of production did not assign permanent property rights to most natural resources, or because Europeans systematically refused to recognize those rights, the consequences for colonial economies were the same. American lands and resources could be had at much lower prices relative to comparable lands and resources in Europe. Unlike the medieval peasant communities Turner had studied under Allen, American settlements rarely had effective feudal landlords. Farmers could own their land in freehold, without paying regular rents. Hard work and comparatively modest capital requirements could thus turn a European class of peasant renters into independent landowners, with all the political and economic consequences that implied. From economic independence flowed political independence as well. Free land was the material foundation of American democracy.

If free land and a return to the primitive were the chief causal forces in Turner's model, then their consequences were the personal qualities Americans shared as a people and the democratic institutions they enjoyed as a republic. Because he had learned from Darwin to think of societies in organic terms, Turner articulated his thesis as a catalog of "character traits" that were the result of American evolution: independence, inventiveness, optimism, a passion for freedom. And because no problem so fascinated Turner's generation as the widespread emergence of nationalism in Europe and the United States, he sought to show how these traits had fused peoples of diverse ethnic backgrounds into a composite "mixed race, English in neither nationality nor characteristics."[36] The analog of the biological race was the political nation, so the final task of Turner's thesis was to assert that frontier character traits had been the defining features of American nationalism. In just this way, so the famous sentence ran, "The existence of an area of free land, its continuous recession, and the advance of American settlement westward, explain American development."[37]

This was the analytical core of Turner's argument, but another feature of his famous essay is too often overlooked: his words. As Ronald Carpenter has pointed out, the 1893 frontier paper was less a historical monograph than it was a piece of oratory. Filled with the classical tropes of parallel repetition, alliteration, prosopopoeia, synecdoche, and especially antithesis, it had more in common with the soaring phrases of Turner's youthful speeches than it did with the plodding academic language of his dissertation.[38] Its most compelling passages gain their power more from rhetoric than from analysis, more from passionate imagery than from close argument. Throughout, the most visual passages and metaphors are the ones that stick in the memory. That so many of them now read like clichés is in fact proof of their long-standing power and fame.

Today, it takes an act of will to imagine the effect they must have had when fresh. And yet if one hears the words as Turner's listeners did, they still conjure vivid images. The frontier itself is the tidal bore of a great oceanic movement, "the outer edge of the wave—the meeting point between savagery and civilization."[39] The Darwinian sequence of staged social development is a pageant and parade, among the most famous in all historical literature:

> *Stand at Cumberland Gap and watch the procession of*
> *civilization, marching single file—the buffalo following the trail*
> *to the salt springs, the Indian, the fur-trader and hunter, the*
> *cattle-raiser, the pioneer farmer—and the frontier has passed by.*
> *Stand at South Pass in the Rockies a century later and see the*
> *same procession with wider intervals between.*[40]

The formation of a mixed nationality is the working of a forge: "In the crucible of the frontier the immigrants were Americanized, liberated, and fused into a mixed race."[41] And, in the most famous, oft-quoted, antithesis-ridden passage of all, the end of the entire process is a nation with all the traits, faults, and virtues of an exuberant adolescent child:

> *The result is that to the frontier the American intellect owes its*
> *striking characteristics. That coarseness and strength combined*
> *with acuteness and inquisitiveness; that practical, inventive turn*
> *of mind, quick to find expedients; that masterful grasp of*
> *material things, lacking in the artistic but powerful to effect*
> *great ends; that restless, nervous energy; that dominant*
> *individualism, working for good and for evil, and withal that*
> *buoyancy and exuberance which comes with freedom—these are*
> *the traits of the frontier, or traits called out elsewhere because of*
> *the existence of the frontier.*[42]

Here was young Fred Turner at his most eloquent, combining the authority of a historian with the power of an orator and the passion of a patriot. The most remarkable accomplishment of the speech was its successful inversion of the anti-western biases that had led Herbert Baxter Adams and his predecessors to emphasize Europe and the eastern seaboard at the expense of other regions of the country. In Turner's hands, the Great West suddenly became not just an important *part* of

American history; it became America itself. The history of its settlement was the essential story of the nation. One might study New England or the South to learn the peculiar features of their unique regional histories, but if one wanted to comprehend the United States as a whole, one must grasp and understand the repeated processes of frontier settlement that had characterized the West. On just this foundation, the entire academic field of western history would be erected in Turner's image, acquiring a centrality and significance that no other argument would likely have given it.

And yet even this was not the essay's most brilliant stroke. That came in the rhetorical frame Turner placed *around* the body of his text. Its first sentence, as every American historian knows, began by quoting a note in the 1890 census that U.S. settlement had proceeded so far that " 'there can hardly be said to be a frontier line' " remaining in the country.[43] Turner's only comment on this announcement was that it marked "the closing of a great historic movement." Rather than elaborate on the idea of closing, he used it as a rhetorical introduction to the historic movement itself and his own thesis about its significance in American history. From that point on, he had nothing more to say about the census announcement until the very last paragraph of the paper. Then, suddenly, he used it to assume that most potent of rhetorical stances, that of the prophet. Ever since Columbus's voyage, he declared, because of frontier expansion, "America has been another name for opportunity." Now the end of the frontier threatened to change forever the material conditions on which the dream of American opportunity had been based. "Never again," he lamented, "will such gifts of free land offer themselves."[44] To the extent that his historical argument was true—to the extent that the frontier really had been the source of American progress, nationalism, and character—the census bureau announcement potentially threatened to undermine everything for which the nation had once stood.

It was a compelling argument, all the more so because it seemed to speak so directly to the common beliefs and anxieties of late nineteenth-century Americans. Theodore Roosevelt described its achievement quite accurately when he wrote that it put "into shape a good deal of thought that has been floating around rather loosely."[45] All elements of Turner's thesis had long been observations made about American society, some for more than a century.[46] Turner's originality was not that he thought of them for the first time, but that he wove them together in a rhetorically compelling way and used them to argue for a new approach to American history. The appeal of what he said was immense. He made a virtue of American provincialism, praising rather than apologizing for his nation's distance and difference from Europe. In a single stroke, he linked American freedom, democracy, and character in a way that placed them at center stage in the history of world civilization, giving Americans (and westerners) unshakable reasons for pride in their national achievements. Had he delivered his speech as a Fourth of July oration, he could scarcely have affirmed more emphatically his compatriots' faith in themselves and their nation.

But because Turner framed his argument prophetically, it also had a darker side. For him as for many of his middle-class peers, America in the 1890s seemed to be on the cusp of great change. Already a great industrial nation, it was clearly leaving its agrarian roots behind. More and more Americans lived in cities, where factory labor seemed to be undermining the individualism and independence that had characterized Jefferson's yeoman vision. Giant corporations had come into being during the previous generation, growing so powerful that their monopolies seemed to threaten the very foundations of democratic rule. Under the yoke of such corporations, farmers seemed increasingly ridden by debt and other troubles, so much so that they had organized great protest movements that Turner's thesis was in no small measure designed to explain. Vast numbers of immigrants were flooding the country and seemed to some to be assimilating less quickly than had been the case with their predecessors from northwestern Europe. Many middle-class and elite Americans worried that their nation was losing touch with its roots and began to evince a deep nostalgia for what seemed the older, simpler world of an earlier America, a land where national values seemed clear. For such people, the present was a time of foreboding, and the future perilous.[47]

The frontier thesis spoke to all of these concerns and seemed to offer a coherent explanation for the anxieties that many of Turner's fellow intellectuals were feeling about their nation. As such, it fulfilled the injunction Turner had offered the public schoolteachers in 1890 that "the aim of history . . . is to know the elements of the present by understanding what came into the present from the past."[48] As orator and prophet, Turner spoke as much to present politics as he did to past history, so that his claims could be mobilized in many arguments about public policy: whether Americans should continue their frontier expansion by seizing the Philippines or Cuba during the Spanish-American War; whether immigration should be restricted; whether the country's last wild lands should be preserved as national parks. The frontier thesis seemed to answer each of these questions in the affirmative.

Although initial reactions to Turner's essay were lukewarm, within half a decade it had gained wide national attention and was being promoted by a number of leading intellectuals.[49] (It hardly hurt Turner's fame that two of his most enthusiastic supporters, Theodore Roosevelt and Woodrow Wilson, would eventually become presidents of the United States.) Starting in 1896, Turner began to be sought by nonacademic journals, especially the *Atlantic Monthly*, to elucidate his ideas for the wider public. Suddenly able to follow the example of his mentor William Francis Allen and fulfill his own earlier ambitions as a journalist, Turner contributed to the popular press broad interpretive essays on such topics as "The Problem of the West," "Dominant Forces in Western Life," and "The Contribution of the West to American Democracy."[50] In each, he adopted his most oratorical style, speaking in broad generalities and resorting to much more vivid and colorful language than was typical of his academic prose. When the national magazines lost interest in Turner's work in about 1905, he continued to write similar essays—usually to be read before an audience as public addresses. Of the thirteen essays that eventually went into Turner's best-known book, *The Frontier in American History*, nearly half began their existence as orations.[51]

This may help to explain one of the curious riddles of Turner's career: his terrible writer's block.[52] Turner was one of the great nonpublishing scholars of his generation, a man who seemed almost congenitally incapable of completing a book. His problems as a writer flowed from many things: his perfectionism, his sensitivity to criticism, his interdisciplinary commitments, and the ordinary demands of a busy academic life. But among the most important was *genre*. The literary form with which Turner was always most comfortable was the one he had mastered earliest: oratory. When forced to present his ideas within the limits of an hour-long speech, he felt liberated to express them in their simplest, most energetic, and compelling form. When freed from those limits and given the hundreds of pages one needed to fill a book, he became overwhelmed by the sheer quantity of material he had to present and the difficulty of mobilizing it on behalf of his grander claims. He was not a skillful storyteller and was disposed to be suspicious of narrative as a form, but he never devised an alternative rhetorical strategy for holding together a book-length argument. Even when he tried to present a closely reasoned analysis and careful reading of sources within the bounds of a shorter academic paper, the shape of the whole too often collapsed into overly detailed fragments as soon as he drifted away from the oratorical rhetoric he understood so well. As works of prose, Turner's monographs are dull; his orations sing.

There is an important parallel here between Turner's own writing and the work he required of his graduate students in seminar. Merle Curti reports that the seminar ordinarily centered upon an arbitrarily chosen period of a decade or two, and that "each student took, for the given period, some field in which he was interested, such as agriculture, transportation, immigration, internal improvements, banking, finance, tariff, land policy, literature, labor, or religion."[53] The narrow period allowed students the diversity of topics that was the hallmark of Turner's interdisciplinary method and still guaranteed that research would remain tightly focused. To force students to keep track of forest and trees together, Turner required each to write two essays. One, known as the "problem paper," was meant to be a limited analysis of a well-defined research question; the other, known as the "correlation paper," gave the student an opportunity "to correlate his problem and to some extent his field with those his colleagues were studying."[54] By the end of the year, in other words, each student had tried to synthesize the research of the entire seminar and relate it to the topic he or she was studying.

Turner's own writing echoed his seminar assignments. His books and academic monographs were "problem papers," each covering a narrow research topic, ranging from agriculture to transportation to the history of presidential administrations—the very subjects his students had examined in seminar. His essays, on the other hand, were "correlation papers," bold attempts to "explain" the history of American settlement in its widest sweep.[55] Turner's fame rests on the very few of those essays that are still read—his orations— while most of his other writings are largely ignored. Struggle as he might to create a work that would equal the fame of his great 1893 essay, he never managed to do so. Indeed, he never even succeeded in expressing the vision of that essay in a book that elaborated the original argument into a systematic presentation of western history as a whole. That task was left to followers of his with broader rhetorical talents, most notably Frederic Logan Paxson and Ray Allen Billington.

Turner's difficulty was intrinsic to both his topic and his method. For Turner, "problem papers" and "correlation papers" somehow never quite came together. They always remained separate assignments, with different analytical frameworks and different rhetorical styles that persistently prevented them from merging. Although Turner during his lifetime was justly famed for having put American history on a new analytical basis that enabled it to escape older narrative historical writing, his books failed to discover a rhetoric to match his analytical vision. Only when he returned to the rhetoric of oratory—and prophecy—did his prose capture that vision, something he did best in the essays whose titles began, "The Significance of . . ." There were no fewer than seven of these, including the three most important: "The Significance of the Frontier in American History," "The Significance of the Section in American History," and that remarkable early speech before the Wisconsin schoolteachers that laid the foundation for everything else, "The Significance of History."[56]

Turner's affection for essays devoted to "significance" revealed the essentially interpretive thrust of his historical projects.[57] Like the prophets, he was drawn as an orator to exegesis and hermeneutics, to creating a web of verbal elaboration around a core set of ideas that never finally changed; like the prophets, he sought not to prove or disprove his vision, but to apply its sweep to all of American history. For all his commitment to problem-oriented history, his central concepts rarely expressed themselves as testable theories. Few could be falsified.[58] The emphasis on "significance" was a black box that avoided the necessity of more rigorous analysis and theory. It is only when one realizes the essentially hermeneutic nature of Turner's work that one understands why his legacy has been at once so powerful and so problematic. Prophets take the events of history and reorder them to give them new meaning, pointing them toward a future moment when history itself will finally come to an end. In that teleological act of interpretation, the past comes to have sequence, significance, direction; it becomes, in other words, a story. Turner's frontier thesis had all of these properties.

Here, then, is one of Turner's central ironies: the man who could not, and did not want to, write narrative history nevertheless codified the central narrative structure that has helped to organize American history ever since. It was Turner who showed that the history of any given American place could be written in terms of a progressive sequence of different economic and social activities, thereby escaping the antiquarianism in local history about which he had complained as early as his 1890 lecture. It was Turner who showed that those activities could be embodied in representative figures who might serve as "types" for the community around them, so that Andrew Jackson became "the champion of the cause of the upland democracy," and Henry Clay "represented the new industrial forces along the Ohio."[59] For lesser figures, the result was to raise ordinary people to heroic stature, so that their stories became "significant" simply by standing for the larger whole. And even if one accepted neither Turner's metaphors of social evolution nor his heroic typologies, there was still the underlying sequence of the frontier itself. Turner showed that one could write the history of the United States according to the order in which different regions of the country had been occupied by Anglo-American settlers.[60] One could thus organize American history along geographical lines that were also temporal: the frontier thesis, in effect, set American space in motion and gave it a plot.

Whatever the merits of Turner's hypotheses about democracy and the national character, his stages and types had great rhetorical attractions. Seen through their lens, previously disparate phenomena and events suddenly seemed to become connected.[61] This, surely, was one of the reasons why Turner's seminar generated such excitement in his students. All those wildly eclectic research topics were related to each other not just chronologically, not just by region, not just by their emphasis on the role of social and economic forces in politics, but by their place in the grand sequence of civilized ascent. The frontier, whether understood as geographic expansion or social evolution, was the "unity and continuity" that held everything together; without it, the "correlation papers" would dissolve into an overabundance of fragmentary detail much as Turner's own books did. Whatever the problems of the frontier thesis, western historians have been unable to replace the rhetorical sequence that Turner synthesized for them: when the chapters of the standard textbook of western history move from Indians to ranchers to farmers, they do so because no other arrangement seems properly ordered.[62] We continue to follow the Turnerian plot.

In the years following Turner's death, his frontier thesis came under increasing attack, so much so that a half-century later many historians are prepared to declare it quite worthless and quite dead. The litany of criticisms is well known.[63] Turner's argument was insufficiently analytical, and his key frontier concept so ill defined that it could be applied to virtually any historical circumstance. A phenomenon that was at once a line, a place, a process, and a state of mind could hardly help but be tautological, so that the apparent explanatory power of Turner's thesis was, in fact, illusory. "Free land" was an ideologically loaded term that ignored Indians and other non-Anglos in a way that erased their existence and reified their conquest. Turner's emphasis on the east–west movement of Anglo-American colonization was geographically inaccurate, culturally biased, and potentially racist, leaving too little room for nonwhite ethnic minorities. Women, too, were absent. His progressive evolutionary metaphors, so modern and scientific at the time they were propounded, were Eurocentric and probably imperialist. Even his core argument was wrong: the frontier had *not* created American democracy. Westerners had looked eastward for most of their democratic institutions, and their lives had been profoundly shaped by the federal government, the corporation, and the city, none of which received adequate treatment in Turner's hands. His model of frontier "closure" made it difficult to study the West in the twentieth century and created a false ending to a regional history that should properly be seen as continuous. And so the list goes on.

The criticisms, for the most part, are fair if not exactly generous. Turner did acknowledge the historical role of Indians, and he never intended his technical use of the term *free land* to deny their existence— but he certainly did read their history through a Eurocentric lens that saw them as savage obstacles to the civilized progress that was his main story. He realized the importance of the traditions and institutions that European and eastern settlers brought with them from their earlier homes—but because he was eager to stress the importance of regions he thought historians had ignored, he emphasized change more than continuity and exaggerated east–west differences. One of Turner's chief fascinations had always been immigration and the varieties of ethnic experience in America, and he was far ahead of his peers in emphasizing what we might today call "history from the bottom up"— but he also shared his generation's unreflectively racist and sexist assumptions about "nations," peoples of color, and women. And yet, such criticisms might not have surprised Turner, however much they would have wounded his vanity. If we find his answers inadequate to the historical questions we ourselves ask, we are doing no less than he predicted back in 1890: *"each age writes the history of the past anew with reference to the conditions uppermost in its own time."*[64]

But does this mean that Turner's frontier history is devoid of value for modern historians? Here, the chance of misreading his work seems greater and more dangerous. In the years since he urged scholars to study something called "western history," the field has followed modern linguistic usage to concentrate more and more on the region we today call "West." Even now we remain unsure of its boundaries: it certainly lies west of the Mississippi, and for many no place east of the Rockies can truly qualify as part of the region. Wherever we locate it, though, fairness to Turner requires us to admit that this most recent West includes neither his West nor any of his frontiers, no matter how loosely or badly he may have defined those words. Turner was generally consistent in accepting as "West" or "frontier" those areas that Americans of any given moment would themselves have called "West" or "frontier." For him, "the oldest West was the Atlantic coast," the Old West lay just beyond the Appalachians, and the West about which he cared most was his own home: the Mississippi Valley, Wisconsin, Portage.[65]

To be sure, Turner also acknowledged the existence of a region lying beyond the Mississippi that he called the "Far" or "Arid" West. Surprisingly, and contrary to what one might think from reading Turner's critics, he said of this Far West almost exactly what subsequent historians would say:

> *The army of the United States pushed back the Indian,*
> *rectangular Territories were carved into checkerboard States,*
> *creations of the federal government, without a history, without*
> *physiographical unity, without particularistic ideas. The later*
> *frontiersman leaned on the strong arm of national power. . . .*
> *When the arid lands and the mineral resources of the Far West*
> *were reached, no conquest was possible by the old individual*
> *pioneer methods. Here expensive irrigation works must be*
> *constructed, cooperative activity was demanded in utilization of*
> *the water supply, capital beyond the reach of the small farmer*
> *was required. . . . The pioneer of the arid regions must be both a*
> *capitalist and the protege of the government.*[66]

Even Turner's harshest critics could hardly disagree with so "un-Turnerian" a West as this, but the important thing to remember is that the Far West he describes in this passage was not *his* West. One must search long and hard to find more than a few references in Turner's work to the West of the Rockies and beyond. The region that most evoked his passion, and against which his arguments can most fairly be tested, was his home, the old Northwest Territory. To complain that his frontier history did not adequately capture the West of our own time is surely a little unfair. Many of the strongest criticisms of the frontier thesis still hold, of course, but at least a few seem less on target when placed back in the trans-Appalachian context that Turner originally intended for them.

There is a deeper problem with the proposal of Turner's critics that "frontier" history be abandoned altogether in favor of a truly "regional" "western" history. For Turner, the chief value of his frontier thesis had been the light it might shed on the development of the nation as a whole. Common frontier experiences had given the United States a national unity it might otherwise have lacked, even as opposing frontier processes produced divergent sectional loyalties. He emphatically resisted his contemporaries' attitude toward western history as "largely antiquarian or of the romantic narrative type devoid of the conception of 'the West' as a moving process."[67] Far from being a regionalist, he saw himself first and foremost as a historian of the United States, reinterpreting the past of the entire nation in terms of settlement and colonization. "I have not," he wrote, "conceived of myself as the student of a region. . . . It is in the *American processes* I have been interested."[68]

It was this national focus that gave Turner his breadth of vision as a scholar. From it came the seriousness with which his views were taken by the public as a whole and the excitement his students felt in one of the leading graduate seminars of his generation. Although Turner himself never managed to combine the rigor of his scientific methods with the synthesis of his oratorical rhetoric, he clearly intended that his frontier model should serve as a heuristic tool for a genuinely comparative history. That tool has served western historians well for nearly a century. Theirs has been the one branch of American history that has consistently looked at the nation as a whole to explore similarities and differences in regional economies, environmental dynamics, political conflicts, and cultural identities. Whether they have looked at Indian–white relations, ethnic cultures, the fur trade, agriculture, mining, or even urban-industrial development, they have retained the comparative approach that Turner first used to give the "West" and its "frontier processes" their national significance. To jettison Turner's frontier in favor of an apparently less problematic "regional" definition runs the grave risk of abandoning the cross-regional and national emphasis he sought to establish for the field. If the regionalists are finally successful in purging western history of its Turnerian frontier legacy, then scholars who wish to study the comparative histories of New England, the Old South and Southwest, the Ohio Valley, the Mississippi Valley, and that broad and ill-defined region called the Middle West will have to find a new home for themselves. That would be an unfortunate loss not just to western history, but to American history as a whole.

It would be a sterile exercise endlessly to reread and revise Turner's frontier thesis so as to try to put flesh on its dry bones. Ray Allen Billington devoted a lifetime to that task, but even his most forgiving interpretations could not overcome the deep analytical problems and contradictions of Turner's essentially rhetorical composition. Turner's organicism, typological taxonomies, crude progressivism, unilineal evolutionary model, and even his proud nationalism are too much the product of his late nineteenth-century context for them to be meaningful at so great a remove. We can safely declare the frontier thesis dead, or at least so badly flawed that any new formulation must be built on an entirely redesigned foundation. But at least some parts of any new foundation must always be Turner's. His writings remain studded with provocative insights, thrown off as suggestive asides in the midst of the grander oratory. Even his arguments about the political and economic consequences of "free land" are not entirely lacking in interest. And if a post-Turnerian western history jettisons the word *frontier* altogether, so long as it defines *West* in the shifting ways that past Americans have used that word, and so long as it takes as its special domain the human occupation of the continent, it will still be following the oldest Turnerian legacy of all. "American history up to our own day," the young scholar wrote in 1892, "has been colonial history, the colonization of the Great West."[69] Whether one speaks of studying comparative frontiers, or colonization, or invasion, or even the legacy of conquest, one proposes to study process rather than region, and the best of Turner's approach will still be very much alive.

In the end as in the beginning, Frederick Jackson Turner made his stand on the search for a meaningful past, a past that would speak to the present in the clear and visionary tones that he had learned as a boy from Emerson. If one could not find the significance of the past, if one could not locate its larger meaning for the generation now living, then the past might just as well be dead. "If I didn't believe that history helps us understand the present," wrote Turner toward the end of his life, "I should not have the interest in it which I have."[70] Turner's own search for significance had led him to understand the West in terms of the nation, America in terms of European colonization, economic opportunity in terms of natural abundance, frontier societies in terms of participation in political governance, and history itself in terms of "a complex of all the social sciences" and "the One-ness of the thing."[71] Whether or not we still share his values about the past or his way of understanding it, we can surely applaud the passion with which he embraced the task of making it meaningful.

As always, it was Turner the orator who captured the feeling best: "Historical study," he told the schoolteachers in 1890,

> has for its end to let the community see itself in the light of the past, to give it new thoughts and feelings, new aspirations and energies. . . . The man who enters the temple of history must respond devoutly to that invocation of the church, Sursum corda, lift up your hearts. No looking at history as an idle tale, a compend of anecdotes; no servile devotion to a textbook; no carelessness of truth about the dead that can no longer speak must be permitted in its sanctuary. "History," says Droysen, "is not the truth and the light; but a striving for it, a sermon on it, a consecration on it."[72]

So spoke the historian. Not all of the Turnerian legacy is worth abandoning. The day scholars forget such words is the day they lose their calling.

NOTES

1. Turner, "The Significance of History," *Wisconsin Journal of Education* 21 (October, November 1891):230–34, 253–56; repr. in Ray Allen Billington, ed., *Frontier and Section: Selected Essays of Frederick Jackson Turner* (Englewood Cliffs, N.J.: Prentice-Hall, 1961), 25.

2. Scholars who have recognized the importance of this once obscure essay include Fulmer Mood, "Turner's Formative Period," in *The Early Writings of Frederick Jackson Turner* (Madison: University of Wisconsin Press, 1938), 30–32; Merle Curti, "Frederick Jackson Turner," in O. Lawrence Burnette, Jr., ed., *Wisconsin Witness to Frederick Jackson Turner: A Collection of Essays on the Historian and the Thesis* (Madison: State Historical Society of Wisconsin, 1961), 184–85; and Billington, in the introduction to *Frontier and Section*, 3–4.

3. The speech for which Turner would eventually become famous was delivered before the AHA at the World's Columbian Exposition in Chicago on July 12, 1893, and was later published in the *Annual Report of the American Historical Association for the Year 1893* (Washington, D.C., 1894), 199–227. It became the first chapter of Turner's *The Frontier in American History* (New York: Henry Holt, 1920), which is the version I quote below.

4. Ray Allen Billington, *Frederick Jackson Turner: Historian, Scholar, Teacher* (New York: Oxford University Press, 1973), 98–99.

5. Turner, "Significance of History," 12–13.

6. Ibid., 14.

7. Ibid., 14.

8. Ibid., 18.

9. Ibid., 19.

10. Ibid., 17.

11. Its idealism, relativism, and sense that history was most relevant when it touched the lives of ordinary people also echoed the writings of Ralph Waldo Emerson, who had been Turner's favorite author as a youth. To my knowledge, no scholar, including Billington, has adequately acknowledged Turner's profound debt to Emerson's writings, which anticipated many of the most important elements both of the frontier thesis and of Turner's idealist philosophy of history.

12. The standard work on the origins of Turner's frontier thesis is Ray Allen Billington, *The Genesis of the Frontier Thesis: A Study in Historical Creativity* (San Marino, Calif.: Huntington Library, 1971). Peter Novick discusses Turner as a New Historian in *That Noble Dream: The "Objectivity Question" and the American Historical Profession* (New York: Cambridge University Press, 1988).

13. Turner, "Significance of History," 18–19.

14. Ibid., 21.

15. Ibid., 24–25.

16. The standard reference for these and other details of Turner's life is Billington's masterful biography, which I rely on without constant re-citation throughout this essay. For Turner's early years, see also Billington, "Young Fred Turner," *Wisconsin Magazine of History* 46 (Autumn 1962):38–48.

17. Billington, *Turner*, 6.

18. Frederick Jackson Turner (hereafter cited as FJT) to Carl Becker, December 18, 1925, reprinted in Billington, *Genesis*, 240.

19. FJT to Constance Lindsay Skinner, March 15, 1922, repr. in Billington, *Genesis*, 215; FJT to Merle Curti, August 28, 1928, in Billington, *Genesis*, 264.

20. FJT to Becker, December 18, 1925, repr. in Billington, *Genesis*, 243.

21. When Turner revised his frontier essay for a national education journal in 1899, he chose, significantly, to preface it with a very suggestive passage from Emerson's "Young American" of 1844. See Turner, "Significance of the Frontier," rev. for *The Fifth Yearbook of the National Herbart Society*, 1899, repr. in Turner, *Early Writings*, 276–77; see also Emerson, *Essays and Lectures* (New York: Library of America, 1983), 216–17, which differs slightly.

22. On Turner's rhetoric, Ronald H. Carpenter's *The Eloquence of Frederick Jackson Turner* (San Marino, Calif.: Huntington Library, 1983) is an important and suggestive work that has been too little appreciated by historians.

23. "The Poet of the Future," in the *University Press* 14 (May 26, 1883):35; repr. in Carpenter, *Eloquence of Turner*, 123.

24. See William F. Allen, et al., *Slave Songs of the United States* (New York: A. Simpson, 1867).

25. See, for instance, William F. Allen, *Essays and Monographs by William Francis Allen: Memorial Volume* (Boston: G. H. Ellis, 1890). On Allen's critical role in

building the University of Wisconsin's history program, see Merle Curti and Vernon Carstensen, *The University of Wisconsin: A History, 1848–1925* (Madison: University of Wisconsin Press, 1949), 1:345–48.

26. See Fulmer Mood and Everett E. Edwards, "Frederick Jackson Turner's History of the Grignon Tract on the Portage of the Fox and Wisconsin Rivers," *Agricultural History* 17 (April 1943):113–21.

27. FJT to Becker, December 16, 1925, repr. in Billington, *Genesis*, 239.

28. The record of Turner's encounter with Allen can be traced in his commonplace book for 1883 and after, in the Frederick Jackson Turner papers, Henry E. Huntington Library and Art Gallery, vol. 3. See Billington, *Turner*, 29–30.

29. FJT to Becker, December 16, 1925, in Billington, *Genesis*, 239.

30. FJT to Mae Sherwood, March 25, 1888, as quoted in Billington, *Turner*, 46.

31. Turner, *The Character and Influence of the Indian Trade in Wisconsin*, in Herbert Baxter Adams, ed., *Johns Hopkins University Studies in Historical and Political Science*, 9th series, 12–13 (November-December 1891), 547–615; repr., ed. David Harry Miller and William W. Savage, Jr. (Norman: University of Oklahoma Press, 1977); page references are to the latter edition.

32. Turner, *Indian Trade*, 3–5, 18, 19; italics in original.

33. Turner, "Significance of History," in Billington, *Frontier and Section*, 17; italics in original.

34. One can see that Turner had put most of it together in his "Problems in American History," (December 1892, repr. in Billington, *Frontier and Section*, 28–36), and in a talk he gave before the Madison Literary Club, in February 1891, entitled "American Colonization" (repr. in Carpenter, *Eloquence*, 176–92). The best close reading of this material is Billington, *Genesis*, but see also Lee Benson's important *Turner and Beard: American Historical Writing Reconsidered* (Glencoe, Ill.: Free Press, 1960); and the various writings of Fulmer Mood, especially "Turner's Formative Period" in Turner, *Early Writings*, 3–39; and "The Development of Frederick Jackson Turner as a Historical Thinker," *Transactions of the Colonial Society of Massachusetts* 34 (December 1943):283–352.

35. See Benson, *Turner and Beard*, 1–40; and Billington, *Genesis*, 134–42, 155–56.

36. Turner, *Frontier in American History*, 23.

37. Ibid., 1.

38. Carpenter's rhetorical analysis of the speech can be found in *The Eloquence of Frederick Jackson Turner*, passim.

39. Turner, *Frontier in American History*, 3.

40. Ibid., 12.

41. Ibid., 23.

42. Ibid., 37. Carpenter devotes many pages to explicating just these two sentences; see *Eloquence*, 53–70.

43. Turner, *Frontier in American History*, 1.

44. Ibid., 37.

45. Theodore Roosevelt to FJT, as quoted by Billington, *Turner*, 130.

46. See, for instance, Fulmer Mood, "Notes on the History of the Word *Frontier*," *Agricultural History* 22 (April 1948):78–83; Mood, "The Concept of the Frontier, 1871–1898: Comments on a Select List of Source Documents," *Agricultural History* 19 (January 1945):24–30; Herman Clarence Nixon, "Precursors of Turner in the Interpretation of the American Frontier," *South Atlantic Quarterly* 28 (January 1929):83–89; and John T. Juricek, "American Usage of the Word 'Frontier' from Colonial Times to Frederick Jackson Turner," *Proceedings of the American Philosophical Society* 110 (February 1966):10–34.

47. The best discussions of these implicit political elements of the frontier thesis remain Benson's *Turner and Beard*, 41–91; and Richard Hofstadter's brilliant *The Progressive Historians: Turner, Beard, Parrington* (New York: Alfred A. Knopf, 1969), 45–164.

48. Turner, "Significance of History," in Billington, *Frontier and Section*, 17.

49. See Billington, *Turner*, 184–208.

50. "The Problem of the West," *Atlantic Monthly* 78 (September 1896):289–97; "Dominant Forces in Western Life," *Atlantic Monthly* 79 (April 1897):433–43; "Contributions of the West to American Democracy," *Atlantic Monthly* 91 (January 1903):83–96. These eventually became, respectively, chaps. 7, 8, and 9 of Turner's *Frontier in American History*. For a bibliography and publication history of Turner's work, see Everett E. Edwards, comp., "A Bibliography of the Writings of Frederick Jackson Turner. . . ," in Turner, *Early Writings*, 231–72.

51. Turner, *Frontier in American History*, chaps. 1, 5, 10–13; to these could be added 7–9, the *Atlantic Monthly* chapters, which although never given as public lectures were very much in that style. There is a palpable difference between these oratorical chapters and the more monographic ones that were originally presented as academic papers.

52. Billington has written about Turner's writing problems, in *Turner* and in "Why Some Historians Rarely Write History: A Case Study of Frederick Jackson Turner," *Mississippi Valley Historical Review* 50 (June 1963):3–27.

53. Merle E. Curti, "The Section and the Frontier in American History: The Methodological Concepts of Frederick Jackson Turner," in Stuart A. Rice, ed., *Methods in Social Science* (Chicago: University of Chicago Press, 1931), 367; "Merle Curti: An Interview Conducted by William Cronon," University of Wisconsin-Madison Archives Oral History Project, Madison, 1986, 10–15; and FJT to Curti, August 8, 1928, in Billington, *Genesis*, 260–64, which contains the fullest exposition of Turner's own thoughts about pedagogy.

54. Ibid. This method was not original to Turner. It was quite close to the pedagogical strategy that William Francis Allen had used to excite Turner himself about history as a field. Curti and Carstensen, *University of Wisconsin*, 1:345–47; Billington, *Turner*, 25–28.

55. The essays that best exemplify Turner's skills at oratorical "correlation" are "The Significance of the Frontier in American History," "The Significance of History," "Problems in American History," and "The Problem of the West," all written during the 1890s. All are gathered in Billington, *Frontier and Section*.

56. The others were "The Significance of the Louisiana Purchase" (1903), "The Significance of the Mississippi Valley in American History" (1910), "The Significance of Sectionalism in American History" (1914), and "The Significance of the North Central States in the Middle of the Nineteenth Century" (1917). See Edwards, "Writings of Turner," in Turner, *Early Writings*, 233–68.

57. Carl Becker furnishes the most incisive observation on this point: "If in all his published work there are five pages of straight narrative I do not know where to find them. His writing is all essentially descriptive, explicative, expository" (Carl Becker, "Frederick Jackson Turner," in *Everyman His Own Historian* [New York: F. S. Crofts, 1935], 227).

58. This criticism applies only to Turner's writing, not to his teaching. His students were consistently struck by his willingness to question any fact or idea and to consider any alternative explanation: Curti remembered that this "impressed me more deeply than any single experience that I had" as Turner's student (Curti to FJT, August 13, 1928, in Billington, *Genesis*, 265). Turner's personal tragedy may well have been that his temperament best suited him to teaching, criticizing, and researching, but his fame demanded that he keep producing works that were synthetic and theoretical.

59. Turner, *Frontier in American History*, 173. Howard Lamar has noted that the only portrait that appears in Turner's *Rise of the New West* is that of Henry Clay (Howard R. Lamar, "Frederick Jackson Turner," in Marcus Cunliffe and Robin W. Winks, eds., *Pastmasters: Some Essays on American Historians* [New York: Harper and Row, 1969], 92). Turner's formulation of frontier "types" in terms of the third-person (male) singular—*the* Indian, *the* trader, *the* rancher, *the* farmer—was one of the ways he unconsciously shied away from examining more closely the pluralism and conflicts of frontier regions. But they were also the way in which society as a whole could become a kind of character in his story, much as different species had functioned for Darwin as emblems of the larger evolutionary struggle for existence.

60. Doing so obviously reveals an ethnocentric bias that especially distorts the experiences of Indians and Hispanic-American peoples, but that bias is hardly Turner's alone. It persists in the writing of much western American history even today.

61. As Becker characterized his master's method, "He studies American history as furnishing a concrete illustration, many times repeated and on a relatively grand scale, of the social process" (Becker, "Frederick Jackson Turner," in *Everyman*, 214). Again, one is grateful for Becker's precise use of language: to "illustrate" a social process meant in this case to take the "process"—whatever that broad phrase might have meant—for granted and to *interpret* the case to fit it. There was no testing of theory by such a procedure.

62. Ray Allen Billington and Martin Ridge, *Westward Expansion*, 5th ed. (New York: Macmillan, 1982), 573–661.

63. The bibliography surveys this literature.

64. Turner, "Significance of History," in Billington, *Frontier and Section*, 17; italics in original.

65. Turner, *Frontier in American History*, 67 and passim.

66. Turner, *Frontier in American History*, 218, 258, 279.

67. FJT to Curti, August 8, 1928, in Billington, *Genesis*, 259.

68. FJT to Skinner, March 15, 1922, in Billington, *Genesis*, 213–14; italics in original.

69. Turner, "Problems in American History," in Billington, *Frontier and Section*, 29.

70. FJT to Curti, August 27, 1928, in Billington, *Genesis*, 280.

71. FJT to Becker, December 1, 1925, in Billington, *Genesis*, 233.

72. Turner, "Significance of History," in Billington, *Frontier and Section*, 27; italics in original.

BIBLIOGRAPHY

WORKS BY FREDERICK JACKSON TURNER

The Character and Influence of the Indian Trade in Wisconsin. In Herbert Baxter Adams, ed., *Johns Hopkins University Studies in Historical and Political Science*, 9th series, 12–13 (November, December 1891):547–615. Repr., ed. David Harry Miller and William W. Savage, Jr. Norman: University of Oklahoma Press, 1977.

Early Writings of Frederick Jackson Turner. Madison: University of Wisconsin Press, 1938.

Frontier and Section: Selected Essays of Frederick Jackson Turner, ed. Ray Allen Billington. Englewood Cliffs, N.J.: Prentice-Hall, 1961.

The Frontier in American History. New York: Henry Holt, 1920.

Rise of the New West, 1819–1829. New York: Harper and Brothers. 1906.

The Significance of Sections in American History. New York: Henry Holt, 1932.

The United States, 1830–1850: The Nation and Its Sections. New York: Henry Holt, 1935.

WORKS ABOUT TURNER

Becker, Carl. "Frederick Jackson Turner." In *Everyman His Own Historian*. New York: F. S. Crofts, 1935, 191–232.

Benson, Lee. *Turner and Beard: American Historical Writing Reconsidered.* Glencoe, Ill.: Free Press, 1960.

Billington, Ray Allen. *America's Frontier Heritage.* New York: Holt, Rinehart and Winston, 1963.

———. *The Frontier Thesis: Valid Interpretation of American History?* New York: Holt, Rinehart and Winston, 1966.

————. *The Genesis of the Frontier Thesis: A Study in Historical Creativity.* San Marino, Calif.: Huntington Library, 1971.

————. *Frederick Jackson Turner: Historian, Scholar, Teacher.* New York: Oxford University Press, 1973.

Burnette, O. Lawrence, Jr., ed. *Wisconsin Witness to Frederick Jackson Turner: A Collection of Essays on the Historian and the Thesis.* Madison: State Historical Society of Wisconsin, 1961.

Carpenter, Ronald H. *The Eloquence of Frederick Jackson Turner.* San Marino, Calif.: Huntington Library, 1983.

Cronon, William. "Revisiting the Vanishing Frontier: The Legacy of Frederick Jackson Turner." *Western Historical Quarterly* 18 (April 1987):157–76.

Edwards, Everett E., comp. "A Bibliography of the Writings of Frederick Jackson Turner. . . ." *Early Writings of Frederick Jackson Turner.* Madison: University of Wisconsin Press, 1938, 231–72.

Gressley, Gene M. "The Turner Thesis: A Problem in Historiography." *Agricultural History* 32 (October 1958):227–49.

Hofstadter, Richard. *The Progressive Historians: Turner, Beard, Parrington.* New York: Alfred A. Knopf, 1969.

————, and Seymour Martin Lipset. *Turner and the Sociology of the Frontier.* New York: Basic Books, 1968.

Lamar, Howard R. "Frederick Jackson Turner." In Marcus Cunliffe and Robin W. Winks, eds., *Pastmasters: Some Essays on American Historians.* New York: Harper and Row, 1969, 74–109, 419–26.

Mood, Fulmer. "The Development of Frederick Jackson Turner as a Historical Thinker." *Transactions of the Colonial Society of Massachusetts* 34 (December 1943):283–352.

Pierson, George Wilson. "American Historians and the Frontier Hypothesis in 1941." *Wisconsin Magazine of History* 26 (September, December 1942):36–60, 170–85.

Putnam, Jackson K. "The Turner Thesis and the Western Movement: A Reappraisal." *Western Historical Quarterly* 7 (October 1976):377–404.

Scheiber, Harry N. "Turner's Legacy and the Search for a Reorientation of Western History: A Review Essay." *New Mexico Historical Review* 44 (July 1969):231–48.

Steffen, Jerome O. "Some Observations on the Turner Thesis: A Polemic." *Papers in Anthropology* 14 (1973): 16–30.

Taylor, George Rogers, ed. *The Turner Thesis Concerning the Role of the Frontier in American History.* Lexington, Mass.: D. C. Heath, 1972.

4

Frederick Jackson Turner and Western Regionalism[1]

MICHAEL C. STEINER

$\mathcal{A}$S THE CENTENNIAL OF
Frederick Jackson Turner's frontier thesis approaches, it is fitting to draw
attention to his equally evocative though surprisingly neglected sectional thesis. Turner is known primarily as the proponent of the frontier
thesis and the progenitor of American frontier history, yet he devoted
most of his career to the sectional thesis and to writing regional history. He is remembered largely for his riveting 1893 announcement that
the four-hundred-year-old American land frontier had closed and that
the continuous push into such "free and open" land had forged the
national character and explained American development. While generations of historians have debated this theory, they have often ignored
its major message: the once vital frontier was dead, and a fresh historical perspective would be needed for a complex, industrial society.

Turner described the frontier as a self-destroying process providing a provisional explanation of American development, and most of
his academic career was devoted to his search for a more lasting explanation. The section seemed to be such a constant, for life had been
shaped by the physiographic framework of the North American continent from the beginning, and Turner argued that this influence would
become increasingly important in a frontierless society as native-born
generations replaced their pioneer parents and restless mobility subsided into attachment to place. Such regional consciousness was both
inevitable and desirable as "crystalized sections feel the full influence
of their geographical peculiarities, their special interests, and their

developed ideals within a closed and static nation."[2] Turner saw Americans as both driven transients and determined settlers, knew that westering engendered a counterdesire for dwelling, and believed that with the passing of the frontier Americans would truly begin to inhabit the land and make it their home.

This, in the barest of outlines, was Turner's sectional thesis—a compelling geohistorical concept that captured his imagination from the mid-1890s until his death in 1932. Although Turner viewed history as a network of forces to which there is no one "key," regionalism and sense of place imbued his thought and overshadowed the frontier as causal forces. "There is no more enduring, no more influential force in our history," he bluntly declared, "than the formation and interplay of the different regions of the United States."[3] Three of his four books are sectional analyses of American history, and one of them—a sectional interpretation of the Jacksonian era—preoccupied Turner for the last twenty-five years of his life.[4] By demonstrating the overriding significance of regional factors in American history, he thought that this book would be the capstone of his career. The mountain of notes, articles, newspaper clippings, maps, slides, and letters he collected for "THE BOOK" on sectionalism fills sixty boxes at the Huntington Library and stands as mute testimony to his devotion to the sectional thesis.[5]

Throughout his career, Turner visualized the frontier and section as "mutually interpretative" concepts to be understood only in their dynamic interaction.[6] In 1925 he admitted to being "possessed with the idea that twenty years from now my Sections paper will travel along with my Frontier as interpretations"; a few weeks before his death he urged Avery Craven to see sectionalism as a larger, more persistent force than the frontier; and two of his most thoughtful students have concluded that compared to the frontier thesis "the concept of the section was if anything even more important in Turner's thinking" and that "the real significance of the frontier . . . was that it created sections."[7] Turner realized that historians would resist such ideas. Knowing that an elusive vision "of the importance of *space* in history" lay at the heart of his thought, he predicted that it would take twenty years "to awaken the brethren to the intimate relationship between regional geography and American history."[8]

It has been harder to awaken the brethren than Turner imagined. Although Turner has attracted more attention than any other American historian, his sectional theory has been largely ignored. A few historians, cultural geographers, political scientists, and bioregionalists have found renewed relevance in the sectional thesis in the 1980s,[9] yet most scholars continue to judge Turner solely for the frontier thesis. He may have suffered the ironic fate of having been too successful too soon; of having expressed such an alluring image of America that much of his subsequent work seemed but an obscure footnote to that dramatic beginning. He may have been trapped by troublesome terminology: *sectionalism* had the unfortunate connotations of cultural divisiveness and civil war; the more honorable term *regionalism* did not appear in the United States until the last decade of his life.[10] His youthful vision of the American as impetuous frontiersman also may have evoked a flattering self-image difficult to relinquish—a powerful "beckoning archetype" that Americans desperately want to believe even though the frontier is dead. "If there is one fact about the United States that can be stated without fear of successful contradiction," James Thurber has observed, "it is that Americans are in love with the Far West, the Old Frontier."[11] For these and other reasons, people persist in treating Turner's work as if it had ended in 1893, neglecting the fact that much of his thought over the next thirty-nine years corrected flaws in the frontier thesis and provided an alternative understanding of America as it moved beyond the frontier and into the twentieth century.[12]

Those who have considered the sectional thesis tend either to slight it or to reject it as a piece of misguided thinking. Aside from a few early appreciative essays and a thorough discussion in Ray Billington's biography,[13] historians have dismissed the sectional concept as a subterfuge hiding the unpleasant fact of class conflict, as a myopic vision of American isolationalism, or as the delusion of a "space-obsessed, geography-bound mind," a case of "arrested development," and an escape from challenging social concerns "into the vast materials of Western Americana."[14] More recently, it has been minimized as a "conceptual straightjacket," and a "vaporous notion" lacking "both analytical precision and narrative force."[15] Even Billington regarded Turner's sectional research as a "plaything" diverting his attention from the more fruitful frontier hypothesis and argued that "when Turner went on to insist that sectional division would continue to deepen, he was flying in the face of common sense."[16]

Many of these criticisms are telling—up to a point. Wishful thinking is indeed part of the sectional concept, but it also contains many valuable insights. Although lacking the oracular panache of the frontier thesis, Turner's regional vision may offer a fuller understanding of modern American culture than its more celebrated sister concept. Nearly one hundred years after the death of the frontier, scholars must move beyond well-worn paths of frontier history into wider realms of thought, to see the West as a complex place in the modern world rather than as a glamorous process in the distant past. Turner himself encouraged this shift, expressing annoyance with those who saw him only as the "patron saint" of the disappearing frontier, and hoping to be remembered as a teacher who encouraged others to "carry on and make new openings in the forest."[17]

More than any other aspect of Turner's thought, the sectional thesis provides openings in the forest and glimpses of something larger than the frontier. Turner's role in frontier history has been endlessly debated; his contribution to postfrontier regional history deserves greater attention. The purpose of this essay is to trace the development of his regional vision and to discuss its relevance for writing western history. An examination of Turner's midwestern background, his intellectual sources, and the sectional thesis as it was fully expressed in the 1920s reveals a valuable though hardly flawless concept for western historians.

Regional Background. Turner's native Midwest shaped his sense of the West. His early years in Portage, Wisconsin, and mature recollections of this area as wilderness, frontier, and settled land affected the sectional thesis in at least two stages. In the late 1880s, Turner's initial speculation about the interaction of frontier and section was spurred by critical affection for his native soil; as the sectional thesis reached its fullest expression in the 1920s, memories of what seemed to be a stable community with a distinctive sense of place provided an image of order and security amid rapid social change and imbued his vision of America's regional future.

During Turner's boyhood, his home town changed from a tumultuous frontier settlement to a more established community. His father had settled in Portage in 1858 to become the local newspaper editor and a Republican politician, and from this secure place within the community, young Turner witnessed the transition from frontier to section.[18] Like Josiah Royce and Walter Prescott Webb, Turner was marked by the process and place he later analyzed. Each of these western regionalists was a child of pioneers; each developed a complex concern for the land and folk of his native region—the Sierra foothills, the open Great Plains, and the forested upper Mississippi Valley—only after leaving it; and each championed regional pride and distinctiveness as a necessary sequel to the frontier and buffer against the excesses of the nation-state.

Being part of an emerging community surrounded by pine forests, swamps, lakes, and rivers left a lasting impression upon Turner. Toward the end of his life, he wrote glowing, detailed accounts of his Wisconsin boyhood; his earlier, more ambivalent reflections are found in a series of letters written between 1886 and 1889 to his fiancée, Mae Sherwood. The letters are full of paeans to the natural landscape—"Blessed be the woods! Wish I might never see a city again"—yet they are also aware of the cultural landscape, depicting farmfolk and villages along the Fox River and "hosts of mounds where rest the antique bones of the mound builders—for this was once *their* fishing and hunting ground."[19]

A critical tone soon tempered this sense of place. Visiting Portage after a year in Madison, he complained, "Ah, but what a barren little town it is, so sandy and dusty and hot. . . . I would sooner keep a fond recollection of the place of my birth but it's impossible." A trip to New England that summer—his first venture beyond the Midwest—intensified Turner's provincial self-consciousness. "I could gladly pitch my tent on Boston Common for the rest of my days," he confessed. Without this trip, he feared he might have become as backward and banal as the bleak towns and scrubby landscape of his native region. Yet exposure to the cosmopolitan East did not inspire rejection of the hinterlands, for within a week of returning home he resolved that his life's work would be to "study chiefly upon the Northwest and more generally upon the Mississippi Valley. The history of this great country remains to be written. . . . I am placed in a *new* society . . . ready to take its course in universal history. . . . The west looks to the future, the east to the past."[20]

This conviction was reinforced as Turner did graduate work in Baltimore. Once again, the East made him sensitive to flaws of his native region and yet committed to writing about it. "My own mind," he recalled, "was warmed and stirred by the change from my more or less provincial life in the West to a new environment, where I could get a more detached view of the significance of the West itself and where I was challenged to try to account for myself and my people, under conditions of a new audience."[21] He returned to Wisconsin in 1889 not simply to promote a particular region, but to analyze critically the formation and interaction of regions within the nation. The strong sense of place that informed Turner's work, therefore, transcends local chauvinism: his regional thought, like Royce's and Webb's, is more profound for being aware of the frailties and strengths of his native soil and for perceiving his region within a larger context.

The immediate product of this period of Turner's life—the frontier thesis—can be interpreted as the first stage of his larger sectional hypothesis. Turner later looked back upon the frontier paper as a sectional manifesto, as "a protest against eastern neglect." A year before delivering this essay, he had objected to the traditional treatment of American history, in which "the older writers on the subject, coming, like all wise men, from the East, have largely restricted their view to the Atlantic coast." By contrast, Turner argued that "the true point of view in the history of this nation is not the Atlantic coast, it is the Mississippi Valley."[22] His 1893 essay was, therefore, an assertion of regional identity: the historiographic counterpart of the farmer's revolt, the Populist campaign, the rise of literary regionalism, and the development of skyscrapers, prairie houses, and the emergence of midwestern and western consciousness at the end of the nineteenth century.[23] Stung by eastern arrogance, Turner described the raw, dynamic West as the seedbed of the national character. He deftly subverted conventional criticisms of the crudeness of western life by arguing that only the intense pressure of the frontier could break the cake of European custom and forge an American culture. James Fenimore Cooper, author of *The Prairie*, winces every time the dull-witted squatter, Ishmael Bush, fells a tree; Turner, on the other hand, applauds the clearing of the forest and ends *Rise of the New West, 1819–1829* with this heroic stroke: "and on the frontier of the northwest, the young Abe Lincoln sank his axe deep in the opposing forest."[24]

Turner admired the aggressive pioneer, yet he also appreciated the wilderness, the very thing that the pioneer destroyed. His autobiographical letters abound with nostalgic portraits of his native soil as wilderness, frontier, and settled section. "What I was *conscious* of was that father had come of pioneer folk, that he loved the forest, into which he used to take me fishing," he recalled. "I have polled [sic] down the Wisconsin in a dug-out with Indian guides . . . through virgin forests of balsam firs, seeing deer in the river . . . feeling that I belonged to it all." But he only saw remants of wilderness: the first stages of the frontier had passed through Portage a generation before his birth, and he had startling memories of the turmoil wrought by that process. "I have seen," he continued, "a lynched man hanging to a tree as I came home from school . . . have seen red shirted Irish raftsmen *take* the town when they tied up and came ashore." Turner remembered the turbulent frontier, but he reminisced in greater detail about the emergence of distinctive regional life. He recalled vibrant Norwegian, Welsh, Scottish,

Swiss, and Irish communities near Portage as well as "Yankees from Maine & Vermont, New York Yankees, Dutchmen from the Mohawk, braw curlers from the Highlands, Southerners—all kinds."[25]

Several themes emerge from such reminiscences. First, Turner's allegiance was pulled in opposite directions: he was attached to a particular place—both in its primal state and as a settled community—at the same time that he was attracted to a moving process. The tension between the dynamic frontier and the sense of place found in the diminished wilderness and the emerging section became a driving force in Turner's work. The frontier process interested him for a while; the land itself—both before and after it had been touched by the turbulent frontier—became his abiding concern.

These recollections also suggest that during an era increasingly affected by cities and machines, Turner held a vision that the Mississippi Valley "was the heart of an agricultural nation and the farmer the real, genuine American, the balance wheel of society."[26] He adhered to this agrarian belief at the same time that he was disturbed by the nation's urban-industrial transformation. Contemplating the advance of civilization into the Ohio Valley, he wrote: "Where Braddock and his men, 'carving a cross on the wilderness rim,' were struck by the painted savages in the primeval woods, huge furnaces belch forth perpetual fires and Huns and Bulgars, Poles and Sicilians struggle for a chance to earn their daily bread, and live a brutal and degraded life."[27] Turner eventually believed that the growth of distinctive regional cultures would counteract such frightening changes; and his regional vision was derived from memories of rural and small town life in the late nineteenth century, a time when—especially through the mist of memory—American society seemed close to the *Gemeinschaft* ideal of intimate, stable, traditional communities for the last time.[28]

Turner's theory, like that of other regionalists, was informed by the places of his past.[29] It was evoked by the tension between mobility and settlement, between the restless frontier and the steadfast community. Turner, who more than any other American has inspired the glorification of the nomadic pioneer, also criticized this migratory itch. He saw the frontier as a fleeting process, the section as an enduring fact of American history. The boisterous movement across the continent, he argued, would eventually subside into attachment to particular places upon the land, encouraging environmental awareness and communal pride that would control the excesses of urban-industrial society. The Midwest furnished the background of the sectional thesis, and it reached sharper focus as Turner reacted to intellectual currents of his day.

Intellectual Influences. A general theory of sectionalism was implicit in Turner's image of the ever-retreating frontier. "I saw at once," he recalled, "that the frontier passed into successive and varied regions, and that new sections evolved in the relations between these geographic regions, and the kinds of people and society which entered them and adjusted to the environment."[30] Thus, for Turner the physiographic "region" existed before colonization, while the cultural "section" emerged afterward as settlers adjusted to new conditions. Of the relationship between culture and environment in the Midwest, Turner wrote that "it took a century for this society to fit itself into the conditions of the whole province. Little by little, nature pressed into her mold the plastic pioneer life."[31] The image of people responding to fresh and varied environments is at the heart of Turner's conception of historical process.

Graduate work at Johns Hopkins under Herbert Baxter Adams should have prepared Turner to slight environmental factors. As high priest of the Teutonic germ theorists, Adams urged historians to turn from shallow American sources to the richer European roots. Turner resisted this logic. His experience in a community developing out of the wilderness forced respect for the American environment, and contact with a young professor from the South, Woodrow Wilson, helped him to visualize the cultural impact of environmental forces. Not only did the two men agree that historians had neglected regions beyond New England, but Turner later recalled that Wilson's "emphasis upon Bagehot's idea of growth by 'breaking the cake of custom' left a deep impression upon me when I came to consider what part the West had played."[32] With this striking metaphor in mind, Turner would assert in his most famous essay that a fresh American culture evolved as people adjusted to a new environment. And the very logic of this environmental explanation compelled him to see American space as composed of many environments evoking many responses.

It was a favorable time for such interests. In the 1880s and 1890s, European and American scholars were particularly concerned with the relationship between culture and environment. In Germany, Friedrich Ratzel was writing influential studies of spatial patterns of cultural diffusion. Having lived briefly in the United States, Ratzel criticized American restlessness and ruthless use of the land. Prefiguring Turner's developing interest in regional consciousness, he predicted that Americans would slow down and cultivate a mature, land-conscious civilization as they occupied their continent.[33] Building upon Ratzel's insights, German geographers Otto Schlutter, Siegfried Passarge, and others visualized each region, or *landschaft*, as a living entity with a distinct texture and spirit. In France, geographer Paul Vidal de la Blache led a similar movement that perceived the natural region, or *pays*, as furnishing both possibilities and limitations to its inhabitants. According to Vidal's theory of *possibilisme*, every region is a reservoir of latent activities that, once chosen and developed, nurtures its full spirit, or *genre de vie*. Still others analyzed the earth's surface as a configuration of "natural regions" rather than nation states, and by 1914 no fewer than twenty-one scholars had proposed boundaries for the natural subdivisions of North America alone.[34]

Turner participated in these efforts. French and German scholarship influenced his own lifelong interest in regional consciousness and psychology. Prefiguring the work of Lucien Febvre, Fernand Braudel, and the *Annales* School by more than a generation, Turner deliberately fused history with geography from the beginning of his career. A member of both the Association of American Geographers and the American Geographical Society, he developed a subtle sense of the relationship between culture and nature. Rarely a simple environmental determinist, he argued that "environment includes both geographical and social factors, and the physical environment itself is changed by changing economic processes and interests," and he perceived sections as "the result of the joint influence of the geologist's physiographic provinces and the colonizing stock that entered them."[35]

Turner also benefited from two emerging traditions in American thought: a growing awareness of the natural landscape, and scientific efforts to delineate the natural divisions of the North American continent. After the Civil War, a significant number of Americans paused to appreciate the land they had passed through and abused for so long. According to Lewis Mumford, only late in the nineteenth century did the pioneer's ruthless land hunger begin to give way throughout the nation to the settler's love of the soil. This emerging reverence for the fragility of the land was foreshadowed in George Perkins Marsh's *Man and Nature* (1864). "Man is everywhere a disturbing agent," Marsh had declared. "Wherever he plants his foot, the harmonies of nature are turned to discord." He was particularly critical of the "incessant flitting" of Americans, whom he urged to settle down and reinhabit rather than ransack their land. At a time when many assumed that the earth made man, Marsh argued that man made the earth.[36]

The perception of man as responsible for the preservation of nature

was reflected in the late nineteenth-century popularity of John Burroughs, John Muir, and Henry David Thoreau; in the emergence of
the Country Life, Back- to-the-Land, and Conservation movements; in
the creation of national parks; and in the pervasive urge to replace the
rational grid with flexibly designed parks, gardens, and suburbs.[37]
Clearly, the sectional thesis developed during a period of incipient interest in the relationship between land and life. Turner's letters abound
with lyrical landscape descriptions echoing Emerson, Thoreau, and
Burroughs. As early as 1893 Turner also responded to the work of
Nathanael Southgate Shaler, a Harvard geologist who applied Marsh's
vision of man's wanton destruction of natural resources to the American scene.[38]

This respect for the natural environment—intensified by an end-
of-the-century awareness of limits to the nation's space and resources—
was paralleled by scholarly efforts to map the continent's natural regions.
The search for the primal rather than the political divisions of the earth's
surface took many forms: American geologists outlined "physiographic
provinces," zoologists mapped "natural life zones," anthropologists
developed the "culture area" concept, and sociologists and literary critics speculated about regional expression and personality types.[39]

The geological surveys of John Wesley Powell were especially influential. After exploring the Colorado Plateau for seven years, Powell
published an 1878 report asserting that American woodland culture
was ill-suited for the dry, treeless spaces west of the 100th meridian. For this arid region, he stressed the desirability of communal
settlement at water sources and proposed a variable system of land
division with boundaries "controlled by topographic features."[40] Powell helped Turner to realize that different environments elicited different settlement patterns, that the agrarian frontier evoked collectivism
as well as individualism, and that in the Far West "the physiographic
province itself decreed that the destiny of this new frontier should be
social rather than individual."[41]

Turner's search for a theory covering other sections as well as the arid
West was furthered by Powell's essay in 1896 on "Physiographic Regions
of the United States," which divided the nation into sixteen natural
regions composed of major slopes and river basins.[42] Turner had been
waiting for such an analysis. In 1892 he had declared a need for
"thorough study of the physiographic basis of our history. When the
geologist, the meteorologist, the biologist, and the historian shall go hand
in hand in this study, they will see how largely American history has

been determined by natural conditions." Powell's analysis provided a geological foundation upon which he could observe the advancing waves of human settlement, and in 1898 he strengthened his understanding of the environmental basis of history by attending Charles Van Hise's seminar on the physiography of the United States.[43]

The following year, Turner reworked the frontier essay in terms of what he had learned from Powell and Van Hise. Designed for history teachers, this revision portrayed the frontier as a "flood of settlement" flowing into "successive physiographic areas." To visualize how civilization had seeped into the geological structure of the continent, Turner urged teachers to place census maps of the advancing frontier line alongside Powell's physiographic maps. The lesson then became clear: the frontier and the West had advanced unevenly, according to the dictates of geography; and the nation had then matured in sections "each with its own inheritance, its own contributions, and individuality."[44]

The sectional thesis reached its final shape as Turner joined his environmental research with Josiah Royce's concept of a "wise provincialism." Where Turner had mixed emotions about what the frontier had done to his native soil, Royce remembered it as an unmitigated evil. In his history of California (1886) and other writings, Royce diagnosed the frontier as a disease that disintegrated community and depleted the land. For Royce, the "real winning of the West" took place in homes, villages, and fields—in the urge to inhabit the land and to build stable communities—not in the mining camps of rootless, isolated individuals. Describing "the reverent memory of the pioneers, the formation of local customs, the development of community loyalty" in the wake of the chaotic frontier, Royce concluded that "in the formation of a loyal local consciousness, in a wise provincialism, lies the way toward social salvation."[45] As Turner shifted his attention from frontier mobility to sectional stability, he turned to Royce's theory. His most important discussion of sectionalism relies upon Royce's belief that wise provincialism would nurture careful use of the earth and support a sense of community amid mass society.[46]

The Sectional Thesis. From the early 1890s until his death in 1932, Turner argued with increasing conviction that subnational places of loyalty had become increasingly important in a frontierless society. As early as 1892, he had begun to visualize the relationship between frontier and section, between process and place in American history, and later called for "the serious study of sectionalism" as "a fundamental fact in American history."[47] He had prepared to answer this challenge by reading

Ratzel, Vidal, Shaler, Powell, Royce, and others, by studying geology under Van Hise, and by rewriting the frontier essay in terms of this knowledge. By 1900, Turner felt confident enough to begin to champion sectionalism as the inevitable and necessary sequel to the frontier.

He approached this task on two fronts. Just as he required students to write two types of essays—an empirical "problem paper" focusing upon a narrow research topic and a theoretical "correlation paper" connecting this data with larger historical themes—Turner promoted the sectional thesis by writing both carefully detailed regional histories and boldly speculative essays. His densely researched histories traced the emergence of sectional identity within particular regions in the past, whereas his speculative essays freely explored the larger implications of sectionalism in the present and possible future. Turner alternated between theoretical and empirical forms of scholarship throughout his career, and the tension between the daring prophet and the cautious positivist—between "the search beyond the skyline for new truth, and the use of such methods of getting there as the need and resources permitted"—was a driving force behind the sectional thesis.[48]

Although Turner outlined a sweeping theoretical essay on sectionalism as early as 1901, he devoted most of his energy over the next five years to narrating the growth of sectionalism during the 1820s. His *Rise of the New West, 1819–1829* (1906), vividly described the passing of the frontier and the creation of sectional consciousness in eastern regions that had once been the West—from New England to the South and from the Ohio to the Mississippi valleys. Emboldened by the success of this book, Turner confidently moved to a more speculative level by promoting environmental theory at professional conferences. In December 1907 the American Historical Association and the American Sociological Society met at Madison. Turner arranged a program on "The Relation of Geography and History" for the historians and urged the sociologists to pay more attention to the spatial variations in culture. At the next AHA meeting he renewed the call for historians to consider environmental factors and to see sectionalism as a fundamental force in our society.[49]

The historians and sociologists were highly skeptical. "Merely mention geographic factors in the Historical Association," one participant recalled, "and the fur flies."[50] Stung by these criticisms, he decided that a more practical way to champion the cause would be to pursue two types of empirical study: a series of essays demonstrating the historical importance of particular sections, and a massive book examining the rise of sectionalism during a particular period of history. To prove the significance of the section by examining New England, the Ohio Valley, the Midwest, and the West became part of his scholarly mission; and retreating to the safer ground established in *Rise of the New West*, Turner began analyzing meticulously the play of sectional forces between 1830 and 1850—a task that consumed him until his death.[51]

Except for another poorly received address on "Geographical Influences in American Political History" in 1914, Turner curbed his desire to proclaim a general theory of sectionalism until the early 1920s.[52] Although the empiricist seemed to prevail over the theorist during these years, Turner continued to refine his larger vision. A combination of factors in the wake of World War I—including reactions to the war itself, the urbanization of American society, and a sense of national and global limits to growth—renewed Turner's prophetic voice and brought the sectional thesis to its highest pitch in three boldly speculative essays written between 1922 and 1926.[53]

The struggle to communicate the sectional thesis may have derived from a deeply rooted conflict in Turner's own mind as well as from resistance by fellow historians. Turner found two compulsions within himself and also deeply entwined throughout American history: the urge to strike out for new territory and the need for attachment to place. Both the compulsion to wander and the desire to settle down, he realized, grew out of the frontier process that bred rampant individualism as well as a collective endeavor. The pioneer who felt the urge to move on at the sight of smoke from a neighbor's campfire also knew that sooner or later he would need help from his neighbor. Turner admired both pioneer traits. He praised the nomadic backwoodsman who "found too little elbow room in town life," yet he extolled frontier communal life and predicted that "in the spirit of the pioneer's 'house raising' lies the salvation of the Republic."[54]

As long as free lands beckoned, the clash between frontier individualism and collectivism could be avoided: Natty Bumppo or Huck Finn could simply leave the jurisdiction of people like Judge Temple or Miss Watson. But once the open West disappeared, the "squatter ideal" of "individual freedom to compete unrestrictedly for the resources of the continent" had to confront the "ideal of democracy—'government of the people, by the people and for the people.' " "The national problem," Turner wrote in 1914, "is no longer how to cut and burn away the vast screen of the dense and daunting forest; it is how to save and wisely use the remaining timber."[55] In a settled nation, in other words, restless individualism would give way to cooperative action and attachment to place.

Turner found the strongest evidence for this change in the emergence of Populist protest and western radicalism. Nomadic pioneer folk who had considered government an evil entanglement were now settled farmers and ranchers seeking legislative protection from eastern plutocracy. Western pride, in particular, was kindled by a sense of dwindling resources and awareness of being a plundered province.[56] Such regional consciousness— which Turner believed grew more vigorously in closed rather than in expanding space—resisted the consolidating forces of Wall Street. With frontier movement halted and land occupied, Turner believed that distinct regional subcultures would grow out of the landscape, cultures potentially as rich and various yet less divisive than those of the war-torn Old World. "The American section," he argued in 1922, "may be likened to the shadowy image of the European nation, to the European state denatured of its toxic qualities."[57]

Sectionalism, therefore, answered many social and psychological needs: it provided a resting place and sense of community after so many centuries of westward movement; it nurtured awareness of the environment that modified the pioneer pattern of mining the land and moving on; it implied a healthy cultural diversity that diverted the urban-industrial glacier and eastern exploitation; it encouraged a sense of American uniqueness; and it offered an alternative to "toxic" European nationalism. Sectionalism also represented a geographical fact that existed before and after the frontier movement across the continent. The "vast and shaggy continent," which Turner described as transforming civilized Europeans into primitive Americans, was composed of many environments, each evoking distinct patterns of life. "The vast spaces over which this forming people have spread," he observed, "are themselves a complex of physiographic sections." "The first clearly marked social integration took place in *sections* rather than in the nation as a whole."[58]

Whereas sectionalism existed along the Atlantic Coast from the beginning, nationalism developed only as settlers moved inland. People from various coastal sections and European nations were thrown together "in the crucible of the frontier" where, through mobility and intermarriage, "the immigrants were Americanized, liberated, and fused into a mixed race."[59] Yet after this nationalizing ferment moved on, people settled back into sections that remained primary places of loyalty. Turner's frontier might be thought of as a turbulent wave passing over an uneven stretch of land. Outstanding features are momentarily submerged as this wave swirls over them, only to reemerge, somewhat smoothed, in its wake. In a similar manner, a slice of the North American continent evolves from a jumble of physiographic regions to an area of frontier activity to a distinct mosaic of sections functioning within the national whole. The homogenizing phase is transitory; a sectional pattern endures. Yet the frontier works an important transformation: it brings a swarm of disparate regions into a federation of sections, into a nation that is, ideally, a creative association of distinct parts: "a nobler structure, in which each section will find its place as a fit room in a worthy house."[60]

Thus, for Turner, sectionalism was an enduring fact of American history that existed before and after the frontier and explained many of the problems and accomplishments of our past. As a historian, he knew the weaknesses of sectionalism: the possible drift toward isolation and small-mindedness, the tendency for one section to exploit other areas and dominate the nation, and the chance for rivalries and conflicts. He believed, nevertheless, that the benefits of sectionalism outweighed these handicaps and that "the Civil War was only the most drastic and most tragic of sectional manifestations"—a terrible deviation from a worthy tradition. Echoing Royce, Randolph Bourne, and Horace Kallen, Turner favored cultural diversity over inflexible nationalism and believed that "the rejuvenation of sectional self consciousness" would enrich rather than disrupt American life. "A measure of local concentration seems necessary to produce healthy intellectual and moral life," he wisely argued. "The spread of social forces over too vast an area makes for monotony and stagnation."[61]

Turner also believed that Americans had developed a political system that balanced the forces of fragmentation and consolidation. Embedded in James Madison's federalism was the conviction that the republic was strengthened by localism: that a diversity of parties, interests, and local governments would clog surges of state oppression and serve as barriers to destructive tides of mass emotion. The opposite drift toward atomistic separatism, according to Turner, was held in check by the growth of cross-sectional interests and political parties. By 1918, Turner compared this *"Pax Americana"* to war-torn Europe and prepared a memorandum for Woodrow Wilson proposing that the "American League of Sections" serve as a model for worldwide peace.[62]

Sectionalism offered Turner the most satisfying solutions to the problems raised by the end of the frontier and the rise of mass society. His

1893 funeral sermon ends with the dismal image of a frontier nation without open space and a pioneer people without free lands to subdue. But sectionalism provided an alternative to this distressing situation and the foundation for the next period of American history. Turner's geographical frame of mind and his emotional attachment to the continent's wild forests and open spaces led him to believe that American mobility halted as soon as open land was occupied. Movement—the "dominant fact" of frontier life—would give way to sense of place, nomadic individualism to community. "As the frontier advance drew to a close," he concluded, "as these provinces were no longer regions to be crossed, or merely exploited, but home-sections of permanent settlers, the final stage was reached."[63] It was a time to establish roots, to shape raw space into familiar place, and Turner believed that Americans would choose to inhabit particular places after so many centuries of restless movement.

But the problem refused to be solved so easily. At the turn of the century, sectionalism had seemed the most desirable sequel to the frontier; by the 1920s, it appeared to be the only way to avoid an unvarying urban-industrial order. In February 1924, Turner began his final course at Harvard by mentioning the swarm of publications concerning the specter of diminishing global resources. He observed that this fear coincided with the 1920 census report that more Americans lived in cities than in the country, with more than one-fifth dwelling in metropolitan areas. This census held as ominous a message for Turner as the 1890 bulletin announcing the end of the frontier. Alluding to Oswald Spengler's theory that the rise of the metropolis marked the decline of the western world, Turner concluded that a nation overwhelmed by cities would lose touch with its sustaining resource base in the countryside.[64]

The prophetic voice returned and the sectional thesis reached its fullest expression as Turner responded to the rise of the city and the sense of a global environmental crisis. In 1922, he outlined an essay on "The Significance of the City in American History," and in 1925 he told Arthur Schlesinger that "there seems likely to be an urban reinterpretation of our history. But we cannot altogether get away from the facts of American history, however far we go in adopting the Old World!"[65] Despite deeply rooted agrarian and exceptionalist biases, Turner recognized that cities and industrial technology had evolved as necessary parts of modern American civilization. It might be appropriate for the industrial metropolis to dominate a few regions, he conceded, but a more balanced, elemental pattern based on farming, fishing, lumbering, mining, and decentralized industry should endure in other sections of the nation and the world.

He thought that such food and resource-gathering regions would become increasingly important in a closed world suddenly aware of limits and the need to conserve its raw materials. He gathered many of his research notes between 1922 and 1925 in files entitled "Alarmist Arguments" and "Strategy of a Saturated Earth," revealing a voracious interest in economic geography, ecology, and regional planning, a familiarity with the work of Carl Sauer, Harlan Barrows, and Patrick Geddes, and a deep concern about global environmental and population problems. A shrill urgency, comparable to his distress about the end of the American frontier in the early 1890s, gripped Turner's imagination as he saw the passing of the global frontier in the early 1920s. "Truly a shrinking earth!" he declared. "An earth compelled by irresistible forces to exercise restraint, to associate, agree, and adjust, or to commit suicide."[66]

This fear, coupled with a regional solution, is most clearly stated in "The Significance of the Section in American History," a work Turner considered the "companion piece" to the frontier essay. The stage is set in two swift sentences: "The free lands are no longer free; the boundless resources are no longer boundless. Already the urban population exceeds the rural population of the United States." He then moved to the heart of his argument, asserting that the surge of eastern urbanism underscored the need for an expanded and self-sustaining resource base in the countryside and especially in the West, that "the natural advantages of certain regions for farming, or for forestry, or for pasturage will arrest the tendency of the Eastern industrial type of society to flow across the continent." In addition to conserving natural resources, such areas were developing distinct cultures of their own—cultures ensuring a more responsible use of the land and acting as mediating structures between the individual and the nation state. With Royce in mind, Turner declared that "the world needs now more than ever before the vigorous development of a highly organized provincial life to serve as a check upon mob psychology on a national scale, and to furnish that variety which is essential to vital growth and originality." American culture, he concluded, would continue to be enriched by the growth and interaction of such primary places of loyalty, and "we must shape our national action to the fact of vast and varied Union of unlike sections."[67]

Turner believed that the intensification of American sectionalism would conserve the nation's natural resources, preserve its rural essence, and sustain its cultural diversity. He interpreted the peaceful growth of sections as a sign of ripeness and maturity, as "exhibiting the larger outlines of a nation's portrait, revealing something of the America that is to be, even as a man's physiognomy takes firmer shape, as the unformed boy's face takes on the features and the lines of character of the man."[68] It was a relief to pass from youthful excess to full-grown stability, from the frenzied activity of the frontier and metropolis to the calmer considerations of sectional life. Turner told Americans that the ever-retreating frontier had vanished and instead of anxiously facing westward from California's shores they must turn around and learn to live upon the land that had been taken for granted for so many generations.

What, finally, is the significance of Turner's regional theory for writing western history? This question may seem perverse, for the man who founded western history in the late nineteenth century has been severely criticized for hampering the field in the late twentieth. Recent critiques follow two paths: Turner's vision of the frontier, it is argued, has trapped western history in the nineteenth century; and his notion of the West as a process has blurred our sense of the West as a place.

The first criticism contends that the image of an exuberant frontier ending abruptly in 1890 has made it painful to see beyond that decade, has "left historians few clues about what to do with the West in the twentieth century: in an odd sense, Turnerian western history almost literally ended at the very moment that Turner created the field."[69] Facing this historical chasm, scholars could either forge new paradigms for a postfrontier West rife with environmental, economic, racial, and urban concerns, or rest in the cozier confines of the frontier past "warmed by fireside fancy . . . of mountain men, miners, cattle wars, and wagon trains." At a "crossroads between romantic antiquarianism and genuine United States history," western historians have usually taken the easiest route, rarely venturing beyond the 1890s in their research and writing.[70]

Just as the siren song of the frontier seems to have stranded historians in the nineteenth century, Turner's understanding of the West as a process appears to glide past the realities of the region. For some critics, his sense of the West as a continual advance into open land is hopelessly amorphous: it has "started historians down a muddy, slippery road that ultimately leads to a swamp" and made it difficult to grasp the West "as a cohesive whole, fixed in space . . . as a distinct place inhabited by distinct people."[71] For others, Turner's supposed fascination with people in motion has obscured our understanding of equally important folk "who stayed behind."[72] Still others complain that Turner's idea of the West as a process and "a form of society rather than an area"[73] is fraught with imperialistic implications. "If the West was at bottom a form of society," Richard Drinnon has remarked, "then on our round earth, Winning the West amounted to no less than winning the world."[74]

Although there is some merit to these criticisms, they usually ignore the full scope of Turner's thought. In almost every case, Turner's sectional concept supplies solutions for the problems he is accused of creating. A fixation upon the frontier thesis, which marked only the beginning of Turner's thought, has often blinded us to his larger historical vision, which stressed the transition from frontier to region, from process to place, from nineteenth to twentieth century. Rather than trapping western historians in the bygone frontier and perpetuating a shadowy image of the West as a process, Turner's sectional thesis visualizes the American West as a complex place in the modern world and anticipates much that is valued in western history today.

Far from encouraging narrow antiquarianism and provincialism, for example, Turner urged western historians to widen their sense of time and space, to extend the history of the West to the present and to analyze the relationship between their region and other parts of the world. Just as he stressed that "we should rework our history from the new points of view afforded by the present," he also believed that "we cannot select a stretch of land and say we will limit our study to this land; for local history can only be understood in light of the history of the world." "The goal of the antiquarian," he declared, "is the dead past; the goal of the historian is the living present."[75]

The living present for Turner was found in the growth of cultural regionalism in the wake of the frontier. As early as 1896, Turner urged western historians to renounce their "antiquarian" and "provincial" tendencies, and offered a prospectus for writing western history that rings true nearly one hundred years later. The West, he argued, was really many Wests: a vast and various land that "requires analysis into the regions that compose it" and awareness of their interaction with each other and with the nation as a whole. He also called for deeper understanding of western "sense of space"; interdisciplinary study of the relations between white, Indian, black, and European immigrant cultures within these western regions; examination of the environmental and social impact of mining, ranching, forest, and agricultural industries; and analysis of the rise of western cities and "the types of life that have been thus created."[76]

Turner perceived the postfrontier, trans-Mississippi West as a configuration of Great Plains, Rocky Mountain, Spanish Southwest, and Pacific Coast regions continually shaped by waves of economic change, environmental exploitation, and urbanization. Generations before geographers coined the term *sequent occupance*, or Webb and Malin unearthed the cultural strata of the Great Plains, Turner visualized regional history as the dynamic layering of people and economic activities upon the land—as an ongoing process within a place.[77] "Wisconsin is like a palimpsest," he declared in 1888. "The mound builders wrote their record and passed away. The state was occupied by various peoples of Indian race—Then came the French. Then a wave of Northern New York and Vermont fur traders." Shifting westward, Turner later observed that "across the Great Plains where buffalo and Indian held sway successive industrial waves are passing" and traced the changes from free range to ranch to homestead to massive irrigation projects.[78] And building upon a lifelong interest in regional consciousness based upon extensive reading of French and German geohistorical theory, Turner speculated about a western "spirit" that arose from a hard-won awareness of geographical immensity and fragility, from a collective sense of inhabiting a daunting, largely arid, and easily depleted land.[79]

The sectional thesis is most compelling when Turner speaks as the spirited visionary rather than as the cautious empiricist. Yet both perspectives are useful for writing western history. His theoretical essays suggest a model of historical change—a sweeping vision of the transition from frontier to region, movement to settlement, process to place—as well as a method for analyzing the interaction of people and place within particular environments. If the essays launch open-ended hypotheses about the larger significance of sectionalism, Turner's exhaustively researched books, *Rise of the New West, 1819–1829* and *The United States 1830–1850*, are remarkable for the interdisciplinary breadth, their sense of the relationships between regions and the nation, and their focus upon ordinary people who stayed behind to forge pluralistic regional cultures rather than upon the "shiftless and indolent" backwoodsmen who mined the land and moved on. These western regions, he concluded, "were not to be a melting pot, with fusion of manifold ingredients, but rather a mixing bowl, with a process of adjustment, of giving and taking. . . . In this plastic society, all the various stocks intermingled, but they did not lose their separate individualities."[80]

The sectional thesis is hardly flawless. It is tinged with agrarian nostalgia and steeped in a Northern European version of cultural pluralism rarely recognizing Indians, Hispanics, Asians, African Americans, and women.[81] Since Turner's time, furthermore, geographical mobility has accelerated, people continue to move from the country to urban centers, and regions have not emerged as the distinct entities that Turner had anticipated. Yet the fact that Turner exaggerated the significance of sectionalism and presented a limited cast of historical actors should not blind us to aspects of the theory that seem increasingly pertinent at the end of the twentieth century.

Turner's sensitivity to the spatial context of history, his awareness of the environmental and social problems incurred by the frontier, and his general concern for cultural diversity amid mass society are potent issues today.[82] Perhaps more than any major American historian, Turner alerts us to the power of place in human affairs; he forces us to acknowledge the truth of Donald Meinig's axiom that "history and geography are bound together by the very nature of things: history takes place and places are created by history," and he underscores David Potter's shrewd observation that "in a nation as vast and diverse as ours there is really no level higher than the regional level at which one can come to grips with the concrete realities of the land."[83]

The sectional thesis also seems ripe for recognition in light of the "new regionalism" that has flourished in our society since the late 1960s. Symptoms of this impulse are vexingly varied, yet many elements— including discussion of the Sunbelt, Frostbelt, Pacific Rim, Ecotopia, Mexamerica, and Sagebrush Rebellion; a surge of backyard environmental protests and concern for cultural "roots" and preservation; a revival of regional studies throughout academia; the establishment of at least a dozen regional studies centers since the mid-1970s; and the global resurgence of ethno-regional passions—all indicate that it is a propitious time to consider the sectional thesis.[84] Turner would be heartened by William Ferris's prediction that "the eighties will be seen as the moment when regional studies emerged as a catalyst for . . . reshaping the traditional image of American culture." More than seventy years after trying to rouse historians to "the intimate relationship between regional geography and American history," he would welcome Richard Maxwell Brown's belief that "the national myth of America is in decline, while the regional myths live on. . . . It is just barely possible that, at last in our history and culture, regionalism will not only rival but surpass nationalism as a source for good in human life."[85]

The sectional thesis is especially pertinent to western history, for it anticipated many trends that are revitalizing the field. Among these are an emphasis upon the West as a distinct "place undergoing conquest"; a concern for common people "who stayed behind" and inhabited the land; and an interest in a distinctive western "sense of identity" and an emerging "cultural voice as strong and as dominant as a prairie wind."[86] These and other perspectives first hinted at by Turner are needed as western historians develop a *"dynamic* sectional thesis" and "push toward a deeper, fuller, more intellectually complex regionalism."[87] At the very least, we should acknowledge Turner's importance "as a remote ancestor" to contemporary regional studies.[88] Even more appropriately, we might understand Turner as he saw himself—as "a porter at the gate, rather than a drill seargent," as a guide suggesting ways toward more sophisticated regional visions and wider realms of thought.[89] Aware of the need for more intimate places of loyalty beneath the veneer of the nation-state and awake to the tragic, often destructive, consequences of the frontier myth in a limited and crowded world, historians would be wise to pay greater attention to the full scope of Turner's sectional concept.

NOTES

1. I wish to thank Richard Etulain, Robert Hine, Wilbur Jacobs, Martin Ridge, and Leila Zenderland for their valuable advice in preparing this essay, which grew out of an earlier article, "The Significance of Turner's Sectional Thesis," *Western Historical Quarterly* 10 (October 1979):437–66. I also express my appreciation for the 1988 Huntington Library Summer Fellowship that helped me complete the research for this paper.

2. Frederick Jackson Turner, "The Significance of the Section in American History" (1925), in Turner, *The Significance of Sections in American History* (New York: Henry Holt and Co., 1932), 45.

3. Frederick Jackson Turner, typescript, "The Significance of the Section in the U.S.," May 1922, File Drawer 14 A, no. 24, Frederick Jackson Turner papers, Henry E. Huntington Library, San Marino, Calif.

4. Turner's three sectional books are *Rise of the New West: 1819–1829* (New York: Harper and Brothers, 1906), and two books published after his death, the Pulitzer Prize–winning *Significance of Sections in American History* and *The United States, 1830–1850: The Nation and Its Sections* (New York: Henry Holt, 1935), which is the skeleton of what Turner hoped would be his sectional masterpiece. Turner's other book, *The Frontier in American History* (New York: Henry Holt, 1920), has a distinctly regional flavor.

5. For an account of the "THE BOOK" on sectionalism that Turner never finished, see Ray Allen Billington, *Frederick Jackson Turner: Historian, Scholar, Teacher* (New York: Oxford University Press, 1973), 367–70, 382–85. Most of the sectional materials are located in File Drawers 14 and 15 A as well as in the sixty boxes that compose File Drawers A–L.

6. Turner, "Introduction to a Lecture on Sectionalism" (April 1922), in Wilbur R. Jacobs, ed., *Frederick Jackson Turner's Legacy: Unpublished Writings in American History* (San Marino, Calif.: Huntington Library, 1965), 47–48, and Turner to Constance Skinner, March 15, 1922, in Ray Allen Billington, *The Genesis of the Frontier Thesis: A Study in Historical Creativity* (San Marino, Calif.: Huntington Library, 1971), 210–11.

7. Turner to Arthur Schlesinger, May 5, 1925, in Wilbur R. Jacobs, *The Historical World of Frederick Jackson Turner: With Selections from his Correspondence* (New Haven, Conn.: Yale University Press, 1968), 164; Avery Craven, "Frederick Jackson Turner, Historian," *Wisconsin Magazine of History* 25 (June 1942):416; Merle Curti, review of *Significance of Sections*, in *American Journal of Sociology* 39 (September 1933): 265; and Craven, "Frederick Jackson Turner," 418.

8. Turner to Charles Homer Haskins, May 19, 1925, in Jacobs, *Historical World of Frederick Jackson Turner*, 157; and Turner to Homer C. Hockett, January 21, 1926, Box 35, no. 7, Turner papers.

9. Historians who have recently found merit in the sectional thesis include Richard W. Etulain, "A New Historiographical Frontier: The Twentieth-Century West," in Gerald D. Nash and Richard W. Etulain, eds., *The Twentieth-Century West: Historical Interpretations* (Albuquerque: University of New Mexico Press, 1989), 2–4; Richard Jensen, "On Modernizing Frederick Jackson Turner: The Historiography of Regionalism," *Western Historical Quarterly* 11 (July 1980):307–22; Richard White, "Frederick Jackson Turner," in John R. Wunder, ed., *Historians of the American Frontier: A Bio-Bibliographical Sourcebook* (Westport, Conn.: Greenwood Press, 1988), 660–81; and Martin Ridge, "The American West: From Frontier to Region," *New Mexico Historical Review* 64 (April 1989):125–41. Recent appreciative analyses of Turner's regional concept by geographers, political scientists, and bioregionalists include Donald G. Holtgrieve, "Frederick Jackson Turner as a Regionalist," *Professional Geographer* 26 (May 1974):159–65; Robert H. Bloch, "Frederick Jackson Turner and American Geography," *Annals of the Association of American Geographers* 70 (March 1980):31–40; Richard Bensel, *Sectionalism and American Political Development, 1880–1980* (Madison: University of Wisconsin Press, 1984); Rene Dubos, *Celebrations of Life* (New York: McGraw-Hill, 1981), 92–94; and Kirkpatrick Sale, *Dwellers in the Land: The Bioregional Vision* (San Francisco: Sierra Club Books, 1985), 137–41.

10. H. L. Mencken, *The American Language* (New York: Alfred A. Knopf, 1963), 183; Fulmer Mood, "The Origin, Evolution, and Application of the Sectional Concept, 1750–1900," in Merrill Jensen, ed., *Regionalism in America* (Madison: University of Wisconsin Press, 1951), 7–9; Hedwig Hintze, "Regionalism," *Encyclopedia of the Social Science* vol. 13 (New York: Macmillan, 1934), 217.

11. James Thurber, "How to Tell Government from Show Business" (1961), in Michael J. Rosen, ed., *Collecting Himself: James Thurber on Writing and Writers, Humor and Himself* (New York: Harper and Row, 1989), 232. Ronald H. Carpenter discusses Turner's frontiersman as "beckoning archetype" in *The Eloquence of Frederick Jackson Turner* (San Marino, Calif.: Huntington Library, 1984). Commenting on the psychological vitality of the defunct frontier, Michael P. Malone argues that "the recency and overwhelming finality of the frontier *is* a fundamental bonding force of western regionalism. If in no other sense, this is true simply because so many westerners *think* it is true—as is witnessed by an endless profusion of 'western' art, music, food and architecture, 'Mint,' 'Longbranch,' and 'Stockman's' bars, pickups with rifles in the window, Skoal, boots, and tight-fitting jeans." "*The Legacy of Conquest* by Patricia Nelson Limerick: A Panel Appraisal," *Western Historical Quarterly* 20 (August 1989):312. Contrary to these positions, Frank J. Popper asserts that the frontier never ended on the land as well as in the minds of people—that it's alive and well in the late twentieth-century west. See his "The Strange Case of the Contemporary American Frontier," *Yale Review* 76 (December 1986):101–21.

12. Most recent discussions of Turner's thought are predictably silent about the sectional thesis. See, for example: David W. Noble, *Historians against History: The Frontier Thesis and the National Covenant* (Minneapolis: University of Minnesota Press, 1965), 37–55, and *The End of American History: Democracy, Capitalism, and the Metaphor of Two Worlds in Anglo-Historical Writing, 1880–1980* (Minneapolis: University of Minnesota Press, 1985), 16–26, 151–52; Gene Wise, *American Historical Explanations: A Strategy for Grounded Inquiry* (Homewood, Ill.: Dorsey Press, 1973), 179–222; Richard Drinnon, *Facing West: The Metaphysics of Indian-Hating and Empire-Buildings* (New York: New American Library, 1980), 460–65; William H. McNeill, *The Great Frontier: Freedom and Hierarchy in Modern Times* (Princeton, N.J.: Princeton University Press, 1983); and Alan Trachtenberg, *The Incorporation of America: Culture and Society in the Gilded Age* (New York: Hill and Wang, 1982), 11–37. Paradoxically, many of these otherwise impressive studies are critical of Turner for discouraging regional, place-related history— the very approach he pioneered with his sectional thesis.

13. Merle E. Curti, "The Section and the Frontier in American History: The Methodological Concepts of Frederick Jackson Turner," in Stuart Rice, ed., *Methods in Social Sciences: A Case Book* (Chicago: University of Chicago Press, 1931), 353–67; Craven, "Frederick Jackson Turner, Historian," 408–24; William B. Hesseltine, "Regions, Classes, and Sections in American History" (1944), in Richard N. Current, ed., *Sections and Politics: Selected Essays of William B. Hesseltine* (Madison: State Historical Society of Wisconsin, 1968), 97–113; Mood, "Origin, Evolution, and Application of the Sectional Concept, 1750–1900," 5–98; and Billington, *Frederick Jackson Turner*, 209–32, 444–71.

14. Louis M. Hacker, "Sections—or Classes?" *Nation* 137 (July 26, 1933):108– 10; Benjamin F. Wright, review of *Significance of Sections in American History, New England Quarterly* 6 (September 1933):630–34; Richard Hofstadter, *The Pro-

gressive Historians: Turner, Beard, Parrington (New York: Vintage Books, 1968), 101, 114, 113.

15. Jensen, "On Modernizing Frederick Jackson Turner," 307; Donald Worster, "New West, True West: Interpreting the Region's History," *Western Historical Quarterly* 18 (April 1987):144–45; and William Cronon, "Revisiting the Vanishing Frontier: The Legacy of Frederick Jackson Turner," *Western Historical Quarterly* 18 (April 1987):168.

16. Billington, *Frederick Jackson Turner*, 379, 470.

17. Turner to Joseph Schafer, January 19, 1931, Box 45, no. 15, and Turner to Merle Curti, September 8, 1930, Box 44 A, no. 9, Turner papers.

18. See Billington's vivid description of this time and place in "Young Fred Turner," repr. in Martin Ridge, ed., *Frederick Jackson Turner: Wisconsin's Historian of the Frontier* (Madison: State Historical Society of Wisconsin, 1986), 13–25.

19. Turner to Mae Sherwood, August 21, 1886, and July 19, 1886, Box A, no. 18 and no. 16, Turner papers.

20. Turner to Sherwood, June 12, June 28, August 24, and September 5, 1887, Box B, no. 3, no. 9, no. 30, and no. 37, Turner papers.

21. Turner to William Dodd, October 7, 1919, in Billington, *Genesis of the Frontier Thesis*, 195–96.

22. Turner to Constance Skinner, March 15, 1922, in Billington, *Genesis of the Frontier Thesis*, 208; Turner, "Problems in American History" (1892), in Ray Allen Billington, ed., *Frontier and Section: Selected Essays of Frederick Jackson Turner* (Englewood Cliffs, N.J.: Prentice-Hall, 1961), 28, 29.

23. See, for example, Lindley M. Keasbey, "The New Sectionalism: A Western Warning to the East," *Forum* 16 (August 4, 1894):579–87, and Hofstadter, *Progressive Historians*, 47–83, for discussions of the creative fervor of turn-of-the-century midwestern and western regionalism.

24. Turner, *Rise of the New West*, 332.

25. Turner to Carl Becker, December 16, 1925, in Billington, *Genesis of the Frontier Thesis*, 243, 240.

26. Frank R. Kramer, *Voices in the Valley: Mythmaking and Folk Belief in the Shaping of the Middle West* (Madison: University of Wisconsin Press, 1964), 74.

27. Turner, "The West and American Ideals," in *Frontier in American History*, 300.

28. For a fuller analysis of nostalgia in the regional expressions of Turner, Hamlin Garland, Frank Lloyd Wright, Sherwood Anderson, and others, see Steiner, "Significance of Turner's Sectional Thesis," 445–47, and Steiner, "Pleasures and Perils of Nostalgia in Local History," *Journal of Orange County Studies* 2 (Spring 1989):46–48.

29. See Paul Shepard, "Place in American Culture," *North American Review* 262 (Fall 1977):22–32; and Edith Cobb, *The Ecology of the Imagination of Childhood* (New York: Columbia University Press, 1977), for discussions of the impact of childhood places upon intellectual development, particularly American regional thought.

30. Turner to Skinner, in Billington, *Genesis of the Frontier Thesis*, 209.

31. Turner, "The Middle West," in *Frontier in American History*, 154.

32. Turner to Dodd, October 7, 1919, in Billington, *Genesis of the Frontier Thesis*, 196.

33. Turner, notes for an essay, "Influences of Geography upon the Settlement of the U.S.," n.d., File Drawer 14 A, no. 2, Turner papers. Turner also cited passages from Ratzel in "The West as a Field for Historical Study," *Annual Report of the American Historical Association for the Year 1896* (Washington, D.C.: G.P.O., 1897), 284. Also see Carl Sauer, "The Formative Years of Ratzel in the United States," *Annals of the Association of American Geographers* 61 (June 1971):253–54.

34. See R. B. Hall, "The Geographic Region: A Résumé," *Annals of the Association of American Geographers* 42 (September 1935), and W. L. G. Joerg, "The Subdivisions of North America into Natural Regions: A Preliminary Inquiry," *Annals of the Association of American Geographers* 4 (March 1914):55–83.

35. Turner to Curti, August 27, 1928, in Billington, *Genesis of the Frontier Thesis*, 279–80, and Turner, *Significance of Sections*, 50. In addition to using the concepts of Ratzel, Vidal, Jean Brunhes, Camille Vallaux, and other European theorists, Turner corresponded with such prominent American geographers as O. E. Baker, Harlan Barrows, Isaiah Bowman, Neven Fenneman, Ellsworth Huntington, A. K. Lobeck, Rollin Salisbury, Ellen Churchill Semple, and John K. Wright.

36. Lewis Mumford, *The Brown Decades: A Study of the Arts in America, 1865–1895* (New York: Harcourt, Brace, 1931), 59–106; George Perkins Marsh, *Man and Nature*, ed., David Lowenthal (Cambridge: Harvard University Press, 1965), 36, 280.

37. See, for example, Peter J. Schmitt, *Back to Nature: The Arcadian Myth in Urban America* (New York: Oxford University Press, 1969), and James Brinckerhoff Jackson, *American Space: The Centennial Years, 1865–1876* (New York: Norton, 1972).

38. N. S. Shaler, *Nature and Man in America* (1891) is part of the 1893 syllabus for Turner's course, "The Colonization of North America from the Earliest Times to 1763," File Drawer 15 A, no. 1, Turner papers.

39. See Michael C. Steiner, *The Regional Renewal of America* (Urbana: University of Illinois Press, forthcoming).

40. John Wesley Powell, *Report on the Lands of the Arid Region of the United States*, ed. Wallace Stegner (Cambridge, Mass.: Harvard University Press, 1962), 40.

41. Turner, "Contributions of the West to American Democracy," in *Frontier in American History*, 258. This theme is elaborated in "The West and American Ideals," *Frontier in American History*, 297–98, 307–10.

42. John Wesley Powell, *The Physiography of the United States* (Chicago: National Geographic Society, 1896), 66–100. Turner's heavily marked copy of this essay is in File Drawer L, Turner papers.

43. Turner, "Problems in American History," in Billington, ed., *Frontier and Section*, 30. Turner's detailed notes of Van Hise's lectures are located in File Drawer 15 A, no. 4, Turner papers.

44. Everett A. Edwards, ed., "A Comparison of Different Versions of 'The Significance of the Frontier'," in *The Early Writings of Frederick Jackson Turner* (Madison: University of Wisconsin Press, 1938), 280, 281.

45. Josiah Royce, "Provincialism, Based upon a Study of Early Conditions in California," *Putnam's Magazine* 7 (November 1909):237. In addition to this essay, see Royce, *California, from the Conquest in 1846 to the Second Vigilance Committee in San Francisco: A Study in American Character* (1886; repr., Santa Barbara: Peregrine Press, 1970), and "Provincialism," in Royce, *Race Questions, Provincialism, and Other American Problems* (1908; repr., Freeport, New York: Books for Libraries 1967), 55–108. Turner's marked copy of the last essay is in File Drawer L, Turner papers.

46. Turner, "Significance of the Section," 45. Other references to Royce appear in "Ohio Valley in American History," and "Middle Western Pioneer Democracy," in *Frontier in American History*, 157–60, 358.

47. Turner, "Problems in American History" (1892), in Billington, ed., *Frontiers and Sections*, 31–33, and Turner, "Problems in American History" (1904), *Significance of Sections*. 9.

48. Turner to Curti, August 8, 1928, in *Genesis of the Frontier Thesis*, 261, 264. See Cronon, "Revisiting the Vanishing Frontier," 162–64, and Ridge, "American West: From Frontier to Region," 140–41, for valuable discussions of this dual approach to research and teaching.

49. See Billington, *Frederick Jackson Turner*, 227–32, for an account of Turner's effort to sway historians and sociologists. Turner's summary of the Madison meeting was printed as "Report of the Conference on the Relation of Geography and History," *Annual Report of the American Historical Association for 1907*, vol. 1 (Washington, D.C.: G.P.O., 1908), 45–47. His address to the sociologists was published as "Is Sectionalism Dying Away?" *American Journal of Sociology* 13 (March 1908):661–75, repr. in Turner, *Significance of Sections*, 287–314.

50. Ellen Churchill Semple to A. P. Brigham, November 28, 1910, cited by Bloch, "Frederick Jackson Turner and American Geography," 39. The harsh reactions of historians and sociologists are cited in Turner's "Report of the Conference on the Relation of Geography and History" and "Discussion of the Paper by Professor Frederick J. Turner, 'Is Sectionalism in America Dying Away?' " *American Journal of Sociology* 13 (May 1908):811–19.

51. The First Official Frontier of the Massachusetts Bay," "The Old West," "The Middle West," "The Ohio Valley in American History," The Significance of the Mississippi Valley in American History," "The Problem of the West," and other essays collected in *Frontier in American History* represent his more succinct form of regional description; Turner's unfinished, posthumously published *The United States, 1830–1850* embodies his encyclopedic approach to sectional history within a national context.

52. Turner, "Geographical Influences in American Political History" (1914), in *Significance of Sections*, 183–92.

53. Turner, "Sections and Nation" (1922), "Significance of the Section in

American History" (1925), and "Geographical Sectionalism in American History" (1926), in *Significance of Sections*, 315–39, 22–51, 193–206.

54. Turner, "Hunter Type," in Jacobs, ed., *Frederick Jackson Turner's Legacy*, 153, and "Middle Western Pioneer Democracy," in *Frontier in American History*, 358. A brilliant analysis of the relationship between frontier individualism and collectivism is Robert V. Hine's *Community on the American Frontier: Separate but Not Alone* (Norman: University of Oklahoma Press, 1980).

55. Turner, *Frontier in American History*, 320, 293.

56. Ibid., 238–42, 277–79, 305–6.

57. Turner, "Sections and Nation," 316.

58. Turner, "Problems in American History," in *Significance of Sections*, 8, and "Development of American Society," in *Frederick Jackson Turner's Legacy*, 175.

59. Turner, "Significance of the Frontier in American History," in *Frontier in American History*, 23, 30.

60. Turner, "Sections and Nation," in *Significance of Sections*, 339. Turner occasionally pushed the argument further, declaring, for example, that "the United States has never been and is not yet a consolidated nation. . . . It is a composite of sections." Turner, "Notes and Writings on Sectionalism," May 1922, File Drawer 14 B, no. 12, Turner papers.

61. Turner, *Significance of Sections*, 26, and Turner, *Frontier in American History*, 160. See *Frontier in American History*, 158, and *Significance of Sections*, 193, 318–19, for further discussion of the "extreme and tragic form of sectionalism" of the Civil War.

62. Turner, *Significance of Sections*, 203, 339. The 1918 memorandum to Wilson is published in William Diamond, ed., "Turner's American Sectionalism and World Organization," *American Historical Review* 47 (April 1942):545–51.

63. Turner, *Significance of Sections*, 197–98.

64. Turner, "Opening Remarks at the Beginning of a Course on the History of the United States, 1880–1920," in Jacobs, ed., *Frederick Jackson Turner's Legacy*, 84.

65. Turner, notes for an essay on "City, Frontier, and Section" or "The Significance of the City in American History," October 1922, File Drawer 14 A, no. 1, Turner papers. Turner to Schlesinger May 5, 1925, is in Jacobs, *Historical World of Frederick Jackson Turner*, 164. Turner's influence was recognized in Arthur M. Schlesinger, "The City in American History," *Mississippi Valley Historical Review* 27 (June 1940):43.

66. Turner, "Since the Foundation of Clark University" (1924), *Significance of Sections*, 233–34. Also see Turner's elaborate research notes, File Drawer 10 A, Turner papers.

67. Turner, *Significance of Sections*, 34–35, 45, 51.

68. Turner, "Introduction to a Lecture on Sectionalism," in Jacobs, ed., *Frederick Jackson Turner's Legacy*, 48.

69. Cronon, "Revisiting the Vanishing Frontier," 159. Related discussions of the reluctance of western historians to deal with the twentieth century include

Richard W. Etulain, "Frontier, Region and Myth: Changing Interpretations of Western American Culture," *Journal of American Culture* 3 (Summer, 1980): 268–84, and "Shifting Interpretations of Western Cultural History," in Michael P. Malone, ed., *Historians and the American West* (Lincoln: University of Nebraska Press, 1983), 414–32; David W. Noble, "American Studies and the Burden of Frederick Jackson Turner," *Journal of American Culture* 4 (Winter 1981):34–45, and *The End of American History*, 16–26; and Earl Pomeroy, "Toward a Reorientation of Western History: Continuity and Environment," *Mississippi Valley Historical Review* 41 (March 1955):579–600.

70. Wilbur R. Jacobs, "Suggestions for a 'New Look' at Frontier History," in John Alexander Carroll, ed., *Reflections of Western Historians* (Tucson: University of Arizona Press, 1969), 275–76, 278. "While Turner in 1920 could afford to slight the history of the West after 1890," Gerald Nash has complained, "we do not have that luxury. No other speciality in the field of history has refused to consider the past 100 years as a legitimate field of inquiry." Nash, "The Twentieth Century West," *Western Historical Quarterly* 13 (April 1982):180.

71. Worster, "New West, True West," 144, 145. See Gerald Thompson, "Frontier West: Process or Place?" *Journal of the Southwest* 29 (Winter 1987):364–75, for a thoughtful overview.

72. Hal S. Barron, *Those Who Stayed Behind: Rural Society in Nineteenth Century New England* (New York: Cambridge University Press, 1984), 2–3; and John Mack Farragher, *Sugar Creek: Life on the Illinois Prairie* (New Haven: Yale University Press, 1986), 51–52.

73. Turner to Curti, August 8, 1928, Box 29, no. 45, Turner papers; and Turner, "The Problem of the West" (1896), *Frontier in American History*, 205.

74. Drinnon, *Facing West*, 465. Also see William Appleman Williams, "The Frontier Thesis and American Foreign Policy," *History as a Way of Learning* (New York: Franklin Watts, 1974), 137–57.

75. Turner, "Social Forces in American History" (1910), *Frontier in American History*, 330, and "The Significance of History" (1891), in Billington, ed., *Frontier and Section*, 20–21.

76. Turner, "The West as a Field for Historical Study," 282, 284, 285. See "The Problem of the West" (1896), "Dominant Forces in Western Life" (1897), "Contributions of the West to American Democracy" (1903), and "The West and American Ideals" (1914), in *Frontier in American History*, for examples of Turner's expansive vision of western history.

77. Derwent Whittlesey, "Sequent Occupance," *Annals of the Association of American Geographers* 19 (March 1929):162–65; Walter Prescott Webb, *The Great Plains* (Boston: Ginn and Co., 1931); Marvin W. Mikesell, "Rise and Decline of 'Sequent Occupance': A Chapter in the History of American Geography," in David Lowenthal and Martyn J. Bowden, eds., *Geographies of the Mind: Essays in Historical Geosophy in Honor of John Kirtland Wright* (New York: Oxford University Press, 1976), 149–69. I am indebted to Richard Etulain for the notion of sectionalism as a "process within a place."

78. Turner to William Francis Allen, December 31, 1888, Tu Box 1, no. 14, Turner papers, and Turner, "The West and American Ideals," *Frontier in American History*, 297–98.

79. Turner, *Frontier in American History*, 219–21, 258–59, 278–79, 293–98. Turner's early interest in the "the *spirit* of various sections" is described in his letter to Walter Hines Page, August 30, 1896, repr. in Fulmer Mood, "The Sectional Concept, 1750–1900," 92–96. Also see Wilbur Jacobs, ed., "Frederick Jackson Turner's Notes on the Westward Movement, California, and the Far West," *Southern California Quarterly* 36 (June 1964):161–68.

80. See, for example, *Rise of the New West*, 84–95, 107–10; *United States, 1830–1850*, 286–97. The quotations are from *Rise of the New West*, 88 and *United States, 1830–1850*, 286.

81. Like most historians of his era, Turner rarely wrote about women and non-Northern European ethnic groups in his published work, yet he consistently recognized the need for such analysis and encouraged younger scholars to begin it. See Billington, *Frederick Jackson Turner*, 491–92. The ideological implications of the sectional thesis are myriad, and I am indebted to Wilbur Jacobs for stressing that "Ulrich Phillips was the symbol of old racist sectionalism. He was an extension of Turner, and he was Turner's disciple." Wilbur Jacobs to Michael Steiner, April 11, 1990, personal communication. With this in mind, it is also important to realize that the sectional thesis has inspired progressive as well as reactionary disciples. See, for example, Constance Rourke's Turnerian-based proposal for a "proletarian regionalism" in "The Significance of Sections," *New Republic* 76 (September 20, 1933):147–51. More recently, William Appleman Williams has advocated a western-flavored regional socialism in "Radicals and Regionalism," *democracy* 1 (July 1981):87–98.

82. Steiner, "Significance of Turner's Sectional Thesis," 464–66.

83. Donald W. Meinig, "The Continuous Shaping of America: A Prospectus for Geographers and Historians," *American Historical Review* 83 (December 1978): 1205; David M. Potter, *The South and the Sectional Conflict* (Baton Route: Louisiana State University Press, 1968), 4.

84. Steiner and Clarence Mondale, *Region and Regionalism in the United States: A Source Book for the Humanities and the Social Science* (New York: Garland, 1988); and Mondale, "Concepts and Trends in Regional Studies," *American Studies International* 27 (April 1989):13–37.

85. William E. Ferris, "Region as Art," in Gene Lich, ed., *Regional Studies: The Interplay of Land and People* (College Station: Texas A&M Press, forthcoming); Richard Maxwell Brown, "The New Regionalism in America, 1970–1981," in William G. Robbins, Robert J. Frank, and Richard E. Ross, eds., *Regionalism and the Pacific Northwest* (Corvallis: Oregon State University Press, 1983), 63–64.

86. Patricia Nelson Limerick, *The Legacy of Conquest: The Unbroken Past of the American West* (New York: W. W. Norton, 1987), 26; Baron, *Those Who Stayed Behind*; and Faragher, *Sugar Creek*, 52; Ridge, "American West: From Frontier to Region," 140; and Robert V. Hine, *The American West: An Interpretive History*, 2d ed. (Boston: Little, Brown and Co., 1984), 358.

87. Cronon, "Revisiting the Vanishing Frontier," 174, and Worster, "New West, True West," 156. Models for a deeper, more complex regionalism in western history include Carl Abbott, "Frontiers and Sections"; David R. Goldfield, "The New Regionalism," *Journal of Urban History* 10 (February 1984):171–86; Frederick C. Luebke, "Regionalism and the Great Plains: Problems of Concept and Method," *Western Historical Quarterly* 15 (January 1984):19–38; Timothy R. Mahony, "Urban History in a Regional Context: River Towns on the Upper Mississippi, 1840–1860," *Journal of American History* 72 (September 1985):318–39; Spencer C. Olin, Jr., "Toward a Synthesis of the Political and Social History of the American West," *Pacific Historical Review* 55 (November 1986):599–611; and Williams, "Radicals and Regionalism."

88. Ray Billington to Michael Steiner, February 17, 1975, personal communication.

89. Turner to Curti, August 8, 1928, in Billington, *Genesis of the Frontier Thesis*, 264.

BIBLIOGRAPHY

TURNER ON WESTERN SECTIONALISM:

The Frontier in American History. New York: Henry Holt, 1920. Essays emphasizing the trans-Mississippi West include "The Problem of the West" (1896), 205–21; "Dominant Forces in Western Life" (1897), 222–42; "Contributions of the West to American Democracy" (1903), 243–68; and "The West and American Ideals" (1914), 290–310.

Rise of the New West, 1819–1820. New York: Harper and Brothers, 1906.

The United States, 1830–1850: The Nation and Its Sections. New York: Henry Holt, 1935.

"The West as a Field for Historical Study." *Annual Report of the American Historical Association for 1896.* Washington, D.C., Government Printing Office 1897, 281–96.

TURNER'S SECTIONAL–REGIONAL THEORY:

Frederick Jackson Turner's Legacy: Unpublished Writings in American History. Wilbur R. Jacobs, ed. San Marino, Calif.: Huntington Library, 1965. Especially useful are Jacobs's Introduction," 1–43, and the previously unpublished lectures and essays on sectionalism gathered under "Frontiers and Sections," 45–78, and "American Social History," 151–92.

"Problems in American History" (1892), in Ray Billington, ed., *Frontier and Section: Selected Essays of Frederick Jackson Turner.* Englewood Cliffs, N.J.: Prentice-Hall, 1961, 28–36.

"Sectionalism in the United States," in Albert Bushnell Hart and Andrew C. McLaughlin, eds., *Cyclopedia of American Government*. New York: Appleton and Co., 1914, 280–85.

The Significance of Sections in American History. New York: Henry Holt and Co., 1932. Important conceptual essays include "Problems in American History" (1904), 3–21; "The Significance of the Section in American History" (1925), 22–51; "Geographical Influences in American Political History" (1914), 183–92; "Geographical Sectionalism in American History" (1926), 193–206; "Is Sectionalism Dying Away?" (1907), 287–314; and "Sections and Nation" (1922), 315–39.

SELECTED SCHOLARSHIP ABOUT TURNER'S SECTIONAL THESIS:

Billington, Ray Allen. "The Genesis of the Sectional Concept," and "The Persistence of a Theory: The Frontier and Sectional Hypothesis." Chapters 9 and 18 of *Frederick Jackson Turner: Historian, Scholar, Teacher*. New York: Oxford University Press, 1973, 209–32 and 444–71.

Bloch, Robert H. "Frederick Jackson Turner and American Geography." *Annals of the Association of American Geographers* 70 (March 1980):31–40.

Craven, Avery. "Frederick Jackson Turner: Historian." *Wisconsin Magazine of History* 25 (June 1942):408–24.

Cronon, William. "Revisiting the Vanishing Frontier: The Legacy of Frederick Jackson Turner." *Western Historical Quarterly* 18 (April 1987):157–76.

Curti, Merle. "The Section and the Frontier in American History: The Methodological Concepts of Frederick Jackson Turner." In Stuart A. Rice, ed., *Methods in Social Sciences: A Case Book*. Chicago: University of Chicago Press, 1931, 353–67.

Etulain, Richard W. "Frontier, Region and Myth: Changing Interpretations of Western American Culture." *Journal of American Culture* 3 (Summer 1980): 268–84.

Hacker, Louis. "Sections—or Classes?" *Nation* 137 (July 26, 1933):108–10.

Hesseltine, William B. "Regions, Classes, and Sections in American History." In Richard B. Current, ed., *Sections and Politics: Selected Essays by William B. Hesseltine*. Madison: State Historical Society of Wisconsin, 1968, 97–113.

Hofstadter, Richard. "Turner and the Western Revolt" and "Frontier and Section and the Usable Past." Chapters 2 and 3 of *The Progressive Historians: Turner, Beard, Parrington*. New York: Vintage Books, 1968, 47–83, 84–117.

Holtgrieve, Donald G. "Frederick Jackson Turner as a Regionalist." *Professional Geographer* 26 (May 1974):159–65.

Jensen, Richard. "On Modernizing Frederick Jackson Turner: The Historiography of Regionalism." *Western Historical Quarterly* 11 (July 1980):307–22.

Malin, James C. "Space and History: Reflections on the Closed-Space Doctrines of Turner and Mackinder" (1944). In *James C. Malin, History and Ecology: Studies of the Grassland*, ed. Robert P. Swierenga. Lincoln: University of Nebraska Press, 1984, 68–84.

Mood, Fulmer. "The Origin, Evolution, and Application of the Sectional Concept, 1750–1900." In Merrill Jensen, ed., *Regionalism in America*. Madison: University of Wisconsin Press, 1951, 5–98.

Ridge, Martin. "The American West: From Frontier to Region." *New Mexico Historical Review* 64 (April 1989):125–41.

Rourke, Constance. "The Significance of Sections." *New Republic* 76 (September 20, 1933):147–51.

Shapiro, Henry D. "The Place of Culture and the Problem of Identity." In Allan Batteau, ed., *Appalachia and America: Autonomy and Regional Dependence*. Lexington: University Press of Kentucky, 1983, 111–41.

Steiner, Michael C. "The Significance of Turner's Sectional Thesis." *Western Historical Quarterly* 10 (October 1979):437–66.

———. "History: Region as Concept." In Michael Steiner and Clarence Mondale, *Region and Regionalism in the United States: A Source Book for the Humanities and Social Sciences*. New York, Garland Publishing, 1988, 233–55.

White, Richard. "Frederick Jackson Turner." In John R. Wunder, ed., *Historians of the American Frontier: A Bio-Bibliographical Sourcebook*. Westport, Conn.: Greenwood Press, 1988, 660–81.

Worster, Donald. "New West, True West: Interpreting the Region's History." *Western Historical Quarterly* 18 (April 1987):141–56.

5

After Turner: The Western Historiography of Frederic Logan Paxson

RICHARD W. ETULAIN

*I*N 1910, IN THE YEAR THAT Frederick Jackson Turner was elevated to his chair of history at Harvard, Frederic Logan Paxson was called from the University of Michigan to become the master's successor at the University of Wisconsin. Taking over Turner's famed "seminary" in western history, Paxson also purchased his predecessor's home in Madison at 629 Frances Street, within skipping distance of Lake Mendota.[1] All this was a tall order—attempting to assume the chair of the best-known historian of western history in the country and trying to supplant him in a college town where he had already become something of a legend. But Frederic Logan Paxson never turned away from challenges; hard work, perseverance, and trustworthiness would find a way.

Still, was Paxson successor to Turner in the larger sense? Did he follow—almost slavishly—Turner's ideas and interpretations, as several commentators have argued? Or, as a few have maintained, did he mark out his own paths in western historiography? Or should his accomplishments be evaluated as an amalgam of imitation and innovation?[2] Whatever one concludes, Paxson's career is worthy of scrutiny because he was a leading western historian of the first half of the twentieth century, publishing three books and a dozen or so notable essays on western topics, training more than two hundred graduate students, and holding the presidencies of three major historical organizations. And for many of his contemporaries, Paxson became, after a generation of teaching and writing and after Turner's retirement in 1924, the best-known interpreter of the American West. The earliest facts of his biography did not suggest, however, that his rise would be so meteoric.

Born February 23, 1877, in Philadelphia to Quaker parents, Paxson was reared among Quakers, attending Friends' schools in Philadelphia and graduating from Friends' Central School in 1894. Despite the early death of his father, Paxson was able to enroll in the University of Pennsylvania in the fall of 1894, where he majored in arts and sciences, with a heavy emphasis in history. Capturing mainly "distinctions" (rather than "goods" and "passes"), Paxson won honors in his sophomore and senior years and graduated as one of five seniors named to Phi Beta Kappa.[3] Writing for several campus publications, "Freddie" Paxson, his class history notes, "was elected class bard because he liked to let his hair grow."[4]

Paxson's commitment to history now seemed set. Named a Harrison Scholar in History and Economics, he entered the University of Pennsylvania Graduate School in the fall of 1898, emphasizing American history and minoring in economics and English history. During the two years after his first two semesters of graduate school, Paxson taught history at Michigan Military Academy in Orchard Lake, Michigan, and at Blees Military Academy in Macon, Missouri. Then, following the practice of history graduate students (particularly those who had taken undergraduate degrees at Penn), Paxson enrolled elsewhere for a year of graduate work—in his case, Harvard—where he was awarded a master's degree after coursework with such well-known scholars as Albert Bushnell Hart and Edward Channing. The next year he returned to Pennsylvania as Harrison Fellow in American history and gained his Ph.D. in June of 1903.[5]

During his two years of graduate work at Penn, in addition to enrolling in courses in bibliography, international law, and economics, Paxson took English history with Edward P. Cheyney and American colonial history with Herman V. Ames. But his major professor and the person who most influenced his training in history was John Bach McMaster, from whom Paxson took courses in American politics and political parties and who gave Paxson his doctoral exam in American history (a "highly credible" ranking) and directed his dissertation. A distinguished historian whose multivolume history of the United States from the Revolution to the Civil War was then appearing, McMaster encouraged his students to read widely, to make use of newspapers and many other popular sources, and, if his own example served as model, to write history appealing to both scholars and general readers.[6]

In this small but notable program in history, Paxson made strong and lasting friendships. Ames, Cheyney, and McMaster, as well as medievalist Dana C. Munro and English historian William E. Lingelbach, played important roles in Paxson's career, as did his fellow graduate students Herbert Eugene Bolton, Claude H. Van Tyne, Issac J. Cox, and James F. Willard. Indeed, these professors or fellow graduates were instrumental in helping Paxson land nearly every position he would hold. And he, in turn, throughout his career, kept strong ties to his alma mater.

Unlike graduate students in more recent times, Paxson took no hours in thesis or dissertation work. He was expected to complete these projects while enrolled as a full-time graduate student. Completing his minor field examinations in International Law in December 1902 and in English history in March 1903, Paxson passed his major exam in American history the following May—all the while finishing his dissertation on "The Independence of the Spanish South American Republics," including a summer's work in the Public Records Office in London. Following accepted practice at Penn, Paxson paid for the printing of 125 copies of his dissertation and was recommended for his doctorate in history on June 13, 1903. Printed without further revisions the same year, Paxson's doctoral dissertation became his first book.[7]

Paxson's initial volume differs in several respects from his later publications. A study in diplomatic and legal-constitutional history, *The Independence of the South-American Republics: A Study in Recognition and Foreign Policy* (1903) drew heavily on Paxson's research in British Foreign Office manuscripts in the Public Records Office in London and the archives of the United States Department of State in Washington.[8] More than any of Paxson's subsequent volumes on the West, this first book is based essentially on published and manuscript primary sources. And while Paxson continued his interests in diplomatic and constitutional history and included sections on those topics in his later writings, he never again wrote full-length books on those subjects.

Other more typical Paxson qualities are also abundantly evident here, however. His endeavors to find balanced perspectives, his use of travelers' accounts and personal memoirs, and his presentist bent are manifest. At the same time, this story of U.S. and British policies toward Latin American republics in the early nineteenth century is told in pleasant and smoothly written prose. Already, Paxson proves he is a skilled and interesting writer, well able to draw readers with his narrative skills.

Paxson's first book opened the doors to his first college job. Probably its forthcoming publication helped Paxson in landing a position at the University of Colorado in the fall of 1903. Interestingly, Turner, after specifically ordering Paxson's volume for his seminar at Wisconsin, referred to the book as "an excellent sketch" and cited it frequently in his own first book *The Rise of the New West*.[9] Indeed, nearly twenty years later, many historians would have agreed with Paxson's confident conclusion that *Independence* remained the best study of its subject.

Even before Paxson completed his doctorate, he had signed a year's contract to teach history at Colorado for twelve hundred dollars. During the next three years at Boulder, Paxson was *the* History Department, except for a lowly assistant. The work load was demanding—four courses each semester, several new preparations, and service on faculty and university committees. On one occasion the routine became too heavy, with Paxson finally breaking under the burden in the fall of 1904 and needing time off to recuperate. More frustrating were the lack of good research libraries and the distance to annual history meetings. But Paxson, ever the professional, attended national conferences and maintained and broadened his contacts. Even Turner sent him a graduate student, though Paxson had to admit that the student was "a lunger and . . . [could] not live in any other place." Although Paxson found Boulder satisfactory, the work "extremely pleasant," and an "excellent outlook" for the future, he could be talked into listening to other offers— and they soon came.[10]

Meanwhile, Paxson lost little time in producing several scholarly essays. Arriving in the fall of 1903, he completed an article that appeared shortly thereafter in the February 1904 issue of the *University of Colorado Studies*, itself just two years old. While this essay, "A Tripartite Intervention in Hayti, 1851," illustrates his ongoing interest in diplomatic history, the remainder of his articles in the Colorado journal focus on frontier topics and are finger pieces for the full-length book he planned, and later abandoned, on Colorado.[11]

The essays in the *University of Colorado Studies*, in fact, bridge Paxson's earliest work in diplomatic history and his growing emphasis on frontier history, just as his work on the nineteenth-century frontier served as prologue to his later stress on recent U.S. history. In tracing the tortured territorial history of Colorado, the evolution of its shifting county boundaries, and the research opportunities in state and local history available to industrious students and scholars, Paxson demonstrated his gradual conversion to western history as he labored in the virgin vineyards of Boulder and its environs.

At the same time, these essays on Colorado reflect Paxson's grow-ing sophistication in western history. If "The Boundaries of Colorado" (July 1904), "The Territory of Jefferson . . ." (November 1905), and "The County Boundaries of Colorado" (August 1906) are useful if entirely factual chronologies, "The Historical Opportunity in Colorado" (Novem-ber 1905) and "A Preliminary Bibliography of Colorado History" (June 1906) demonstrate that Paxson had acquainted himself with the most notable primary and secondary sources of Colorado history.[12] But the essay on "Historical Opportunity in Colorado," which Frederick Jackson Turner praised as a valuable piece of work, proved to Turner and others that Paxson evidenced a "grasp of the significance of western history" and an ability "to handle a problem."[13] He had shown that he had thoughtfully considered the major research opportunities available to students and how they might, like Turner, demonstrate the ways in which the West molded American society; or, on the other hand, how they might, in the fashion of the New History, show how the past illu-minates and guides the present.

Concurrently, Paxson began to read papers at national conferences and to contribute to such scholarly outlets as the *Quarterly of the Texas State Historical Association*, the *Annual Report of the American Historical Association*, and the *American Historical Review*. In the latter prestigious journal, Paxson placed his essay "The Territory of Colorado," which asserted that discussions about slavery had overshadowed other prob-lems in previous histories—such as "the problem of the expansion of the agricultural West, the settlement of new areas, and the providing of adequate institutions of government for citizens of the frontier" (p. 53). Although Paxson's goals for his brief essay were too ambitious, he had moved unmistakably beyond the localism of his earliest western research to cast his arguments in larger frameworks—all in a space of less than three years.[14] Obviously, ambition, hard work, and a quick grasp of research materials and opportunities characterized Paxson's career from its beginning.

And new opportunities followed Paxson early in his career like a medievalist collecting footnotes. When Andrew C. McLaughlin re-signed at the University of Michigan to take a position at the University of Chicago in 1907, Paxson was called to Ann Arbor as Assistant Pro-fessor of American History to take over McLaughlin's courses in con-stitutional history and to join his graduate school colleague Claude Van Tyne, recently promoted to Professor of American History at Mich-igan.[15] Another milestone occurred the first Christmas after Paxson's move to Ann Arbor when he married Helen Hale Jackson, whom one of his students described as a "tall, handsome, imperious woman of Philadelphia Main Line standards who respected conventions and showed some disdain for those who did not." To the Quaker couple three daughters were eventually born: Jane Taylor (1909), Emma Fell (1911), and Patricia (1915). Mrs. Paxson was a skilled hostess who entertained well and often and thus helped Paxson in important social aspects of his career.[16]

Paxson's position at Michigan offered a larger view of his profession, and he speedily capitalized on the broader vista. Attending and reading papers at professional conferences and cementing friendships and contacts with Turner, J. Franklin Jameson, and other leading historians, Paxson quickly became known as an able younger American historian on the rise. In 1908, in the same year that Paxson was promoted to Junior Professor of American History, McLaughlin considered Paxson as a possible candidate for a professorship then open at the University of Chicago, and in the same year Paxson was tendered a position at Cornell at a salary higher than he had received at Michigan.[17] Meantime, Jameson, a much-respected professor and the doyen of historical editors in the United States, added to the mounting chorus of praise for Paxson. When Charles Francis Adams asked Jameson for a short list of promising candidates for the directorship of the Massachusetts Historical Society, Jameson named several well-known senior men and then added:

> *Among younger men the best choice might be Mr. Frederic L.*
> *Paxson. . . . I do not know him personally, but I have been told*
> *that he is a man of excellent address and well liked. Certainly he*
> *has plenty of scholarship, and I have observed that wherever he*
> *has been placed, sometimes in rather unpromising soil, he has*
> *turned to the local materials for history and has extracted from*
> *them good matter for the general history of the United States.*
> *Therefore, though I do not know that he has given much*
> *attention to New England history I see that he could do so with*
> *rapid effect and would do it with an eye to what is important*
> *rather than with a merely antiquarian predilection.*[18]

Adding to this vein was Albert Bushnell Hart, one of Paxson's teachers at Harvard, who said of the Michigan professor: "Paxson is a brilliant and rising man who will make his mark wherever he goes."[19]

A large part of Paxson's growing reputation came from his publications. When the established scholar Clarence W. Alvord made preliminary plans with publisher Arthur H. Clark for a series of western biographies, which he hoped Turner would edit, he included Paxson prominently, along with several leading specialists, as a prospective author for the series. Although the series did not materialize, Paxson was busy publishing a major essay on the Pacific railroads and the closing frontier and other pieces.[20] Even more important, Paxson had wisely given up his book on Colorado so that he could broaden his focus to the western frontier. Once he had signed the contract with Macmillan, he set quickly to work on the book.

He made remarkable progress, considering that he was not teaching western history at Michigan and that he was removed from major holdings on frontier topics. Working rapidly through a host of new primary and secondary published sources, Paxson completed his volume in the late spring or early summer of 1909, and the book appeared in early 1910—just at the right time, as we shall see, in Macmillan's series entitled Stories from American History.[21]

As Paxson's second book and his first on the West, *The Last American Frontier* illustrates his major emphases as well as the strengths and limitations of most of his books and his two major western volumes.[22] Intending his book for students and general readers, Paxson nonetheless wanted scholars to accept the study as sound, well-researched history. As a gifted writer with obvious strengths of synthesis, Paxson presents a readable overview of several aspects of frontier history from roughly 1821 to 1885, but he also essays, in the first chapter, to cast his story in a Turnerian framework of emphasizing the shaping power of the frontier on American history. Still, if Paxson produced a useful, readable overview, on the one hand, he failed to achieve his goal of conceptualization and synthesis on the other.

In the opening chapter of *The Last American Frontier* Paxson strikes notes already familiar to western specialists early in the twentieth century. Declaring that "the greatest of American problems has been the problem of the West" (p. 1) and that "the influence of the frontier has been the strongest single factor in American history" (p. 3), Paxson suggests, in terms reminiscent of Turner, that his work will demonstrate the dramatic role of the frontier in determining American character. But, for the most part, his volume does not follow these promising remarks, moving instead toward a more popular stance emphasizing the peristaltic-like movements of pioneers westward and their continued conflicts with Indians, especially in the Great Plains and Rocky Mountains.

More than Turner and other contemporary western historians and more than in his later writings about the West, Paxson devotes extraordinary attention to conflicts between Indians and settlers in his first western study. Throughout his volume, Paxson seems sympathetic to the plight of the Indians and critical of the pioneers for the ways in which their juggernaut steamrolled nations along the frontier, but he also concludes "the conflict . . . could not have ended in any other way than that which has come to pass" (p. 15). Labeling Indians as "wild beasts," as savage and yet childlike innocents, and as an "inferior race," he also depicts whites as rapacious and selfish but still a "superior" and "stronger" race. Although Paxson thought that the American government and the country's institutions may have been fair in their attitudes toward and treatment of these "savages," most Anglo Americans were usually unwilling to stand up to grasping and greedy frontiersmen bent on gobbling up Indian lands. Generally, Paxson's volume coheres around the thrusts of pioneers westward and their gradual displacement of Indians as lords of frontier lands.

Attempting to cover more than six decades of frontier history and a host of new topics forced Paxson to center on a few subjects and to omit or overlook others. In addition to focusing on clashes with Indians, he places notable stress on the roles that means of transportation—particularly overland trails, stages, and railroads—played in closing the frontier. Devoting several chapters to these topics, Paxson concludes that the meeting of the Central Pacific and Union Pacific at Promontory Point in 1869 was profoundly significant—"for the immediate audience, or for posterity"—as a symbol of the "struggle for the last frontier" (pp. 337–38). The railroads not only brought hordes of new settlers; they also provided the lasso that the intrepid pioneers, with the aid of the army, threw around the Indians and pulled them onto reservations. In providing these mental maps of the swiftly closing frontier, Paxson also depicts the iron horse as a wedge, as a spearhead gradually allowing for the division and then the encircling of the final frontier.

Paxson was not able to push much beyond these extended sections on conflicts with Indians, transportation, and two or three dealing with mining rushes and mining camp life. Indeed, probably much more than he intended, the narrative stance is that of writer poised on the eastern slopes of the Rockies, watching white settlers flooding past the "bend of the Missouri," pressuring and supplanting Indians, skirting the mountains, and moving toward the Pacific Northwest and California. Three generations of frontiersmen flow westward to the Rockies and Great Plains, but Paxson follows few of them past the ridge of the mountains. His focus is on the northern Great Plains and Rockies, with little treatment of the Pacific Coast and the Southwest.

If Paxson's geography is telescoped, his topical focus is equally narrowed. Surprisingly, he omits or severely limits discussions of livestock, territorial organizations and politics (except those of Colorado), land policies, and farming. As Max Farrand bluntly pointed out in the most unfriendly review of the volume, Paxson attempted too much, overlooking major western topics and providing little new information for specialists.[23] Farrand admitted, however, that the book was "written in an easy, readable style" that might please general readers. And, like other reviewers, Farrand gratefully mentioned the appended section of sources for further reading. Finally (and a point that Farrand and other readers did not make), Paxson was limited in another way. Following the perspectives of most western historians before the publications of Walter Prescott Webb and James Malin in the 1930s and 1940s, Paxson does not deal with changes over time *within* the West. Although he moves settlers into or toward Oregon, California, and Utah during the 1840s, he avoids tracing sociocultural, economic, and political occurrences within those newly settled areas during the next two generations after the first arrivals. Instead, he joined his contemporaries in emphasizing contact with the land and Indians, not the decades of social organization and institution-making that followed these initial years of cultural contact and confrontation.

One must not downplay, however, how much Paxson accomplished in such a short time. In less than five years, he mastered enough western history to produce a more-than-satisfactory popular introduction to several facets of the nineteenth-century frontier. As several commentators have concluded, Paxson's smoothly written, well-organized, and pleasantly presented volume provided readers with a serviceable overview of the pioneer West. And for Paxson, the volume could not have appeared at a more auspicious moment.

Late in the fall of 1909, serendipity again blessed Paxson. A few months before Paxson's *Last American Frontier* appeared, Frederick Jackson Turner unexpectedly resigned from the University of Wisconsin to take his chair in American history at Harvard. Now, the best-known professorship of western history in the country was vacant, just as Paxson was seeing his first western book through the press. When Yale historian Max Farrand, the first choice of the Wisconsin men, rejected their overtures, they turned to Paxson. In January, Turner asked for proof sheets of Paxson's forthcoming volume, and one month later additional supporting material traveled from Ann Arbor to Madison. Wisconsin history chairman Dana C. Munro, an instructor at Pennsylvania when Paxson was a graduate student, then visited Ann Arbor to woo Turner's successor. Although his colleague and good friend Claude Van Tyne was certain that Paxson would not leave Michigan, by the end of March Paxson phoned Munro of his "readiness to accept and come to Madison." Further details were untangled in the early spring, with both communities announcing in May Paxson's removal to Wisconsin.[24] In the unusually hectic summer that followed, Paxson spent three months in London helping prepare a guide to manuscript materials about the United States in British archives, in addition to moving his family to Madison. Despite these complications, Paxson must have been euphoric; in seven short years he had catapulted to the top of the "western men" and now occupied the most important position in western history in the United States.

The brightness of Paxson's rising star neither faded nor blinked out after he reached Wisconsin in 1910. Indeed, in the next few years his light shone even more brightly in the galaxy of leading young American historians. In his ever-widening personal, public, and professional circles, Paxson gained additional notice and helped spark a new generation of interest in western history at the University of Wisconsin and in the nation during his years at Madison from 1910 to 1932. In these more than two decades Paxson reached his zenith as a well-known western historian.

A long-lasting love affair among Paxson and his family, Madison, and the University of Wisconsin blossomed soon after the Paxsons' arrival. Except for his natal Philadelphia, Paxson was never more tied to one place than to Madison. The town, the university, the invigorating mix of politicians, intellectuals, and colleagues seemed just the right combination to Paxson. Many years later he told Merle Curti, who replaced Paxson's student John D. Hicks at Wisconsin, that "you will like Madison and Madison will like you. . . . I almost wish I could turn back the clock for thirty odd years and begin again on the exciting life I had there. It is a good and stimulating place."[25]

Paxson found his new colleagues particularly to his liking, especially Harvard-educated Carl Russell Fish, Winfred T. Root (another McMaster-trained product of Pennsylvania), and Dana Munro, the departmental chair. Soon, Paxson, Fish, and Root became the "big three" in U.S. history, and so successful were they that by the mid-1920s, even after Root left to head the history department at Iowa, J. Franklin Jameson considered the Paxson–Fish duo the outstanding team in the country specializing in American constitutional and political history.[26] And Paxson's colleagues reciprocated his good feelings toward them, finding him able, hard-working, and unfailingly congenial. Paxson might not be the intellectual equal of Turner, but most members of his department considered him a likeable, talented, and valuable colleague.

Paxson the indefatigable worker also assumed a large teaching load and several demanding committee assignments within the department and university. Unlike Turner, Paxson taught a full load of three courses each semester (Turner had a one-semester reduction each year for research), and by the late teens had large enrollments in all his courses in addition to training increasing numbers of graduate students. Although not as active in local political matters and organizations as Turner had been, Paxson became a valued member of several faculty and university committees. For example, President Van Hise singled out Paxson's diligent work on the University Committee in 1916–17 as a major reason for boosting his salary to four thousand dollars when a call to the University of Iowa came in 1917 to chair its department.[27] As one indication of his strong support within the history department, Paxson was elected departmental chair during World War I and served again from 1927 to 1932.

Nor did Paxson slack off in his professional activities. In fact, he lost no time in taking advantage of the wider window on the profession that his position at Wisconsin afforded him. Continuing to take part in the American Historical Association, he served on the General Committee of the association, engineered a circular to build membership in the Midwest, and chaired a committee looking into the teaching of history in high schools.[28] Seeming to thrive on committee work, he built a reputation as a solid, hard-working professional. Not surprisingly, then, when a small band of outspoken critics accused AHA leadership, including Jameson and Turner, of high-handed methods and even malfeasance, Paxson quickly and easily sided with the AHA leaders in the brouhaha.[29]

A bit earlier, when a coterie of "western men" called for a new organization and journal to provide outlets for a burgeoning interest in western history, Paxson became a member of the Mississippi Valley Historical Association. Serving on a variety of the association's committees and on the Board of Editors of the *Mississippi Valley Historical Review*, Paxson was elevated to the presidency of the organization in 1917, another indication of how quickly he had risen among the ranks of western specialists. Assuming office one year early because of the death of the incumbent, Paxson had to preside over a crisis when the death of the secretary-treasurer threatened to throw the association into disarray.[30]

When the U.S. entered World War I, Paxson's Quaker backgrounds did not keep him from taking part in the war effort. Commissioned a major in July 1918, he went to Washington to participate in the Historical Branch of the War Plans Division of the General Staff. As part of his "war work," he served as an editor for the Committee on Public Information, headed by the controversial George Creel, in preparing its *War Cyclopedia* (1918) and other publications.[31]

Probably adding most to Paxson's reputation as a rising historian, however, was the large number of his publications appearing while he was at Madison. As he did with most of his first books, Paxson whipped out his *Civil War* (1911) in a matter of a few months.[32] Drawing primarily on well-known secondary sources, including "the profound, judicial, and enlightened pages of James Ford Rhodes" (p. x), Paxson hurried through the research and writing of the slim volume intended more for general readers than for specialists. After a brief, general overview of the 1850s, Paxson's twelve-chapter book runs quickly year by year through the Civil War with a minimum of interpretation and analysis. As part of the well-known Home University Library of Modern Knowledge, the 250-page book achieves its modest purpose of introducing a controversial topic to general American and British readers.

Hardly had *The Civil War* appeared when Paxson began work on another topic, a subject that demanded more research but one that vied with the West as the major focus of Paxson's scholarly energies during the next two decades. *The New Nation*, published in 1915 as the final installment of the four-volume Riverside History of the United States, allowed Paxson to trace American history from the Civil War to World War I.[33] In addition to his frontier and western lecture courses and seminar, Paxson had begun to give a course in recent U.S. history, a course he evidently offered for the first time at Wisconsin; *The New Nation* drew heavily on the written lectures for this new course. Indeed, in the last twenty-five years of his career Paxson turned increasingly to contemporary American history and pioneered research and writing in that field much as he had done in western historiography from his first years at Colorado to about 1930.

Like most of Paxson's volumes written before the late 1920s, *The New Nation* endeavors to provide a general account of its subject. Or to use Paxson's words, the volume attempted "to narrate the facts of the last half-century and to show them in their relations to the larger truths of national development" (Preface). To provide focus and context for his narrative, Paxson balanced chapters of regional and national concerns in dealing with the periods of Reconstruction, Gilded Age, and the Nineties and then centers on national topics in the first fifteen years of the new century. If sections on the Civil War, Reconstruction, and the New South center on the South, Paxson balances that coverage with chapters on "The West and the Greenbacks," "The Last of the Frontier," "The Farmers' Cause," "Populism," and "Free Silver" that largely deal with the trans-Mississippi West. Other chapters on major political figures and economic issues supply connecting tissue between the discussions of regional topics.

The chapters on the West contain no major surprises and draw heavily on Paxson's previous publications, particularly *The Last American Frontier*. In "The Last of the Frontier," for instance, Paxson stresses the establishment of the Interstate Commerce Commission, the Dawes Act (1887), agricultural organization and irrigation legislation, and the admission of the Omnibus States of 1889 and 1890 as four indications of a closed frontier. This section does not emphasize frontier influences on American society and culture, and the other three chapters on farmers, Populists, and Free Silver often diverge from those topics and treat such subjects as American literature, national elections, and other nonwestern matters. While Paxson argues that the West was more liberal politically than other regions (p. 250) and that Populism much influenced Progressivism and other reforms in the first two decades of the twentieth century, he avoids placing major stress on the West here, even though he mentions women's suffrage, railroads, and land settlements as noteworthy western activities. Curiously, in fact, his chapters on the West seem more catchall divisions than explicit statements about western activities, and material from several of the important books dealing with the West cited in the chapter-ending bibliographies seems not to have been worked into those chapters. Generally, too, extensive discussions of western (as well as other regional) topics disappear from the text after the 1890s.

In the late teens and early twenties Paxson completed several other writing projects. Among these were a brief, informative essay on "The Cow Country" in the *American Historical Review*, filling in a major gap in *The Last American Frontier*, and his presidential address before the Mississippi Valley Historical Association in 1917, "The Rise of Sport," a lively piece of sociocultural history based primarily on Paxson's thorough newspaper research.[34] He also found time to rewrite *The New Nation* and publish it as *Recent History of the United States* (1921), a pioneering text on the post–Civil War period that, in several revisions (each brought up to the present), was widely adopted in classrooms throughout the 1920s and 1930s.[35] The treatment of the West in this text is much as it was in *The New Nation*: a sideshow affair to the main attraction of national history.

Then, in the early 1920s, realizing that Turner would probably never write his overview of the West, Paxson decided to move ahead with his own thorough study of the frontier.[36] Like his other early books, this one, once begun, zipped ahead. Although teaching full time, directing the work of numerous graduate students, and participating in national and regional organizations, Paxson completed the 575-page book in less than two years.

Just as Theodore Roosevelt noted that Frederick Jackson Turner had pulled together many ideas "in the air" in his famous frontier essay of 1893, so one might have observed in 1924 that Paxson synthesized and reflected many widely held conclusions concerning the American frontier experience in his Pulitzer Prize–winning volume *History of the American Frontier 1763–1893*.[37] In the preface of *The Last American Frontier*, Paxson had promised before long to provide a thorough study of the frontier based on a wide reading of sources; fourteen years later, then, he was fulfilling his earlier pledge.

No one should approach Paxson's volume as a revisionist study of frontier history. It was instead a thorough, readable synthesis of contemporary research and conclusions about the significant shaping power of the frontier on American history. As the author points out in one of his typically terse prefaces, "the time is ripe for this synthesis, in which an attempt is made to show the proportions of the whole story." Further, Paxson contends that though later students may reach beyond him in interpreting the full impact of the frontier, "none will complete his task with a firmer conviction than . . . [he possesses] that the frontier with its continuous influence is the most American thing in all America." Although this explicit conclusion is rarely baldly stated in the pages that follow, Paxson's position as a Turnerian (in his emphasis on the frontier but not in his failure to stress analysis ["significance"], sectionalism, or the social sciences) is as clear as Paxson's limpid syntax and diction throughout his long volume.

The contents of Paxson's second book about the West reflect how much his thinking and reading had expanded in the decade and a half since the publication of *The Last American Frontier*. Beginning in medias res by discussing "The American Frontier of 1763" in his first chapter, Paxson then devotes the next ten chapters to the eighteenth century before dealing with the eastern frontiers of the first half of the nineteenth century in roughly the next twenty chapters. Boundaries, formation of colonies, territories, and states, and economic policies, along with the roles of Thomas Jefferson, Andrew Jackson, and Henry Clay are major topics here. The final chapters treat events east and west of the "bend in the Missouri," Paxson's favorite dividing point between the Midwest and the further West. Averaging about ten pages, most of the chapters are arranged chronologically. Nearly all emphasize what happened as the frontier moved west, but few try to elaborate on the significance of these happenings.

Comparisons and contrasts between Paxson's two narrative histories of the West suggest continuities and changes in his vision of the West. Dealing with a much greater expanse of place and time in his second volume, Paxson still hesitates to treat the colonial frontier that so intrigued Turner and many of his followers. If fully two-thirds of *History of the American Frontier* narrates the westward movement from eastern frontiers to the 95th meridian and in doing so introduces new material about which Paxson had not previously written, the sections on the trans-Mississippi West both follow and break with coverage in *The Last American Frontier*. Conflict with Indians is still a major theme, but here the native peoples are not "beasts" or "savages" innocent of rational thought or learning. Rather, they are barriers to an inexorable movement of pioneers pushing them westward. Clearly, the tone and point of view of Paxson's discussions of Indians have been greatly moderated and have become more balanced in the fifteen years between his books.

Paxson likewise continues to stress state-making, transportation means and routes, and railroad building in his later volume.[38] Always fascinated with the writing of territorial and state constitutions and the other processes by which territories became new states, Paxson persists in indulging that interest. And the lengthy chapters on railroads and other forms of transportation so apparent in 1910 remain much in evidence here. Throughout his writings on the frontier, Paxson used clashes with Indians, the coming of railroads, and the organizing of new states as major symbols of a closing frontier.

Contrasts between the two volumes are equally evident. Perhaps remembering the omissions that reviewers pinpointed in *The Last American Frontier*, Paxson remedies several of these limitations in his later book. New chapters on land policies, economic problems, and the cattle country correct some of the most glaring lacks, and his coverage of the Southwest is now more than adequate with additional sections on Texas and the Mexican War. Notably, however, Paxson does not deal with the Populists or several of the problems that led to their insurgency in the 1890s. He continues to view state-making and the completion of the transcontinental railroads as notable symbols of a vanishing frontier, but unlike Turner and many other historians writing before the mid-1920s, Paxson omits mentioning the rise of Populism as a signal sign of a closed frontier. He would, however, soon deal with the Populists.

Other limitations of Paxson's second volume stand out. Although his reasons for beginning his story in 1763 seem evident, the causes for his ending the narrative in 1893 are less clear. Was he stopping with the Panic of 1893, with the appearance of Turner's pathbreaking frontier speech, or for other reasons? In fact, the final chapters on the disappearing frontier, like many chapters in nearly all of Paxson's books, are too often grab bags of several topics. Nor is he as successful in achieving his purpose as he could have been. He promises that his book will show how frontier experiences molded America and made it significantly different from earlier European and eastern experiences. Although showing what happened during the movement westward and clarifying some of the unique ideas that emerged over time from eastern frontiers, Paxson is less successful in demonstrating how these experiences and resulting ideas redirected the larger experiences of the country.

Paxson's contemporaries were less critical of his second western volume, however. Many thought his work deserving of the Pulitzer Prize, and nearly all reviewers praised his book as a notable volume providing the much-needed overview of the frontier in America. They undoubtedly would have agreed that *History of the American Frontier* was his major contribution to western history and proved him a worthy successor to Turner as the leading western historian in the country. And for professional historians, Paxson's book furnished just the text they needed and used in their classrooms. Here was the book Turner had not produced and that for a quarter of a century, until the appearance of Ray Billington's *Westward Expansion* in 1949, served as their core text. Here was an authentic and well-written guide to a large and important topic, much as Billington's massive volume would be for a later generation.[39]

Less clear to Paxson's contemporaries was the position that his 1924 volume occupied in the development of western historiography. At least no one in the 1920s noted that his book placed him more in the camp of western historians stressing *process* (to-the-West) over *place* (in-the-West). Like Paxson's student Robert Riegel in his text *America Moves West* (1930, 1947), like LeRoy Hafen and Carl Coke Rister in their *Western America* (1941, 1950), and like Billington in *Westward Expansion*, Paxson charted the successive tides of westward-moving peoples through a series of floods; but, unlike western historians Walter Prescott Webb, James Malin, and Paxson's student, Earl Pomeroy, Paxson was less interested in showing changes over time and institution-building within a specific region or section. In pitching his tent with historians emphasizing *process*, Paxson joined the largest and most influential group then interpreting the West. Not until the last generation or two have regionalist or in-the-West historians vied on nearly even terms with the advocates of the frontier school, in which Paxson early became and remained a proponent.

Paxson's first two books on the West more than proved he could produce lively narratives about the frontier, but his third book on that subject, *When the West Is Gone* (1930), called for a different kind of performance. Invited to deliver the Colver Lectures at Brown University in 1929, Paxson was expected to offer high-quality, provocative "think pieces" rather than another narrative history. Clearly, Paxson was in distinguished company as a Culver lecturer, for in the 1920s biologist Vernon Kellogg, historian Charles Homer Haskins, jurist Roscoe Pound, and classicist (and former Paxson colleague) M. Rostovtzeff had added luster and scholarship to the lecture series.

Although Paxson's third book was a different kind of performance, it owed much to his previous work on the West. If his earlier volumes were fact-filled narratives emphasizing eastern and trans-Mississippi frontier processes, *When the West Is Gone* (1930) proves more speculative and philosophical than most of his writings about the frontier. Arguing that his listeners needed to understand what had happened to the West (that is, the frontier), Paxson devotes his first lecture to "When the West Was New," a brief overview of frontier development up to the 1890s. The second lecture, "The Middle West," attempts to show the legacies that the frontier bequeathed to American life; but Paxson turns more philosophical in the last lecture, speculating what will happen to a frontierless America.

Drawing heavily on his previous work, Paxson asserts that George Washington, Thomas Jefferson, Andrew Jackson, and Abraham Lincoln epitomized earlier frontier experiences. But with the defeat of William Jennings Bryan and the Populists in the 1890s, the frontier, for the first time, tasted political defeat, and in the subsequent three decades no new political party had arisen to represent the frontier or its lasting legacies. In commenting on the large significance of the Populists, Paxson treats a topic missing from his two previous books on the West but a subject that he increasingly emphasized in his frontier lectures during the 1920s and 1930s.[40]

If the three lectures read well, illustrate Paxson's strong abilities as a narrator, and are well suited for oral delivery, the third lecture seems more tentative and less convincing than the material presented in the first two sections. Paxson had warned his audience of the difficulties historians found in lifting the curtain of the future and peering into that uncertain era. More than he probably wished, Paxson seems too circumspect, too uncertain of what he wishes to say about the United States devoid of a frontier. Clearly, one reason for Paxson's uncertainties was his unfamiliarity with the twentieth-century West. It was foreign country to him, as it was to most historians writing before 1950. Although three decades had elapsed since the political demise of the Populists, Paxson, similar to Turner, wrote little about the history of the West between the 1890s and the 1920s. While Walter Prescott Webb, James Malin, and Bernard DeVoto, for example, would publish significant essays or books about this new West before the 1940s, Paxson and Turner were more intrigued with studying legacies of the frontier than in scrutinizing a postfrontier West.

Second, while Paxson had written a good deal about twentieth-century U.S. history previous to these presentations in 1929, many of the insights in *The New Nation* and *Recent History of the United States* are lacking in these lectures. In his nonwestern volumes, for example, he argues for the later, widely accepted theory of continuity between the Populists, Progressives, and other reformers; but that carryover is not mentioned here. Nor does Paxson speculate about western influences on women's suffrage, labor activism, and conservation policies—influences that he noted elsewhere.

Third, Paxson's definitions are sometimes too hazy. He speaks about several Wests, but these varied geographical, cultural, and economic experiences are not as clear as they should be. And what is one to make of his contention that midwesterners are alike in their "ambition" but that the several Wests differ in their "alien" ingredients? New social and political historians of the last generation would particularly wince at the inadequate hard evidence Paxson presents to substantiate his spread-eagle generalizations.

In the end, *When the West Is Gone* is disappointing. Paxson's uneasiness about speculation, his unwillingness to deal with the postfrontier West, and his large and inexact generalizations about images of the frontier vitiate the otherwise sparkling quality of his prose.[41] No doubt the lectures were an enjoyable aural experience, but unfortunately the performances seem more warmed-over observations from Paxson's previous writings than stimulating and provocative new insights into a society and culture bereft of a frontier. Perhaps Paxson's major energies were focused on other projects; possibly he had to write the lectures without time for further research; or, most likely, he was gradually shifting from the frontier toward modern America as his specialty. Whatever the problem, the lectures, his final book-length study of the West, were not a major achievement.

Then Paxson's career took a sharp new turn. Even though his translation to the University of California in 1932 was sudden, it was not entirely unexpected. The chairman of the History Department, Herbert Eugene Bolton, a friend of Paxson's since graduate school days, had hinted to his acquaintance a year earlier about his moving to the coast. And previous summer school teaching stints at Berkeley and UCLA had whetted the interest of the Paxsons in California. Bolton began in earnest to twist Paxson's arm in the late fall of 1931, and by the next spring Paxson declared that he would listen carefully to what California had to offer.

When Wisconsin matched an earlier bid, Bolton and President Sproul of California sweetened the offer with the new Margaret Byrne Professorship of History at 9,000 dollars plus moving expenses (Paxson was earning 6,500 dollars at Madison), and Paxson agreed to come, though he never wanted to leave Wisconsin.[42] The proposal of the Byrne Professorship to Paxson and the concurrent offer to Professor James Westfall Thompson of the University of Chicago for another chair at California—at a nadir of the Depression—captured the attention of national magazines and newspapers.[43]

While Paxson had finished his major books about the frontier before removing to California, he continued to write a few essays about the West, to teach his lecture and seminar courses on the frontier, and to direct dozens of theses and dissertations on western topics. In addition to this continuing work in western history, Paxson chaired the History Department from 1939 until his retirement in 1947 at the age of seventy and wrote his three-volume magnum opus on early twentieth-century America, *American Democracy and the World War* (1936–1948).

The move to Berkeley did not lessen Paxson's professional commitments nor his energetic roles in campus affairs.[44] He continued to be active in the American Historical Association and was named president of that august body in 1937. Meanwhile, as a member of the Pacific Coast branch of the AHA, he succeeded to its presidency in 1942. Heavy teaching loads and large class enrollments were also typical of Paxson's work at Berkeley. Continuing his lecture courses in western and recent history, he likewise offered lectures on World War I and seminars on frontier and contemporary U.S. history. Not only were his lecture courses filled with students, so were his seminars—sometimes so packed that Paxson had to offer two sections of his seminars. If the University of Wisconsin was deservedly famous for its western history offerings under Turner, Paxson, and the latter's student, John D. Hicks, for a half-century after 1890, Berkeley surpassed Madison's notoriety in the 1930s and into the 1940s when students overflowed the lecture courses and seminars of Paxson and his colleague Bolton. Unfortunately, after Paxson's retirement in 1947 and Bolton's series of leave-takings in the 1940s, interest in frontier and western history fell dramatically at California, only to be revived later at such universities as Yale, Oklahoma, Oregon, Colorado, and New Mexico.

Paxson's students at California vividly recall his lectures and seminars in frontier history. Although his published books seemed to emphasize narration, he lectured more interpretatively and avoided merely repeating his textbooks in his lectures. For the most part, he used *History of the Frontier* in his large western courses, but assigned no readings in his seminar, in which students gave oral reports tied directly to their theses and dissertations. Paxson also encouraged his seminarians to avoid limiting their graduate projects to fact-filled, local histories that lacked larger focus.

Paxson's students likewise recall the appearance, style, and work habits of their mentor. Always well dressed, often with a boutonniere in his lapel, Paxson impressed listeners as a man of energy and force, well prepared for his lectures, which were frequently written out in full but not read. Some thought he had timed his performances since he would often finish his last sentences just as class ended. Others were impressed with his style of notetaking, from newspapers and other sources but even, sometimes, from the seminar papers of his students. Carried on for more than forty years, this notetaking on three-by-five cards eventually jammed dozens of card files and so influenced some of his students that they became disciples of his methods.[45] Still other Paxson students remember that he always had newspapers spread on his desk when they visited his office. Like his mentor McMaster, Paxson was convinced that newspapers might be the best source for capturing the history of a large body of people. And while Paxson did little manuscript work himself in later years, he urged thesis and dissertation writers to make use of manuscripts in their projects.

Paxson's major research project during the last fifteen years of his career—his three-volume *American Democracy and the World War*—clearly reveals that regionalism was not a major theme in his work on modern America.[46] In the more than twelve hundred pages of text in this trilogy, Paxson briefly mentions such political westerners as Hiram Johnson, William Borah, and George Norris, and he recounts the trips of Charles Evans Hughes, Woodrow Wilson, and Warren G. Harding into the West to raise political support. In abbreviated compass, Paxson also deals with the activities of the Industrial Workers of the World and the Ku Klux Klan in the West, with even briefer mention of Hollywood and the Panama Pacific International Exposition. A bit more extensive are the commentaries on western farmers, the Nonpartisan League, and the Farm Bloc. But none of these sections on western topics—or his comments on the South—betray Paxson as a regionalist or as a historian eager to demonstrate the impact of the twentieth-century West on the nation.

In his final notable essay about the West, however, Paxson provides intriguing glimpses of what he might have dealt with in discussing the twentieth-century West. Drawing upon his extensive research in Bay Area newspapers and utilizing information from his students' recent dissertations on the modern West, Paxson details the nearly twenty-five-year struggle to build a naval station at Alameda, near Oakland, California.[47] Pointing out the important economic development of the West Coast and its growing importance to national defense, Paxson produces provocative regional history: local trends reflecting—and refracting—national and even international circumstances. Here, Paxson demonstrates the burgeoning significance of the modern American West to U.S. history—a notable topic on which his students John D. Hicks and Earl Pomeroy and others such as Gerald D. Nash and Roger Lotchin have expounded.

In another area, Paxson finally commented on the importance of Frederick Jackson Turner to western history. Early on, he limited his

obsevations on Turner and his writings to a line or two in textual, footnote, or bibliographical references, but after Turner's death in March
of 1932, Paxson ventured more extensive evaluations of Turner's ideas.
His essay, "A Generation of the Frontier Hypothesis: 1893–1932," the
first extended evaluation of Turner's frontier theory, other than those
by Turner's students, not only summarizes Paxson's views of Turner's
conclusions but also clarifies his own view of western history and
historiography.[48]

Initially, Paxson summarizes Turner's pathbreaking frontier thesis,
his commitment to conceptual history, and his avoidance of romantic,
fact-deadened, local history. If Turner's followers and other historians
had been less fanatical in preaching what was actually a hypothesis to
be tested, had they been more aware of Turner's continual stress on
the "significance" of the local materials they lovingly hoarded, and had
they been less inclined to study such narrow topics, Paxson asserts,
they might have avoided the provincial and unanalytical studies that
were misleading examples of Turner and his historical approaches. "No
investigation may be properly called Turnerian," Paxson rightly adds,
"unless its goal is more than the description of a set of facts" (p. 41).

Then Paxson discusses specific ingredients of Turner's theories—for
example, corporate society, democracy, individualism, and national
identity. Generally, he sees little in Turner's conclusions from which to
dissent. Paxson agrees that the frontier helped to make Americans more
democratic, although he notes that other forces and European trends
were also moving toward democracy. Perhaps, Paxson continues, less
Americanization took place on the frontier than Turner thought, but
more research is needed before further conclusions can be advanced.
And certainly the social laboratory of the frontier helped to spawn individualism, thus encouraging both local autonomy as well as federal ties
to the frontier. Finally, to Paxson (and to Turner) the inexorable pressures of the newest pioneer areas unified disparate areas, peoples, and
ideas. After examining these facets of Turner's writings, Paxson contends
that the Turner frontier thesis "stands today as easily to be accepted as
it was when launched." Perhaps, he adds, in a ringing conclusion, we
can "account for the weakness of the straggling attack upon his hypothesis by the inherent weakness of the case against it" (p. 51).

In this essay Paxson says little about Turner the man, but elsewhere,
especially in his portrait of Turner in the *Dictionary of American Biography*, Paxson mentions several of Turner's notable characteristics.[49]
Turner, Paxson notes, "was a teacher with unusual power to inspire

devotion, and an appearance of youth and simplicity that never quite deserted him" (p. 63). Friendly, open, and painstaking in his research, Turner was a marked man; students, colleagues, politicians, and popularizers, taking advantage of his helpful and gregarious qualities, kept him from his study and from writing more. At the same time, the force of his ideas and the suasive power of his writings encouraged his contemporaries to rewrite American history, assaying the influences of the frontier while gradually abandoning a too-strict adherence to interpretations of American society and culture as primarily the results of "religious liberty and revolt against the tyranny of England" or "the triumph of the principle of democracy" (p. 63). In these two essays and in nearly all of Paxson's other writings, his admiration of Turner as historian and man shine through. Although Paxson confided in his diary that he was "not much like Turner," those differences never foreshortened his enormous respect and admiration for his predecessor.[50]

So evolves the career of western historian Frederic Logan Paxson. Gradually abandoning his early interest in diplomatic history and moving toward a new specialization in western history largely because he was isolated from national sources in Colorado, Paxson quickly developed in the next decade a national reputation as a notable western historian, especially after the publication of *The Last American Frontier* in 1910 and his assumption of Turner's position in western history at the University of Wisconsin in the same year. His activities in several professional organizations, his training of dozens of graduate students in western history, and the publication of his *History of the American Frontier* (1924) and *When the West Is Gone* (1930) solidified Paxson's position as a leading western historian. After moving to California in 1932, Paxson turned increasingly to modern U.S. history but continued to teach numerous graduate students in frontier history. And before his death in 1948 he turned out several other essays on the West, including revealing commentaries on Frederick Jackson Turner.

In some ways Paxson was a loyal Turnerian. He not only championed Turner's frontier thesis of 1893; he also repeatedly urged his colleagues and students to rewrite American history, emphasizing the signal importance of the frontier in shaping the country's past and present. Sixteen years younger than Turner and beginning his research in frontier history a decade after Turner had announced his frontier thesis, Paxson in all his writings about the West never broke markedly from what Turner had to say about the frontier.

But from other perspectives Paxson differed a good deal from Turner. He never betrayed much interest in Turner's concept of section, was less intrigued than Turner with "significance" (analysis), and, except for minor census and map research, was less fascinated than Turner with the application of social science techniques to the study of history.

These comparisons and contrasts, however, tend to lessen the importance of Paxson's contributions, to suggest that he was little more than a follower or an imitator. He was manifestly more than that. He moved beyond Turner in producing two influential syntheses of frontier history, something Turner often promised but was never able to accomplish. Indeed, as an apt student of himself, Paxson delivered on his promises and gained a reputation as a dependable synthesist not only in frontier history but also for his pioneering overviews of recent American history. And his amazing productivity carried over into other areas. During his nearly forty-five years in the classroom, he lectured to thousands of students in frontier history courses and trained more than two hundred masters and doctoral students. Many midwestern and far-western colleges and universities had at least one Paxson-trained historian during the 1920s, 1930s, and 1940s.

Whereas Paxson's books tracing the frontier in America became standard texts in hundreds of college courses from 1910 to the 1940s, he never ventured on to carry out systematic studies of a postfrontier West. His later contemporaries, Webb, Malin, and DeVoto, for example, had begun to do so by the 1930s and 1940s, but by that time Paxson's focus had shifted largely to nonwestern topics. On the other hand, Ray Billington, an undergraduate in Paxson's frontier course in Wisconsin, also wrote an overview in *Westward Expansion* that, though more comprehensive and longer than Paxson's volume of 1924, reminds some readers of Paxson's earlier survey. And two of Paxson's best-known students, John D. Hicks and Earl Pomeroy, as well as a host of others, undertook notable studies about the frontier as well as the modern West.

What was the Paxson legacy? Two influential, well-written surveys of frontier America and a series of lectures on the closed frontier; a nearly forty-year stint of teaching western history; and two generations of graduate students trained in frontier and western subjects. After Turner, Frederic Logan Paxson was perhaps the most significant teacher and writer of frontier history in the first half of the twentieth century.

NOTES

1. Details concerning Paxson's purchase of Turner's home are clarified in Paxson to Turner, November 2, 1910, Frederick Jackson Turner papers (hereafter cited as FJTP), Box 15, Henry E. Huntington Library (hereafter cited as HEH), San Marino, Calif. Unfortunately, Paxson left no major collection of letters. Since he inexplicably destroyed most of his papers when he moved from Wisconsin to California in 1932, much of his career must be pieced together from other sources, especially from his letters in the collections of other scholars. The beginning place for information on Paxson's research methods and ideas, and an essay to which I am much indebted, is Earl Pomeroy, "Frederic Logan Paxson and His Approach to History," *Mississippi Valley Historical Review* 39 (March 1953):673–92. See also Ira G. Clark, "A Dedication to the Memory of Frederic Logan Paxson, 1877–1948," *Arizona and the West* 3 (Summer 1961):107–12. The most recent treatment of Paxson is Tully Hunter, "Frederic Logan Paxson," in John R. Wunder, ed., *Historians of the American Frontier* (Westport, Conn.: Greenwood Press, 1988), 458–69. I want to thank Earl Pomeroy, Edwin R. Bingham, Gerald D. Nash, Merle W. Wells, Ira Clark, and Russell R. Elliott for reading earlier versions of this essay.

2. Pomeroy makes a strong case for Paxson's contributions to the study of history, while Howard R. Lamar questions the value of some of those contributions in "Frederick Jackson Turner," in Marcus Cunliffe and Robin W. Winks, eds., *Pastmasters: Some Essays on American Historians* (New York: Harper and Row, 1969), 74–109, especially pp. 80, 420 n.22.

3. Details of Paxson's early years, particularly his undergraduate and graduate years at the University of Pennsylvania, are available in the records of the Franklin Inn Club, State Historical Society of Pennsylvania, Philadelphia; and in his student records at the University of Pennsylvania (hereafter cited as UP) Archives, Philadelphia.

4. *The Record of the Class of 98: University of Pennsylvania College Department* (Philadelphia: Penn Printing and Publishing Company, 1898), 89.

5. "Frederic Logan Paxson," Graduate School, UP, Record Sheets, October 15, 1898–October 15, 1900, and October 15, 1900, to October 15, 1904, UP Archives.

6. On McMaster, see Eric Goldman, *John Bach McMaster, American Historian* (Philadelphia: University of Pennsylvania Press, 1943). The experiences of Herbert Eugene Bolton, contemporary of Paxson and doctoral student under McMaster and the person most responsible for wooing Paxson from Wisconsin to California in 1932, are chronicled in John Francis Bannon, *Herbert Eugene Bolton: The Historian and Man, 1870–1953* (Tucson: University of Arizona Press, 1978), and in Bolton's letters to his brother Frederic, in the Frederic Bolton papers, Bancroft Library (hereafter cited as BL), University of California, Berkeley (hereafter cited as UCB).

7. Graduate School Records, UP.

8. Paxson, *The Independence of the South-American Republics: A Study in Recognition and Foreign Policy* (Philadelphia: Ferris and Leach, 1903). Page references to this and subsequent Paxson writings appear in the text.

9. F. J. Turner to Reuben Gold Thwaites, August 27, 1903, FJTP, Box 4, HEH.

10. Paxson to Claude H. Van Tyne, October 22, 1905, March 17, 1905, Claude H. Van Tyne papers (VTP), Michigan Historical Collections (MHC), Bentley Historical Library (BHL), University of Michigan, Ann Arbor.

11. Paxson, "A Tripartite Intervention in Hayti," *University of Colorado Studies* 1 (February 1904):323–30. Paxson to Van Tyne, May 16, 1904, VTP, MHC, BHL.

12. All of the essays appeared in the *University of Colorado Studies*: "The Boundaries of Colorado," 2 (July 1904):87–94; "The Territory of Jefferson: A Spontaneous Commonwealth," 3 (November 1905):15–18; "The Historical Opportunity in Colorado," 3 (November 1905):19–24; "A Preliminary Bibliography of Colorado History," 3 (June 1906):101–14.

13. Turner to Paxson, January 12, 1906, FJTP, Box 5, HEH, repr. in Wilbur R. Jacobs, ed., *The Historical World of Frederick Jackson Turner. . .* (New Haven: Yale University Press, 1968), 203.

14. "The Territory of Colorado," *American Historical Review* 12 (October 1906):53–65. J. Franklin Jameson to Paxson, July 16, 1906, American Historical Association papers, *AHR* Correspondence, Box 270, 1906, Library of Congress (hereafter cited as LC), Washington, D.C.

15. Telegram from Paxson to President James B. Angell, April 27, 1906, Angell papers, MHC, BHL.

16. John D. Hicks, *My Life with History: An Autobiography* (Lincoln: University of Nebraska Press, 1968), 157. Interview with Jane T. Paxson, June 11, 1988, Berkeley, Calif.

17. Turner to President Charles Richard Van Hise, March 31, 1908, copy in FJTP, HEH; original in the Van Hise papers, University of Wisconsin (hereafter cited as UW) Archives, Box 10; Charles H. Hull to Van Tyne, May 14, 1908, VTP, MHC, BHL.

18. Elizabeth Donnan and Leo F. Stock, eds., *An Historian's World: Selections from the Correspondence of John Franklin Jameson* (Philadelphia: American Philosophical Society, 1956), 109.

19. A. B. Hart to Van Tyne, April 22, 1910, VTP, MHC, BHL. Charles Homer Haskins had a few reservations about Paxson, however. Although he appreciated Paxson's "good ability" and "energy," he wondered if Paxson were not "somewhat superficial." Haskins to F. J. Turner, April 29, 1908, FJTP, Box 10, HEH.

20. Alvord to Turner, January 27, 1909, FJTP, Box 12, HEH. Paxson, "The Pacific Railroads and the Disappearance of the Frontier in America," *Annual Report of the American Historical Association for the Year 1907*, vol. 1 (Washington, 1908), 107–18.

21. Paxson to Turner, March 22, 1909, FJTP, Box 12, HEH.

22. Paxson, *The Last American Frontier* (New York: Macmillan Company, 1910).

23. Farrand, review of Paxson, *The Last American Frontier, American Historical Review* 15 (July 1910):892–93.

24. Paxson to Turner, January 17, February 10, March 30, 1910, FJTP, Box 14, HEH; Max Farrand to Turner, December 5, 1909, FJTP, Box 13, HEH; Farrand to Dana C. Munro, December 5, 1909, Max Farrand papers, Box 7, HEH; Van Tyne to Arthur L. Cross, March 17, 1910, A. L. Cross papers, Box 1, MHC, BHL.

25. Paxson to Merle Curti, August 13, 1942, Merle Curti papers, Box 29, State Historical Society of Wisconsin, Madison.

26. J. Franklin Jameson to Colonel Hiram Bingham, January 9, 1924, in Donnan and Stock, *Historian's World*, 295–96.

27. Letters from President Van Hise to Paxson, from November 7, 1916, to February 5, 1917, Van Hise Collection, Paxson folder, UW Archives.

28. Paxson to E. C. Barker, October 16, 1910, August 21, October 5, 1911, May 19, 1912, E. C. Barker collection, Barker Center, University of Texas, Austin.

29. Paxson to J. Franklin Jameson, October 11, Jameson to Paxson, October 13, Paxson to Jameson, October 16, 1915, AHA Collection, AHR Correspondence, Box 284, LC; Paxson to Turner, January 23, 1915, FJTP, Box 23, HEH.

30. Margaret F. Stieg, *The Origin and Development of Scholarly Historical Periodicals* (University: University of Alabama Press, 1986). Paxson's central role in the MVHA is amply demonstrated in the association's files, particularly from 1913 through 1918, MVHA papers, Boxes 16, 18, Nebraska State Historical Society, Lincoln.

31. Paxson to General Alumni Society, October 11, 1947, Paxson file, UP Archives; additional information on Paxson's "war work" is available in the Paxson file, UW Archives; and Paxson to Miss Forbes, August 22, 1921, Houghton Mifflin papers, Houghton Library, Harvard University (HL–HU).

32. Paxson, *The Civil War* (New York: Henry Holt and Company, 1911). Paxson details the writing of this volume in a series of letters to his publisher, from June 21 to November 3, 1911, Henry Holt correspondence, Princeton University Archives, Princeton, N.J.

33. Paxson, *The New Nation* (Boston: Houghton Mifflin Company, 1915).

34. Paxson, "The Cow Country," *American Historical Review* 22 (October 1916):65–82; "The Rise of Sport," *Mississippi Valley Historical Review* 4 (September 1917):143–68.

35. Paxson, *Recent History of the United States* (Boston: Houghton Mifflin Company, 1921).

36. Paxson to Mr. Hoyt, February 11, 1921, Houghton Mifflin collection, HL–HU.

37. Paxson, *History of the American Frontier 1763–1893* (Boston: Houghton Mifflin Company, 1924).

38. Paxson spoke several times of writing a book on western railroads but eventually gave up the project.

39. For a cross-section of reviews of Paxson's volume, see Cameron Rogers, *The World's Work* 50 (July 1925):304–8; Walter Prescott Webb, *Southwest-*

ern Historical Quarterly 28 (January 1925):247–52; Samuel Eliot Morison, *English Historical Review* 40 (July 1925):441–42. The most searching and provocative review is that by H. C. Dale in the *American Historical Review* 30 (April 1925):603–5.

40. Paxson's scattered lecture notes, Paxson papers, BL, UCB.

41. Howard Lamar calls *When the West Is Gone* (New York: Henry Holt and Company, 1930) "one of the most militant defenses of the frontier thesis in existence" and adds that "it is possible that many of the criticisms directed at Turner should have been pointed at Paxson," Lamar, "Frederick Jackson Turner," 420 n.22. For a survey of historical interpretations of the modern West, see Richard W. Etulain, "The Twentieth-Century West: A New Historiographical Frontier," in Gerald D. Nash and Richard W. Etulain, eds., *The Twentieth-Century West: Historical Interpretations* (Albuquerque: University of New Mexico Press, 1989), 1–31.

42. The details of the offers to Paxson are in correspondence between Paxson and Bolton, March-May 1932, Bolton papers, BL, UCB.

43. *Time* 19 (May 30, 1932):32.

44. For Paxson's years at Berkeley, I have drawn heavily from Pomeroy, "Frederic Logan Paxson," Clark "Frederic Logan Paxson," and on correspondence and interviews with Pomeroy, Clark, Russell R. Elliott, Merle W. Wells, and Robert E. Burke.

45. Pomeroy, "Frederic Logan Paxson," describes in detail this intriguing system of notetaking. The Paxson collection, BL, UCB, contains the enormous collection of his note cards.

46. Paxson, *Pre-War Years 1913–1917* (Boston: Houghton Mifflin Company, 1936); *America at War 1917–1918* (Boston: Houghton Mifflin Company, 1939); *Postwar Years: Normalcy, 1918–1923* (Berkeley: University of California Press, 1948).

47. Paxson, "The Naval Station at Alameda 1916–1940: A Case Study in the Aptitude of Democracy for Defense," *Pacific Historical Review* 13 (September 1944):235–50. An understanding of these regional-national configurations in the early twentieth century also informs Paxson's "The Highway Movement, 1916–1935," *American Historical Review* 51 (January 1946):236–53.

48. Paxson, "A Generation of the Frontier Hypothesis: 1893–1932," *Pacific Historical Review* 2 (March 1933):34–51.

49. Paxson, "Turner, Frederick Jackson," *Dictionary of American Biography*, vol. 29 (New York: Charles Scribner's Sons, 1936), 62–64.

50. Paxson note card, Paxson collection, BL, UCB, quoted in Pomeroy, "Frederic Logan Paxson," 686. Paxson's ideas about Turner and the frontier thesis are expanded upon in Paxson to Arthur Cole, November 16, 1936, and Paxson to "My dear Mr. Kane," September 28, 1936, Paxson collection, Box 2.

BIBLIOGRAPHY

WESTERN WRITINGS OF FREDERIC LOGAN PAXSON

"The Cow Country." *American Historical Review* 22 (October 1916):65–82.

"A Generation of the Frontier Hypothesis: 1893–1932." *Pacific Historical Review* 2 (March 1933):34–51.

"The Highway Movement, 1916–1935." *American Historical Review* 51 (January 1946):236–53.

History of the American Frontier 1763–1893. Boston: Houghton Mifflin Company, 1924.

The Last American Frontier. New York: Macmillan Company, 1910.

"The Naval Station at Alameda 1916–1940: A Case Study in the Aptitude of Democracy for Defense." *Pacific Historical Review* 13 (September 1944):235–50.

"The New Frontier and the Old American Habit." *Pacific Historical Review* 4 (December 1935):309–27.

"The Pacific Railroads and the Disappearance of the Frontier in America." *Annual Report of the American Historical Association for the Year 1907*, vol. 1 (Washington, 1908), 107–18.

"The Territory of Colorado." *American Historical Review* 12 (October 1906):53–65.

"Turner, Frederick Jackson." *Dictionary of American Biography*, vol. 29 (New York: Charles Scribner's Sons, 1936), 62–64.

When the West Is Gone. New York: Henry Holt and Company, 1930.

WORKS ABOUT FREDERIC LOGAN PAXSON

Clark, Ira G. "A Dedication to the Memory of Frederic Logan Paxson, 1877–1948." *Arizona and the West* 3 (Summer 1961):107–12.

Hicks, John D. *My Life with History: An Autobiography.* Lincoln: University of Nebraska Press, 1968.

Hunter, Tully. "Frederic Logan Paxson," in John R. Wunder, ed., *Historians of the American West.* Westport, Conn.: Greenwood Press, 1988, 458–69.

"Paxson, Frederic Logan." *The National Cyclopaedia*, vol. 39 (New York: James T. White and Company, 1954), 159.

Pomeroy, Earl. "Frederic Logan Paxson and His Approach to History." *Mississippi Valley Historical Review* 39 (March 1953):673–92.

6

Walter Prescott Webb
and the Search for the West

ELLIOTT WEST

$\mathscr{F}$OR ANYONE INTERESTED IN
western history, 1893 was quite a year. In July, Frederick Jackson Turner
unveiled his "frontier thesis" at the annual meeting of the American
Historical Association in Chicago. Scholars would look back on this
presentation as a hallowed hour. But even as Turner spoke, something
equally important was happening a thousand miles to the southwest.
The family of Casner and Mary Webb was settling on a hardscrabble
homestead just west of Fort Worth.

Later, Walter Prescott Webb said that he had started research on
his life's work when his parents carried him, at age five, from the east
Texas pine forests to the edge of the Great Plains. With his first gaze
onto that "open, arid country that stretched north and west farther
than a boy could imagine," young Walter Webb began a remarkable
intellectual odyssey.[1] Along the way, he would influence the writing
of western history as much as anyone ever has, Turner included.

Seasoned historians will find Webb's books and articles full of
insights into the larger meanings of the western past. For apprentices
in the guild, he poses fundamental questions about the historian's craft.
And for the general reader, Webb demonstrates how the light of history can illuminate the present and even, perhaps, give a glimpse of
the future.

He is, besides, a fascinating study of the role of personality and
character in historical scholarship. Webb's work was highly personal,
as much as that of any recent historian. He traced each of his major

works to some part of his early life. Other writers have drawn inspiration from their experiences, of course, but Webb was doing more. His sense of who he was seems to have evolved with his work; writing history, he was also somehow explaining himself to himself. The two threads—autobiographical and scholarly—were always entwining. No one hoping to understand the man will ever untangle them.

The Webbs came to west Texas by the classic pattern of southern pioneers, from Mississippi to the humid piney woods of Panola County, Texas, where Walter was born in 1888, and then to the south plains near Ranger. They arrived late on one of the state's last homesteading frontiers. Their land was stingy. Although Walter grew up absorbing the sights and stories of that country, he had little affection for farming and less for poverty. For diversion he read whatever he could find, but the local supply of books was slim, so on impulse he wrote an Atlanta periodical, *The Sunny South*, asking readers to send him any castoff books or journals. Years later, Webb began his autobiography: "My life has been a successions [sic] of deep humiliations and pleasant surprises."[2] Of the latter, surely the most important came in the form of a letter from a William E. Hinds, a Brooklyn importer, who wrote with encouragement ("Keep your mind fixed on a lofty purpose") and a promise to send the sixteen-year-old something to read.

Webb never met his benefactor, but for more than ten years the mail from Brooklyn brought books, kind words, and eventually loans. After a stint at schoolteaching, Webb borrowed enough from Hinds to enroll at the University of Texas. There he drifted, a decidedly average student, until he took a class from Lindley Miller Keasbey. This Harvard-trained professor had ideas and teaching techniques so unusual that he had been given his own department, that of Institutional History. At a time when most social scientists were carving out carefully limited fields of study—economics, anthropology, sociology—Keasbey argued that any society could be understood only in the grandest frame of reference. He was ahead of his time, for his approach is much like that of the *Annales* school that would gain increasing influence after World War II. A student must think of his subject as a series of layers, Keasbey argued, then peel them back, one by one; after reaching the bottom, a proper reconstruction could begin. So to understand the Roman Republic or Bismarck's Germany, Keasbey said, start with geology and climate and work upward through plant and animal life, human social structures, popular attitudes, and finally formal institutions and high culture.

Webb credited Keasbey for his basic orientation toward history. Surviving papers from Webb's student years show the young man's fascination, especially, with the ways geography had shaped human history.[3] Webb also took some of his persona from his mentor. Keasbey was outspoken and slightly eccentric; Webb became an iconoclast who cultivated the reputation of a professional maverick and a gadfly to bureaucrats. The similarities stopped, however, with the men's careers. Webb rose late from obscurity to the top of his profession; Keasbey began brilliantly, then lost his job for his opposition to World War I. When Webb's first book was published, his mentor was running a kennel of chihuahuas in Tucson.[4]

After graduation in 1915, Webb taught school and studied briefly at the University of Wisconsin. Then came another surprise—a call to return to Austin as an instructor in the teaching of history in public schools. Except for a few short absences, Webb would remain on the faculty of the University of Texas until his death. He soon felt pressure, however, to push up the path toward tenure by pursuing the doctoral degree. Webb would never place much stock in the Ph.D. He compared it, in fact, to suspenders. The doctorate protected many men of mediocre ability from exposure—or, as he wrote in his autobiography, the degree "holds up a lot of academic pants." But for himself, it offered an end to nagging by superiors. Like suspenders, the Ph.D. would turn him loose to work with both hands.[5]

So he set to work. On the advice of others, he chose as a thesis topic a history of the Texas Rangers, then enrolled in the doctoral program at the University of Chicago. There, Webb suffered probably the most painful of his life's "deep humiliations." Impatient and homesick, he took his qualifying oral examination after less than a year of preparation. He failed. The rejection left him bitter. He would not greet his professors in the halls, he later wrote, and in class, as the ultimate revenge, he would not laugh at their jokes. He soon returned to Texas, though he technically remained enrolled in the northern school. Webb remembered this as a passage toward home and himself. He was determined now to follow his own instincts, to write history informed by his own experience.

That was his life's turning point. Webb, in fact, already had chosen his subject. Two years before leaving for Chicago, he had what one psychologist has called an "A-Ha!" experience—a moment in which years of thought and impressions suddenly crystallize into an original idea. In Webb's case, the lessons and disappointments of his recent schooling reflected back on his early years. As he told it, the insight was literally heaven-sent. It came as rain on the roof.

In February 1922, he had been working on a short article on the Texas Rangers. Re-reading Emerson Hough's *Way to the West*, he was struck by Hough's statement that the new country had been won with four tools—the horse, the boat, the axe, and the long rifle. This conclusion seemed odd to Webb. The horse was certainly crucial in the West of his youth, but if eastern settlers needed the other items on the list, the plainsmen did not. Then, as a cold winter rain hammered above him, the thought came. The arid, treeless West had accepted some tools of the humid East, such as the horse; it had rejected others, like the Kentucky rifle; it had demanded new ones, like the six-shooter. Here was the germ of a much broader idea. What was true of tools applied to all institutions, from laws and literature to ways of thinking. Culture grew from the place. His own civilization, that of the plains, could be understood only in those terms.

This proposition, simple and full of implications, was the basis for *The Great Plains*, the book that established Webb's reputation as an important American historian and as one of the great influences on western history.[6] Webb spent four years after his return from Chicago elaborating on the concept—clipping magazine articles, studying animal life and Indian sign language, and reading geology texts and John Wesley Powell's famous report on arid lands. Then, in the spring of 1928, he started to write. Students and colleagues later agreed that an inspired Webb was a wonder to behold. He prowled the library for anything that seemed remotely pertinent. Back in his office, he raced through books and articles, picking out what he needed. For twelve hours a day the staccato of his two-fingered typing could be heard from behind his door in Garrison Hall.

As some critics later suspected, this project was no investigation in the usual sense. Webb was not seeking facts to help him solve a problem; he began with the solution, then looked for confirming details. *The Great Plains* already had been written in his head. "The whole story . . . was in my mind," he later explained. "I lived in a mental cocoon which I had spun about myself through imagination. . . . I was . . . building a world into which all the pieces seemed to fit." He identified his historical quest with the story he was telling, and he linked both to his reconstruction of his early years. Just as the plains pioneers had cast about until they found what suited their needs, he wrote, "my procedure was one of intellectual stumbling, picking up a clue here, a bit of evidence there, remembering always my own childhood on the edge of the land that I was now coming to know."[7] Whatever else could be said of this approach, it was undeniably productive. In the summer of 1929 Webb sent off his manuscript, and two years later it was published.

The Great Plains is properly considered Webb's masterpiece. It is a showcase for his most impressive strengths and his most irritating weaknesses; through it he has had his greatest influence, both good and bad. The book's thesis is easily stated in three points. First, the western environment—in its geology, climate, and landforms—differs fundamentally from that of the East. Certain traits are especially significant. Most of the land is arid or semiarid; much is relatively flat; much is treeless, or nearly so. Only in the plains proper, that corridor of land stretching from west Texas into Canada and from roughly the 98th meridian to the Rockies, can all of these traits be found. But in most of the remaining West one or two of those characteristics apply.

Second, this distinct environment has shaped everything that has managed to live within it. Grasses, grasshoppers, curlews, wolves, and humans—all have conformed. The first Europeans to approach the region pulled back, unable or unwilling to adapt. Later, Anglo-Americans also failed at their first try at invasion. Just beyond the Mississipi, westering pioneers ran against an "institutional fault," a line they could cross only if they changed their ways. Accustomed to well-wooded, well-watered locales, they finally succeeded by two strategies: learning to do without timber and plentiful rain, and using the fruits of the industrial revolution to meet the challenges before them. The result was a distinctive society molded by and reflecting the environment.

These two points lead to the third. The West is truly a region. This means that it is more than a place separated from other areas of the continent. The West has unique, enduring physical characteristics, a distinctive history with ancient roots, and a character and mood drawn from both. It will be forever different. It can be understood only on its own terms. It will continue to play a role in national life that is all its own.

In making these points, The Great Plains was not nearly as original as some of its admirers have claimed. Truly original works rarely enjoy the immediate, widespread praise that Webb's book did, for it takes time for new insights to be understood and appreciated. The Great Plains received almost instant recognition because it expanded upon well-established ideas, some more than a generation old.

Webb spoke to a growing interest in America's regional diversity. By the late 1920s there had appeared in many areas figures of intellectual and cultural life who interpreted and often celebrated the various values, customs, and idiosyncracies growing from the nation's several regions—Frank Lloyd Wright in architecture; Grant Wood, John Steuart Curry, and Thomas Hart Benton in art; Allen Tate, John Crow Ransom, and Robert Penn Warren in literature and literary criticism; to name but a few. Turner himself, America's preeminent western historian, had also turned to the study of sections and their significance in the nation's history. When Webb provided a historical definition of another distinctive part of the American land, he found a large and receptive audience.

At the heart of this definition was an account of how the western environment had given birth to a new society. In this, Webb was continuing a rich tradition in both scholarship and popular culture. Since the time of Daniel Boone and Leatherstocking, Americans had been infatuated with the belief that something exceptional had happened when their ancestors confronted an unfamiliar landscape. This historical process was closely akin to the basic notion of *The Great Plains*. In particular, Webb stressed the continuous, shaping role of geography, but that, too, had been gospel among many historical geographers for a generation. Listen to Ellen Churchill Semple on the role of geography in history: "It never sleeps. This natural environment, this physical basis of history, is for all intents and purposes immutable in comparison with the other factor in the problem—shifting, plastic, progressive, retrogressive man."[8]

Webb's originality and appeal took subtler forms. No one had ever described a region so ingeniously as a historical evolution within a changeless landscape. *The Great Plains* is also one of the most seductive books ever written by an American historian. It rests upon a few simple ideas. Webb states these ideas clearly at the outset, then develops them in a grand march through historical and topical chapters. The gathering details coax the reader into Webb's way of thinking. The reader feels involved in the work, partly because of the book's engaging style. Facing his typewriter, Webb had imagined he was sitting across from a reasonably intelligent businessman who knew nothing of the book's subject. Webb then wrote as if he were explaining to his friend what he had learned. The result was an easy, conversational prose that appealed to the general reader. Above all, there is in *The Great Plains* an undeniable feel of authenticity, a confidence and conviction that reach below thought to experience.

Webb also said his piece at just the right time. The idea and story of the West, full of high drama and inspiration, had fascinated Americans since the early days of the republic. It had helped them in explaining who they were. But after generations of reading and dreaming western history, Americans had reached a crisis in their thinking on the subject. Intentionally or not, Webb spoke to these doubts.

Among the intellectual community, questions centered on Turner's "frontier thesis." To Turner, the West was no particular part of the United States; rather, it had been the advancing edge of European-American settlement, the "line between civilization and savagery" that had moved gradually across the continent during the three centuries after 1600. The special conditions along that frontier—an abundance of undeveloped resources, the needs of an ambitious people, the threat posed by native inhabitants, the absence of social and legal restraints, for instance—had transformed those who lived there. New values and traits had evolved, characteristics that together defined a distinctive American character.

Turner's ideas had dominated the writing of American history for nearly thirty years. But soon after his death in 1932, and coincident with the widening fame of *The Great Plains*, critics had begun to pick away at the frontier thesis. Some questioned the connection between the frontier and the national character. How could the frontier, by definition an isolated and thinly settled part of the country, have had such a profound impact on the nation as a whole? In trying to answer that, readers ran into a second problem—Turner's vagueness. His writing was highly abstract. Describing the birth of a new society, he wrote mainly about attitudes and values—individualism, a practical and inventive turn of mind, an instinctive democratic urge. These were certainly important, but Turner never defined them, so they remained ephemera, inviting different meanings and conflicting claims about their origins. In fact, Turner gave few specifics to illustrate any of his ideas. Although some readers found Turner's essays an intellectual feast, others left the table hungry for particulars.

Finally, Turner's West was an elusive place, everywhere and nowhere. The West, as frontier, had passed over each part of the nation, and now it was gone. But when had it been where? What combination of conditions made any place "western"? Kentucky obviously qualified in 1780, and Nebraska in 1870, but when exactly did the moving West pass on, leaving these places to become something else? Many decided that Turner's ideas, so intriguing and stimulating at first reading, were on closer inspection a confusing snarl.

Webb's version of western history, appearing on the eve of Turner's death, was convincing and appealing precisely where Turner's was weakest. He claimed no special connection between his West and the national character. His main point was just the opposite—that plains lifeways make no sense anywhere else. Webb wrote of things easily visualized—flora and fauna, reclamation projects, the plainsman's tools and techniques. There was a refreshing concreteness about the cultural evolution pictured on the pages of *The Great Plains*; after all, it is easier to describe a windmill, say, than democracy. Certainly no one could complain about a lack of specifics. There were yipping prairie dogs, Indian sign language, longbarreled revolvers, branding irons, and riparian legislation.

And Webb's readers had no trouble in finding the West. After reading *The Great Plains*, anyone could point to a map and say, "Here." Webb's West was defined in terms of the land's timeless traits, not the rather fuzzy characteristics of a shifting, moving line of settlement. It reached from just beyond the first tier of trans-Mississippi states to the Pacific slope. That was where it was, had been, and always would be.

In saying that, Webb was appealing to a far larger audience, most of whom had never heard of Turner. For years Americans had been hearing that the "Old West" was dying or dead. With several widely publicized episodes—the final defeat of the Indians, the fencing of the open range, and the widening web of railroads over the continent's interior, among others—this unique part of our history was over. Now Webb wrote that if the frontier was gone, the West, in another sense, was immortal. The region he defined, with its vast deserts, looming mountains, and sweeping plains, had been the backdrop for Cody's extravaganzas, thousands of dime novels and potboilers, respectable fiction like that of Owen Wister, and hundreds of movies. Here, the essential appeal of the popular western—the story of people trying to master a challenging environment—remained rooted in reality. So take heart, Webb seemed to say. The West as stage for dramatic struggle would be around forever.

The Great Plains, then, recast western history by combining familiar elements into a strikingly original form. He drew upon a popular interest in regional life and long-standing ideas of geographical determinism. He took one of the oldest, most evocative themes of the American story—that of process and becoming, particularly of the changes that follow when ordinary people confront extraordinary places—and restated it clearly and simply in geographical terms. Doing this, he transformed western history into the study of a unique and fascinating region.

The West was no moving, shifting spirit, he wrote; it had enduring traits and coordinates on the map. Its story began centuries before the arrival of Turner's pioneers, and it continues until today.

But there was a price for this change. As Turner conceived it, western history might have been vague and shot through with contradictions. Yet it also spoke, in a most personal way, to everyone in every part of the nation. The moving frontier had touched every American acre. No matter where one lived, there was something out of the years of conquest and settlement from which to take pride or umbrage—and, through that, to feel, however vaguely, some attachment to a distinctive experience common to all. Webb gave the West specificity and permanence. But he also surrendered western history's special claim—the notion that it provided a unifying vision for all Americans.

The Great Plains soon attracted critics of its own. Some wondered whether the plains could correctly be called a region, given the many variations of terrain within them. Others applauded Webb's attempt to define the plains and the West as a distinct section, but they complained that his approach (and thus his conclusions) were too simplistic. James C. Malin argued that Webb's conception of the plains was too static. People changed the land as much as the land changed them; the natural setting, human minds, and social institutions always were influencing one another; and this made for a range of possibilities infinitely greater than Webb suggested. The history of the region, Malin argued, has been far more fluid, dynamic, and complex than described in *The Great Plains*.[9]

Still others thought that Webb overemphasized how much the settlers' lives changed when they moved onto the plains. A lot that they brought with them—their government and laws, family and community customs, folklore and language—remained much the same. Because Webb wrote only of adaptations, ignoring continuities, he distorted badly the plains experience. The reader will find no hint, for example, that the northern plains was the most ethnically diverse part of the nation in the late nineteenth century, a patchwork of Germans and Russian-Germans, Swedes, Czechs, Finns, Norwegians, French, and others. Perhaps Webb drew too heavily on the more homogenous south plains of his own youth. More than that, Webb simply screened out all survivals of tradition, including the rich ethnic heritage found in the West even today.[10]

The most outspoken among Webb's critics was Fred Shannon, professor of history at the University of Illinois. His attack came in 1939 at a conference sponsored by the Social Science Research Council to evaluate *The Great Plains* as one of the most important works of interdisciplinary scholarship in recent years. Several other distinguished figures in history, sociology, and economics attended the meeting. Most were complimentary. Shannon was not. His face-to-face showdown with Webb was one of the most dramatic episodes in the history of the profession.

Shannon's bill of particulars was long, his tone often sarcastic. He charged that *The Great Plains* was full of misleading, contradictory, and erroneous statements. Innovations that Webb said were responses to the needs of the plains had been used for years in country far to the east. When some of these phenomena, such as barbed wire and the Colt revolver, were brought into the area, they did not have the profound effects that Webb had claimed for them. On and on, Shannon chipped away at Webb's presentation. He agreed that lifeways had changed when they entered the plains. But those changes were not nearly as abrupt as Webb had described, and in fact they were best understood as a gradual adjustment typical among pioneers for centuries.[11]

All this Shannon submitted to Webb before the conference. Webb was angry, even bitter. Here was another instance of a member of the historical establishment unfairly attacking honest efforts to say something new about the West. Webb gave no detailed response to Shannon. Instead, he wrote that Shannon had entirely missed the point. Not once had the critic considered the validity of the book's thesis—that the generally flat, treeless, and arid conditions of the plains were so different as to constitute a distinct region with its own institutions—or its method: "to attempt to view the entire round of life in the Great Plains, from the geological foundations to the literary and mystical superstructure."[12] In short, there had been no real appraisal, so there would be no reply.

Facing one another at the conference, the two antagonists touched on the fundamental difference between them. "My sole concern is the integrity of history," Shannon said:

> I claim that generalizations can be established if you collect
> enough data of the proper kind and analyze them sufficiently;
> that only by this means can epochal contributions to historical
> science and significant new interpretations be made. . . . I have

been trying to point out that we need a return to the objectivity of historical research.[13]

Webb answered that he had no apologies for his book:

The concept upon which it is based came accidentally. . . . It was not my business to write the history of any movement which I treated. It was my business to take these various movements, use the best material I could get, and fit these various parts into a picture which would give people a better understanding of this great region. The idea was so clear to me that I wondered why the work had not been done before. . . . It was not necessary for me to document this book at all. . . . There are different kinds of students; we have different ways of doing things. The Great Plains *was done in a way that suited me at the time I did it. That is the way I hope to write any book.*[14]

Here was a classic confrontation on an issue all students of history must face—the role of intuition in understanding the past. Shannon had no quarrel with moments of insight, such as Webb's "A-ha!" experience. But, he was saying, concepts "accidentally" acquired must be tested against exhaustively amassed evidence. Better yet, we should gather details first, then systematically puzzle out their meaning. Whichever approach is taken, the data in all their specifics should produce the conclusion. If not, that conclusion must be tossed aside, no matter how correct it "feels."

Webb, in turn, was not rejecting the gathering and analysis of evidence. But, he said, a deep and general acquaintance with a subject sometimes leads to an instant when one sees a connection among facts that illuminates more—far more—than the facts themselves. That kind of vision, comprising what Webb called "patterns of truth," is not history in the usual sense. A book like *The Great Plains* does not bring together bits of evidence to produce a finished picture of anything. It is less an end than a beginning, not an explanation but a way of thinking that spins off explanations. As such, Webb argued, it should be judged by different standards. Will thoughtful readers continue to find in it clues toward understanding a topic of great complexity? If so, that book, errors and all, will have measured up.

By that standard, *The Great Plains* has been a success. It has kept its value as a frame of reference for understanding the West. Those who live there generally agree that the people of the West, their methods of supporting themselves, their lifeways, and attitudes are different from those of the world outside. Historians trying to trace those differences have typically found their way back to the environment—its resources, appeal, and limitations. Webb still has much to say about the West as a unique part of the American whole and a continuing presence in national life.

Within weeks of its publication, reviews in both the *New York Times* and *Herald-Tribune* praised *The Great Plains*. A year later the book was awarded Columbia University's Loubat Prize. In 1932, with Webb's star on the rise, his department surprised him by proposing to accept *The Great Plains* as his doctoral thesis. He notified the Chicago faculty that he would not be back, then took the Ph.D. from his employer. Finally, Webb had his suspenders.

Respect for *The Great Plains* grew with the years, and so, naturally, did Webb's professional standing. He was chosen for two prestigious visiting appointments, first as Harkness Professor at the University of London (1938) and later as Harmsworth Professor at Oxford (1942–43). In 1950 a panel of scholars selected *The Great Plains* as the most influential historical work by a living author. During the next decade, Webb was elected president of both the Mississippi Valley Historical Association and the American Historical Association.

But the Texas farmer's son never seemed comfortable with this recognition. He rejected the notion that he had become part of the historical establishment, which he thought was dominated by faculties of eastern schools, scholars with little understanding of or sympathy for his country and its people. Mingled with these opinions, furthermore, were hints of insecurity. Even in his presidential address before the A.H.A., Webb was self-deprecating, referring to his "plebeian field of Western America." He remained hypersensitive to criticism, especially from anyone in the more venerable institutions of the East. In Webb's mind, at least, he would remain always a professional outsider.

His second book was *The Texas Rangers* (1935). It was his least successful book. Although extensively researched, it is uncritical, even worshipful of its subject, and its portrayal of Indians and Hispanics is at best insensitive and sometimes appalling. This book did, however, suggest Webb's pride in Texas and his strong belief in the value of regional and local history. He never wavered in either of those commitments. He was the inspiration and editor of the monumental reference work, *The Handbook of Texas*, and he took deep satisfaction from helping found the Junior Historians, a group dedicated to encouraging public school students to investigate their towns and neighborhoods. Graduate students, too, should leave the library often to learn as he had, by laboring "in the garden, the field, the street, or the market place" of the West. Through local history, Webb wrote, westerners would "come to feel that they have a culture and a civilization of their own and not something borrowed or brought in from a summer trip."[15]

He was arguing a kind of prideful particularism, urging westerners to find strength and self-understanding by reconstructing the story of their most immediate and intimate surroundings—counties, towns, neighborhoods, families. In this he was not alone. Two other distinctive personalities on the university faculty, the folklorist J. Frank Dobie and Roy Bedichek, a classical scholar turned naturalist, also were earning reputations for their books and essays on Texas and Texans. Webb, Dobie, and Bedichek were close friends, and as public presences they symbolized an intellectual respectability for the study of what had often drawn jokes and condescension—their state's past, its people and culture, and its landscape.

Yet, perhaps inevitably, Webb's perspective expanded with his maturing thought and his exposure to the world beyond Texas. As he encouraged regional and local history, he also was exploring how the West fit within a national context. In a short book and an article, published twenty years apart, Webb carried some of the implications of *The Great Plains* into the present. Both pieces questioned public policy and comfortable assumptions; both rubbed hard against sensitive feelings of the West and the nation. These statements provoked a wide controversy, by far the most heated of Webb's career.

At first glance *Divided We Stand* (1937) seems to have little in common with Webb's other work.[16] It is as much a political tract as a piece of history. It is largely concerned with the grinding economic problems of the South, and it reportedly spurred President Franklin Roosevelt to step up efforts to deal with Dixie's blight.

Behind this political appeal, however, was a fundamental issue of modern American history—the economic balance of power among the major regions of the United States. The nation can be divided into three sections, Webb observed. The West and South together included nearly all of the country's natural resources, yet most of the wealth generated by these raw materials had gone to the Northeast, the smallest and most resource-poor of the three. To make this point, Webb used a variety of measures, from the "Fortune 500" list of largest corporations, to bank deposits and insurance policies, to advertisements in the *Saturday Evening Post*. All led to the same conclusion: modern America had become a feudal empire, and the westerners and the southerners were the serfs.

This book was a landmark in establishing the most persistent theme in twentieth-century western history and politics—colonialism. Webb's charge, that the Northeast held the rest of the country in an economic stranglehold, was hardly new. It had been made by the Populists and more recently by Bernard DeVoto, the western-born columnist for *Harper's* who was an enthusiastic admirer of *The Great Plains*. But Webb's analysis gave historical weight to the discussion. He was arguing that the West's special characteristics had led to its economic fate. For reasons explained in *The Great Plains*, the western interior was the last part of the country to be settled. By then the industrial revolution was well underway. Here was an ugly joke. The same industrial flowering that had given the pioneers many tools needed to settle the West had also made the Northeast the center of the nation's banking, business, and corporate life. Capitalists there had used their vast economic clout to command the new country's rich farmlands and vast stores of precious metals, timber, petroleum, and other resources. Geography and history had conspired to deny westerners the benefits of their own land.

The timing of *Divided We Stand*, like that of *The Great Plains*, was significant. The book appeared in the midst of the Great Depression. Staggering from the national economic calamity and the regional disaster of the Dust Bowl, westerners were angry, frustrated, and in the mood for a reassessment. On one level, Webb's book was a polemic about the present. On another, it was a fresh, tough look at the future. The West's problems, he wrote, lay only partly with the Depression. The Northeast gouged the rest of the country in good times and bad, so the return of prosperity would mean only fatter profits for Wall Street. The West was in bondage. Until that relationship changed—presumably through hard-fought political campaigns—the western states would never achieve their ambitions.

But would they even then? What was the truth behind the perennial dream of the West as a place of boundless promise for any and all with the gumption to move there? Allowed to grow with little interference from the outside, would the region still be limited by itself, by its own shortcomings? Webb answered these questions in an article published in *Harper's* in 1957, "The American West: Perpetual Mirage."[17]

In *The Great Plains* Webb had listed the section's three most distinctive geographical traits. Now he singled out one—aridity—as most important. The West is a desert, he wrote, and that is the key to understanding it. Its core, from the high plains to the Sierra Nevada and southern California, receives only about a dozen inches of rain a year. The desert rim gets about twice that much, which is still much less than country to the east. The lack of rainfall has stunted western plant life, "put horns on its toads," and forced rattlesnakes to slither sideways. Most important, the desert has determined patterns of human development. People have avoided the core in favor of the rim, and everywhere they have clustered in water-blessed "oases" like Lubbock, Los Angeles, Denver, and El Paso. Only recently, in fact, had true civilization intruded into the region at all. Western history has been "brief and . . . bizarre," like stunted grama grass. The desert has produced few events and persons of significance. For the raw stuff of boasting, westerners have had to rely on spectacular scenery and manufactured heroes like Calamity Jane.

Pettifoggers could obscure the truth, and fools ignore it, but the desert "is the great designer of the American West," Webb concluded. The implications were—and are—obvious. The West might be a storehouse of resources. Yet it would remain forever a section of scant population and limited influence, culturally retarded and historically "thin."

The response was predictable. "Sincerely hope you avoid lynching," a concerned reader wrote Webb. Despite the sentiment, Webb was strung up, editorially at least, in newspapers throughout the region, and a blizzard of outraged letters blew into Austin. One westerner promised to spit on Webb's building.[18] These assaults can be passed off as wounded pride. Other, more telling criticism came in time. The comment that civilization and history began only with the Anglos' arrival was ethnocentrism of the rankest sort. Some said that Webb's rigid geographical determinism, his claim that aridity spelled the West's "inevitable destiny," underestimated the ability of westerners to overcome this one deficiency, or at least to make the best of it. At first glance, in fact, Webb seems a remarkably poor prophet. During much of the time since 1957 the region that he predicted would be forever underpopulated has been America's boomland. With that has come rising political power; of the six presidents elected during those years, four have been from the desert rim.

Yet the "Mirage" article, as well as *Divided We Stand*, still has much to say about present debates and future problems, particularly the West's fortunes and inequities and the unbridgeable gap between its people's hopes and reality. Western growth in many ways has confirmed, not contradicted, what Webb wrote. As he predicted, newcomers have gravitated toward the cities, which have exhausted local water supplies and now rely on distant sources. As several works have shown, the region's rivers are being drained and its vast underground lakes sucked lower and lower. Most specialists agree that the West is living on borrowed water, and so on borrowed time. Other scholars continue to find in aridity the key to the West's past and future evolution. The lack of rainfall has led to two dominant "ecological modes," the environmental historian Donald Worster has written. Both the "pastoral" mode of cattle and sheep grazing and the "hydraulic" of irrigated agriculture are unique to the West; both have encouraged large landholdings, the concentration of wealth and power in few hands, and an excessive reliance on government aid and a technocratic elite.[19] *Divided We Stand*, though in some ways out of date, is still pertinent to western studies. Anyone concerned with the pressing issue of colonialism would likely agree with Webb's basic premise—that the West's history, resources, and environmental conditions have threatened to make it a ward of the national government and the pawn of concentrated wealth.

Together, these two works were a fascinating follow-up to Webb's original insight. And once again Webb was mingling the historical and the autobiographical. Having declared the West as unique, he now told his readers that being different was not always to the good. The West, like he himself, was an outsider by history and temperament, Webb seemed to say. Whatever rightful pride its people felt, the region was and would remain on the periphery of national power, just as Webb, loyal to his Texas roots and sensitive to criticism from outlanders, always would place himself on the circumference of academic circles. The perspectives of man and subject had become much the same—looking eastward toward the center of political authority, economic control, and professional respectability.

In his final book, *The Great Frontier*, Webb tried to put the West's story within the broadest context of all, that of world history.[20] To do so, he abandoned the theme that had first carried him to national prominence. Up to this point, he had portrayed the West as a region. Now, ironically, he returned to the approach rejected in *The Great Plains*. The West, once again, became a stage of development, an era of rapid change that swept over America and much of the earth.

The Great Frontier rested on a single idea—the "boom hypothesis." By this, Webb argued that Europe's early, tentative efforts at exploration triggered phenomenal changes that eventually transformed the institutions and values of the continent and much of the world. Europe on the eve of the Age of Discovery was densely populated, at least by standards of that day. Webb dubbed it the "Metropolis." Its society was static. Virtually all resources and political power were controlled by a small elite. The commonfolk of the continent, accustomed to conditions that had prevailed for centuries, could scarcely imagine anything different.

When Columbus stumbled upon a new world, all this changed. European nations embarked on increasingly aggressive voyages of discovery and conquest. This extraordinary expansion, the "Great Frontier," brought all of the Western Hemisphere, Australia and parts of Africa and Asia, under the domination of the Metropolis. Suddenly a small part of the world's people, the Europeans, had access to a huge portion of global resources. The amount of precious metals, commodities, and land available to Europe shot upward far more rapidly than its population. The most obvious and immediate result for the continent was an economic growth unprecedented in world history. This new wealth at first was controlled by the old elite, but inevitably its blessings were spread to an ever-larger part of the populace.

This rising standard of living brought in turn other transformations. A new figure appeared—the man on the make, fired by a lust for profits. For even the average citizen, the future seemed one of open-ended possibilities of individual gratification. A static view of life gave way to one in which rapid, intoxicating change was the norm. New World riches inevitably reduced the economic distance between rich and poor, and as class distinctions eroded, old political systems no longer made sense. The flood of wealth swept away European autocracies along with the rest.

In short, the Great Frontier was largely responsible for the modern world's distinctive features, among them capitalism, individualism, parliamentary democracy, and a respect for civil liberties, all institutions that most readers would applaud. But there was a catch, Webb wrote. The "boom" was over. By about 1890, four hundred years after it began its outward sweep, the Great Frontier had expanded as far as it could. Meanwhile, the world population was growing at such a pace that it would soon catch and surpass available resources. The growth that had spawned and sustained those modern, salutary changes was slowing to a crawl. The old, static life soon would return, and with it, perhaps, the rigid and repressive institutions of the pre-Columbian world. When seen in the context of millenia past and future, the Great Frontier would be an aberration. On history's long timeline, the "boom" would be only a blip.

The debt to Turner is obvious here. In fact, there is a wonderful symmetry to the evolving ideas of these two most influential western historians. Reading their work is like watching an intellectual round dance, with the partners bowing and changing places. Webb's first book answered doubts about the young Turner's frontier thesis by describing the West as a region with a unique, enduring history. The maturing Turner, by the 1920s, turned from the frontier to the study of regions as a more promising theme in American history. Webb, in his turn, revived the idea of the frontier, extended it far beyond Turner's conception, and proclaimed it to be the primary force in shaping modern history.

Nonetheless, Webb wrote that he was not inspired by Turner or any man. His own life, not the ideas of others, had given him the truth. His west Texas youth had planted the seed of *The Great Frontier* as well as *The Great Plains*. In the Cross Timbers he was "on the tag end of frontier life." The "flavor and tang" of its spirit was all around.[21] In his acquisitive, optimistic neighbors he saw the product of four centuries of expansion; with them he also knew the frustrations of facing the boom's final years.

The Great Frontier was Webb's most ambitious book, and he thought it was his best. Of all his works, however, it received the harshest reviews. J. R. Hexter's comment summed up the response: Webb had "simply wasted his time." Such remarks can be explained partly by the climate of the day. In the scholarly community, any interpretation smacking of Turner was out of fashion; Webb's thesis, wrote Oscar Handlin, "reduces the frontier conception to its ultimate absurdity."[22] In American society at large, *The Great Frontier*'s glum forecast came when the public was warming itself in the postwar glow of unmatched prosperity and faith in the institutions that Webb suggested were doomed.

Its timing aside, the book had undeniable weaknesses, many of them by now familiar to Webb's readers. Once more, he overstated his case to make a grand point. Leaving the Metropolis for the frontier, he wrote, "man stepped forth with old human restraints stripped off, old institutions of aid or hindrance dissolved."[23] Taken at face value, statements like this were preposterous. David Potter, among others, added that Webb woefully underestimated the ability of modern man, with the help of technology, to continue wringing benefits from the land. European historians scoffed at the simplistic explanations of the continent's complex changes. Webb's warmest admirers pursed their lips, shook their heads, and looked for excuses; Jacques Barzun would write that Webb was "out of his element."[24]

Equally telling was criticism of the book's point of view. Exceptionally broad in one sense, its perspective was quite narrow in another. For those looking from Europe outward, the results of the expanding frontier were happy indeed. But what if one imagined the consequences from other angles? The areas invaded were certainly not, as Webb described them, *a vast body of wealth without proprietors* [italics in original]."[25] The Metropolis profited through conquest and dispossession of tens of millions of persons. And as recent research shows, the wave of European influence was biological as well as institutional. Diseases sweeping through the New World reduced native populations by at least half, perhaps by as much as 95 percent. The Great Frontier triggered the greatest human calamity in history. Exploitation of resources, furthermore, demanded far more labor than Europe was able or willing to provide. As a result, by one estimate, the conquerors carried nearly eight million African slaves to the New World by 1820. Or, put another way, for each of Webb's frontiersmen who departed Europe with "human restraints stripped off," at least four left Africa in chains. When we view the "boom" from the perimeter inward, its history is not the sunny tale that Webb told; it is a nightmare almost beyond imagination.

That said, *The Great Frontier* has also gained considerable respect. Webb built a framework, a bare scaffolding meant to suggest the general shape of history over four centuries. As in *The Great Plains*, the details he chose to hang on this scaffolding told a story that was distorted, neglectful of many influences, and insensitive to experiences of groups other than Webb's own kind. But as with Webb's first book, scholars have found that the framework itself is sound. Although Immanuel Wallerstein's award-winning volume, *The Modern World System*, gives *The Great Frontier* only a brief, favorable comment, its sophisticated argument—that a "European world-economy" arose after 1500 from the complex exchange between the continent and its newly conquered "periphery"—might have been written by a Webb disciple.[26] An entirely new field, that of comparative frontier studies, has taken inspiration from the book that was given such a rough ride when it first appeared.

Probably the highest praise has come from William H. McNeill, renowned world historian from, of all places, the University of Chicago.[27] McNeill agrees with most of the usual criticisms of Webb's book,

and he adds that it, as well as Turner's works, has encouraged a romantic, parochial view of the past. In its statement of the grand themes of
global history since Columbus, however, McNeill finds *The Great Frontier*
exceptionally perceptive. Europe's explosive expansion did determine
the contours of continental and world development. The catastrophic
die-off of conquered peoples left a void into which European institutions and technology quickly moved. The continent's standard of living and population both spiraled upward, fed by resources and New
World foods that revolutionized the Old World's diet. These changes,
in turn, were most responsible for others, including the political and
industrial revolutions that in many ways define modern life. But the
reverberations set off in the Age of Discovery have finally subsided,
McNeill observes. Like Webb, he concludes that we are entering a new,
uncertain era.

Whatever its differences from Webb's other work, *The Great Frontier* sits comfortably with one of his major themes—that of the modern
West's narrowing possibilities and its manipulation by outside forces.
Here, he was suggesting how these were part of a phenomenon encompassing a half-millenia and much of the planet. Shrugging off the early,
hostile reviews, he predicted that by 1990, at the centennial of the
boom's demise, thoughtful readers would find this thesis full of truth.
Now that time of reckoning is here, and Webb surely would be com-
forted. *The Great Frontier* may not be, as Ray Allen Billington once predicted, "one of the most significant books of our time," but as historians
refine its ideas, the value of its fundamental insight into modern history seems confirmed.[28]

Walter Webb was an "idea" historian. He rarely touched primary
documents, though he gratefully used the archival diggings of his seminar students. His best work was based on books by others and on countless hours of coffee conversation with colleagues and friends. He liked
to say that he did his research while driving and thinking on the roads
around Austin. So it was perhaps fitting, if deeply regrettable, that he
died in an automobile accident south of the city in March of 1963.

By then Webb's contribution was clear. He grounded western history in a place. With that, he gave historians a vast field to work, a
subject embracing dozens of cultures and ranging over twenty thousand years, from the arrival of the first humans until the present. His
most persistent theme—that of the intricate relationship among the environment, people, and their institutions— is still essential to understand-

ing western life, whether the topic is the cliff dwellers or modern Denver. This approach naturally leads to a hardened, sometimes pessimistic view of western life befitting this uncertain and often difficult century. In this warning is a valuable message. Describing how the land has always set the limits of what man can do, Webb reminds us of the need for restraint and continuing accommodation with our surroundings. If Turner spoke for those reared with the Myth of Abundance, Webb is a historian for today, the Age When Things Are Running Out.

Webb, as a craftsman, wrote engaging history that challenged and never condescended. His style was clear and direct. As we try to puzzle out the past, he reminds us of the value of intuition and personal experience. As we present our results, he shows what can be done through an impassioned involvement with our subjects and a respect for the simple declarative sentence.

Some of these very strengths, however, raise troubling questions about the man and his legacy. Today, western history does not hold the prominent place it did fifty years ago. Books on cattlemen and fur traders have lost much of their mass appeal. Despite recent interest in the "new western history," specialists in other academic fields typically pay scant attention to the work done by western historians, who too often return the favor. For this, Webb must bear some responsibility. By concentrating on the study of a single region, Webb denied to western history what Turner had given it—an intimate, unifying connection to the story of the American people. People in New Jersey, asked to read books on an interesting, unique but alien part of the country, might be tempted to ask, "Why?"

As a champion of local and regional history, Webb strove to place his work within a national and global context. But among lesser mortals, his regional concentration and his pride in the West could become a narrow provincialism, a smug unconcern with history beyond the region or even the county line. As for his methods, Webb seemed to say that the best history is written by those who have "lived" it. He helped set the personal tone and the experiential, almost testimonial tradition so characteristic of the writing and criticism of western history today. Of the great man's work, for instance, the scholar and native westerner Donald Worster writes that "I know in my bones, if not always through my education, that Webb was right."[29] This approach is well suited for someone of Webb's intuitive brilliance. But it implies that only those who have spent most of their lives in the region should write about it. Is an understanding of the West ultimately beyond the reach of anyone who has not experienced the country and partaken of its spirit? Is western history, then, a kind of closed society?

Perhaps Webb's final lesson is the unavoidable conflict between defining his field absolutely on its own terms and keeping it always within a larger historical setting. Students must work with that tension if they are to give western history its proper perspective. Only then will they earn for it a due respect. To do that, while writing with Webb's vitality and insight, is a formidable challenge indeed.

NOTES

1. Walter Prescott Webb, "History As High Adventure," in *An Honest Preface and Other Essays*, ed. Joe B. Frantz (Boston: Houghton Mifflin Company, 1959), 206.

2. Walter Prescott Webb, "Autobiography," 1, typescript, Walter Prescott Webb Papers (hereafter cited as WPW), Eugene C. Barker Texas History Center, University of Texas, Austin.

3. "Geographic Features as a Factor in the History of the United States of America" and "Influences Determining the Political Theory of the American Revolution," Walter Prescott Webb Papers, 2–22/788, Texas State Archives, Austin, Texas.

4. "Background on Lindley Miller Keasbey," in Lindley Miller Keasbey file, 2M/253, WPW. There is an odd epilogue to the story of Keasbey's influence. When Webb sent his mentor a copy of *The Great Plains*, Keasbey congratulated his student warmly, then revealed an entirely new theory of historical change that Keasbey claimed was far superior to his ideas presented in class. Reaching into a fourth dimension, this theory included, among other things, the mathematics of triangles, the mystery of the Christian Trinity, and the musical principle of the major and minor third. See Lindley Miller Keasbey to Walter Prescott Webb, October 10, 1931, Lindley Miller Keasbey file, 2M/253, WPW.

5. Webb, "Autobiography," 177–78.

6. Walter Prescott Webb, *The Great Plains* (Boston: Ginn and Company, 1931).

7. Webb, "Autobiography," 149.

8. Ellen Churchill Semple, *Influences of Geographic Environment on the Basis of Ratzel's System of Anthro-Geography* (New York: Henry Holt and Company, 1911), 2.

9. James C. Malin, "Webb and Regionalism," in *History and Ecology: Studies of the Grassland*, ed. Robert P. Swierenga (Lincoln: University of Nebraska Press, 1984), 65–111.

10. Frederick C. Luebke, "Regionalism and the Great Plains: Problems of Concept and Method," *Western Historical Quarterly* 15 (January 1984):19–38.

11. Fred A. Shannon, *An Appraisal of Walter Prescott Webb's "The Great Plains: A Study in Institutions and Environment,"* Critiques of Research in the Social Sciences, vol. 3 (New York: Social Sciences Research Council, 1940).

12. Ibid., 123.

13. Ibid., 186–87.

14. Ibid., 210–13.

15. Webb, "Autobiography," 160, and "Foreword from *Texas County Histories*," in Frantz, ed., *Honest Preface*, 70.

16. Walter Prescott Webb, *Divided We Stand: The Crisis of a Frontierless Democracy* (New York: Farrar and Rinehart, 1937).

17. Walter Prescott Webb, "The American West: Perpetual Mirage," *Harper's Magazine* 214 (May 1957):25–31.

18. Barry Reiche to Webb, n.d., C. L. Bloom to Department of History, May 15, 1957, 2M/267, WPW.

19. Donald Worster, "New West, True West: Interpreting the Region's History," *Western Historical Quarterly* 18 (April 1987):141–56.

20. Walter Prescott Webb, *The Great Frontier* (Boston: Houghton Mifflin Company, 1952).

21. Webb, "Autobiography," 20, 50.

22. Reviews in *American Historical Review* 58 (July 1953):963, and *The Nation*, January 10, 1953, 34.

23. Webb, *Great Frontier*, 29.

24. David M. Potter, *People of Plenty: Economic Abundance and the American Character* (Chicago: University of Chicago Press, 1954), 160–65; Jacques Barzun, "Walter Prescott Webb and the Fate of History," in *Essays on Walter Prescott Webb and the Teaching of History* (College Station: Texas A&M University Press, 1985), 23.

25. Webb, *Great Frontier*, 13.

26. Immanuel Wallerstein, *The Modern World System: Capitalist Agriculture and the Origins of the European World-Economy in the Sixteenth Century* (New York: Academic Press, 1974).

27. William H. McNeill, *The Great Frontier: Freedom and Hierarchy in Modern Times* (Princeton, N.J.: Princeton University Press, 1983).

28. Ray A. Billington, "Frederick Jackson Turner and Walter Prescott Webb: Frontier Historians," in Harold M. Hollingsworth and Sandra Myres, eds., *Essays on the American West* (Austin: University of Texas Press, 1969), 114.

29. Worster, "New West, True West," 146.

BIBLIOGRAPHY

WESTERN WRITINGS OF WALTER PRESCOTT WEBB

"The American Revolvers and the West." *Scribner's Magazine* 81 (February 1927): 171–78.

"The American West: Perpetual Mirage." *Harper's Magazine* 214 (May 1957): 25–31.

Divided We Stand: The Crisis of a Frontierless Democracy. New York: Farrar and Rinehart, 1937.

"Geographical–Historical Concepts in American History." *Annals of the Association of American Geographers* 50 (June 1960):85–93.

The Great Frontier. Boston: Houghton Mifflin Company, 1952.

The Great Plains. Boston: Ginn and Company, 1931.

The Handbook of Texas. ed. 3 vols. Austin: Texas State Historical Association, 1952–1976.

An Honest Preface and Other Essays. Boston: Houghton Mifflin Company, 1959.

"Search for William E. Hinds." *Harper's Magazine* 223 (July 1961):62–69.

The Texas Rangers: A Century of Frontier Defense. Boston: Houghton Mifflin Company, 1935.

"The West and the Desert." *Montana: The Magazine of Western History* 9 (January 1958):2–12.

WORKS ABOUT WALTER PRESCOTT WEBB

Billington, Ray A. "Frederick Jackson Turner and Walter Prescott Webb: Frontier Historians." In Harold M. Hollingsworth and Sandra Myres, eds., *Essays on the American West.* Austin: University of Texas Press, 1969, 89–114.

Dugger, Ronnie, ed. *Three Men in Texas: Bedichek, Webb and Dobie: Essays by Their Friends in the Texas Observer.* Austin: University of Texas Press, 1967.

Friend, Llerena. "Walter Prescott Webb and Book Reviewing." *Western Historical Quarterly* 4 (October 1973):381–404.

Furman, Necah Stewart. *Walter Prescott Webb: His Life and Impact.* Albuquerque: University of New Mexico Press, 1976.

Jacobs, Wilbur R., John W. Caughey, and Joe B. Frantz. *Turner, Bolton and Webb: Three Historians of the American Frontier.* Seattle: University of Washington Press, 1965.

Luebke, Frederick C. "Regionalism and the Great Plains: Problems of Concept and Method." *Western Historical Quarterly* 15 (January 1984):19–38.

McMurtry, Larry. *In a Narrow Grave: Essays on Texas.* Austin: Encino Press, 1968.

McNeill, William H. *The Great Frontier: Freedom and Hierarchy in Modern Times.* Princeton, N.J.: Princeton University Press, 1983.

Morris, Margaret F. "Walter Prescott Webb, 1888–1963, A Bibliography." In William F. Holmes and Harold M. Hollingsworth, eds., *Essays on the American Civil War,* Austin: University of Texas Press, 1968.

Owens, William A. *Three Friends: Roy Bedichek, J. Frank Dobie and Walter Prescott Webb.* Garden City: Doubleday and Co., 1969.

Philp, Kenneth R., and Elliott West, eds. *Essays on Walter Prescott Webb.* Austin: University of Texas Press, 1976.

Reinhartz, Dennis and Stephen E. Maizlish, eds. *Essays on Walter Prescott*

Webb and the Teaching of History. College Station: Texas A&M University Press, 1985.

Rundell, Walter Jr. "Walter Prescott Webb and the Texas State Historical Association." *Arizona and the West* 25 (Summer 1983):109–36.

———. "Walter Prescott Webb as Businessman." *Great Plains Journal* 18 (1979): 130–39.

———. "Walter Prescott Webb: Product of Environment." *Arizona and the West* 5 (Spring 1963):4–28.

———. "W. P. Webb's *Divided We Stand:* A Publishing Crisis." *Western Historical Quarterly* 13 (October 1982):391–407.

Tobin, Gregory M. *The Making of a History: Walter Prescott Webb and "The Great Plains."* Austin: University of Texas Press, 1976.

———. "Walter Prescott Webb." In John R. Wunder, ed., *Historians of the American Frontier: A Bio-Bibliographical Sourcebook.* New York and Westport: Greenwood Press, 1988, 713–28.

Worster, Donald. "New West, True West: Interpreting the Region's History. *Western Historical Quarterly* 18 (April 1987):141–56.

7

Herbert Eugene Bolton:
The Making of a Western Historian

DONALD E. WORCESTER

*B*ORN ON A FARM IN RURAL
Monroe County, Wisconsin, on July 20, 1870, Herbert Eugene Bolton
did not appear destined for a prominent place among American scholars. He was quick to learn, inquisitive, and determined to excel, but
his educational opportunities were exceedingly limited. His parents,
although largely self-taught, encouraged their children to do their best
in the little country schools. Herbert's father knew that his tall, blond
son ("my Norwegian") would be successful at something, but he could
not predict what it might be.

After his father's death in 1885, Herbert supported himself by odd
jobs while attending high school in Tomah. Upon graduation, he and
his brother Frederick, four years his senior, took turns teaching or serving as high school principals to help each other through the two-year
Milwaukee Normal School and the University of Wisconsin. "For over
a dozen years there was no time when either he or I was not in debt to
the other," Frederick recalled.[1]

Herbert's studies at the University of Wisconsin under Frederick
Jackson Turner and Charles Homer Haskins helped him decide to
become a historian. Turner's pioneer work in American history especially intrigued him, for he had the good fortune to arrive at the University of Wisconsin shortly after Turner had delivered his epochal
paper, "The Significance of the Frontier in American History," at the
1893 American Historical Association convention in Chicago.

After graduating in 1895, Bolton married Gertrude Janes and served a year as high school principal to earn money for graduate school. He avidly read American history to prepare for his M.A. work. The next year he entered graduate school at Wisconsin and served as Turner's part-time assistant. When he received the M.A., Bolton, now with a family to support, found no fellowships available for history students at Wisconsin. On Turner's recommendation he was granted the six-hundred-dollar Harrison Fellowship at the University of Pennsylvania, where in two years he earned a Ph.D. in American history under John Bach McMaster. His 1899 dissertation was "The Free Negro in the South before the Civil War."

The writing of history in that period was greatly influenced by scholars trained in Germany, among them Herbert Baxter Adams. He had introduced the seminar method of instruction at the Johns Hopkins University, where many of the historians in the major universities earned their degrees. In seminars at Wisconsin and Pennsylvania, Bolton was grounded in a critical historical methodology similar to that taught in European universities.

Bolton's attitude toward and view of America's past would have to undergo an enormous change before he could develop a sympathetic understanding of other cultures. As he explained, "My early environment and outlook were typically Yankee 'American,' that is to say, provincial, nationalistic." His unquestioned historical beliefs included the following: "The Americans licked England; they licked the Indians; all good Indians were dead; the English came to America to build homes, the Spaniards merely explored and hunted gold; Spain failed in the New World; the English always succeeded," and so forth. "Every one of these concepts is false in whole or in part, but it took half a lifetime to discover it."[2]

History departments were small and openings were few, so Bolton taught various subjects at Milwaukee Normal School for one thousand dollars a year while awaiting an opportunity to join a history department. That came in 1901, when he accepted a one-year appointment at fifteen hundred dollars to teach medieval and European history at the University of Texas in place of Lester G. Bugbee, who was ill. This was a crucial move to the right place at the right time, although that was not immediately apparent. Texans, Bolton observed, are interested in the history of their own state and the Holy Land, but not much else.[3] Bugbee never returned to teaching, and Bolton stayed on in his place.

Although his work under Haskins at Wisconsin and Edward Potts Cheyney at Pennsylvania had prepared Bolton for teaching the history of the Middle Ages and of Europe, his real interest remained American history. But at the University of Texas that field was the exclusive domain of departmental chairman George P. Garrison, while a young colleague, Eugene C. Barker, was becoming the authority on Stephen F. Austin and the Texas Republic. It appeared that Bolton was trapped in European history.

Early in January 1902, however, he wrote his brother that he was scheduled to teach a course "that will bring me into American history—'European Expansion, commercial and colonial activities of the sixteenth and seventeenth centuries'—I think that in time I shall be able to block out a field of *my own* here."[4] He would make it a course on the Spaniards in America. This was his first step in the direction of his future work, but at the time he saw the Spaniards merely as an opportunity to edge into the periphery of American history.

No one in the department was interested in research on Spanish Texas, but in 1900 Garrison had visited the archives in Mexico City and Saltillo, where he had begun a program for collecting transcripts of Spanish documents that concerned the state of Texas. He had also written two articles, "The Archivo General de México" and "Some Southwestern History in the Southwest," about the San Antonio archives.[5] Although Bolton had read Prescott's *Conquest of Mexico*, it was undoubtedly these articles as well as conversations with Garrison that first aroused his interest in the Mexican archives; his new course would take him into the early period of Spanish American history.[6]

Later, in January 1902, Bolton wrote Frederick that "Texas has the key to Spanish American history. I am grubbing Spanish, so that I may be able to turn the lock. My new course is a triumph for me, for it is Garrison's permission to tramp on his ground."[7] In July he added that he wanted "to get into the heart of Spanish civilization and the mine of sources that lie in Mexico."[8] His future was taking shape. Six weeks in Mexico at the end of the summer session helped confirm the direction that his career would take. At the time he apparently was thinking only of Spanish Texas.

On Sundays, when the archives were closed, Bolton spent some time following Cortés's route to the Aztec capital. Later, he would always try to cover the same ground as the men he wrote about, to see firsthand the country they had described, a process that became a unique feature of Bolton's work.

Back in Austin, he wrote Frederick that his trip had been successful. "It will keep me in powder for shooting off historical fireworks for most of the year. I shall get one or two articles in the October publications."[9] Eager to make the archival treasures known to other scholars, he wrote the first part of "Some Materials for Southwestern History in the Archivo General de México," which appeared in the October issue of the Texas State Historical Association *Quarterly*. Although he focused on Texas, he also noted the vast amount of material he had seen on Nuevo México.

"The above sketch is, of necessity, incomplete," he stated, "and aims . . . to be illustrative rather than exhaustive. But it may serve to indicate the nature of some of the apparently considerable material on Southwestern history, in the volumes examined, still largely unused." This article attracted much favorable comment. "I opened up a relatively unexplored field here. I hope to exploit part of it myself," he wrote to his brother.[10] In the summer of 1903 Bolton returned to Mexico City, and in January 1904 the second part of his article appeared in the *Quarterly*.

Those first summers in Mexico City opened for Bolton a new and continually expanding horizon. The wealth of materials that Spanish explorers, conquerors, civil and military officials, and missionaries had left for posterity astonished him. They offered an unrivaled opportunity to develop a significant but neglected aspect of American history, although at first his interests remained limited to Texas.[11]

In another fortunate development for Bolton, the Carnegie Institution began supporting the preparation of a series of guides to materials pertinent to the United States in foreign archives. This far-sighted program would make an enormous contribution to the development of historical scholarship in the United States; it also gave Bolton an opportunity that his ability and capacity for hard work enabled him to exploit. Historian J. Franklin Jameson had been named general editor of the series, and he selected the men to produce the guides.

On January 4, 1906, Jameson wrote to Bolton, "As I am writing to Dr. Garrison, I have concluded to ask you to undertake for us the important task of making a comprehensive guide to materials for the United States which may be found in the Mexican archives." He asked about expenses and when Bolton could come to Washington to discuss the project.[12] Garrison was delighted at this recognition of his department, but since Barker was to be on leave to complete his doctoral work, Bolton could not begin his survey until 1907–1908. Bolton was naturally elated at this extraordinary opportunity for a fledgling scholar. "Things have opened up for me since I last wrote you," he informed Frederick in April.

After spending the summer of 1906 in Mexico, Bolton visited Jameson in December. He found himself in select company, for the others in the program were all established scholars.[13] He and Jameson agreed on funding and on his plans for the survey of archives.

Leaving Austin for Mexico on June 20, 1907, Bolton embarked on the great enterprise that would last for fifteen months and establish his reputation. His wife and five daughters joined him in Mexico City. Although he hired assistants to help with the cataloging and making of transcripts, he realized that he needed to examine each item personally. The listings were incomplete or inaccurate, and he found only one printed list or catalog. He often discovered significant items of which archivists had been unaware. He had learned, he wrote to Frederick, not to place confidence in reports of rich holdings; "neither do I pay any attention as a rule, to archive keepers and other officials when they tell me that they have nothing. I humor them by saying, 'Of course not, but I'd like to look around a little' and generally find what I expect to find."[14] In March he mentioned that Turner had advised the University of California to look him up as one who might help them "develop their field there."[15]

Bolton sent in monthly progress reports. In April 1908 Jameson wrote to him to express his gratitude and admiration: "Your Guide is more likely than any other so far constructed to give a great impulse to historical production in the United States."[16] His prediction proved to be correct.

At the Archivo General de la Secretaría de Relaciones, Bolton made one of his most important early discoveries, the papers taken from Zebulon M. Pike in 1807 when he was arrested for entering Spanish territory illegally. Jameson asked Bolton to make copies for publication. The appearance of these papers in the *American Historical Review* in July 1908 aroused a new interest in Pike and also made Bolton's name better known.

The publication of his preliminary report, "Materials for Southwestern History in the Central Archives of Mexico," in the April 1908 issue of the *AHR*, had already established Bolton as the leading authority on the archives of Mexico. He had read the paper at the December 1907 American Historical Association meeting in Madison, where it attracted much favorable attention. The University of Texas also appreciated his work and, while he was still on leave, promoted him to associate professor with a base salary of twenty-four hundred dollars. His courses, however, were still those he had inherited from Bugbee.

In July 1908 Bolton began visiting provincial archives, the final part of his project. That month he received a telegram from Stanford University offering him a one-year appointment as associate professor. He replied that he would consider only a permanent appointment, and believed the matter was closed.

While Bolton was still in Mexico, publisher Arthur H. Clark approached him about preparing ten volumes of documents on American history from the Spanish and Mexican archives. He wanted to begin the series in January 1910 and to continue it at the rate of one volume a month. Bolton, confident of his ability to do more than was humanly possible, agreed to translate and edit the series. He went even further, signing contracts with Clark for preparation of the many documents concerning Athanase de Mézières and the "Favores Celestiales" of Padre Eusebio Francisco Kino. Mézières had served both France and Spain in Louisiana and Texas. The "Favores Celestiales," Kino's history, had long been believed lost until Bolton found it. Bolton's enthusiasm and eagerness to produce would lead to unconcealed disappointment for several editors and publishers when he found it impossible to meet deadlines.

After surveying the Saltillo archives, Bolton returned in October to Austin to put his enormous collection of cards and notes in shape for publication, expecting to complete the task in a few months. It was not until mid-September 1910, however, after he had left Austin, that Bolton finally sent off the bulky manuscript. Three more years passed before the *Guide to Materials for the History of the United States in the Principal Archives of Mexico* appeared in print. It was his most important work, well worth all the time, effort, and delay, for its impact on future American historical writings was exceptional. His students would call it "Bolton's Bible."

The archival surveys had made Bolton keenly aware of the magnitude of Spain's activities and accomplishments in North America, and through articles and translations of documents he set out to inform Texans about their long-ignored Spanish past. Thereafter, too, he took great pleasure in shattering the popular stereotypes of Spaniards that he had once taken for granted.

Spanish documents also aroused Bolton's interest in Indians. Spanish policy, he discovered, was largely Indian policy, and the writings of missionaries and colonial officials were replete with descriptions of Indians, their customs, and their multitude of languages and dialects. Many of the tribes described, such as the Jumanos of Texas, had disappeared by the mid-nineteenth century.

About the time that Bolton's articles began appearing regularly, the Bureau of American Ethnology of the Smithsonian Institution initiated a project for preparing *The Handbook of Indians North of Mexico* under the editorship of Frederick Webb Hodge. Early in January 1906 Bolton had written to the Bureau offering his services. Bureau chief W. H. Holmes asked him to join his editorial staff, and although much involved with his other projects, Bolton contributed upwards of one hundred articles on Texas Indians to the *Handbook*. According to anthropologist Alfred L. Kroeber, concerning Indians of the Southwest, "He succeeded in putting on record more data than the total which anthropologists had had available to them previously."

Other scholars, such as Frederick W. Hodge and John R. Swanton, gratefully acknowledged his generous assistance in obtaining information on Texas tribes. He had, Hodge wrote, "made students of the Indians of the Southwest his debtors to an extent only they can appreciate."[17]

Holmes proposed that Bolton also write a monograph on Texas Indians, which he began. He soon realized, however, that he could not manage a task of such magnitude without abandoning his many other projects. He did write a manuscript on the Hasinai, his favorites, but he refused to allow it to be published, except in part.[18]

Although he had as yet published only articles, by 1908 Bolton's name was already well known outside Texas. Shortly before his return to Austin from his guide survey, a long letter from E. D. Adams, history chairman at Stanford, caught up with him in Saltillo. Adams had been in Europe when the earlier offer was made. Had he been present, he wrote, "I would not have thought of proposing to a man in your position and of your reputation a temporary appointment." He wanted to hear from Bolton concerning his interests.

His work under Turner and McMaster, Bolton replied, had oriented him toward western and socioeconomic history, and his research had focused on Texas. After his work in the Mexican archives he had broadened his perspectives to include New Mexico, Arizona, and California. He preferred to teach undergraduate courses on the West, Spanish Southwest, and U.S. social-economic history. At the graduate level he wanted seminars on the Spanish Southwest and the Anglo-American West.

After more correspondence, Stanford raised its offer to full professor at thirty-five hundred dollars. Texas countered by offering three thousand dollars and five hundred dollars for archival transcripts. It was a difficult decision; except for his courses, Bolton was happy in Austin. He finally decided to move, "but I shall look forward, not back, and try to make good there, as I managed to do here," he wrote to his brother.[19] In the summer of 1909 he left Austin for Palo Alto. He was thirty-nine years old and had been teaching at the university level for eight years, but this was his first opportunity to teach American history. In January, however, he wrote Frederick that he had lost a solid year of research and was no better off otherwise than he would have been at Texas.

In July 1910 Dr. Garrison died, and Texas offered the chairmanship to Bolton, who again faced a difficult decision. He missed Texas, and now he would be able to teach courses there that were of his own choosing. He also received many letters from Texans urging him to return "to the state where I belong." While Bolton seriously considered the offer, Stanford took steps to induce him to remain.

His predicament became more complicated yet more easily solved in early August when he was invited to have lunch at the University of California Faculty Club with Henry Morse Stephens, chairman of the history department. The enterprising Stephens had concluded earlier that American history needed a new emphasis at Berkeley and that Turner could best provide it. He had offered him a position, but Turner was already committed to Harvard. Perhaps recalling Turner's advice to keep an eye on Bolton, and aware that he was likely to return to Texas, Stephens invited him to lunch. "If we cannot have Turner," he wrote, "let us have Turner's most promising pupil. With Turner lost, I know of no one whom I would rather have by my side as my special colleague to handle American history than yourself."

The Texas invitation was tempting, but California had more to offer than the professorship at four thousand dollars. In 1905 the university had acquired Hubert Howe Bancroft's rich collection of books, manuscripts, and other research materials on Mexico and the West, which Bolton had used more than once. In writing to Frederick about the offer, he stated that "the great Bancroft Collection, the greatest in my field, is there."[20] The move to Berkeley in August 1911 finally placed him in the perfect position to utilize his unusual ability and prodigious energy to the fullest. In a sense, he had just crossed the threshold to his career.

By this time Bolton had fully determined his role as historian. He had become convinced that history can be best observed and understood by reaching beyond the confines of a single nation. "I am an

American historian," he said by way of introducing one of his speeches, "and therefore I do my research in foreign archives."[21] His West was New Spain's North; his arena, the whole Western Hemisphere. His students might write on topics ranging from the Yukon to Tierra del Fuego. As a result, his influence on Latin American history in its formative years equaled his impact on western history.

All of his major works were published after he was at Berkeley, although several had been started earlier and the *Guide* had been completed in Palo Alto. He had been in Berkeley only a few months when he wrote President Benjamin Ide Wheeler a memorandum on the need to publish a comprehensive body of documents relating to the history of Spanish activities within the present limits of the United States. In it, he outlined much of his future work and that of many of his students.

"For nearly three centuries the Southwestern half of the present United States constituted a portion of the Spanish possessions of North America," he began. From 1762 to 1800, furthermore, Spain had possessed the whole trans-Mississippi West, with posts and fur traders as far north as Nootka Sound, the upper Missouri River, and southern Minnesota. These Spanish possessions were an object of utmost interest in world politics and on them turned some of the principal diplomatic contests of the period. They also had an internal history distinct from that of the United States. That history embraced Spanish exploration and conquest; missions, presidios, pueblos, mines, and ranches; Anglo-American trappers, explorers, contraband traders, and filibusters into the Spanish domain; independence from Spain and development under Mexico; and finally, Anglo-American settlement, diplomacy, and conquest. "It is needless to state that his long period of Spanish occupation and the half century of conflict between the Spanish and Anglo-American frontiers constitute a most important portion of American history, or that the subsequent development of the West—the portion of the Spanish dominions with which we are most concerned—cannot be properly interpreted without first devoting to their antecedents a complete and thorough study."

He went on to say that the importance of the Spanish period in American history had never been properly recognized. Much more was known of French than of Spanish activities in North America, leading to the erroneous conclusion that French influence was the more important of the two. "Spanish exploration, missionary work, industrial development, and settlement in North America at all times far exceeded that of France," even in the area that was to become the United States.

"But this fact is not generally known, for the reason that France in America had a Parkman while Spain in America had none."

Another reason for the neglect of the Spanish period and of the West in general, he continued, was that until recently the history of the United States had been written solely from the standpoint of the East and the English colonies. Turner had lately directed attention to the West, "but his West is a moving area which began east of the Appalachians and has not thus far reached the Mississippi Valley. The lead in this field of investigation must be taken by us here in the West, and it is on this field that the history department of the University of California is concentrating its efforts."

Bolton pointed out that developing the field depended on adding to the body of materials already available. The archives of Mexico and Spain contained a wealth of sources for early western and southwestern history never before utilized or even known by scholars. He cited a number of examples from his three-thousand card references to documents about California in the archives of Mexico, some of the cards representing whole volumes of manuscripts. "I think no more need be said . . . to demonstrate the existence of a world of unused material, or to show that the early history of the Southwest and West is yet to be written."

To be useful, Bolton added, these materials had first to be gathered and published, for as long as they existed only in foreign archives, few scholars could utilize them. Even if transcripts were made, their availability would still be limited. "The only way to make them properly available, therefore, is to publish them." He proposed publishing twenty-five volumes of documents, if funds could be obtained. "I have suggested for the collection the title 'Spain in the United States,' but even under that title I should favor putting emphasis on Spanish activities in the West and the contiguous Southwest. Nevertheless, Western history is interwoven with that of the whole country, and it must not be studied narrowly if the best results are to be secured."[22]

In a letter to Turner in June 1914, Bolton explained why his works and those of his students were so detailed. The details would disappear in the writing of the general history, he said, but he realized that in a new field that was foreign to most American students, the exact setting was needed along with the general results, so that later generalizations would have meaning. "As I see it, until the field is covered by monographs of this kind, we shall have no basis for a clear understanding of the work of the Spaniards in the American West. This helps to explain the dreariness of most of what I have written."[23] It also explains why Bolton concentrated on making available the raw materials rather than writing syntheses and generalizations that necessarily would have been based on insufficient evidence.

After leaving Austin, Bolton began directing some of his research toward Spanish California, but his earlier interest led to more articles and several books on Spanish Texas. The *Guide*, which he had completed in 1910, finally appeared in 1913; if Bolton had produced nothing else, it alone would keep his name alive.

In a 1917 letter to his friend William E. Dodd of the University of Chicago, Bolton explained his goal. "Since you mention Parkman you may be interested to know that I am planning to 'Parkmanize' the history of the Spanish Southwest. I have been gathering materials and writing painful monographs for a long while, but one of my aims is to present the story of the Spanish advance into the Southwest in a series of scholarly but graphic sketches, much as Parkman wrote for the history of the French in North America. The subject is much larger and the materials richer than he had, and with a pen equal to his one could win immortal fame, and at the same time make money for his publishers."

He went on to list the volumes he planned to write, but the project was too vast for one man, even one with Bolton's energy and ability. A number of the topics were, therefore, pursued by his students with his blessing.[24]

Just as he learned Spanish in order to translate documents, Bolton mastered whatever skill he needed for his work. To understand thoroughly the subject he was writing about, he became explorer, cartographer, geographer, and ethnohistorian. His Berkeley workday began when he reached his office at eight o'clock each morning. At six he went home for dinner and a brief chat with Mrs. Bolton, then returned to his office and worked until midnight. Despite his busy schedule and numerous projects, he always found time for graduate students needing help or encouragement.[25]

Because preparing the *Guide* for publication had taken about two years longer than expected, Bolton had made little progress on any of the projects for Clark. By 1910 Clark had ceased even mentioning the documentary series and prodded Bolton only for the Mézières work, but he did not receive the fourteen-hundred-page manuscript until early in 1913, three years late. Bolton was also painfully slow in returning the galley proofs, and he made substantial and costly changes in them. His perfectionism was of little comfort to Clark, who saw his losses rising steadily. Bolton suggested that the Mézières volumes could be the first two in a series entitled "Spain in the West." The Kino materials would form the third and fourth volumes, and Morfi's history of Texas, the fifth.

The Mézières volumes appeared in 1914, to great praise from the reviewers, especially for Bolton's long "Historical Introduction." Sales soon fell off, however, as the nation turned its attention to the war in Europe. Clark warned Bolton that the Kino volumes might have to be delayed, so Bolton arranged for joint publication with the University of California Semi-Centennial Committee and promised the manuscript by the end of the summer of 1916, but because of other commitments, he missed the deadline.

One of these other commitments was preparing a paper for the prestigious Faculty Lecture Series, to be delivered on March 31, 1917. The paper was not one he could dash off in a hurry, for, as he wrote Frederick, being invited to lecture in the series was "equivalent to an honorary L.L.D."[26] His paper, "The Mission as a Frontier Institution in the Spanish Colonies," became a classic. In it he pointed out how the Spaniards, "with a handful of men," took possession of more than half of two continents. Spain's culture, language, laws, and religion still predominated in the regions once occupied. "These results are an index of the vigor and virility of Spain's frontier forces; they should give pause to those who glibly speak of Spain's failure as a colonizing nation, and they suggest the importance of a thoughtful study of Spain's frontier institutions and methods."[27]

Another commitment had been made when, in the fall of 1916, he learned that Yale University Press had launched the "Chronicles of the Americas" series with Allen Johnson of Yale as general editor. These were to be popularly written books by top scholars. Bolton was disturbed by the fact that only two in the proposed series promised to touch on the Spaniards and their contributions to American history. That impelled him to write to Johnson, proposing a volume on Spain in the Southwest. Johnson accepted and set June 1917 as the deadline. Bolton got to work on it immediately, further delaying the Kino manuscript. In 1916, moreover, he was named curator of the Bancroft Library.

Even before moving to Berkeley, Bolton wanted to accomplish so many things at once that he had committed himself to more projects than he could possibly manage. Failure to meet deadlines got him into some rather heated exchanges with editors. In June 1917 he finally sent the Kino manuscript off to Clark and then turned to the one for Johnson. He could not have been delighted when the first of the Kino galley proofs reached him in August. Despite Clark's frantic pleas, Bolton did not return the galleys until January 1918. One reason for the delay was that the perfectionist Bolton had again made many changes; he did the same to the page proofs, which considerably increased the cost of printing. The two volumes finally appeared in 1919; Clark lost money on Kino as well as Mézières, and that ended the series the two men had agreed on. Morfi's history would have to wait for another scholar to translate it.

Bolton was nearly six months late with the manuscript for John son, although he had been hard at work the whole time. Someone involved in the series suggested "The Spanish Borderlands" as a subtitle. Bolton liked that suggestion so much it became the main title, but all was not smooth sailing. Johnson found the manuscript much too detailed for a popularly written series and wanted it completely rewritten; at the same time, Clark was pressing Bolton for the galleys of the Kino volumes. Discouraged as well as overextended, Bolton finally returned the Yale volume completely rewritten in late March 1919. Johnson was still not satisfied—it contained piles of building materials but no building, he said. He suggested having an author of literary distinction rewrite it.

Bolton was naturally crushed and humiliated, but he submitted to the embarrassing process. He went over the suggested changes, corrected mistakes, restored key passages that had been deleted, and returned the manuscript in October 1920. *The Spanish Borderlands: A Chronicle of Old Florida and the Southwest* (1921) was one of the most costly in the series but also one of the best. Of all Bolton's books and articles, none reached as many readers or better linked his name with the Borderlands. As a result of the experience, Bolton rewrote and polished his manuscripts to good effect thereafter.

Adding to Bolton's distractions and responsibilities was the sudden death of Henry Morse Stephens on April 16, 1919. Bolton took over as chairman, an office he held until he retired. He also had to devise a course to replace Stephens's popular freshman course on Europe, History 1. The result was two courses: History 4, a European survey, and History 8, the History of the Americas, which Bolton would teach. He expected only a few students and was shocked when more than seven hundred enrolled. Thereafter, History 8 attracted between eight hundred and a thousand students every semester. His responsibilities increased again in 1920 when he became director of the Bancroft Library.

In the fall of 1922 Bolton received an accolade from a Frenchman named Pasquet, who wrote that Bolton was among the few men who had done the best work in rescuing American history from the rut of tradition. "You have proved conclusively that there is something else to be said on the topic of American colonization besides Plymouth Rock, Pocahontas, and other time-honored stories."[28]

Texas had not forgotten Bolton, nor had Bolton forgotten Texas. In 1924, when the presidency of the University of Texas was vacant, the faculty and many others wanted Bolton to fill the post. He finally declined the offer, but agreed to meet with the Regents in Austin to present his views on what was needed to make Texas a great university.

Back in Berkeley, Bolton's work was greatly aided by generous financial support from San Francisco attorney Sidney M. Ehrman, who in 1926 subsidized publication of the four-volume *Historical Memoirs of New California by Fray Francisco Palou, O.F.M.* Over the years Ehrman's contributions amounted to nearly fifty thousand dollars. Although he was primarily interested in California history, Ehrman also underwrote publication of *Arredondo's Historical Proof of Spain's Title to Georgia* (1925), so that Bolton could get on with his California studies.

Excellent maps had become a feature of Bolton's works. For the Palou volumes he also wrote a comprehensive book-length historical introduction. Because he felt that the cost of the four volumes of documents would be too much for most scholars, he advised the University of California Press to publish the introduction separately. It accepted the idea, and *Palou and His Writings* (1926) proved to be a success. His volume on Crespi followed in 1927.[29]

In 1929 the historians of the Anglo-American West held a conference at the University of Colorado to exchange ideas and information on their particular areas of interest and invited Bolton to give one of the major addresses. His paper was "Defensive Spanish Expansion and the Significance of the Borderlands." In it, he stressed the importance of the area as a point of contact between the Anglo and Latin civilizations. He also pointed out the universal defensive character of border regions.[30]

When working on *Anza's California Expeditions*, Bolton had the first real opportunity to combine fieldwork with the editing of documents and the writing of biography. He retraced Anza's trail from southern Arizona to San Francisco. He would employ this technique with great success in his later studies—especially the biographies of Kino, Coronado, and Escalante. It became, in fact, a Bolton hallmark.

The fifth and last of the Anza volumes appeared in 1930, followed in 1931 by *Font's Complete Diary: A Chronicle of the Founding of San Francisco*. In the same year, *Outpost of Empire: The Story of the Founding of San Francisco* was published by Alfred A. Knopf. The introduction to the Anza volumes, it completed Bolton's California series.

Always pressed for money, Bolton had never been able to gratify his ambition to visit Europe. The Native Sons of the Golden West, who annually gave two fellowships to graduate students for research in Europe, combined the two and made Bolton their fellow for 1931–32. The three-thousand-dollar grant enabled him to spend four months in Europe, where he visited the archives and libraries in Spain, Italy, and Holland, making lists of items to be copied later. He was also ready to undertake his long-delayed biography of the famous Jesuit pioneer, Father Kino—a mere dozen years after the publication of his translation of Kino's history. After stopping in Rome, he traveled to Segno in the Tyrol, Kino's birthplace, then visited Bavaria, where his favorite Black Robe had received his Jesuit training. Upon his return to Berkeley, friends soon provided funds for copying the documents he had selected for the Bancroft Library.

Before leaving for Europe, Bolton was elected vice president of the American Historical Association, which meant that he would automatically become president the next year. His presidential address at the 1932 convention in Toronto was "The Epic of Greater America." It was a summary of his History of the Americas course and stressed the need for a broader treatment of American history to supplement the customary nationalistic histories. Each local story would have a clearer meaning when studied in the light of others, he said. Historians may have agreed, but none attempted to write a history of the Western Hemisphere.

At the meeting, the University of Toronto gave Bolton one of the eight honorary degrees he would receive, and his former students presented him with a two-volume festschrift, *New Spain and the Anglo-American West*. His students' tribute delighted him even more than the honorary degree.

Despite his many responsibilities and his busy schedule, Bolton found time to spend several months in Kino's country, Sonora and Arizona, having already visited his birthplace. By mid-1935 the manuscript was ready for the publisher. "I literally followed his footsteps from the cradle to the grave," Bolton said.[31] In July 1936 Macmillan brought it out as the *Rim of Christendom*.

In February 1937 Bolton received a telephone call from a Beryle Shinn, who described a metal plate he had found the previous summer in the hills of Marin County across the bay. The plate, he said, had writing on it, but the only word he could make out was "Drake." Bolton often had told students to be on the lookout for the plate Sir Francis Drake had nailed to a tree on his voyage around the world. Now Shinn brought the Drake plate to his office. Although tests proved the plate to be authentic to the satisfaction of most, doubters remained.

The National Park Service called on Bolton a number of times to join its regional surveys, such as those of the Colorado River basin and the Big Bend country of Texas. On these and similar occasions, Bolton was able to follow parts of the Coronado and Escalante trails.

Another opportunity to travel came in December 1938, when Bolton represented the university at the Seventh Pan American Conference in Lima. He made the most of the opportunity, crossing the Andes to visit Cuzco and La Paz, Bolivia. Then he went to Chile as one of the U.S. delegates to the Conference on Cultural Cooperation. Afterward he flew to Buenos Aires, then visited Montevideo, Uruguay, and Ascunción, Paraguay. In Brazil he stopped at São Paulo, Rio de Janeiro, and Recife before flying on to Caracas, Venezuela. His two-months journey fulfilled a long-standing dream; it came just before mandatory retirement at seventy and what was expected to be his last year of teaching.

During World War II, Bolton's student and chosen successor, Lawrence Kinnaird, was called on by the State Department for a mission in Chile. In 1941 Bolton had returned from retirement to take charge of the Bancroft Library when its director, Herbert I. Priestley, suffered a stroke; then he was asked to teach in place of Kinnaird. When Bolton retired again in March 1944, departmental chairman Frederic Logan Paxson requested information to be used in his annual chairman's report. Bolton supplied it. "Before closing," he added, "I wish to tell you how greatly I have appreciated the opportunity to return to teaching, which has always been my favorite sport."[32]

After his second retirement, Bolton was finally able to get back to work on the Coronado volume that George P. Hammond had requested in 1939 for the University of New Mexico's Coronado Cuarto Centennial Publications. He had worked on the biography intermittently, and over the years he had covered the explorer's trail. Dr. Agapito Rey occasionally sent him new Coronado materials, and he took the time to incorporate them. Although Hammond and Bolton both understood he was writing the book for the Coronado Cuarto Centennial series, no contract had been signed.

About the time that Bolton completed the manuscript, which he re-wrote and polished a number of times, the Whittlesey House division of the McGraw-Hill Book Company announced a Southwestern Fellow-ship Award of one thousand dollars for the best manuscript on the area. Joseph Henry Jackson, long-time reviewer for the San Francisco *Chroni-cle*, informed Bolton of the award and also wrote Whittlesey House editor William E. Larned about Bolton's work on Coronado. Larned immediately offered Bolton a twenty-five-hundred-dollar advance against future royalties and expressed hope that his manuscript might also win the award.

Never one to concern himself with money matters, Bolton had been forced to teach two courses at San Francisco State College to supple-ment his insufficient retirement pay. His previous writings had brought recognition, not money. As one of his daughters quipped: "But money to him was only a game; he brought up his family on honor and fame."[33] As a result, the McGraw-Hill offer tempted him beyond his capacity to resist. He sent off the manuscript to Whittlesey House in August 1947.

Hammond, a former Bolton student and now director of the Ban-croft Library, was in a difficult situation, but after some exchanges between Fred E. Harvey of the University of New Mexico Press, Larned, and Bolton, a compromise solution was reached. The New Mexico press took over the McGraw-Hill contract and in 1949 published Coronado on the Turquoise Trail as the first volume of its long-delayed Cuarto Centennial series. McGraw-Hill took the University of New Mexico Press printings, gave the volume the Whittlesey House joint imprint, and assumed responsibility for national distribution. Its edition appeared as *Coronado: Knight of Pueblos and Plains.*

The Coronado volume did well for Bolton. In addition to winning the Whittlesey House Southwestern Award and receiving reviews that praised both its scholarship and readability, it was chosen as the His-tory Book Club selection for January 1950. It also won the coveted George Bancroft Prize for the outstanding book in American history that year.

In mid-1949 Joel E. Ricks of Utah State University and president of the Utah Historical Society wrote to Bolton to declare that Utah people were eager to see a book on Fray Silvestre Vélez de Escalante. In 1776 the young priest and others had tried to open a trail from Santa Fe to Monterey and had traveled over much of Utah. Bolton had followed parts of the trail in 1926, when he taught a summer session at the Uni-versity of Utah, and he had covered the rest of it later. The historical society offered twenty-five hundred dollars for translating Escalante's diary. Bolton delivered the diary in December 1950 and his historical introduction to it early in 1951. In July, *Pageant in the Wilderness: The Story of the Escalante Expedition to the Interior Basin, Including the Diary and the Itinerary of Father Escalante* was in his hands. It was his last book, completed shortly before his eighty-first birthday. In June 1952, while at work in his office, he suffered the first of a series of disabling strokes. He died on January 30, 1953.

The contributions of Herbert Eugene Bolton to western history were many and varied, and in most cases unrivaled. After three-quarters of a century, his *Guide* is still invaluable to researchers in the Mexican archives. He translated and edited at least sixteen large volumes of Spanish documents concerning the West and Southwest, providing scholars and students with the raw materials of early western history. He wrote a number of excellent histories and biographies as well as dozens of shorter pieces. His articles on southwestern Indians were important to ethnohistorians, and his translations provided anthropologists with a wealth of material for cultural and linguistic studies of many tribes, some already extinct.

Yet this was only one side of Bolton's work. He trained more than 300 M.A. students and 105 Ph.D.s, about equally divided between the histories of the West and Latin America. It is doubtful that any American historian has ever had an equal impact on the teaching of history at the university, college, or high school levels. Several generations of Boltonians and their students continue to spread his influence.

As an administrator, Bolton built the Bancroft Library into an outstanding research collection of more than a million volumes on the West and Latin America. Under his guidance, the history department grew into one of the strongest in the country. Although he was often overcommitted and overextended, his enormous energy and dedication enabled him to excel in all of his various activities. Both the volume of his publications and his record of training historians are still unequaled. His biographer and former student, John Francis Bannon, S.J., best summed up his career: "Explorer of archives and trails, cartographer, ethnographer, director of a great research library, teacher extraordinary, author of historical classics—he was the most innovative and versatile historian of America."[34]

NOTES

1. Frederick E. Bolton, "The Early Life of Herbert E. Bolton," *Arizona and the West* 2 (Spring 1962):72.

2. Quoted in Lewis Hanke, *Do the Americas Have a Common History?* (New York: Alfred A. Knopf, 1964), 12.

3. John Francis Bannon, *Herbert Eugene Bolton: The Historian and the Man, 1870–1953* (Tucson: University of Arizona Press, 1978), 32.

4. John Francis Bannon, "Herbert Eugene Bolton: His *Guide* in the Making," *Southwestern Historical Quarterly* 73 (July 1969):37.

5. The first appeared in *The Nation*, May 30, 1901. The second was in the *Annual Report of the American Historical Association for the Year 1901* (Washington, 1902).

6. Garrison's *Texas: A Contest of Civilizations* (1903) was strongly pro-Anglo. E. G. Bourne's *Spain in America* (1904) was fairer and more accurate.

7. Bannon, "Bolton: His *Guide*," 37; John Francis Bannon, "Herbert Eugene Bolton—Western Historian," *Western Historical Quarterly* 2 (July 1971):269; Bannon, *Herbert Eugene Bolton*, 33.

8. Bannon, "Bolton: His *Guide*," 37; Bannon, *Herbert Eugene Bolton*, 34.

9. Bannon, "Bolton: His *Guide*," 38; Bannon, "Bolton—Western Historian," 270; Bannon, *Herbert Eugene Bolton*, 35.

10. Bannon, "Bolton—Western Historian," 270.

11. In the last quarter of the nineteenth century, Hubert Howe Bancroft produced a large set of thick volumes on the history of the West and Southwest as well as of Mexico and Central America. Presumably, Bolton was familiar with them.

12. Bannon, "Bolton: His *Guide*," 35.

13. Among them were Charles McLean Andrews, William R. Shepherd, and James A. Robertson.

14. Bannon, "Bolton: His *Guide*," 52.

15. Bannon, *Herbert Eugene Bolton*, 71.

16. Bannon, "Bolton: His *Guide*," 49.

17. Russell M. Magnaghi, "Herbert E. Bolton and Sources for American Indian Studies," *Western Historical Quarterly* 6 (January 1975):37, 46.

18. That earlier study has now been published as *The Hasinais: Southern Caddos as Seen by the Earliest Europeans*, edited with an introduction by Russell M. Magnaghi (Norman: University of Oklahoma Press, 1987).

19. Bannon, "Bolton—Western Historian," 273.

20. Ibid, 272–76; Bannon, *Herbert Eugene Bolton*, 58–70.

21. John W. Caughey, "Herbert E. Bolton," in Wilbur R. Jacobs, John W. Caughey, and Joe B. Frantz, *Turner, Bolton, and Webb: Three Historians of the American Frontier* (Seattle: University of Washington Press, 1965), 44.

22. John Francis Bannon, ed., *Bolton and the Spanish Borderlands* (Norman: University of Oklahoma Press, 1964), 23–31.

23. Bannon, *Herbert Eugene Bolton*, 150–51.

24. Bannon, *Bolton and the Borderlands*, 9–10.

25. Francis Haines, "Go Write a Book: Nez Percé, Horses, and History," *Western Historical Quarterly* 4 (April 1973):128.

26. Bannon, *Herbert Eugene Bolton*, 108.

27. Bannon, *Bolton and the Borderlands*, 188.

28. Bannon, *Herbert Eugene Bolton*, 151.

29. Herbert E. Bolton, *Fray Juan Crespi, Missionary Explorer on the Pacific Coast, 1769–1774* (Berkeley: University of California Press, 1927).

30. It was published in the *American Historical Review* 23 (October 1917) and repr. in Herbert E. Bolton, *Wider Horizons of American History* (Notre Dame: University of Notre Dame Press, 1939), and Bannon, *Bolton and the Borderlands*.

31. Bannon, *Herbert Eugene Bolton*, 196–97.

32. Ibid., 222.

33. Ibid., 231.

34. Ibid., ix.

BIBLIOGRAPHY

WESTERN WRITINGS OF HERBERT EUGENE BOLTON

Anza's California Expeditions. 5 vols. Berkeley: University of California Press,1930.

Athanase de Mézières and the Louisiana–Texas Frontier, 1768–1780. 2 vols. Cleveland: Arthur H. Clark Company, 1914.

Coronado, Knight of Pueblos and Plains. New York: Whittlesey House, 1949.

Fray Juan Crespi, Missionary Explorer on the Pacific Coast, 1769–1774. Berkeley: University of California Press, 1927.

Font's Complete Diary: A Chronicle of the Founding of San Francisco. Berkeley: University of California Press, 1927.

The Hasinais: Southern Caddos as Seen by the Earliest Europeans. Edited with an Introduction by Russell M. Magnaghi. Norman: University of Oklahoma Press, 1987.

Historical Memoirs of New California, by Francisco Palou, O.F.M. 4 vols. Berkeley: University of California Press, 1926.

Kino's Historical Memoir of Pimería Alta: A Contemporary Account of the Beginnings of California, Sonora, and Arizona, by Father Eusebio Francisco Kino, S.J., Pioneer Missionary Explorer, Cartographer, and Ranchman, 1683–1711. 2 vols. Cleveland: Arthur H. Clark Company, 1919.

Outpost of Empire: The Story of the Founding of San Francisco. New York: Knopf, 1931.

A Pacific Coast Pioneer. Berkeley: University of California Press, 1927.

The Padre on Horseback: A Sketch of Eusebio Francisco Kino, S.J. Apostle to the Pimas. San Francisco: Sonora Press, 1932.

Pageant in the Wilderness: The Story of the Escalante Expedition to the Interior Basin, Including the Diary and Itinerary of Father Escalante. Salt Lake City: Utah State Historical Society, 1950.

Palou and His Writings. Berkeley: University of California Press, 1926.

Rim of Christendom: A Biography of Eusebio Francisco Kino, Pacific Coast Pioneer. New York: Macmillan, 1936.

The Spanish Borderlands: A Chronicle of Old Florida and the Southwest. New Haven: Yale University Press, 1921.

Spanish Exploration in the Southwest, 1542–1706. New York: Scribner's, 1916.

Texas in the Middle Eighteenth Century: Studies in Spanish Colonial History and Administration. Berkeley: University of California Press, 1915.

WORKS ABOUT HERBERT EUGENE BOLTON

Bannon, John Francis. *Bolton and the Spanish Borderlands*. Norman: University of Oklahoma Press, 1964.

———. *Herbert Eugene Bolton: The Historian and the Man*. Tucson: University of Arizona Press, 1978.

———. "Herbert Eugene Bolton—Western Historian." *Western Historical Quarterly* 2 (July 1971):261–82.

Bolton, Frederick E. "The Early Life of Herbert E. Bolton: From Random Memories of An Admiring Brother." *Arizona and the West* 2 (Spring 1962):65–73.

Weber, David J. *Myth and the History of the Hispanic Southwest*. Albuquerque: University of New Mexico Press, 1988.

———. "Turner, the Boltonians, and the Borderlands." *American Historical Review* 91 (February 1986):66–81.

8

James C. Malin:
A Voice from the Grassland

ALLAN G. BOGUE

THE BACKGROUND

*J*AMES C. MALIN WAS WELL
fitted to make the North American grassland his particular interest.
He was a true child of the plains country, born on a homestead in 1893
in the Edgeley-Kulm district of North Dakota, with the family residential coordinates falling between the 98th and 100th meridians. Here,
his father, Jared, was intermittently farmer and townsman—grocery
store clerk, real estate man, hardware and implement salesman, and
sometime lay preacher. Ten years after the birth of young James, his
father abandoned the struggle in North Dakota and moved to Edwards
County, Kansas, where he had lived briefly before his marriage and
where his brother James farmed. Here, Jared once more worked the
land and once more left it, moving into the hamlet of Lewis to return
to the farm implement business. As a boy, Malin experienced the rig-
ors and challenges of western farming, as well as the life of small-town
middle America in a region just leaving its frontier era. He entered a
new world in 1910 when he enrolled at Baker University, a small institution in Baldwin, Kansas.[1]

Young Malin decided to major in mathematics, declaring history as
a minor. Although conscientious and interested, he was not, reports a
biographer, a brilliant student, perhaps because his initial plans did
not suit ideally his talents. After deciding to major in history, however,
he not only completed the requirements in that area but had also worked
up majors in philosophy and combined psychology and biology by the
time of his graduation in 1914. Knowledge gained in his science con-

centration, including the subjects of botany, physiology, and zoology, proved to be a unique intellectual resource in later years. His teachers at Baker found him enthusiastic but somewhat retiring, and his fellows on the football team respected his ability as a lineman but noted that he departed to his room or to the library after games or practices rather than joining them in more gregarious settings.

Before the end of his first semester as a high school teacher of science and mathematics in Buffalo, Kansas, Malin had decided that such work was not for him. He obtained a fellowship in the University of Kansas graduate program in history for the year 1915–16. Another year of high school teaching followed, and in 1918 he was called into the army, returning thereafter to the secondary school classroom, this time in Oklahoma City. But most summers saw Malin enrolled in the graduate studies program at the University of Kansas, and each year the personal bonds strengthened between Malin and Frank Heywood Hodder, his adviser in the History Department there. Until this time, the Kansas history faculty members had advised their graduate students who aspired to complete the doctorate that they should enroll in one of the eastern universities. Indeed, Frank E. Melvin, Malin's instructor in French history, helped him in making tentative arrangements to pursue doctoral studies in that area at the University of Pennsylvania. But meanwhile, during 1919, Malin was working on a paper on United States Indian policy that Hodder suggested should be revised to meet the dissertation requirement at Lawrence. Although it was shorter than most dissertations, Hodder believed that the research "makes up in originality what it lacks in bulk."[2]

Yielding to Hodder's advocacy, the Kansas department offered Malin an instructorship on the completion of the doctorate in 1921. In that year he assumed a teaching load of fifteen hours per week, including an English history survey course and a new offering to be developed in contemporary American history. He was to spend his whole teaching career at the campus on Mount Oread, where the Old Overland Trail had climbed out of the Wakarusa bottoms and where the statue of the pioneer (foot on shovel) and "prairie acre" became almost as familiar to him as wife and family. Although Malin was not completely ignored by the recruiters of other departments, such interest came too late in his career for him to consider moving seriously and, still later, both his health and his research commitments dampened any flickerings of desire to join the footloose Fulbright junketeers.

MALIN THE TEACHER

About five feet ten or eleven in height, Malin was thick-chested and shouldered and in his middle and later years inclined to weigh more than he wished. Late in his career, one of his graduate students dubbed him "Big Jim," a tribute perhaps to his intellect, in part, since in physique Malin did not match George L. Anderson, his former student, chairman, and friend, or various others among the faculty community. His eyes were brown and, as late as his mid-fifties, his black hair was luxuriant if a bit receding. Typically during the 1940s and 1950s he entered the undergraduate lecture room unobtrusively, carrying a manila folder or battered brown brief case—often with a map under his arm or, in season, a small sheaf of bluestem grass or bundle of barbed wire segments—and walked slowly to the front of the room where he seated himself at the desk and arranged lecture notes in front of him. His lecturing voice was soft, somewhat higher in pitch than the norm and inclined at times to be husky. He spoke in a conversational tone, utterly bereft of rhetorical artifice. Sometimes in answering questions he seemed to inspect one of the upper rear corners of the room before giving a qualified response. A Republican at the ballot box, he was not politically active, nor avowedly partisan in the class room.

Malin did not assign conventional texts in his courses on the History of the Trans-Mississippi West and the History of Kansas, nor was his lecture material much influenced by such sources. He had published, or would publish, much of the lecture material and his approach was analytical rather than narrative.[3] Taking his courses as a dissertator during 1948–49, I found the lectures interesting and sometimes fascinating as Malin demonstrated how state and regional history courses could be used to address larger issues of social change and politics. But I sympathized a bit with the undergraduate education major who leaned over to whisper, "What is he talking about?"

Even some graduate students found Malin to be lacking in humor, and he *was* a very serious man. But his conversation and lectures were not devoid of gentle fun or colorful incident. He liked word play and when an assistant rented accommodations on the attic floor of Professor Paul Roofe, Malin introduced him to colleagues on occasion with the explanation that he had a room under the roof at the Roofes. In class, he punned upon Everett Dick's title *The Sod House Frontier*[4]—"sod" really should be spelled "sawed," he maintained. He was accustomed to reading a long passage from the writings of Bill Nye in which that worthy mourned the passing of the frontier of '49. With a pronounced twinkle,

Malin read to the students in his western history course from a Kansas newspaper in which the editor described the adaptation of prim house-keepers from the older states to the use of buffalo chips. First, a shovel was used to stoke the fire, but "familiarity breeds contempt" and soon the hands emerged from the biscuit dough to charge the stove and then returned to the floury mass without benefit of wash basin. He lectured on the Battle of the Little Bighorn, and there was real emotion in his voice when he referred to "that fourflusher Custer"; his sympathies did not run with the Seventh Cavalry's "royal family."

Malin, however, made no pretense of being a crowd pleaser. During the 1940s and 1950s he and the economist John Ise were some-times identified as the two most distinguished members of the Kansas faculty, but Malin engaged in none of the pyrotechnics that led mem-bers of Ise's classes in introductory economics to recurrent bursts of clapping, stamping, and cheering as they listened to the demolition of the capitalist system. Late in Malin's career, complaints from under-graduates about his teaching led his dean to remove him from the class-room. This was a painful blow, only partially assuaged when a chancellor who had once been in Malin's class directed that he be returned to the classroom because some students would find study with him to be one of the great experiences of their university careers.

Until well after World War II, the doctoral program in the Kansas History Department was modest in size; only seven students completed doctorates under Malin's direction. But during the 1920s and thereaf-ter, dozens of masters candidates, mainly teachers, were enrolled. Malin supervised the writing of almost one hundred M.A. theses. Onerous as the work of direction could be, it helped Malin to develop his ideas and enlarge his knowledge of source materials.[5]

During the last third of his career, Malin's direct influence upon younger scholars spread well beyond the KU campus. William B. Hesseltine, Roy F. Nichols, and particularly Paul W. Gates brought Malin's work to the attention of graduate students, and some of them established enduring relations with him. During the mid-1950s, the University of Kansas History Department obtained foundation funds that allowed the convocation of three summer seminars to which were invited groups of promising young historians to discuss presentations by senior scholars, including Malin. Not all of them were impressed by him, but some kept in touch with him for years. He was delighted to explain to one or two students why the lands stretching beyond a rain-drenched field of alfalfa must have been the claims of the John

Brown family or to stop the car and conduct an impromptu seminar on prairie grasses at the edge of an adjacent field. An out-of-state doctoral candidate sought advice from him in 1972, some ten years after his official retirement, and remembers a "somewhat grizzled man (he looked like a *younger* brother of Vince Lombardi) in a boiler suit who was prepared to devote hours to a graduate student setting out on a new research project."[6] Such helpfulness was not new; Malin's papers contain many critiques of manuscripts done for both junior and senior scholars and evidence as well of errands run at the Kansas State Historical Society for eastern scholars.

THE RESEARCH SCHOLAR

The mathematics, science, and philosophy that Malin studied at Baker University seem to have imparted an analytical cast to his thinking that always set his work apart from that of more conventional historians. Frank Heywood Hodder was his mentor in history as well as advocate and firm friend at the University of Kansas. A student of Charles Kendall Adams, who had also studied at Goettingen and Freiburg, Hodder exemplified the virtues of scientific history and was possessed of "remarkable ability to analyze complex problems and conflicting evidence."[7] His approach and enthusiasm also stimulated Malin's tendency to view historical issues as problems to be solved, and throughout the last third of his scholarly career he often spoke and wrote about "problems," rather than "topics" or "subjects," and of the necessity of "thinking things through."

Hodder's experiences somewhat colored Malin's understanding of academic administration and the outside world. The older scholar's efforts to portray the historical development of Kansas government had drawn sharp fire from self-appointed guardians of the free state heritage—a fire that accounted to some degree in Malin's view for Hodder's relatively short list of publications. Another professor, Frank E. Melvin, a specialist in French history, was enthusiastic, broadly learned, and erratically brilliant, and he also influenced Malin. His contribution to Malin's intellectual armory was visible as late as 1961 in two chapters on the Napoleon theme in a book that Malin entitled *Confounded Rot About Napoleon . . .* "[8] But it was Hodder's interests in mid-nineteenth-century expansionism, Stephen A. Douglas, and the Kansas-Nebraska Act that provided the context for Malin's doctoral dissertation.

James C. Malin's publications included seventeen books (plus second editions and reprintings) and dozens of articles, dictionary or encyclopedia pieces, and book reviews. Given his teaching load, the lack of research leave, and the health problems that were recurrent subsequent to a partial collapse and diagnosis of high blood pressure during the late 1930s, the volume of his publications was amazing. "The secret of a long life," he was accustomed to say, "is to contract an incurable disease at an early age and then look after oneself." When his health weakened, he installed a cot in a small room off the front entrance to the southwestern-style house that he and his wife Pearl E. Keene had built on University Drive in 1938; and there, recumbent, a clipboard balanced on his chest, he wrote the drafts of much of his later work. Mrs. Malin committed much of her time to typing his manuscripts. Several projects might be going forward at the same time, and visiting their home in 1956 Lee Benson found that the Malins had developed work stations throughout the house, at each of which were segregated the materials related to a particular study. "Their house, the one time I was in it," wrote Rodney O. Davis, "was totally taken over by books, journals and papers, stacked on chairs, tables, couches, the floor, and even the piano and piano bench."[9]

During the first twenty-plus years of Malin's scholarly career his publication outlets were conventional. He published his dissertation and an interpretive monograph on recent American history in the *Bulletin of the University of Kansas: Humanistic Studies*, and the Century Company printed the second work in a revised form. Ginn and Company issued a recent American history text for Malin in 1930.[10] He also published articles and reviews in the *Mississippi Valley Historical Review, Agricultural History*, and other respectable historical journals. A great stream of contributions appeared subsequent to 1930 in the *Kansas Historical Quarterly*, of which he was an associate editor for many years. The American Philosophical Society and the University of Kansas Press published major books for him during the early 1940s.[11]

Believing that he had been promised a favorable reception, in mid-decade Malin submitted a substantial manuscript to the University of Kansas Press. It dealt in general with historical adaptation to the subhumid grassland environment, but included chapters that bore upon the nature and methods of historical writing. The press director returned the draft to Malin, suggesting that it be divided and one or the other part resubmitted. Malin believed that in making this offer the director reserved the right of the press to rewrite and edit as its staff saw fit.

Malin purchased a new typewriter, and Mrs. Malin prepared *Essays on Historiography* for lithoprinting in paperback by Edwards Brothers of Ann Arbor.[12] Malin continued his venture in private printing through the publication of some eight books.

Some admirers deplored Malin's new mode of publication, and during the early 1950s Roy F. Nichols of the University of Pennsylvania persuaded Malin to submit the manuscript of *The Nebraska Question* to his university's press.[13] Agreement on publication was apparently reached, but Malin balked when he found that the copy editor proposed to take undue liberties with the manuscript. His resort to personal publishing reflected Malin's belief that his ideas were unpopular and that only thus could he bring his work before the public in the form that most accurately presented his findings. So defensive was Malin that Fred A. Shannon once told him that he had a "persecution complex." And unfortunately Malin's later method of publication denied his contributions to American history and historical method the circulation that they deserved.

Malin's view of history was broad, as were his research interests. He was interested in the political history of postbellum America and in agricultural policy;[14] as a mature scholar he was increasingly challenged by problems of historical theory, method, and historiography. But since the primary focus of this volume is upon western history, we shall concentrate here on Malin's contributions to that area of study. These can be grouped in four general categories.

Malin's doctoral dissertation, *Indian Policy and Westward Expansion*, announced his interest in the westward expansion of America in the central Mississippi and lower Missouri river regions during the antebellum era, the problems of establishing territorial government in that region, and the implications of these processes for the settlement of Kansas. Malin intermittently published articles and notes on these themes throughout most of his career, as well as major books on John Brown's role in frontier Kansas and the Kansas-Nebraska Act. During the 1930s Malin began to develop a second major research theme—that of human adaptation to the subhumid climate of the grassland. The research on adaptation to the grasslands led him, in turn, into reconsideration of the contributions of Frederick Jackson Turner and Walter P. Webb and the problems of generalizing about the westward movement, a third emphasis of much interest to historians of the American West.

Finally, during the 1950s and thereafter, Malin published various books and articles dealing with the "folk culture" of Kansas during the late nineteenth century, as revealed in the lives and institutions of Kansans. Groping toward a methodology of historical cultural analysis and dealing with the Kansas theatre, Kansas poetry, Kansas political careers, and even the hostility of Kansas doctors to female competitors, Malin displayed continuing curiosity, breadth, and vitality in these contributions. But they did not interest other scholars as had his earlier work. Thoughtful, provocative, and useful as many of these materials are, space is too limited to consider them here.

INDIANS, TERRITORIES, AND SECTIONAL STRESS

In his dissertation, "Indian Policy and Westward Expansion," Malin wrote, "The early history of the Trans-Mississippi Valley is essentially the history of the relation between the Indian and the advancing frontier placed in proper perspective with all the other related problems." This short monograph grew out of Malin's earlier research on the career of Senator David R. Atchison of Missouri, who was for a time chairman of the Senate Committee on Indian Affairs. Here, Malin describes the development of the Indian removal policy and its elaboration during the Jackson administration. He shows that by the late 1830s public sentiment supported a policy of consolidating Indian tribes in the Southwest, beyond the western boundaries of Missouri and Arkansas and below the Kaw. But the transcontinental migration and the Santa Fe trade, as well as the Mexican accession, caused the years from 1840 to 1848 to be a period of transition and rethinking. Four "great factors" now influenced Indian policymakers: "westward expansion and the settlement of the Pacific Coast"; the movement to build a railroad to the Pacific; the relation of an expanding population to the organization of Nebraska; and the "changed living conditions and civilization of the Indians."[15]

Discussion of the four factors and the efforts of administrators and law makers to react to them comprises almost half of the monograph. Malin's text concludes with the emergence of a policy designed to win permission for uncontested passage through the territories of the indigenous and intruded plains country tribes to the settlements on the western coast and a removal policy designed to concentrate tribes on the northern plains and most particularly in an Indian territory to the southwest of Missouri. Thus, the federal government prepared for the settlement of the region west of Iowa and Missouri under territorial organization and the building of a transcontinental railroad. By the time of the passage of the Kansas-Nebraska Act in 1854, these policies had been almost completely effected; the lands of what was to become eastern Kansas and Nebraska lay waiting for the settler.

In writing *Indian Policy and Westward Expansion*, Malin displayed a remarkable ability to generalize and trace the ways in which institutional change reflected social factors or forces. Hodder was delighted with the study, perhaps because it set in place various pieces of the puzzle that intrigued him throughout his career—the motivation of Stephen A. Douglas in shaping and supporting the Kansas-Nebraska Act. Malin's dissertation also provided the scholarly foundation for his continuing interest in that fateful law and the territorial struggles within "Bleeding Kansas."

Between the publication of his doctoral dissertation and the early 1960s Malin published two major books and at least eighteen articles or notes bearing upon Kansas territorial themes. Like Hodder, he was iconoclastic. The first article in the series dealt with "The Proslavery Background of the Kansas Struggle," and here Malin quoted with approbation Theodore Parker's evaluation of the "Kansas struggle": " 'I know of no transaction in human history which has been covered up with such abundant lying.' " When Malin prepared "An Essay to Accompany An Exhibition of the Kansas Statehood Centennial," he concluded: "The first one hundred years of the history of Kansas statehood is not in all respects a model to be followed for the second century. Thus it is better to commemorate, not celebrate, the one hundredth anniversary of Kansas statehood." There were, argued Malin, two basic issues involved in territorial Kansas: at the time "the fundamental question" involved the fate of slavery there, but in short order the "question, who should receive credit for saving Kansas from slavery [?]" became highly controversial as well.[16] In Malin's eyes, the major protagonists in territorial Kansas melded sectional objectives with blatant self-seeking, even crime, and obscured their own objectives and actual events in a haze of misleading propaganda. Mythmakers and apologists were immediately at work.

Malin's article, "The Proslavery Background of the Kansas Struggle," appeared in 1923. In it, he sought to analyze dispassionately the objectives and plans of Missouri Senator David R. Atchison and other proslavery leaders in territorial Kansas. These men, he showed, had encouraged proslavery settlers, mainly from Missouri, to occupy the timberlands of eastern Kansas and seize political control of the territory. But the

political maneuvers of the free state party practically nullified the
proslavery gains. Organized immigration from the south as well
as from the north was a failure and the proslavery domination
could not be maintained. The intense excitement attending those
efforts gradually grew out of bounds and, in a measure carrying
the leaders with it, resulted in the Kansas civil war. Natural
forces and the weight of numbers balanced the scale in favor of a
free Kansas.[17]

In 1929 Malin again picked up the territorial Kansas theme in a minor publication that had bizarre consequences, strongly influencing his views of the academic institutional context. At issue was the destruction during the spring of 1856 of the hotel of the free-state faction in Lawrence. The United States Marshal led a large posse of proslavery men into the town to serve several warrants. The task completed, he disbanded his force and its members rallied to the call of the Douglas County sheriff, who led them in destroying the New England Aid Company's new hotel. Subsequently, the officers of the company unsuccessfully presented a demand for reimbursement to the federal government in the amount of twenty-one thousand dollars. Immediately prior to the dissolution of the company in the 1890s, the board of directors transferred this claim to the University of Kansas.

University authorities pressed vigorously for compensation, and on one occasion they were almost successful. The omens appeared favorable again under the Hoover administration, since the vice president of the United States was a Kansan and other well-disposed individuals occupied key positions in the Congress. At this point, the *Daily Kansan*, the student newspaper at the University of Kansas, published a story suggesting that the university might soon win reimbursement. The writer's account of the burning of the hotel followed the Emigrant Aid Company and university version of the incident. Unaware that Chancellor Ernest H. Lindley was deeply involved in pressing the unversity's case, Malin wrote a letter to the student newspaper, maintaining that the sheriff and his men were not acting under federal authority. The university claim, Malin suggested, was groundless.[18]

Lindley berated the young professor on the street, hectored him in the chancellor's office, and ordered him to cease publishing on the territorial period. The acting chairman of the History Department was pressed to obtain Malin's approval of an amended version of the hotel incident. Malin refused to cooperate, and only the intervention of Hodder saved his job. Malin did not remain muzzled for long. Three years later, his article describing the activities of one of the major free-state guerrilla-force leaders, James A. Harvey, appeared under the defiant title, "Colonel Harvey and His Forty Thieves."[19] Viewed within the context of Hodder's earlier problems, this incident helped to engender the belief in Malin's mind that hostile vested interests might threaten the historian's freedom of expression at any time.

Among Malin's publications on territorial themes is the book that he later acknowledged to be his best in terms of the canons of conventional history, *John Brown and the Legend of Fifty-Six*.[20] During the 1930s the federal government replaced the Federal Building in Topeka with a new structure, and the State Historical Society obtained many documents that had been stored on the top floor of the old building. Among them were the federal court records from the territorial period, and Malin discovered that these bore upon the activity of John Brown and his sons during the bloody spring and summer of 1856. Was John Brown, Sr., the leader of the free-state men who murdered five pro-slavery "ruffians" in their settlement along Potawatomie Creek in eastern Kansas shortly after the sack of Lawrence in May of 1856? Free-state historiography had answered "no." Did the older Brown lead guerrilla forces in the war of bushwhacker against jayhawker that ensued for some months thereafter? This, too, would be denied. Were theft and intimidation no less involved in these struggles than the issue of whether Kansas was to accept slavery? The victors of the free-state movement rejected the possibility. Malin developed his answers to such questions in a tour de force of some eight hundred pages, based upon land and court records, newspapers, correspondence, reminiscences, and secondary materials.

Malin likened the organization of his narrative concerning John Brown in Kansas to Robert Browning's device in *The Ring and the Book* in which all parties to the case delivered their testimony in turn and the Pope provided the final summation. In Part One he followed the story through the local and eastern newspapers of 1856 and 1857. Part Two examined the "The Growth of the Legend," as participants, observers, publicists, and biographers contributed to the growth of myth and legend about the events on Potawatomie Creek. Finally, Malin reconstructed the crime in the light of his painstaking analysis of the geography of eastern Kansas and the wealth of new evidence that he had assembled. He discussed the competition for claims and town sites and the rustling of cattle and horses occurring at the time and concluded that the most likely motivation for the murders of the proslavery men lay in the efforts of the free-state men to thwart the working of the courts under the proslavery code of laws. He admitted that not all of the trustworthy evidence conformed with that interpretation, but he believed that it was more credible than any other.

Given his training under Hodder, the misrepresentations abounding in the historiography of early Kansas history, and Malin's previously unfortunate experience in correcting free-state myth, he may have approached John Brown and his family with something less than forgiving sympathy. Although Ralph Volney Harlow noted that Malin had failed to explain Brown's ability to impress eminent easterners as a man of "compelling personality and even an admirable character," this reviewer pronounced Malin's book to be revolutionary in its impact. Other eminent reviewers praised the book, and both David Potter and Allan Nevins cited it in their later work with apparent approbation.[21]

After a very different attitude toward abolitionism and its leaders had been established in American historiography, the prolific biographer Stephen B. Oates denounced Malin's study of Brown in 1971 as "not a scientific study but a partisan work of the anti-Brown school" and criticized Malin for his failure to use "indispensable Brown materials" and related documents in various repositories, mostly outside the Middle West or in the hands of private collectors. Oates accused Malin of bias and of misrepresenting the details of Brown's earlier career and his deep commitment to abolition. A grudging paragraph admits that Malin made some contributions, but, Oates added, the book was "essentially a biased and one-sided study of Brown the man." Had he responded, Malin might have replied that his book was never intended to be a multisided study of Brown the man but rather, as he attempted to make clear, an analysis of the development of the John Brown legend and a reconstruction of the local circumstances and details of the Potawatomie massacre. The Kansan admitted that he had not exhausted the John Brown theme. In terms of "cultural history," he wrote, "the study of it is only begun"—and indicated that his eastern sources were only "fairly representative." Oates did not explain in his article or biography of Brown how the materials in the unused archives would have changed Malin's story significantly, nor do the relevant chapters in Oates's biography of Brown reveal major contributions to the factual substance of our knowledge about the Potawatomie murders and their perpetrators. The interpretation, of course, is different.[22]

Malin published his final book on territorial issues in 1953. In *The Nebraska Question: 1852–1854* he conducted an intensive analysis of the regional background of the Kansas Nebraska Act.[23] This volume was the culmination of the research begun long before upon David Rice Atchison and national Indian policy. In its opening pages, Malin presented evidence that Hodder and others interested in the motives of Stephen A. Douglas had long sought—a letter in which the Little Giant specifically explained that his objectives in seeking territorial organization for the Nebraska country involved the opening of the central region of the Louisiana Purchase for the construction of transcontinental railroads and the development of settlement there that would bind the West Coast communities firmly to the older regions of the country.

Malin argued that it was inappropriate to view the political positions and legislative activity of Douglas as merely an aspect of the slavery issue. The Illinois senator was responding primarily, he maintained, to the changing technological imperatives of the times. But, also, Douglas saw the squatter sovereignty of the compromise legislation of 1850 as a step forward in the conception of American freedom, and the Kansas-Nebraska Act as a still further advance. Malin implied that Douglas would have seen the disintegration of American slavery—a doomed institution—as a still further step. A major feature of *The Nebraska Question* was Malin's effort to depict the interaction between national and regional policymakers and the frontier population of northwestern Missouri. On the basis of the newspapers serving them, Missourians of this region, Malin believed, were initially not much concerned about slavery, seeing territorial development to the West in much the same perspective as did Douglas. But then extremists, both North and South, seized the issue and launched the nation upon the path to "Bleeding Kansas."

A close student of antebellum territorial expansion, Holman Hamilton praised the "book's tremendous strength and importance . . . intriguing discoveries, resourceful analysis, and the historian's care and courage in supporting his revisionist position." Roy F. Nichols also found it to be a "significant contribution" and commended Malin for once again demonstrating "his great capacity for fact finding and keen analysis, his wide reading, and the far-flung horizon of his vision." Avery Craven remarked that there were "few books on present-day shelves that throw more light on the events leading to the American Civil War." He also joked that Malin did not "seem to realize that there are 'controversial' fields in history, and to think and draw conclusions will only lead to the charge of 'bias.' He will find himself called a 'revisionist'—a very nasty word in a profession where respectability and mediocrity are one and the same thing."[24]

In the *Mississippi Valley Historical Review*, however, the reviewer found it "no pleasant task" to "struggle through the entire volume of 450 closely printed pages" to understand the book's "conclusions or interpretations." Nichols, too, faulted the "heaviness of style." By this stage of his career, Malin was interested only in the clear expression of his ideas. Elsewhere, he extolled "sound history" that was "neither a popularized and emasculated product that acts like a sedative, nor a patronizing one dressed up in artificial 'literary' forms. Sound history at any level challenges the intellectual capacity of the author and the reader, both in form and substance."[25]

THE RIDDLE OF THE GRASSLAND ·

During the early 1930s Malin began to develop another major area of research interest—the adaptation of Euro-American institutions to the subhumid environment of the central American grasslands. Keeping in mind the publication of Walter P. Webb's *The Great Plains* during 1931, one may hypothesize a chain of cause and effect. Malin, so the scenario might run, was intrigued by Webb's picture of frontiersmen repulsed initially at the 98th meridian and marking time for a generation until industrial America had produced the six-shooters, barbed wire, and windmills necessary to conquer a hostile land.[26] The Kansan thereupon designed a research study that would test the impact of changing environment upon human behavior in Kansas. From East to West he divided the four-hundred-mile breadth of Kansas into five rainfall belts—the most eastern receiving thirty-five inches plus of precipitation each year and the westernmost but twenty inches or less. Within each subregion he selected comparable numbers of townships, forty-eight in all, and using the manuscript federal (1860–1880) and state (1865–1935) censuses, he compared the persistence of farm operators in each belt from census year to census year. Thus, Malin was able to generalize about the impact of Webb's frontier on the general "success" of settlers in adapting to the region and also to examine other aspects of the behavior of the population in the pioneering and ensuing eras. The result was a far richer analysis of population movement and behavior in the settlement era of the central plains and thereafter than that provided by any previous historian of the frontier.

The background of the article on "The Turnover of Farm Population in Kansas" was actually very different from our imaginary script. The catalytic agent, as Malin identified it, was an invitation from his former high school in Lewis, Kansas, to give the commencement address in 1933.[27] In preparing a history of Wayne township, the site of Lewis, for the occasion, he explored the manuscript census data available at the Kansas State Historical Society and found the story that they told of settlement in Edwards County, Kansas, to be significantly different from the generalizations that he had derived from reading the work of historians working within the historiographic framework built upon the writings of Frederick Jackson Turner. Later, Malin conceived the idea of expanding his analysis to embrace the state of Kansas as a whole.

The "Turnover" article is one of the most innovative and ingenious contributions in the broad field of western American history. Malin demonstrated that the replacement of settlers was high in the frontier period of all regions in Kansas, irrespective of the available moisture, and noted subsequent stages of somewhat greater stability, including the years of the 1930s. Fluctuations in resident population were related most directly to variations in the inflow of settlers. Malin found the proportion of farm operators provided by the descendants of the pioneers to be roughly in the one-quarter to one-tenth range after some fifty years of settlement. Malin's study of farmer turnover and persistence demonstrated the utility of the manuscript census returns. He was apparently the first scholar to put the manuscript census data in state repositories to intensive scholarly analysis. With modifications, Malin's techniques of estimating persistence served as a model for important research by both rural and urban historians after 1950. In describing his methods in the "Turnover" and related studies in 1940, he was, he suggested, writing history "from the bottom up," a phrasing popularized in the 1960s by a rather different kind of historian.[28]

Preparation of the Lewis High School commencement address confirmed Malin's belief that "one of the most interesting problems in the history of the westward movement in the United States is the adaptation of the agricultural system to the environment." A succession of papers and books from the 1930s to the 1950s enhanced the historical profession's understanding of such matters. Malin understood that the process of western community building involved the interaction of town or village and country, and during 1935 he published a two-part article on "The Kinsley Boom of the Late Eighties," a masterful analysis of western town promotion. But the adaptation of the agricultural system was to be of greater interest to him, and the historical sources of Edwards County also included information on the activities of the farmers' club in Wayne township, an organization that settlers there used as a forum during the late 1880s and early 1890s to discuss their experience in identifying appropriate crops and cultivation practices for their locality. The club discussions provided Malin with the basis for an important article on adaptive processes. In experiencing great turnover of population, Malin thought frontier communities must have experienced major difficulties in developing stable institutions and accumulating the knowledge of appropriate crop and livestock combinations and cultivation practices.[29]

Malin's publications on adaptation document a widening geographical focus. From Wayne township, he moved to other aspects of community development in Edwards County and then turned his attention to a four-county area at the eastern margin of the central wheat belt and to the bluestem pastures region. Concerning the latter area he published only one major article, but continuing attention to the former culminated in the publication of *Winter Wheat in the Golden Belt of Kansas*. Thereafter, Malin extended his range still more to follow the theme of adaptation through broader regional manifestations and issues.[30]

In his study of the emergence of the winter wheat economy Malin used the local newspapers and agricultural press brilliantly. He traced the painful processes through which the settlers of the Golden Belt of Kansas discarded corn as their staple crop and fixed upon hard winter wheat as the central element of their cropping combinations and the adoption of the listing process as an important regional adaptation. He noted the importance of the Mennonites in bringing Turkey Red wheat to the area and their exemplary farming practices. Adaptation here by trial and error, he emphasized, was a kind of folk process, sometimes painful but successfully pursued at times against the specific recommendations of both the milling interests and spokesmen of academic agricultural science. In explaining the success of individual farmers, Malin also emphasized personal factors: "Managerial ability plus . . . the acquisition of skills in the handling of machines and soils . . . make one man a success while the lack of them make his neighbor a total failure even with identical machinery."[31]

As Malin worked on these questions, his interest in the broader issues of regional perception and adaptive reaction increased. In his research on the winter wheat belt and the bluestem pastures area, he drew upon the research of geographers and farm economists, but the gasoline shortages and restrictions on travel during World War II forced him to curtail even his hitherto frequent visits to the State Historical Society in Topeka. Necessity again fostering innovation, Malin decided to expand his knowledge of work in disciplines that he believed might enhance his understanding of the unique environmental challenges of the grassland. He had entered his career with a broader knowledge of science and its classic documents than most young historians. Now he began to read widely in the professional literature that would bring him abreast of research in the various branches of ecology, climatology, geography, geology, and soil science insofar as these served to illuminate his understanding of the grassland. From this study came the *The Grassland of North America: Prolegomena to its History*, the book that he identified in 1972 as his most interesting and useful contribution "because it opened up so many things."[32]

No graduate student has ever reported that *The Grassland of North America* is easy to read. In it, Malin summarized relevant scientific thought and research about the plains country and examined past descriptions and efforts to understand it as a unique region or to develop relevant broader frameworks of historical interpretation. Here are terse descriptions of the ideas and contributions of dozens of individuals to the understanding of grassland regionalism—"the relation of natural environment to man's specialized utilization of regional resources, and the recognition of regional adequacy, and regional interdependence."[33] The chapters are stubbornly analytical rather than narrative in form, and the reader must strain at times to fit ideas and evidence into the structure of what Malin apparently had in mind. But no other historian of his generation equaled the range of relevant ideas and evidence that he brought to bear upon the "problem" of the grassland nor developed the scientific understanding necessary to critique scientific positions with the sureness demonstrated here. A final series of chapters drew upon his local and quantitative investigations of the previous decade to provide models for research that might be done in other areas of the region or, indeed, of other regions. The methodology of agricultural community studies has been on a higher plane ever since.

Malin did not work in an intellectual vacuum. As he thought about the problems of grassland adaptation during the 1930s, federal planners, drawing upon the theories of physical and natural science of the day as well as contemporary social science, were criticizing the resource policies and cultivation practices that had, they believed, turned the plains into a land of exodus, in part a ravaged Dust Bowl. Malin did not read the past as did the proponents of a new order. He knew that high rates of population turnover were not new to the grassland and indeed were less striking in the early 1930s than in past eras. The

Resettlement Administration filmmakers adopted the view popular in Washington that the Dust Bowl was the product of *The Plow That Broke The Plains*, and Hugh H. Bennett of the Soil Conservation Service claimed that the streams of the plains country had run clear in presettlement days, inferring that soil and wind erosion were postsettlement phenomena. Malin's sources told him a different story. While working on the *Grassland* manuscript, he published a three-part series of articles on dust storms in Kansas, showing that such phenomena had been recurrent in the nineteenth-century history of the state. He also found evidence that muddy streams had preceded agricultural settlement.[34]

Malin suggested that the Russian-derived system of soil classification endorsed by government soils specialists in the United States had been inadequately adapted to the characteristics of the grassland. In a region where much of the soil was windblown in origin, wind erosion might, he argued, be less serious than to the east of the Mississippi where topsoil losses could presumably be offset only by the slow weathering of parent materials. Writing in the 1940s, Malin noted bumper yields of wheat in Kansas counties believed to have been severely damaged during the 1930s. Although stimulated by the findings of the ecologists, he found the climax and organismic conceptions of the grassland held by Frederic E. Clements and his followers to be excessively arbitrary and the "deserts on the march" theme of one of them, Paul B. Sears, to be bad history as well as alarmist.[35]

During the decade after the publication of the *Prolegomena*, Malin continued to develop and rethink grassland themes. In the first and—as it happened—last volume of a projected series of *Grassland Historical Studies*, Malin considered the influence of geology and geography and their interaction with technology in the development of the plains region and more specifically in the development of Kansas City as a regional center of commerce. Between 1950 and 1955 he prepared a series of papers that brought recent scientific thinking upon pleistocene geology, archeology, and plant and animal ecology to bear upon his previous efforts to understand grassland soil formation as well as the role of mankind and animals in the process. He pondered the significance of changing ecological perspectives concerning plant communities and the appropriate perspective within which to view Euro-American occupancy of the region. Although Malin did not forsake history, these papers were in general prepared with scientific audiences in mind and included a contribution to the distinguished symposium collection published under the title *Man's Role in Changing the Face of the Earth*.[36]

Some historians immediately recognized Malin's grassland research as path-breaking of a high order. In 1950 Thomas LeDuc published a review essay dealing with four of Malin's recent studies: *Winter Wheat, Essays on Historiography*, the *Prolegomena*, and *Grassland Historical Studies: I* (all available for the grand total of eleven dollars) and hailed the author as a "creative worker of prodigious industry, immense learning, and disciplined imagination." Malin was the first historian to understand and to make constructive use of ecological theory and concepts, even formulating an appropriate conceptual framework for the historian. But strangely enough, when Donald Worster essayed a history of ecology, he expressed no admiration for the scholar who had been first to try to bring the knowledge of ecology within the competence of the historian. Rather, he derided Malin for accepting the position of the wrong ecologists and charged that he was "prompted by his . . . intense ideological biases."[37]

Yet Malin had not dismissed conservation out of hand, explaining rather that "conservation theory" should be written "in terms of control measures derived from appreciation of the ecology of the grassland in its natural condition." Ecologists were divided among themselves as to the correctness of the views of the Clementsian school about the grassland, and surely not all critics were merely motivated by the ideology of laissez faire, as Worster suggested was true of Malin. If Ronald C. Tobey's analysis of the Clementsian ecologists is to be believed, one of the leading members of the group during the 1930s, John Weaver, had concluded by the end of the decade that various of his earlier conceptions of the grassland must be revised. Malin's prescience in raising objections on the basis of his evidence was worthy of respect, and Worster's critique appears to be one of the crueller efforts to commit intellectual patricide in the historiography of the American West.[38]

MALIN AS CRITIC AND THEORIST
OF WESTERN HISTORY

Malin also contributed to western American history as a critic of orthodoxies and advocate of different perspectives. Western historian that he was, Malin never succumbed to the lure of western American history as interpreted by Frederick Jackson Turner and his followers. He never doubted that the frontier was well worthy of consideration, and in discussing the making of "the nationalized federal state" between 1865 and 1887 in his second monograph, Malin noted that "the union of the East and the Trans-Mississippi West is fully as important and

significant to the history of the new America as the restoration of the
South and justifies as full treatment." And the economic and political
implications of the frontier, he suggested in the same publication, had
been inadequately considered in their relation to antebellum sectionalism and metropolitan rivalries.[39]

Malin, however, also emphasized the role of technology in social
change and tried to provide a balanced treatment of the internal and
external influences that helped to shape American development. "The
significance of the frontier in American history is such a well-known
theme," he wrote, "as to require little more than mention of it here as
a democratizing and nationalizing influence."[40] He apparently came
to view the Turnerian approach increasingly critically as a result of
reviewing various books in the 1920s and early 1930s cast in that mold,
his failure to reconcile the findings of his research into frontier social
processes with the generalizations of Turnerian scholars, and his out-
rage at efforts of New Deal proponents to use the loss of the frontier as
rationalization for their economic and social programs. By the mid-1940s
Malin had developed a rather sweeping critique of Turner's theories.

Malin's analysis of Turner does not reflect the exasperation, logic
chopping, or even derision that some other critics revealed. "A good
part of the Turnerian controversies," he maintained, "turned on quib-
bles over verbalisms." Turner was a "creative genius," a man of "such
unusual accomplishments," who, as a historian, "gave the world the
most significant statement of a particular application of the idea" of
space as an opportunity for American expansion and conversely of the
problems that might be encountered when a country instead faced the
problem of "closed space."[41] Somewhat later, Malin noted, the British
geographer, Halford J. Mackinder, applied these ideas to a Western
world that had seemingly reached the end of colonial opportunities.

Malin pictured a Turner who in the beginning recognized the broader
relationships of American development and endorsed the theory of mul-
tiple hypotheses, the concept that society grows, as well as the importance of interdisciplinary methods, but who over time had narrowed his
focus. Broad-ranging in his knowledge, Turner in the end organized
that information basically in terms of his twin concepts of frontier and
section—they became his only independent variables. Nor did Turner
always provide satisfactory definitions—this, however, was understand-
able, Malin believed, because "anyone trying to express a new idea or
meaning must always experience this difficulty in proportion to the
novelty and complexity of the innovation." The stage theory to which

Turner committed himself was flawed, and his understanding of physiographic regions was based solely on the work of the geologist and
geographer. He ignored other relevant sciences, paid too little attention to science and technology, and missed the significance of changing systems of communications. The role of the city "was particularly
a blind spot in Turner's historical outlook."[42] Malin noted the possibility of European precedent and example in various cases that Turner
or his followers believed to demonstrate frontier-derived innovativeness.
(His suspicion that Achille Loria's writing had significantly influenced
Turner was a forecast of Lee Benson's brilliant work on that subject.)
Once Turner found himself in the era of closed space, he had, Malin
believed, no satisfactory explanation of American development.

When he referred to Turner's disciples Malin was less sympathetic. They wrote a history that was one-sided and terminated in 1890.
Their legend-making had produced serious distortion of the frontier
hypothesis. And "in the hands of the advocates of a collectivist revolution" Turner had become a "Legend and his use of the frontier a
Social Myth."[43]

Given his emphasis on regionalism and the plains country, Malin's
attitude toward Walter P. Webb is of particular interest. Apparently, he
did not write a review of *The Great Plains*. But in the *Prolegomena* he devoted a chapter to a discussion of "Webb and Regionalism." There, he
termed Webb's book a "landmark in the regional approach by historians
to the Trans-Mississippi West." In discussing the famous confrontation between Fred A. Shannon and Webb at the Skytop Conference
sponsored by the Social Science Research Council in 1939, his sympathies appear to lie somewhat with Webb. He noted that Webb had not
exhausted the sources available to him, particularly the scientific literature, but "in a pioneer work, in which he was feeling his way, it would
have been most unusual had he, or anyone, done so."[44]

More regrettable, believed Malin, was the tendency of scholars to
allow Webb's methods and findings to harden into orthodoxy. Malin
noted problems and issues of adaptation to the grassland that Webb
had omitted, and he indicated ways in which his particular areas of
interest could be further developed. The Kansan was less kind when
he critiqued Webb's paper at the American Historical Association meeting in 1950, where the Texan outlined the basic thesis of his forthcoming book *The Great Frontier*. Malin dismissed it as a restatement of the
Turner–Mackinder closed-space hypothesis and termed the presentation an exercise in philosophy rather than history.[45]

During his most creative years, from the mid-1930s to the mid-1950s, Malin developed a general philosophy of history in which men and women worked within an open system where options were limited primarily by the fertility of the human brain and the ingenuity of the human hand. He rejected determinism; individuals, he believed, were usually free to choose from a number of possible courses of action. Eventually, Malin saw a parallel between the study of ecology and history. "Both history and ecology," he wrote, "may be defined as the study of organisms in all their relations, living together, the differences between plant, animal, and human ecology being primarily a matter of emphasis. Therefore, all forms of single—or limited—factor interpretations are rejected as fragmentation of knowledge, with its resultant distortion of facts." Robert W. Johannsen was to write that Malin had "developed a view of man's past that [was] as broad and wide and all-encompassing as the prairies and plains of his native region. . . . His work bears a universality of purpose and meaning that few historians have even tried to achieve."[46]

Some respected historians have tilled narrow fields of interest rewardingly throughout their careers. Malin, on the other hand, constantly found new grain for his mill. Even in retirement he was trying to "think through" new problems and reevaluate old positions in the light of new considerations and evidence. It is not surprising, therefore, if his publications over many years occasionally show some inconsistencies. But he always believed that historians could be objective within reasonable limits in their treatment of evidence, although he denied that any one history could be truly definitive.

Against this background we can try to sum up the debt that western historians owe to Malin. His publications relating to expansion and territorial growth on the antebellum frontier of the Nebraska country cleared away a tremendous undergrowth of partisan misinformation and myth. They brought a great mass of new primary source material into the realm of scholarship and effected a major reevaluation of the motives and plans of major politicians and minor actors, as well as materially clarifying the general context within which they moved.

Malin singlehandedly moved the historical study of grassland regionalism to a new level of discourse. Based on household-level census data, his local studies pioneered a methodology that has produced a new kind of agricultural history and was transferred with important results to the field of urban history. From his beginnings flow our current understanding of the tremendous local-population mobility of the nineteenth century and our detailed knowledge of frontier demographics. His imaginative use of travel and exploration narratives and of local Kansas newspapers pioneered the study of the perception of landscape a generation before such work became a priority interest among historical geographers. He went far beyond Webb in describing the ways in which changing sources of mechanical power, other technological innovations, and the improvement of domestic animals and plants were involved in the American adaptation to the plains country. In his exploration and use of the work of the natural and physical sciences, Malin also far surpassed Webb.

Was there a Malin hypothesis? Robert P. Swierenga has tried to define a central thesis in Malin's work on the grassland: "agricultural adaptation by European forest-culture people to the treeless grassland environment was a painfully slow and disorganized folk process that succeeded only because of the ingenuity and resourcefulness of individual settlers."[47] This summary does catch much of the Malin message, but, as Swierenga realized, it disregards Malin's emphasis on technological change, the interaction of regions, his denial of determinism and related belief in an open system, and the diversity of his interests.

A scientist noted Malin's "amazing faculty for grasping the essentials of fields seemingly alien to his own."[48] He developed a special interest in ecology, perhaps because he found clues in that discipline to approaches that would allow historians to avoid the kind of environmental determinism that in his view flawed much western history and the "subjective relativism" that had, he feared, been used in some cases as justification for history that served as rationalization for statism. He was not, however, willing to accept all of the positions of the Nebraska school of grassland ecologists.

As a critic of Turner, Malin was insightful, respectful, and firm. The frontier–section theories were inadequate as full explanations either of the American or the West European experience. Nor was any other single factor adequate to those tasks. Similarly, Malin gave Webb his due—*The Great Plains* was a trail breaker of major importance, but it should not be considered the state of the art some fifteen years after its publication. Malin was much less considerate of Turner's followers, who exacerbated the failings of the master, or of those who, in his eyes, perverted the frontier message in extentuation of particular governmental policies. In cases of disagreement he could be brutal. He damned the relativist for instance as "Man-Afraid-of-His-Mind." Malin's tendencies toward strong views on current issues caused Roy F. Nichols, on one occasion, to temper his praise of the Kansan. Nichols wrote admiringly of Malin's efforts to develop techniques of cultural analysis and urged him to write a concise history of Kansas that would incorporate the findings of his many writings. But, he cautioned, Malin should not bring the story past World War I. Not surprisingly, Malin was unpopular in some sectors of the historical profession, and derision was sometimes expressed in asides at historical meetings. We have seen that members of a later generation were to fault Malin's ideological biases concerning his views both on antebellum territorial issues and grassland ecology. Time will place these criticisms in perspective and a later generation doubtless identify the ideological inclinations of the critics.[49]

Finally, Malin's career suggests another legacy to western historians and, indeed, to all historians. His career is an inspiring example of commitment. Malin called the shots as he saw them. He never regretted that he exposed the flimsiness of the free-state hotel claim. He did not stop his research when others disagreed with him or he suffered professional disappointments. He always stood true to his obligations as a professional historian. Robert Galen Bell characterized Malin with a quotation: "The real historians are those who love history for its own sake, who love it when they are old as when they were young. . . . To them history is a profession, a profession worthy of its hire, and in itself a sufficient reward for the hardest efforts."[50] Malin was indeed a "real historian."

NOTES

1. Robert Galen Bell accurately summarizes Malin's personal background and surveys his career and writings to the mid-1960s, in "James C. Malin: A Study in American Historiography" (Ph.D diss., University of California, Los Angeles, 1968). Burton J. Williams, ed., included a comprehensive bibliography of Malin's writings in preparing *Essays in American History in Honor of James C. Malin* (Lawrence: Coronado Press, 1973), 239–50. Subsequent to Professor Malin's death on January 26, 1979, Pearl E. Malin compiled a supplementary list of his publications. During 1972, Gould P. Coleman of the Cornell University Libraries staff interviewed Malin; the 118-page transcript will be cited hereafter as Malin, "Oral Interview." A considerable collection of Malin's correspondence, teaching materials, research notes, and miscellaneous items constitute Collection 183 at the Kansas State Historical Society, Topeka. During academic year

1948–49, I was Malin's research assistant and took his course in the History of the Trans-Mississippi West and a broadly defined graduate-readings course in the History of Agricultural Policy, as well as auditing his course on the History of Kansas. Thereafter, we corresponded sporadically until well into the years of Malin's retirement, and also I was able to renew our personal contact during the summer of 1955 when I attended the first of several summer conferences for young historians organized by the Department of History at the University of Kansas.

2. Frank Heywood Hodder to James C. Malin, December 4, 1919, James C. Malin Collection, Kansas State Historical Society, cited by Bell, "A Study in Historiography," 10.

3. Malin, *A Concern About Humanity: Notes on Reform, 1872–1912 at the National and Kansas Levels of Thought* (Ann Arbor, Mich.: Edwards Brothers, 1964), and *Power and Change in Society with Special Reference to Kansas, 1880–1890* (Lawrence: Coronado Press, 1981), particularly explore themes that Malin treated in his course in the History of Kansas.

4. Everett Dick, *The Sod-House Frontier, 1854–1890: A Social History of the Northern Plains* (New York: Appleton-Century, 1937).

5. Williams, ed., *In Honor of James C. Malin*, 251–56, provides a listing of Malin's graduate advisees and the titles of their theses or dissertations.

6. D. Aidan McQuillan to Allan G. Bogue, March 15, 1989. A number of those who attended one or more of the conferences of the 1950s have recently shared their recollections with me. I much appreciate the kindness in this respect of Lee Benson, Robert H. Bremner, John A. Denovo, Robert H. Ferrell, Dewey W. Grantham, Otis A. Pease, Roland Stromberg, David Van Tassel, and Bennet H. Wall.

• 7. George L. Anderson, "Frank Heywood Hodder and the Kansas-Nebraska Act, 1854–1954," *Your Government: the Bulletin of the Governmental Research Center, University of Kansas* (1954). James C. Malin, "Frank Heywood Hodder, 1860–1935," *Kansas Historical Quarterly* 5 (May 1936):115–21.

8. Malin, *Confounded Rot About Napoleon: Reflections Upon Science and Technology, Nationalism, World Depression of the Eighteen-Nineties, and Afterwards* (Ann Arbor: Edwards Brothers, 1961).

9. Rodney O. Davis to Allan G. Bogue, February 15, 1989.

10. James C. Malin, *Indian Policy and Westward Expansion. Bulletin of the University of Kansas, Humanistic Studies*, vol. 2, no. 3 (Lawrence: University of Kansas, 1921); *The United States, 1865–1917: An Interpretation. Bulletin of the University of Kansas, Humanistic Studies*, vol. 3, no. 2 (Lawrence: University of Kansas, 1924): *The United States after the World War* (Boston: Ginn and Company, 1930).

11. Malin, *John Brown and the Legend of Fifty-Six.* Memoirs of the American Philosophical Society, vol. 17 (Philadelphia: American Philosophical Society, 1942); *Winter Wheat in the Golden Belt of Kansas: A Study in Adaptation to Subhumid Geographical Environment* (Lawrence: University of Kansas Press, 1944); *Essays on Historiography* (Ann Arbor: Edwards Brothers, 1946).

12. Malin, *Essays on Historiography*.

13. Malin, *The Nebraska Question, 1852–1854* (Ann Arbor: Edwards Brothers, 1953).

14. Malin was president of the Agricultural History Society in 1943. During the late 1920s and early 1930s he wrote a manuscript "History of the Recent Agricultural Policy of the United States" that was never published. Malin assigned the manuscript as reading in his graduate reading course in the History of American Agricultural Policy. There is a copy in the Malin Collection in the Kansas State Historical Society.

15. Malin, *Indian Policy and Westward Expansion*, 5, 41.

16. Malin, "The Proslavery Background of the Kansas Struggle," *Mississippi Valley Historical Review* 10 (December 1923): 285; "In Commemoration of the Centennial Anniversary of the Admission of Kansas into the Union 1961" (Lawrence: University of Kansas Library, 1961), 9.

17. Malin, "Proslavery Background," 305.

18. "Claims for Burning of Old Free State Hotel Bring Reminiscences of Episodes in Lawrence History," *University Daily Kansan*, January 6, 1929; Malin to the Editor, *Daily Kansan*, January 10, 1929; Clifford S. Griffin, "The University of Kansas and the Sack of Lawrence: A Problem of Intellectual Honesty," *Kansas Historical Quarterly* 34 (Winter 1968):409–26.

19. Malin, "Colonel Harvey and his Forty Thieves," *Mississippi Valley Historical Review* 19 (June 1932):57–76.

20. See n. 11 above.

21. Ralph V. Harlow, "Review," *Journal of Southern History* 9 (August 1943):419; James G. Randall, "Review," *American Historical Review* 48 (July 1943):819–20; Philip M. Hamer, "Review," *Mississippi Valley Historical Review* 30 (March 1944):581–82.

22. Stephen B. Oates, "John Brown and His Judges: A Critique of the Historical Literature," *Civil War History* 17 (March 1971):13, 19. See also Oates, *To Purge this Land with Blood: A Biography of John Brown* (New York: Harper and Row, 1970), 70–180. Malin, *Legend of Fifty-Six*, vii, viii.

23. Malin, *The Nebraska Question, 1852–1854* (Ann Arbor: Edwards Brothers, 1953). But also note two useful territorial centennial pieces: "The Nebraska Question: A Ten-Year Record, 1844–1854," *Nebraska History* 35 (March 1954):1–15, and "The Topeka Statehood Movement Reconsidered: Origins," *Territorial Kansas: Studies Commemorating the Centennial*. University of Kansas Social Science Studies (Lawrence: University of Kansas, 1954), 33–69.

24. Holman Hamilton, "Review," *Pacific Historical Review* 23 (November 1954):509; Roy F. Nichols, "Review," *American Historical Review* 59 (July 1954):947; Avery Craven, "Review," *Journal of Southern History* 20 (May 1954):270–71.

25. Joseph H. Parks, "Review," *Mississippi Valley Historical Review* 41 (June 1954):132; Nichols, op. cit. For Malin's comment on style, see his "On the Nature of Local History," *Wisconsin Magazine of History* 40 (Summer 1957):230.

26. Walter P. Webb, *The Great Plains* (Boston: Ginn and Company, 1931).

27. Malin, "The Turnover of Farm Population in Kansas," *Kansas Historical Quarterly* 4 (November 1935):339–72.

28. Joseph Schafer's research in Wisconsin local history antedated Malin's work, but his use of census data was much more descriptive than the Kansan's. Harriet and Frank Owsley and his students—the "Vanderbilt School"—used manuscript census data to good effect, but Harriet Owsley informed me on February 7, 1989, that they were not aware of their availability or potential utility until the fall of 1937.

29. Malin, "The Kinsley Boom of the Late Eighties," *Kansas Historical Quarterly* 4 (February, May 1935):23–49, 164–87; "The Adaptation of the Agricultural System to Sub-Humid Environment," *Agricultural History* 10 (July 1936): 118–41; quoted passage, p. 118.

30. Malin, *Winter Wheat in the Golden Belt of Kansas* (Lawrence: University of Kansas Press, 1944), and *The Grassland of North America: Prolegomena to Its History* (Ann Arbor: Edwards Brothers, 1947); rep. as *The Grassland of North America: Prolegomena to Its History with Addenda and Postscript* (Gloucester, Mass: Peter Smith, 1967).

31. Malin, *Winter Wheat*, 251–52.

32. Malin, "Oral Interview," 24.

33. Malin, *Grassland*, 31.

34. Malin, "Dust Storms, 1850–1900," *Kansas Historical Quarterly* 14 (May, August, November, 1946):129–44, 265–96, 391–413.

35. Paul B. Sears, *Deserts on the March* (Norman: University of Oklahoma Press, 1935).

36. Malin, *Grassland Historical Studies: Natural Resources Utilization in a Background of Science and Technology*, vol. 1: *Geology and Geography* (Ann Arbor: Edwards Brothers, 1950). Four of the papers of these years are presented as chaps. 23–26 in *Grassland of North America* (1967). A fifth, "The Grassland of North America: Its Occupance and the Challenge of Continuous Reappraisals," appears in William L. Thomas, Jr., ed., *Man's Role in Changing the Face of the Earth* (Chicago: University of Chicago Press, 1956).

37. Thomas H. LeDuc, "An Ecological Interpretation of Grasslands History: The Work of James C. Malin as Historian," *Nebraska History* 31 (September 1950):226–33. Donald Worster, *Dust Bowl: The Southern Plains in the 1930s* (New York: Oxford University Press, 1979), 205. See also Worster, *Nature's Economy: The Roots of Ecology* (San Francisco: Sierra Club Books, 1977). Malin, *Grassland*, 119.

38. Ronald C. Tobey, *Saving the Prairies: The Life Cycle of the Founding School of American Plant Ecology, 1895–1955* (Berkeley: University of California Press, 1981), 196–222.

39. Malin, *The United States, 1865–1917*, 9.

40. Op. cit., 18.

41. Malin, *Grassland of North America*, 264; *Essays on Historiography*, 1, 37.

42. Op. cit., 24, 32.

43. Op. cit., 11, 36.

44. Malin, *Grassland*, 255, 264.

45. "Comments upon the Papers of W. P. Webb and Lee Benson at the Annual Meeting of the American Historical Association, Chicago, December 28, 1950." Typescript bound with a collection of review reprints assembled by Pearl E. Malin. My colleague, Stanley K. Schultz, was present as an undergraduate when Webb presented a lecture before the History Department at the University of Kansas during the early 1960s and was challenged by Malin, who suggested that Webb's concept of regionalism was somewhat inferior to his own.

46. Malin, *Grassland* (1967 ed.), 408; see also Malin, *The Contriving Brain and the Skillful Hand in the United States: Something about History and Philosophy of History in the United States* (Ann Arbor: Edwards Brothers, 1955). Robert W. Johannsen, "James C. Malin: An Appreciation," *Kansas Historical Quarterly* 38 (Winter 1972):457.

47. Robert P. Swierenga, ed., *James C. Malin, History and Ecology: Studies of the Grassland* (Lincoln: University of Nebraska Press, 1984), xix.

48. Calvin McMillan, "Grassland Perspective," *Ecology* 38 (July 1957): 542.

49. Malin, "Adventure into the Unknown: Relativist 'Man-Afraid-of-His-Mind,' " in Helmut Schoeck and James W. Wiggins, eds., *Relativism and the Study of Man* (Princeton: D. Van Nostrand, 1961), 175–96; Roy F. Nichols, "Kansas Historiography: The Technique of Cultural Analysis," *American Quarterly* 9 (Spring 1957):85–91.

50. John Spencer Bassett, *The Middle Group of Historians* (New York: Macmillan, 1917), 136.

BIBLIOGRAPHY

MAJOR WESTERN WRITINGS OF JAMES C. MALIN

"The Adaptation of the Agricultural System to Sub-Humid Environment." *Agricultural History* 10 (July 1936):118–41.

"Dust Storms: Part One, 1850–1860; Part Two, 1861–1880; Part Three, 1881–1900." *Kansas Historical Quarterly* 14 (May, August, November, 1946):129–44, 265–96, 391–413.

Essays on Historiography. Ann Arbor: Edwards Brothers, 1946.

Grassland Historical Studies: Natural Resource Utilization in a Background of Science and Technology. Vol. 1: Geology and Geography. Ann Arbor: Edwards Brothers, 1950.

The Grassland of North America: Prolegomena to Its History with Addenda and Postscript. Gloucester, Mass.: Peter Smith, 1967 (rep. and supplement to 1947 edition).

Indian Policy and Westward Expansion. Bulletin of the University of Kansas, Humanistic Studies, Vol. 2, No. 3. Lawrence: University of Kansas, 1921.

John Brown and the Legend of Fifty-Six. Philadelphia: American Philosophical Society, 1942.

"The Nebraska Question: A Ten Year Record, 1844–1854." *Nebraska History* 35 (March 1954):1–15.

The Nebraska Question, 1852–1854. Ann Arbor: Edwards Brothers, 1953.

"The Proslavery Background of the Kansas Struggle." *Mississippi Valley Historical Review* 10 (December 1923):285–305.

"The Topeka Statehood Movement Reconsidered: Origins." *Territorial Kansas: Studies Commemorating the Centennial.* Lawrence: University of Kansas, 1954.

"The Turnover of Farm Population in Kansas." *Kansas Historical Quarterly* 4 (November 1935):339–72.

Winter Wheat in the Golden Belt of Kansas: A Study of Adaptation to Subhumid Geographical Environment. Lawrence: University of Kansas Press, 1944.

WORKS ABOUT JAMES C. MALIN

Bell, Robert Galen. "James C. Malin: A Study in American Historiography." Ph.D. dissertation, University of California, Los Angeles, 1968.

Bogue, Allan G. "The Heirs of James C. Malin: A Grassland Historiography." *Great Plains Quarterly* 1 (Spring 1981):105–31.

Griffin, Clifford S. "The University of Kansas and the Sack of Lawrence: A Problem of Intellectual Honesty." *Kansas Historical Quarterly* 34 (Winter 1968):409–26.

Johannsen, Robert W. "James C. Malin: An Appreciation." *Kansas Historical Quarterly* 38 (Winter 1972):457–66.

LaForte, Robert S. "James C. Malin, Optimist: The Basis of His Philosophy of History." *Kansas History: A Journal of the Central Plains* 6 (Summer 1983): 110–19.

LeDuc, Thomas H. "An Ecological Interpretation of Grasslands History: The Work of James C. Malin as Historian." *Nebraska History* 31 (September 1950): 226–33.

Nichols, Roy F. "Kansas Historiography: The Technique of Cultural Analysis." *American Quarterly* 9 (Spring 1957):85–91.

Swierenga, Robert P., ed. *James C. Malin: History and Ecology, Studies of the Grassland.* Lincoln: University of Nebraska Press, 1984.

Williams, Burton J. "James C. Malin, Creative Iconoclast." *Heritage of the Great Plains* 16 (Spring 1983):18–33.

————, ed. *Essays in Honor of James C. Malin.* Lawrence: Coronado Press, 1973.

III

*Recent Western
Historians*

9

Henry Nash Smith's
Myth of the West

LEE CLARK MITCHELL

"*O*NE OF THE MOST PERSISTENT
generalizations concerning American life and character is the notion
that our society has been shaped by the pull of a vacant continent drawing population westward through the passes of the Alleghenies, across
the Mississippi Valley, over the high plains and mountains of the Far
West to the Pacific Coast."[1] So it was that Henry Nash Smith opened his
magisterial *Virgin Land* (1950), a study that itself has "shaped" the dominant view of the American West more fully than any since Frederick
Jackson Turner's. In part, Smith's triumph can be traced to the sheer
ambitiousness of his scope—his willingness to venture bold speculations about a diverse array of western materials, and then to move like
Turner beyond the bounds of a narrowly regional history in order to pose
much larger questions of cultural meaning and national identity. Like
Turner as well, he succeeded through a graceful, sometimes colorful
style that deftly captured the turn of events in a series of memorable
turns of phrase.[2] Yet where Turner's broad rhetorical strokes carried a
thesis that the frontier had created Americans, Smith chose to turn his
eye inward to focus on figures of speech themselves, on the vivid language invoked by Americans to create a West as image of their desires.
Both men captured contemporary imaginations by writing western history metaphorically, but Smith trumped Turner by reading as metaphor
the language others had accepted as literally true. By reading metaphor
historically, in other words, Smith revealed how powerfully rhetoric
itself can invert historical patterns of cause and effect. This working

assumption is nowhere better exemplified than in the altered formulation that he adopted for the West: not "free land," with Turner's
straightforward economic and political connotations, but "virgin land,"
which implies a blank slate, an unexplored region, an uncontested terrain open to imaginative conquest and the transformation that will
finally allow history to begin.

So convincing was Smith's thesis, and so influential for scholars
outside the field of western history, that he is often cited as an "originating figure," even *the* "originating figure" of the American Studies
movement that emerged in full force during the 1950s. The reason is
not simply that he was the first to receive a doctorate in American Civilization from Harvard (after all, similar degrees had already been
awarded for some years at Yale); nor was it that *Virgin Land* is often
lauded as the first book that could genuinely by deemed as belonging
to American Studies (even though interdisciplinary texts on American
culture had certainly preceded it). Smith's stature rests, instead, on
the force of the kinds of questions he found worth asking, and the
kinds of answers that he found convincing. All but singlehandedly, he
generated a new perspective for Americanist scholars by drawing
together ideas from psychology, philosophy, and anthropology, from
history and literature "high" and "low," in an interdisciplinary mélange
that continues to define the field. Much as Turner exerted a strong if
covert influence over Smith—which Smith himself came to realize only
long after the fact when he was rereading his own book—so the materials and methods of *Virgin Land* still continue to influence us, inform-
ing the work of Americanists in a number of varied disciplines and
altering the assumptions of those with otherwise little interest in the
West.[3] Far more than any other western historian, Smith forced an
awareness of the ways in which history is as much made as found, as
much an account of imagery and desire, as of actual topographies or
real events.

Smith came of intellectual age at a time when the study of religion,
literature, history, and art had become increasingly specialized—fostered
by scholars whose interests had shifted toward more and more local
studies, as well as more neatly disciplinary concerns. Resisting such
specialization, Smith self-consciously broadened the scope of scholarly investigation in order to trace the indigeneous "myths" and "symbols" that might explain American culture. In the process, he fostered
a set of assumptions about popular images and collective beliefs that
have since themselves been called into question—assumptions about

the connections linking private intention with public behavior, cultural belief, and social control. Yet he also offered an engagingly powerful vision of cultural process that no longer seemed imposed from above or simply imported from the East—one that emerged instead through the accumulated experience of Americans living in the West. A westerner himself, he remained perpetually curious about vernacular forms, alert to the vitality of regional idioms, local lore, and subcultural modes of behavior that vigorously (if only insidiously) contested the dominant culture. Such western habits of expression effectively spoke across lines of eastern authority, giving the lie to standard claims for cultural "integrity" or homogeneity "from the top down," and revealing a web of cultural meanings inaccessible to more traditional methods of inquiry.

Smith can, in other words, be seen as reacting fiercely against the intellectual Balkanization that fractured mainstream scholarship during the years of his apprenticeship and early maturity. From his earliest essays in the 1920s (on contemporary Texas) to his late studies in the 1970s (on popular literature), he was intent upon breaching divisions that others had taken as obvious or natural. Whether it was simply the split between "high" and "low" culture, or between the established academic disciplines of anthropology, psychology, politics, and art, Smith invariably strove to rescue meanings obscured by such divisions. His innovative practice eventually led (from the perspective of hindsight, all too predictably) to revisionist attacks on his consensus ideal of culture. Yet the power of his reading of the American West was based on just that willingness to see it whole—as not simply a separate region of unique events and idiosyncratic assumptions, but as an essential component of what he took to be a national consciousness. Integrating history with literature in order to address broad questions of cultural meaning, Smith transformed our understanding of the West's effect on Americans, and vice versa. Ironically, given his attention to cultural polyphony and his enduring distaste for ad hoc divisions, he would eventually be accused of ignoring contestatory voices and minority views. The very comprehensiveness of his thesis—establishing how an imagined "West" has continuously transformed social, economic, and political issues unrelated to it—was taken as a damning sign of elitist assumptions.

Over a long career, Henry Nash Smith would investigate various aspects of American culture. But his major, distinctively western efforts—*Virgin Land* and the books on Mark Twain—grew from his earliest experiences as a child growing up in Texas. In his own words, written late in life, "my childhood and youth in Texas . . . stored up in me an almost unnoticed feeling for the Western past."[4] Born in Dallas in 1906, he graduated in 1925 from Southern Methodist University and was persuaded to cross the Mississippi for the first time only to spend a disappointing year in Harvard's English Department. Returning eagerly to Texas with an M.A. in hand, he began teaching Chaucer, Milton, and literary criticism at S.M.U., where he remained for more than a decade. During this period, he also coedited the *Southwest Review*, writing a regular column for the journal that enthusiastically championed the new western regionalism. The movement had been inspired by the work of friends like J. Frank Dobie and Walter Prescott Webb and was oriented specifically toward the art and life of the Great Plains and Rocky Mountains. Also during this period, Smith began to read unsystematically in a broad range of disciplines, exploring a curious medley of ideas that would later coalesce in his best work. Intellectuals like Bergson, Frazer, Freud, Boas, Lévy-Bruhl, and Otto Rank, among others, transformed his understanding of myth, dreams, and collective behavior, intriguing him with the possibility of a new perspective on the American West wholly unlike that introduced by Turner.[5]

In 1937, attracted by Harvard's new American Civilization program, Smith again went east and was immediately drawn to Frederick Merk's course on the Westward Movement. As he later acknowledged, "it was precisely the impact of Merk's richly factual approach to Western history on my earlier flights into the stratosphere of epistemology that set in motion the mental process that became *Virgin Land*."[6] Working under the supervision of Merk and Howard Mumford Jones, he completed a dissertation finally entitled "American Intellectual and Imaginative Attitudes toward the Great Plains and the Rocky Mountains, 1803–1850." The carefully chosen, cumbersome title conceals the fact that Smith had been forced to abandon his original and ambitious plan of surveying the entire century. As countless other graduate students have likewise been forced to acknowledge, the materials he needed to research were far more extensive than his finances. In 1940, as a rather mature student of thirty-four, he was awarded the program's first doctoral degree.

Smith returned once again to S.M.U. to found a program in the "History of American Civilization," but was lured away only a year later by the offer of a position at the University of Texas. He remained at Austin through the war, moved on to Minnesota in 1947, and then in 1953 he accepted the permanent appointment at Berkeley that would be his last. Repeatedly, his liberal principles and devotion to the ideal of academic freedom placed him in embattled positions against a reigning conservative orthodoxy.[7] At Texas, he wrote a documentary pamphlet for the Students Association that opposed any of the political or racial constraints prescribed by the Board of Regents. At Minnesota, he openly defended the right of faculty to join the Communist party and went on to challenge an emergent McCarthyism in a series of forthright published statements. At Berkeley, during the Loyalty Oath controversy, then the Free Speech movement, followed in turn by the Vietnam, Cambodian, and Third World protests, he continued to espouse deep liberal principles, but increasingly operated behind the scenes as a conciliator and trusted negotiator. Over a half-century in academic life, Smith never failed to champion the university as a unique and necessary forum for the expression of unfavorable ideas. At the height of his career, as president of the Modern Language Association, he was nonetheless compelled to face down protestors at the annual convention in 1969. Having been led (by his liberal ideals) into an open confrontation with militant radicals, he was publicly charged as the representative of a sexist, racist, elitist institution by those whose very right to be heard he himself would once again fiercely defend.[8]

The irony, however, may not be as great in fact as it seems, since Smith's own scholarship did represent the hegemony of interests against which the radicals were protesting. Despite the heterogeneity of his materials, despite his sensitivity to vernacular or otherwise marginal voices, he had nonetheless invariably sought to identify the dominant discourse within a largely middle-class, largely white, largely male experience. And students and colleagues influenced by him at Minnesota and Berkeley—including most notably Leo Marx, Tony Tanner, and Alan Trachtenberg—not only themselves represented such an exclusive group, but likewise encouraged the further study of those similarly privileged. True, Smith's devotion to a pluralism of voices had the salutary effect of enabling a critique of premises in his own work. But that would occur only twenty-odd years after the first appearance of *Virgin Land*, following the intellectual and social upheavals that occurred in the late 1960s and 1970s.

Less dramatic (and more enigmatic) than this shift in Smith's perceived political persona—from champion of radical causes to formal apologist for the status quo—is the transition in his professional career from innovative cultural historian to rather more traditional literary critic.

He had initiated a powerful new mode of studying the American West, relying upon a creative mix of disciplines and materials to sustain a set of daring claims for the significance of "region" in national thought. Yet following *Virgin Land*, he metamorphosed into a seemingly more cautious and conventional scholar, committed all but exclusively to editing and interpreting the works of Mark Twain. The years at Berkeley were spent not in American Studies but in an English Department, and on the whole he no longer chose to address large cultural questions with the same ambition. Yet even as one wonders what contributed to this transformation, it may be appropriate (given Smith's own lessons in historical self-consciousness) to ask ourselves why we must construe it as a dramatic turn in his thought, as an abrupt volte-face rather than a gentle and congruent transition.

Part of the answer lies once again in the human tale of Smith's intellectual biography and comes down to the fact that his considerable stature as historian and critic is based, like Turner's, on a surprisingly small body of work. The long gestation of *Virgin Land*, as well as the difficulties he exerienced in securing its publication, meant that he was forty-three before his first book had even appeared.[9] And not until his mid-fifties, a dozen years later, would his second book be published, *Mark Twain: The Development of a Writer*, followed two years later by his third, *Mark Twain's Fable of Progress: Political and Economic Ideas in "A Connecticut Yankee."*[10] Different from each other as these books are in subject matter and overall treatment, each one succeeds as an exemplary model of scholarly expertise, each has been highly influential, and each focuses on a set of characteristically "western" motifs. It is also clear that each was conceived and written by the same person, since through them all runs a persistent concern, even obsession, with questions of identity—and in particular, with the ways that regional and cultural identity are peculiarly shaped.[11]

Smith's "turn" to Twain was mediated by this overriding obsession, and more particularly by the persistent vision of identity as in great measure the product of language, created through the suasions of rhetoric. Twain can, of course, be seen as embodying (perhaps more than any other American writer) the uncertainties of identity—not only in his gaudily divided public persona, but in the recurrent themes of his fiction. Smith's early fascination with the meaning of the West in the construction of a unique American identity, then, far from switching abruptly to a scholarly investigation of Twain, simply mutated into a more crabbed, more precise, less easily satisfied curiosity about a deeply conflicted writerly personality. In both cases, early and late, Smith probed the underside of a supposedly integrated American self, questioning what many had assumed was simply an unproblematic construction. Working amid an unusual constellation of texts and documents—in *Virgin Land*, of a region; in his books on Mark Twain, of a famous career—he proposed ambitious, controversial analyses of western icons. And by probing the contradictions that emerged from these powerful images, he disclosed a hitherto unobserved richness within American culture, past and present.

These large issues were already intriguing Smith in his early twenties, as confirmed by the rather confident title he attached to his very first essay: "Culture." He protested vehemently against the way that "cultural" and "business" interests in Texas worked at odds to each other, and lamented: "Unable to find culture, we have tried desperately to content ourselves with soporific or artificially stimulating amusements of escape." By contrast, "the deep satisfaction of an indigenous culture" both contributes to and emerges from great art, which consists in "products of a common enthusiasm . . . expressing desires near the hearts of the common people."[12] This was a somewhat paradoxical vision that at once celebrated indigenous forms of art and entertainment, yet decried their inability at the moment to sustain any serious intellectual life—a vision expressed by countless Americans from James Fenimore Cooper through Henry James. During the next two decades, this paradox increasingly troubled Smith, who, in essays for the *Southwest Review*, repeatedly disparaged the lack of genuinely indigenous forms of response, wryly challenging the bureaucratic logic behind "Hoover's Philosophy of Comfort," invidiously comparing the charms of Europe with "Living in America," and in general proposing that Texans ignore the "opiate" of mass culture in favor of authentic traditions and local idioms.[13] Long before Adorno and Horkheimer would blast the "culture industry" on behalf of the claims of art, Smith had staked out a similar position as the proponent of culture from the bottom up.

If *Virgin Land* emerged, then, from a persistent Emersonian concern with the local and particular, it did so as a response to questions raised by Smith's troubled view of American culture. Perhaps what we sense as the desire for a strong overarching thesis, the longing for a comprehensive account that impels so much of the argument in *Virgin Land*, might be traced back to this uneasiness about the integrity of cultural life in modern America. For Smith seems everywhere to doubt that the "indigenous culture" he celebrated had in fact yielded the kinds of "deep satisfactions" he claimed or that it had otherwise succeeded in generating a coherent, sustaining intellectual vision. Thus, in *Virgin Land* he set himself the task of discovering an unspoken order to nineteenth-century ideas, to show how a range of popular beliefs, common assumptions, and government policies had all coalesced in a set of powerful images. Those images could obviously be linked to expectations evoked by a singular landscape, and that iconographic hoard was, in turn, the precursor to human action. As he expressed the general thesis some twenty years after, "history cannot happen . . . without images which simultaneously express collective desires and impose coherence on the infinitely numerous and infinitely varied data of experience."[14] Instead of offering a narrowly economic or political study of the West, or a colorfully biographical and anecdotal account (of the kind frequently written prior to 1950), he experimented with a method of relating events to cultural responses by concentrating on the popular images that linked western history with literature.

Where Herbert Eugene Bolton, Frederic Logan Paxson, James Malin, and even Walter Prescott Webb had earned fine reputations as historians by explaining aspects of the region's development, Smith began by turning his attention to a distinctively figurative question: what did it mean that the West had previously been conceived as a blank space outside of history, and how did that misconception affect the ideas that Americans held of themselves? By assessing words as generously as other historians had evaluated events, he fastened upon what Americans thought they were doing as well as what they actually had done. He attended to the language they used in the effort to transform a continent and discovered how fully the continent, in turn, had transformed them through their language. As much as anyone else since Turner, Smith believed an otherwise regional history had created a national consciousness. But he believed it in a special way: that Americans' altering view of the West itself figured forth the meaning of America. As he explained some thirty-five years later, he had identified a distinctive "political unconscious" to American life long before Fredric Jameson had labeled the concept.[15]

Virgin Land explores the capacity of language to effect historical change. Yet, as Smith saw it, this protean verbal activity was born of human desire, specifically the desire of nineteenth-century Americans to embrace a landscape they did not know. This not-knowing—the empty epistemological space that constituted the West for so many—enabled a process of self-definition that was also one of self-projection, revealing far more about those who wanted to possess the West than of the West itself. In separate sections, Smith assesses three prevalent images of the West—images that existed simultaneously but that were dominant at slightly different periods. The first section, on "The Passage to India," traces the changing conception of the unexplored continent from little more than a geographical stumbling block to a lauded and valued end in itself. Through the century, this notion of a far-flung empire somewhere beyond the Pacific loomed large. Gradually, however, the high plains and coastal woodlands themselves—conceived at first as nothing but a gateway to empire in the Orient—began to be imaged as the locus of imperial power. Turning from the writings of Thomas Jefferson to the speeches of Thomas Hart Benton, linking the railroad proposals of William Gilpin with the bardic mysticism of Walt Whitman, Smith argued that a constantly changing national faith was represented by an invariable symbol: the old "passage" to the Far East mutated into a golden highway, in the transition "from an outward-looking to an introspective conception of empire" (29). Ideas of Manifest Destiny were gradually associated with the western landscape itself, as America *became* the empire whose location had been sought for so long. That transformation explains a long history of government policies, domestic and foreign, whether on behalf of internal improvements or isolationism.

Part Two plots a metamorphosis in the equally persistent image of "The Sons of Leatherstocking," rugged personifications of the wilderness who appeared first as escapees from civilization, then as civilizing figures themselves. This section shifts away from historical personages to fictional characters (or, in the case of Daniel Boone and Kit Carson, to a fictionalized reality), and in the process it shifts from political conceptions of empire to the increasingly social problems of law and order, authority and violence. Deadwood Dick, Calamity Jane, and a host of other dime-novel figures are given a lineage that extends back through novels by Charles Webber and James Fenimore Cooper, and forward to Buffalo Bill's Wild West shows and the emergence of the cowboy hero. As Smith nicely observes, the ambivalence of this western figure—self-reliant yet advocating social good, freed from the trappings of civilization yet prompted by Christian ethics—reflects a deeper division that Americans felt about their culture.

A long, last section on "The Garden of the World" depicts an evo-

lution in the way the West was visually imagined: from barren desert
to fruitful garden, from threatening wilderness to agrarian paradise
where the ideal of a yeoman society could still be achieved. As Smith
points out, neither of these disparate images accurately described the
Far West in the late nineteenth century, as it was being transformed by
industrial capitalism (the yeoman farmer had little place in a realm where
farms were increasingly mechanized, where huge land grants were given
to railways and then quickly sold to speculators). Yet as fully as the collapse of that image was detailed in the bleak accounts of local-color
realists, its strength was nonetheless reflected in a host of public-land
policies that culminated in the 1862 Homestead Act. That crowning
tribute to a republican ideology based on the idea of free labor would
prove in the end a dismal failure, all because the image of the West on
which it was based was simply fantastic.

Criss-crossing the century in pursuit of these diverse set of images,
Smith pulled together an assortment of material culled from his reading in "books, magazines, newspapers, promotional pamphlets, emigrants' guides, government reports (including records of debates in
Congress and legislatures), novels, everything I could lay hands on."[16]
He carefully transgressed conventional categories, as if aware that the
clarity they secured for issues political, social, or economic was purchased at the price of some obscurity for issues cultural and sociopsy-
chological. As Richard Bridgman tellingly observes:

> *Smith's patient harvest of diverse testimonies indicated what*
> *insights were available when one ignored, as it were, the limits*
> *of any specifically defined academic discipline. In the opening*
> *pages of one chapter of* Virgin Land, *the sources for Smith's*
> *argument are successively: Tocqueville's* Democracy in
> America; *an essay by Whitman; Lewis Evans's* Geographical,
> Historical, Political, Philosophical Essay *(1775); Jonathan*
> *Carver's* Travels Through the Interior Parts of North
> America in the Years 1766, 1767, and 1768; *Nathaniel*
> *Ames's* Astronomical Diary; *a poem by Freneau; a letter and*
> *an essay by Franklin; an article from the* William and Mary
> Quarterly *and one from* Agricultural History; *and George*
> *Logan's* Letters, Addressed to the Yeomanry of the United
> States *(1791). Each source constitutes a part of the extremely*
> *intricate mosaic that Smith was assembling. One never feels that*
> *their function is to crush the reader with authority, but rather to*
> *enlighten by means of establishing unexpected conjunctions of*
> *evidence.*[17]

Beyond the electric illumination generated by such startling juxtaposi-
tions, Smith's writing also carried conviction enforced by its unusual
literary strategies. His history, in other words, depended—as much as
that of the culture he unlayered—on the force of language per se. Thus,
as historian he melded genres, mixing the force of traditional historical documentation with a rich admixture of the artifice inherent in literary narrative. In effect, he convinced the reader of his "unexpected
conjunctions of evidence" through a series of otherwise silent fictional
techniques.

   "Historical" here refers not only to amassed evidence and documentary citations but to the book's chronological structure; each section tends to focus on a different time span, moving, in turn, from the
first to the middle, to the last third of the nineteenth century. "Fictional"
suggests, on the other hand, the various gestures toward rhetorical
shape, the tropes, figures, and oppositions that animate Smith's verbal
landscape. The three sections, for instance, are organized around quite
different epicenters: the first around the largely political implications
of the image of empire; the second around the social issue of reasonable
constraints on individual behavior; and the third around economic
problems associated with western development. Moreover, each section
nicely defines itself in terms of a binary opposition: of the West as merely
a passage to empire, or as the setting of empire itself; of the westerner
as eager refugee from the trappings of civilization, or as its harbinger;
of the land as desert, or garden. Despite an impressive amassing of
materials that might in other hands simply fall apart, Smith threads
his way (and ours) through a complex history of ideological conflict.

   Indeed, Smith's argument benefits from the particular way *Virgin
Land* unfolds, a pattern that only becomes apparent from a narrative
or rhetorical perspective. Each of the three separate sections extends
twice as long as the one preceding, which lends a certain onward motion
to the underlying thesis: the first image of the West is depicted in four
chapters of thirty-three pages; the second requires six chapters and sixty-
nine pages to illustrate; and the last, more than half the book, is detailed
in twelve chapters and 137 pages. At the same time, the narrative focus
becomes more relaxed as the book progresses: the concentration on a
few powerful historical figures in the first section gives way to a discussion of broader, less coherent, more impersonal movements in the
third. The story, that is, grows more evocative the farther one reads.
And topping off Smith's effective disposition of materials is the compelling rhetorical way in which he characterizes ideas. The headings
to sections, for instance ("The Sons of Leatherstocking" or "The Gar-

den of the World"), deftly capture his dominant themes, as do his larger descriptions of the "anonymous popular mind" and an "objectified mass dream" (34, 91). There is even a curious mixing of metaphors hidden in the suggestive implication of the title itself, of a virgin land pregnant with possibilities.

Smith persuasively reveals the capacity of an image like "virgin land" to incorporate ideas of egalitarianism, individualism, and progress—indeed, all that Turner had meant to suggest by the phrase "free land." Yet Smith's metaphor and the questions he asks derive from premises never considered by Turner, including, first, the notion that a symbiotic relation exists between artists and their social contexts and that the collective myths and symbols cherished by a society are the property of no individual effort but, rather, are jointly produced. Second, Smith assumes that these apparent "timeless images" have a broadly ordering effect on popular attitudes and beliefs, and that ideological contradictions are resolved at any given time through the images people cherish (viii). Finally, he holds to the idea that myths and symbols are accepted as more or less true by everyone in a culture, whether or not those images "accurately reflect empirical fact" (vii). Their power lies precisely in their capacity to order ideas by lending an apparent logic to political, economic, and social movements, as well as by more self-consciously structuring an assortment of fictive expressions.

This uniting of image and idea, of literary expression and historical event, as well as the atmospheric evocation of history conveyed by the narrative structure of *Virgin Land*, proved both a powerful performance and an immediate success—one that continued to influence American scholars through the next two decades. Indeed, so many others replicated Smith's effort that it became known (as it were, on the street) as the "myth and symbol" school—a sobriquet not originally as comically cosmic as it now seems. Few of these practitioners were, as it happens, concerned with the West itself, having turned instead to other metaphors and organizing images in order to reveal the supposedly constitutive structure of "American life and character." It is instructive, moreover, that few of these were trained as American historians. In general, they came instead from departments of English literature and turned their attention to novels and poems far more than to government reports or political speeches.[18] The point is that Smith succeeded in capturing the imagination of a generation of scholars, few of whom were interested in the issues that western historians knew, through a study that posited the West's importance to any understanding of America. And what made Smith successful was less the logic of his argument or the character of his evidence than the persuasiveness of his rhetoric and the power of his overstatement. Like Turner, whose troubling premises allowed for a daring quality of analysis, what appears most original in Smith's strong claims would also be finally least defensible.

Before assessing the problem of premises, however, it is worth admiring once again the considerable virtues in Smith's effort. Not least of these is his astonishing ability to fuse disparate materials into a cogent account. Government documents, dime novels, effete poems, political speeches, crude posters, and an array of otherwise diverse texts rub elbows in his book, as Bridgman observed. Smith turned away from canonized literature as well as from standard historical methods, crossing disciplinary divisions to reveal a set of common cultural concerns. With a mixed methodology that integrates literary and social history, public policy and private desires, he revealed the shifting contradictions that lay hidden just below the surface in an array of popular images. James K. Paulding's well-known poem, *The Backwoodsman* (1818), for instance, extols a set of ideals that are denied by its poetic construction, reflecting in its very structure constraints upon its expressed aspirations. As Smith nicely reveals, "Paulding was a prisoner of literary convention, . . . trying to write about the fluidity of classes in a measure which proclaimed with every caesura that order was Heaven's first law" (138). Countless others committed to federal and regional projects, or popular drama, or imperialist excursions expressed themselves through a similar array of contradictory images and paradoxical explanations.

Smith's triumph as a western historian was to reveal as rarely before the occasionally disastrous impact of collective belief on the course of public events. The idea that somehow "rain follows the plow," for instance, may seem nothing short of extraordinary today, and yet the widespread faith that cultivation would alter climate and that an increase in rainfall would be permanent, not cyclical, encouraged countless failed settlements and informed a disastrous land policy. Likewise, an image of "virgin land" enforced the widespread belief in exceptionalism, an ideology that would have the effect of crippling national policies, both foreign and domestic. The singular advantage of Smith's approach was that it allowed one to mark a distinction between image and action, between consciousness (false or otherwise) and the actual conditions of labor, without diminishing the former as an important intellectual construction. In doing so, he offered a model for other investigations, a powerful paradigm to help explain a broad spectrum of events and ideas having little to do with the West.

As something of a "father figure" to American Studies, Smith established the working assumptions by which the fledgling field defined itself—assumptions enthusiastically adopted after the appearance of *Virgin Land* and nearly as quickly held up to close scrutiny. In particular, critics were troubled most by the logic behind his central pairing of the anthropological terms, *myth* and *symbol*—terms he had succinctly asserted to be "larger or smaller units of the same kind of thing, namely an intellectual construction that fuses concept and emotion into an image" (xi). That definition raises a number of interesting theoretical issues—issues, however, that a pragmatic Smith was not disposed to pursue. Primary among these was the problem of how images and expressions emerge in the first place, as responses to what kinds of differing pressures, in anticipation of what kinds of probable ends.[19] Just such questions prompted a number of former students and colleagues—including Barry Marks, Alan Trachtenberg, and, most notably, Bruce Kuklick—to offer corrective views, the most telling of which focused on Smith's distinction between "myth" and empirical fact. After all, how does one go about isolating what people supposedly thought from what was actually true—and in any event, what is gained by trying to establish such a rigid dualistic distinction between the imagined and the real?[20]

The energy devoted to the theoretical attack on Smith's premises was, of course, largely generated by his remarkable success in explaining so diverse an experience as the West, and doing so through images that supposedly reproduced American self-consciousness. As if to confirm his celebrated stature, even he would criticize the methods he first introduced. In the twentieth-anniversary edition of *Virgin Land*, he conceded weaknesses in his rigidly dualistic model, "of symbols and myths on the one hand, and on the other a supposed extramental historical reality" (viii). But when push came to shove, he still felt his earlier conclusions had stood unshaken. Sixteen years after this first, long backward look (and shortly before his untimely death in an auto accident), he made an even more sweeping bow of regret for shortcomings he now acknowledged in the book: in particular, its exclusion of minority voices (notably Indians) and its casual dismissal of popular literature (notably cowboy Westerns). Once again, however, he reaffirmed the strength of his basic method by identifying "myth" with Jameson's

concept of the "political unconscious" and with Sacvan Bercovitch's
ideal of an "American consensus." His concept of "virgin land" defines, so he triumphantly reasserted at last, the "central ideology or
myth of America."[21]

For the moment, it may be less important to question the terms of
this final judgment than to recognize how much the strengths of Smith's
analysis are intimately linked with its weaknesses. This may well be because any attempt at more than local truths of "American culture"—at
more than isolated observations about, say, regional fiction, or western
politics, or the shape of provincial boosterism—only seems to lead us
directly back into the larger quandary of "meaning," with all the troubling assumptions that inflect *Virgin Land*. The point is that Smith's
sweeping conclusions, which generated such enthusiasm for his mode
of analysis, rest on a set of social and psychological premises that fail
to withstand close scrutiny. To opt for the alternative process of a more
cautious, restrained sifting of evidence, however, seems to preclude
the possibility of reading a larger "meaning" into the West (or into any
other regions, individuals, or icons)—a prospect that would seem to
condemn western history once again to a local and regional status. Nonetheless, it is important to keep in mind how often Smith's conclusions
gain their dramatic force by exceeding the limits of warrantable assertion. And one of the most interesting aspects of those otherwise excessive claims is that they so often rest upon problematic assumptions
about intention and belief.

The basis of the argument in "The Sons of Leatherstocking," for
example, is that the most ubiquitous images in popular literature and
public speeches inform the myths and symbols that work hegemonically
to constrain social behavior. If the ultimate source of those images is
never made clear, Smith does at least offer a famous description of the
formula writers for Beadle's Dime Novels that illustrates how amaz-
ingly productive such writers were (in one spectacular case, of an author
who penned a thirty-five-thousand-word tale in a day and a night):

> *Fiction produced in these circumstances virtually takes on the
> character of automatic writing. The unabashed and systematic
> use of formulas strips from the writing every vestige of the
> interest usually sought in works of the imagination; it is entirely
> subliterary. On the other hand, such work tends to become an
> objectified mass dream . . . The individual writer abandons his
> own personality and identifies himself with the reveries of his*

readers. It is the presumably close fidelity of the Beadle stories to
the dream life of a vast inarticulate public that renders them
valuable to the social historian and the historian of ideas.

This vivid image of the writer closeted away in his room encapsulates Smith's premise of shared belief: that the very absence of any evident craft or creativity in popular literature renders it thereby a more accurate barometer of contemporary opinion. "Automatic writing" becomes a form of cultural ventriloquism in which the least common denominator of attitudes and beliefs speaks through a passive, even comatose, deindividualized body. And we can supposedly therefore best understand the ideological terrain of the nineteenth century by looking to its least self-conscious, most poorly constructed artifacts.

It should be clear that this model neatly obscures a number of major issues. Apart from the fact that the nineteenth century may not have considered such popular literature "bad," this reading ignores how much of what we now count as "great" literature was composed in a similar white heat. "Automatic writing," in other words, does not necessarily mean that cultural norms are being expressed, any more than culture alone speaks through bad writing while genius sings its own voice in masterworks. Smith's model likewise assumes a passive, uniform audience for such texts, failing to address specifically who was reading what and why—the sexes, classes, age groups, and regional identities, among other variables, and the conflicting functions such literature may well have served for them.[22] But more than this: how do we know that these readers (any or all of them) did not find such literature as transparently silly as we do?

The problem lies in assuming a direct relationship between a book's reception and the message it has for us—between its immediate success and the later readings we happen to give it. Smith created a short-circuit between nineteenth-century texts and a twentieth-century reader, assuming the spark that leaped between the poles represented some secure, nineteenth-century "understanding" of the words he examined. Yet it is possible that "bad" writers simply communicate badly and that he (and we) retrieve a message from their technical incompetence when no similar communication had originally taken place. After all, since we construct texts as we read to match our own expectations, why should we somehow believe that nineteenth-century readers did any differently, creating meanings that we (because distant, alien, or otherwise changed) are no longer able to recover? On the other hand, it may be that writers we consider "bad" fail only by our standards, not their contemporaries', and that our valuation of them as insufficiently talented measures our distance from the culture we are attempting to understand.

Smith's claims for the success or failure of popular literature are based, in fact, on mid-twentieth-century axioms drawn from the New Critics, in particular the premise that a text need not depend on its context to be adequately understood.[23] As useful as this formalist approach can be in certain interpretive circumstances, the one thing it cannot do is to tell us what other readers in other times have thought they were reading: it is a fundamentally antihistorical gesture. That inability means that Smith is unable to prove the pattern he traces, for instance, of "progressive deterioration in the Western story as a genre," from the novels of James Fenimore Cooper through the Beadle writers (119). Even were one to agree that the genre declined to a "near-juvenile level" (and Smith himself later regretted having made this claim), such a deterioration can be variously caused, resulting as much from the failing skills of individual authors as the demands of their audience or the constraints of a formula. Some popular writers have continued to produce best-sellers over long careers (Ian Fleming and Louis L'Amour most obviously come to mind), while others reveal a loss of inventive powers as soon as their second book. The problem, however, is more complicated, as revealed in Smith's description of the most popular western stories, whose success allegedly resists either analysis or explanation. All we can claim is the tautology that such texts succeeded because of their contents, and that their contents, in turn, explain their success.

> It may be that Deadwood Dick's appeal to readers of the Beadle
> novels depended on Wheeler's eclecticism, the device of ascribing
> to the hero all the skills, functions, graces, and successes that
> had ever fallen to the lot of any Western character, plus other
> powers derived from folk heroes of a forgotten past, and still other
> accomplishments prophetic of the coming reign of the dime novel
> detectives. (101–2)

After this, Smith can only conclude that the character "reflects the kind of sensationalism that increased so markedly in the later 1870s."

Where his earlier standard for measuring the "deterioration" of a genre had been an arbitrary (possibly inappropriate) value judgment, based on little more than Smith's mid-twentieth-century literary standards, here the explanation for the genre's popular success is so eclectic as to preclude any judgment. In both cases, however, the relation of audience to popular text remains indistinct, and Smith's sheer assertion that certain themes mattered does not suffice as proof that they did. Again, he may well take too seriously what audiences at the time did not, which is to do little more than patronize past readers. The point is that no clear way exists to prove the kind of claim that Smith wants to make. And to respect the enigma of readers' responses, either then or now, is to acknowledge how fully popular literature performs a complex mediatory function connecting the reader to his or her culture.[24]

A more general problem in Smith's analysis emerges from the fact that the reading public in the nineteenth century constituted only a small proportion of the general population. Yet Smith repeatedly conflates this literate group with all Americans, assuming they shared the same beliefs on the basis of similar behavior and that in any event those beliefs meant similar things to all who held them. Any such version of the functionalist fallacy is problematic; belief is too easily flattened out, thinned into correspondence with the ideas of those who report them. But belief operates in a much richer, more varied environment than this suggests, and people respond in a wide variety of ways to simple expressions of trust or faith. Smith most often broaches this issue in "The Garden of the World," which turns from popular literature to examine the effect of belief on land policy. At one point, he asserts, "It is likely that most Americans would have said during the 1880's that the Homestead Act had triumphantly borne out the predictions of the 1860's" (189). But as Bruce Kuklick caustically (and incisively) observes, "If opinion polls today are any indication of people's knowledge, it is much more likely that most Americans of the 1880s would not have heard of the Homestead Act or predictions about it."[25]

The point is that imputing collective beliefs is an extraordinarily difficult process, not simply to be assumed, as Smith tended to do. Consider, for instance, his description of the land system of the 1870s as

> *a cruel mockery, humane in its pretensions but in practice a speculator's dream. Were the Western representatives ignorant of these facts at a time when Easterners like Hewitt and Atkins understood them? Or, if they did understand how completely the land system had failed to foster the yeoman ideal cherished by its authors, are we to accuse them of deliberately cynical misrepresentation? (199–200)*

Smith dismisses this latter interpretation as "unlikely," and opts instead for a reading of the representatives' "sincere" motives based on their acceptance of "the dream of a yeoman society." But lacking other evidence, what confidence can we invest in the conclusion that these politicians truly shared "the dream"—perhaps especially given the reputation of politicians then and now? Why should we not simply assume a more "deliberately cynical" intent with at least as much justification? The point is not to compel a claim for one position or the other, but simply to enjoin some caution in reading belief from behavior—a process that requires considerable respect for the variousness of human motivations and ideals.

Despite (and also to a large extent, because of) its problematic premises, *Virgin Land* emerged as the most influential history of the West since Walter Prescott Webb's *The Great Plains* (1931). In the thirty years following its publication, the book became a standard source for scholars committed to emulating Smith with "symbols" of their own. Yet they would be followed by critics rather less sympathetic—the feminists, popular culture enthusiasts, African- and Native-American scholars intent on breaking through the exclusions that Smith's model had reinforced. They certainly have helped us to see that any symbolic order is imposed on the past and that to determine the "meaning" of an age is as difficult as identifying the meaning of yesterday. But their debt to Smith, if inverted, is deep. Smith first forced us to consider the significance of the West in other than purely political or economic terms. He extracted a cultural meaning from the West that others have found alternately inadequate, monological, and elitist; but the important point is that he succeeded in turning us back to the study of cultural meaning. To put it paradoxically, Smith made American Studies in mismaking it, opening out the interpretive possibilities of popular images even as he fostered doubt about what those images could be made to bear.[26] He forms at once an inspiring and a cautionary instance, replicating in his own work what has sometimes seemed a peculiarly American penchant for global explanations.

As for the biographical enigma—the riddle of why Smith turned away from this stunningly comprehensive view of the West to devote his career to reading the region's chief literary lion—no clear answer emerges. Perhaps, if we are to elude Smith's own too-satisfying "fictive" closures to history, none should. But at least part of the reason surely was that upon appointment at the University of California in 1953, he was named coeditor of the Mark Twain papers and in the course of the decade was called upon to edit two selections of journalism and to coedit a volume of letters: *Mark Twain of the Enterprise; Mark Twain: San Francisco Correspondent;* and the *Mark Twain–Howells Letters, 1872–1910.*[27] Whether this editorial work precluded further projects like *Virgin Land,* it clearly prepared him for the work that students of western American literature know best, *Mark Twain: The Development of a Writer* (1962).

Any reader of *Virgin Land* is aware of how attentive Smith was to matters of literary style and particularly to the stylistic tensions that emerged when a civilizing eastern discourse confronted an intractable western experience. In his discussion of Fenimore Cooper and Timothy Flint, he was struck by the fundamental "conflict of allegiances" at the heart of their western plots—by the ways in which they (like others) became "prisoners[s] of literary convention" (61, 141, 138). What he sensed as the essentially conflicted nature of western narrative is evident nowhere more clearly than in the works of Mark Twain, and the effect of Smith's reading and editing of Twain was to turn him even more fully to the process by which discourse itself reproduces cultural values. Granted, his immediate focus had narrowed to one writer's long career, but only as a means of pondering further the "conflict between the dominant culture of [Twain's] day and an emergent attitude associated with the vernacular language of the native American humorists" (vii). Thus, a writer who makes only a fleeting appearance in *Virgin Land* comes later to embody, indeed to serve as the most potent personification of, the conflicts that the West represents for the East. Yet as Twain discovered (and Smith made clear), the inability of the vernacular perspective to challenge seriously dominant cultural values would contribute not only to the breakdown of Twain's career but to larger tensions in American culture.

After laying out in an opening chapter his opposition of "two ways of viewing the world"—the western vernacular and the eastern ideal— Smith carefully examines nine of Twain's principal works in terms of that binary opposition, which structures everything from early apprentice pieces to late philosophical fragments. Twain had from the beginning realized the subversive power of western expression—not simply as a peculiar (and peculiarly threatening) manner of speech, but as the embodiment of humanistic values imperiled by a crassly oppressive dominant culture. The vernacular voice, whether that of the jovial "sinners" in *The Innocents Abroad* (1869) or the bumptiously naive narrator in *Roughing It* (1872), offers a humorously skeptical, sometimes bewildered, often deflating perspective on a world that is everywhere structured by arbitrary social forms and complacent pretensions. Yet Twain's comic response to these circumstances reveals a divided sensibility, one unable to master the conflict between vernacular and ideal that he repeatedly represented. Even as late as *The Gilded Age* (1873) and *The Adventures of Tom Sawyer* (1876), so Smith declares, Twain was still "discovering a role and an identity for himself" as a performer, trying to please two audiences at once through an unlikely mix of nostalgia and satire (111).

Not until he was fifty would he resolve this split satisfactorily through the distinctive voice that springs from *Adventures of Huckleberry Finn* (1885). Plotting the novel's ordeal between "a sound heart and a deformed conscience," Twain moved beyond any simple strife of regions or classes to a profound examination of the conflict that Smith sees as characteristically American:

> *The conflict in which Huck is involved is not that of a lower against an upper class or of an alienated fringe of outcasts against a cultivated elite. It is not the issue of frontier West versus genteel East, or of backwoods versus metropolis, but of fidelity to the uncoerced self versus the blurring of attitudes caused by social conformity, by the effort to achieve status or power through exhibiting the approved forms of sensibility. (122–23)*

Unable to resolve the competing claims of East and West, Twain transformed the vernacular voice from a protest against the genteel tradition into a denunciation of all forms of cultural coercion—with the constraining vernacular mode itself very much included. In doing so, he created not only a distinctively western text, but also what many argue is our first distinctively American novel.

Huckleberry Finn effectively split Twain's career in two, since he was now forced to realize that the vernacular values embodied in Huck and Jim were not "capable of being reconciled with social reality" (132). For Smith, this disillusionment explains the strained ending of the novel as well as the ambitious failures of the next decade. Twain's confidence in a subversive, transgressive western perspective slowly disintegrated, as did his belief in progress, technology, and an egalitarianism he also identified with the West. His novels now take place in distinctly unwestern locales—Arthurian England for *A Connecticut Yan-*

kee in King Arthur's Court (1889) and the antebellum South for *The Trag-edy of Pudd'nhead Wilson* (1892)—but the conflict of values that generated plot was much the same as in his earlier books. And the despair that Twain felt in the 1890s was less a response to his life than to his art, the logical result (or so Smith argues) of an earlier inability to reconcile vernacular and ideal. Unable to resolve the conflict of West and East that was the source of his comic power, he could only descend into anecdotal and apothegmatic carping at "the damned human race."

After completing this book, Smith felt dissatisfied with his treatment of *A Connecticut Yankee* and returned to it in a series of lectures published as *Mark Twain's Fable of Progress* (1964). Expanding on points he had made earlier, he attempted to sort out the novel's confusions by exam-ining its stages of composition, the illustrations commissioned from the socialist Dan Beard, and the larger context of businessman novels that appeared at about the same time. According to Smith, *Connecticut Yankee* was "one of the most characteristic productions of the decade when Americans generally first realized they were entering the mod-ern world."[28] And the novel can therefore be read not simply as a west-ern tall tale, but as a fable of capitalism: "Mark Twain was asking himself whether the American Adam, who began as representative of a pre-industrial order, could make the transition to urban industrialism and enter upon a new phase of his existence by becoming a capitalist hero" (69). In fact, the answer was no, revealed in the novel's puzzling med-ley of burlesque, satire, and utopian treatise. As Smith unravels its tech-nical problems in terms of its larger philosophical contradictions, he exposes the inconsistency in Twain's dual commitment to a western vernacular and an agrarian order.

Smith's two studies are among a handful of trenchant assessments of Twain, advancing close readings of texts in a way that makes sense of the overall career as few others have done. It is instructive, however, to observe how the problematic assumptions of his earlier scholarship resurface in these later, more directly literary analyses. The grandiose idea of "broad cultural consensus" that informed *Virgin Land* returns as an unmodified version of Santayana's 1911 thesis "that in the nine-teenth century the United States was a country of two mentalities" (*Development*, 20). This loose distinction between a vernacular and a "genteel tradition" makes sense of Twain's career in terms of a Mani-chean plot, by envisioning him at the mercy of two coherent sets of impulses, analogously western and eastern. Again, a supposedly monological vernacular voice is made to carry too much ethical weight, which becomes clear when one begins to consider not the similarities but the differences among, say, Pap Finn, Colonel Sherburne, Scotty Briggs, and Hank Morgan.[29] Again, the power of Smith's thesis depends upon conflating a variety of voices and beliefs.

At points, Smith does admit to the immense "confusion of tastes and attitudes in nineteenth-century America" and further acknowledges the problem of making "inferences from fragmentary data" (*Development*, 109–10). But, as earlier, the force of his conclusions derives from a willingness to infer an almost operatic dualism to the culture and then to imagine the dramatic "scenes" that ensue from so strict a binary division. He gains a clarity of vision as well by reducing complex cultural issues to straightforward economic terms, setting forth the conflict of the late nineteenth century as simply one between industrial capitalism, on the one hand, and agrarianism, on the other. Twain's artistic decline can thus be read as an inability to accept the implications that progress would have for an America steeped in traditional western values.

Other problematic assumptions from *Virgin Land* reemerge in Smith's treatment of intention and belief, and particularly in his assumption that Twain's characters must directly reflect their author's biases. The conflation of fictional representation with authorial self leads to a self-confirming psychology, one that allows Smith to read back into Mark Twain's own body and psyche the conflicts, instabilities, and crises he discovers in the plots. To be sure, few others have had as close familiarity as Smith with Twain's life and papers; but the connection between art and life is precarious, and the identification of protagonist "fully" with its author is more problematic than Smith is ever willing to allow (*Fable*, 107). The risks of this kind of analysis loom even larger for those contemptuous of an author's enthusiasms, and Smith's disdain for "lowbrow" culture (whether Mickey Spillane, TV Westerns, stage melodrama, or dime novels) suggests little understanding of the kind of popular entertainment that Twain himself found engaging.[30] Again, he fails (as many do) to resist his own projected beliefs in the attempt to recover a historically alien experience, to interpret its significance.

Henry Nash Smith's career as a leading historian of the American West is atypical for many reasons, not least for his training primarily in cultural and literary criticism rather than in history. That unusual emphasis gave him a perspective on the region altogether different from others who come to mind with the phrase "western history." Smith invariably strove to see the larger place of the West in American life, and his powerful influence on more local practitioners lay in his ability to show how aspects of a region that had earlier been dismissed or trivialized were, in fact, central to whatever most distinguishes our cultural heritage. True, he worked, as historians must, with tools that a later generation finds inadequate: in his case, axioms about high and low culture, intention and belief, image and idea. But as never before, he wove together a variety of texts about the West, wresting from anthropology and literary criticism a concern for larger meanings as they emerge from the complex structure of what otherwise seem like merely irrelevant details. In the process, he made us realize how necessary the West has been to our history, and how our altering conceptions of it have shaped and been shaped by our sense of ourselves as Americans. In lucid prose, he transformed our study of the West from simply a concentration on the economics or sociology of a place to the contemplation of the profound effects of an image, one whose commanding grip on the nineteenth-century imagination has shaped the terms of our deepest cultural dialogues. That we now are better positioned to understand why those terms have so often taken on a life of their own is largely due to Smith's recognition of the influence our beliefs have had on the West, more so than the other way around.

NOTES

1. Henry Nash Smith, *Virgin Land: The American West as Symbol and Myth* (rev. ed., Cambridge: Harvard University Press, 1970), p. 3. Subsequent references to this edition are included parenthetically in the text.

2. Richard Hofstadter has claimed, "It is in large part the vagueness, the impression, the overstatement in Turner's essays that has given them their plasticity and hence their broad acceptance." See *The Progressive Historians: Turner, Beard, Parrington* (New York: Knopf, 1968), 84. Still an incisive critique, Hofstadter's book exposes Turner's elision of assumptions about cultural transmission, the historical inaccuracy of treating the West as "safety valve" for free labor, and the theory's crippling isolationist implications for foreign policy. Moreover, as he observes, Turner concentrates on individuals and environments to draw unsupportable conclusions about institutions, habits, and ideas.

3. "When I imagined I was operating without hypotheses," Smith claimed on rereading his book thirty-five years later, "I was sometimes unwittingly using those of Turner." See "Symbol and Idea in *Virgin Land*," in Sacvan Bercovitch and Myra Jehlen, eds., *Ideology and Classic American Literature* (Cambridge: Cam-

bridge University Press, 1986), 27. For efforts influenced by Smith's approach, see Sacvan Bercovitch, *The Puritan Origins of the American Self* (New Haven: Yale University Press, 1975); Annette Kolodny, *The Land before Her: Fantasy and Experience of the American Frontiers, 1630–1860* (Chapel Hill: University of North Carolina Press, 1984); T. J. Jackson Lears, *No Place of Grace: Anti-Modernism and the Transformation of American Culture, 1880–1920* (New York: Pantheon, 1981); Richard Slotkin, *The Fatal Environment: The Myth of the Frontier in the Age of Industrialization, 1880–1890* (Middletown, Conn: Wesleyan University Press, 1985); and Alan Trachtenberg, *The Incorporation of America: Culture and Society in the Gilded Age* (New York: Hill and Wang, 1982).

4. Cited from the author's copy of Smith's unpublished lecture, "Seminar on *Virgin Land*," given at Harvard University, February 22, 1979, p. 8. Much of the following also relies on Richard Bridgman's excellent biographical account, "The American Studies of Henry Nash Smith," *American Scholar* 56 (Spring 1987):259–68.

5. According to Smith's recollection, during this period he read Henri Bergson's *L'évolution créatrice* and *Les deux sources de la morale et de la religion*; Franz Boas's *The Mind of Primitive Man*; James Fraser's one-volume condensation of *The Golden Bough*; Sigmund Freud's *The Interpretation of Dreams*; Lucien Lévy-Bruhl's *La mentalité primitive*; Alfred Loisy's *Les mystères paiens et le mystère chrétien* and *Essai historique sur le sacrifice*; Thomas Mann's *Joseph and His Brothers*; Karl Mannheim's *Ideology and Utopia*; Otto Rank's *Das Inzest-Motiv in Dichtung und Sage*; Hans Vaihinger's *Die Philosophie des Als Ob*; and Jesse Weston's *From Ritual to Romance*. See author's copy of unpublished lecture, "Seminar on *Virgin Land*," given at Harvard University, February 22, 1979, 5–6; and correspondence with Richard W. Etulain, May 22, 1976.

6. "Seminar on *Virgin Land*," 7.

7. At Southern Methodist, he had risked institutional reprisals by defending William Faulkner's early fiction. So offended was his chairman that Smith had to be reappointed in the Department of Comparative Literature.

8. In his published statement on the events of December 1969, Smith agreed to "open the discussion" in response to attacks made on the "pluralism and eclecticism" of the association's scholarly journal, *PMLA*. But in later agreeing that a problematic relation inhered between political action, on the one hand, and teaching and study, on the other, he forcefully asserted that "radicals incur an obligation to propose" new aims, not simply to criticize the old. See "Something is Happening But You Don't Know What It Is, Do You, Mr. Jones?" *PMLA* 85 (May 1970):419.

9. In the half-dozen years after leaving Harvard, Smith continued to read and research in order to extend the scope of his project to the end of the nineteenth century. A year's fellowship at the Huntington Library in 1946–47 allowed him to write virtually the whole of *Virgin Land*—only 15 percent of which, according to recollection, was based dirrectly on his dissertation. Knopf held onto the manuscript for six months in 1948 before rejecting it, and Harvard

University Press brought it out early in 1950. This information is based on Smith's unpublished "Seminar on *Virgin Land*," 8, and on correspondence with Richard W. Etulain, May 22, 1976.

10. *Mark Twain: The Development of a Writer* (1962; rev., New York: Atheneum, 1967). Subsequent references to this edition are included parenthetically in the text.

11. Richard Bridgman claims that "Smith's whole career was involved in studying the problems and illusions of identity." See "The American Studies of Henry Nash Smith," 259.

12. Henry Nash Smith, "Culture," *Southwest Review* 13 (January 1928):249–55.

13. See "The Dilemma of Agrarianism," *Southwest Review* 19 (April 1934): 215–32; "Hoover's Philosophy of Comfort," *Southwest Review* 14 (October 1928):111–18; "On Living in America," *Southwest Review* 16 (October 1930):22–31; "What Is the Frontier?" *Southwest Review* 21 (October 1935):97–103.

14. *Virgin Land*, ix.

15. See "Symbol and Idea in *Virgin Land*," 22.

16. Smith, "Seminar on *Virgin Land*," 17.

17. Richard Bridgman, "The American Studies of Henry Nash Smith," 264.

18. See John William Ward, *Andrew Jackson: Symbol for an Age* (New York: Oxford University Press, 1953); R. W. B. Lewis, *The American Adam: Innocence, Tragedy, and Tradition in the Nineteenth Century* (Chicago: University of Chicago Press, 1955); Charles L. Sanford, *The Quest for Paradise: Europe and the American Moral Imagination* (Urbana: University of Illinois Press, 1961); Leo Marx, *The Machine in the Garden: Technology and the Pastoral Ideal in America* (New York: Oxford University Press, 1964), Alan Trachtenberg, *Brooklyn Bridge: Fact and Symbol* (New York: Oxford University Press, 1965); Richard Slotkin, *Regeneration through Violence: The Myth of the American Frontier, 1600–1860* (Middletown, Conn.: Wesleyan University Press, 1973).

19. In his original "Preface," Smith simply offers his own definition of "myth" and "symbol" without engaging the considerable literature on the subject or adducing other definitions (xi). In the "Preface to the Twentieth Anniversary Printing," he admits to a "chastening realization" of having oversimplified, only to claim: "Yet it might be argued that the materials presented in *Virgin Land* are abundant and various enough to compensate for this inadequacy of method" (vii–viii).

20. See Barry Marks, "The Concept of Myth in *Virgin Land*," *American Quarterly* 5 (Spring 1953):71–76; Alan Trachtenberg, "Myth, History, and Literature in *Virgin Land*," *Prospects* 3 (1977):125–33; and Bruce Kuklick, "Myth and Symbol in American Studies," *American Quarterly* 24 (October 1972):435–50.

Smith himself ventured an early theoretical justification in "Can 'American Studies' Develop a Method?" *American Quarterly* 9 (Summer 1957):197–208. In opening this influential essay, he declared: "By 'American Studies' I shall mean 'the study of American culture, past and present, as a whole'; and by 'culture' I shall mean 'the way in which subjective experience is organized.'" He then attempted to mediate between the formalist claims of literary criticism and the behavioralist claims of sociological analysis in describing how American cultural studies might best be undertaken. His famous (perhaps notorious) resistance to any single "method" for approaching such issues was expressed as a commitment to "principled opportunism" (207). See also Leo Marx, "American Studies—A Defense of an Unscientific Method," *New Literary History* 1 (October 1969):75.

21. Smith, "Symbol and Idea in *Virgin Land*," 27. This phrase is repeated twice on the page.

22. See Janice A. Radway, *Reading the Romance: Women, Patriarchy, and Popular Literature* (Chapel Hill: University of North Carolina Press, 1984); and Michael Denning, *Mechanic Accents: Dime Novels and Working-Class Culture in America* (London: Verso, 1987).

23. In "Seminar on *Virgin Land*," among the authors Smith describes as having been the most exciting to teach, he lists "I. A. Richards, Empson, my friends Brooks and Warren, John Crowe Ransom, T. S. Eliot, and Edmund Wilson" (5).

24. Or as Bruce Kuklick, Smith's most severe and astute critic to date, has stated, "we simply don't *know* why many people read mysteries, science fiction or sensational best sellers." See "Myth and Symbol in American Studies," 444. See also Janice Radway, *Reading the Romance*, for an excellent discussion of the problems of interpreting the effects of popular literature.

25. Kuklick, "Myth and Symbol in American Studies," 445. Smith was understandably dismissive of Kuklick's critique, and in his "Seminar on *Virgin Land*" offers a series of rebuttals that culminate in what he takes as an absurdity: "Pushed to a logical extreme, Kuklick's position would apparently be that statements about what 'most Americans' thought at any time should be excluded from historical writing. But of course no one, including Kuklick, means anything quite so drastic" (16). After acknowledging that he had read exhaustively in the period, and admitting that he had no special "access to the minds of a numerical majority of the population," Smith nonetheless urges that "there is such a thing as a climate of opinion from which relatively few members of the population dissent, and I believe my data are sufficiently numerous and varied to establish a climate of opinion" (17).

26. See Richard Slotkin, *Regeneration through Violence*; John Cawelti, *Adventure, Mystery, and Romance: Formula Stories as Art and Popular Culture* (Chicago: University of Chicago Press, 1976); and Edwin Fussell, *Frontier: American Literature and the American West* (Princeton: Princeton University Press, 1965).

27. Ed., *Mark Twain of the Enterprise* (Berkeley: University of California Press, 1957); ed., *Mark Twain: San Francisco Correspondent* (Berkeley: University of California Press, 1957); and with William Gibson, eds., *Mark Twain–Howells Letters* (Berkeley: University of California Press, 1960). In retirement, Smith also completed an important study entitled *Democracy and the Novel: Popular Resistance to Classic American Writers* (New York: Oxford University Press, 1978). But this book is not germane to work in western history.

28. *Mark Twain's Fable of Progress: Political and Economic Ideas in "A Connecti-cut Yankee"* (New Brunswick, N.J.: Rutgers University Press, 1964).

29. On this point, see David Sewell, *Mark Twain's Languages: Discourse, Dia-logue, and Linguistic Variety* (Berkeley: University of California Press, 1987).

30. For examples, see *Development*, 66–67; *Fable*, 61.

BIBLIOGRAPHY

WESTERN WRITINGS OF HENRY NASH SMITH

"Can 'American Studies' Develop a Method?" *American Quarterly* 9 (Summer 1957):197–208.

"Culture." *Southwest Review* 13 (January 1928):249–55.

"The Dilemma of Agrarianism." *Southwest Review* 19 (April 1934):215–32.

Coeditor with William Gibson. *Mark Twain–Howells Letters.* 2 vols. Berkeley: University of California Press, 1960.

Ed. *Mark Twain of the Enterprise.* Berkeley: University of California Press, 1957.

Ed. *Mark Twain: San Francisco Correspondent.* Berkeley: University of California Press, 1957.

Mark Twain: The Development of a Writer. Cambridge, Mass.: Harvard University Press, 1962.

Mark Twain's Fable of Progress: Political and Economic Ideas in "A Connecticut Yan-kee." New Brunswick, N.J.: Rutgers University Press, 1964.

"On Living in America." *Southwest Review* 16 (October 1930):22–31.

"Origins of a Native American Literary Tradition." In Margaret Denny and William H. Gilman, eds., *The American Writer and the European Tradition.* Minneapolis: University of Minnesota Press, 1950, 63–77.

"Presidential Address to the Modern Language Association." *PMLA* 84 (March 1969):344.

"Seminar on *Virgin Land.*" Given at Harvard University, February 22, 1979. Unpublished lecture in typescript.

"Something is Happening But You Don't Know What It Is, Do You, Mr. Jones?" *PMLA* 85 (May 1970):417–22.

"Symbol and Idea in *Virgin Land.*" In Sacvan Bercovitch and Myra Jehlen, eds., *Ideology and Classic American Literature.* Cambridge: Cambridge University Press, 1986, 21–35.

Virgin Land: The American West as Symbol and Myth. Cambridge, Mass.: Har-vard University Press, 1950.

"*Virgin Land* Revisited." *Indian Journal of American Studies* 3 (June 1973):1–8.

"The West as an Image of the American Past." *University of Kansas City Review* 18 (Autumn 1951):29–40.

"Western Chroniclers and Literary Pioneers" and "The Second Discovery of

America." Chapters 45 and 48 in Robert E. Spiller, Willard Thorp, Thomas H. Johnson, et al., eds., *Literary History of the United States: History.* 1948; 3d ed. rev. London: Macmillan, 1963, 758–70, 789–97.

"What Is the Frontier?" *Southwest Review* 21 (October 1935):97–103.

WORKS ABOUT HENRY NASH SMITH

Bridgman, Richard. "The American Studies of Henry Nash Smith." *American Scholar* 56 (Spring 1987):259–68.

Cawelti, John G. *Adventure, Mystery and Romance: Formula Stories as Art and Popular Culture.* Chicago: University of Chicago Press, 1976.

———. "Myth, Symbol, and Formula." *Journal of Popular Culture* 8 (Summer 1974):1–9.

Etulain, Richard W. "The American Literary West and Its Interpreters: The Rise of a New Historiography." *Pacific Historical Review* 45 (August 1976):311–48.

Kuklick, Bruce. "Myth and Symbol in American Studies." *American Quarterly* 24 (October 1972):435–50.

Lenz, Guenter H. "American Studies—Beyond the Crisis?: Recent Redefinitions and the Meaning of Theory, History, and Practical Criticism." *Prospects* 7 (1982):53–113.

Marks, Barry. "The Concept of Myth in *Virgin Land.*" *American Quarterly* 5 (Spring 1953):71–76.

Marx, Leo. "American Studies—A Defense of an Unscientific Method." *New Literary History* 1 (October 1969):75–90.

Sklar, Robert. "The Problem of an American Studies 'Philosophy': A Bibliography of New Directions." *American Quarterly* 27 (August 1975):245–62.

Sykes, Richard E. "American Studies and the Concept of Culture: A Theory and Method." *American Quarterly* 15 (Summer 1963):253–70.

Tate, Cecil F. *The Search for a Method in American Studies.* Minneapolis: University of Minnesota Press, 1973.

Trachtenberg, Alan. "Myth, History, and Literature in *Virgin Land.*" *Prospects* 3 (1977):125–33.

Veysey, Laurence R. "Myth and Reality in Approaching American Regionalism." *American Quarterly* 12 (Spring 1960):31–43.

Wise, Gene. "'Paradigm Dramas' in American Studies: A Cultural and Institutional History of the Movement." *American Quarterly* 31 (Bibliography Issue 1979):293–337).

———. "Some Elementary Axioms for an American Culture Studies." *Prospects* 4 (1979):517–47.

10

Persistent Traits and the Persistent Historian: The American Frontier and Ray Allen Billington

PATRICIA NELSON LIMERICK

*I*N *LAND OF SAVAGERY, LAND of Promise* (1981), Ray Allen Billington told of curious scenes and actions in popular European novels set on the American frontier. In one, an enterprising group of adventurers took a river journey from San Diego to Santa Fe; in another, unrestrained hunting by the Blackfeet Indians threatened to exterminate the vast, indigenous ostrich herds.[1] To read *Land of Savagery, Land of Promise,* full of mad images like these, is to recognize that there are few limits to the fantasies that human imagination has unloaded on the American West.

The river journey to New Mexico and the Blackfeet ostrich hunt carry one additional charm: they are both indisputably, provably inaccurate, a fact on which both Turnerians and non-Turnerians can agree. As statements of western experience, they did not, and do not, pose problems of historical interpretation. No latter-day, revisionist historian is going to argue that a thriving river-freighting culture, in fact, tied the Pacific to New Mexico or that the ostriches were a key part of the delicately balanced Blackfeet ecosystem. The wilder European writers of western novels thus provided Billington and his readers with a rare opportunity in the writing of western history: the chance to say, without the least possibility of historiographic dispute, what was false and what was true.

In Billington's long campaign to revive and restore Frederick Jackson Turner's frontier hypothesis, such moments of utter certainty were hard to come by. In book after book, article after article, Billington fought to keep the cold winds of historiographical change from extinguishing the flame lit by Frederick Jackson Turner in 1893. A reading of his major works,* from the first edition of *Westward Expansion* (1949) to *Land of Savagery, Land of Promise* (1981), provides a remarkable case study in loyalty and persistence, in the working out of one man's conviction that Turner's frontier thesis held a significance so central that American scholars who rejected the thesis did so at the nation's peril. But Billington was also fully aware that Turner's ideas had experienced a rough passage through the 1930s and 1940s. Taking the most compelling criticisms into account while also maintaining allegiance to a core of Turnerian ideas, Billington would spend his career navigating through a maze of conflicting interpretations of frontier reality. That journey came close to making a river passage from San Diego to Santa Fe look easy by comparison.

Billington was a comparative latecomer to his frontier enthusiasms. Born (in 1903) and raised in Michigan, he seemed well launched on a career in journalism. Then, editing a student newspaper at the University of Michigan, he fell afoul of administrators' standards of propriety in student publications and found himself disenrolled. Landing at the University of Wisconsin, he found a new interest in the serious study of history. Although he did study with the western historian Frederic Paxson, Billington was by no means an instant convert to the field. He was nonetheless an indirect beneficiary of Frederick Jackson Turner, coming to life intellectually in the History Department that Turner had raised to prominence several decades before.[2]

Moving on to Harvard for graduate school in 1927, Billington took one seminar with Frederick Merk, the man chosen to wear Turner's mantle at Harvard. The appeal of the frontier aside, Billington chose to specialize in American cultural and intellectual history, working with the influential Arthur M. Schlesinger, Sr. Billington's dissertation, later published as *The Protestant Crusade, 1800–1860: A Study of the Origins of American Nativism* (1938), gave few indications of his future interests. Indeed, as Martin Ridge has pointed out, this first book includes an explicit, if also somewhat off-hand denial of the significance of the frontier:

---

*Billington wrote and published prolifically, but limits of space have confined this appraisal to his five most substantial works.

> *Theoretically, the settlers should have been won from their*
> *intolerance by the liberalizing influence of the frontier; actually*
> *they continued to think of the Pope as an "old rogue, who had a*
> *respectable pair of horns."*[3]

Beyond this statement that, in Ridge's words, "the frontier had no impact on American behavioral patterns whatsoever,"[4] *The Protestant Crusade* made clear that Billington was no fan of nativism, no supporter of racial prejudice. In 1938, the difficulty that Billington would face in combining a rejection of racial exclusiveness with conventional Turnerian frontier studies was far in the future.

In the early 1940s, James B. Hedges, whom Billington had known at Harvard, offered a partnership in the writing of a western history textbook. Originally, Hedges and Billington planned to share the burdens of writing; as it turned out, Hedges contributed only three chapters, and Billington wrote the bulk of *Westward Expansion.*

The project was of a scale that would either demolish a person's interest in frontier history, or confirm it for all time. In a few short years, Billington did an enormous amount of reading in frontier history, as the sizable and useful bibliographical essay showed, and synthesized that widely scattered literature into a coherent narrative. *Westward Expansion* both triggered and certified the conversion of Ray Allen Billington to the cause of frontier history.

"This book," Billington wrote in its first sentence, "attempts to follow the pattern that Frederick Jackson Turner might have used had he ever compressed his voluminous researches on the American frontier within one volume."[5] The publication of *Westward Expansion* in 1949 made clear that Turner had acquired, posthumously, a spokesperson and supporter who evidently never suffered a twinge of the writer's block that plagued Turner himself.

Billington's chosen task was not made any easier by the accumulated criticisms and rejections of the frontier thesis. From the apparent monocausal assumptions of Turner's enormously influential 1893 essay, "The Significance of the Frontier in American History," to the irrelevance of rural frontier history in a nation struggling with depression and war, the frontier thesis had taken a beating—a beating, Billington persuaded himself, that had gone too far. Turner's critics, he believed, had indiscriminately tossed out propositions of real and lasting value, along with a few claims that Billington himself was willing to find doubtful.

It was, therefore, impossible to follow Turner unthinkingly. Some of Turner's grander statements simply had to be cut back, modified, restrained. And thus Billington found himself launched on a long-term enterprise that from time to time made him the intellectual equivalent of an alterations tailor, a specialist in expanding and tightening, lengthening and shortening, letting out and taking in, adding and trimming. Without modification, Turner's frontier thesis could not retain credibility; to serve the cause, Billington had to become a specialist in modification, developing finely tuned instincts to tell him when to hold firm and when to retreat, when to assert Turner's fundamental accuracy and when to acknowledge Turner's errors.

The result was a body of writing with a paradoxical quality: a collection of words that are, on one count, clear, and on another, confusing. Billington wrote clear and fluent sentences; he rarely fell into pedantic or jargonized language. His beginning ties to journalism never left him, and the result was a level of readability and intelligibility all too uncommon in academic prose. But the reader's confusion comes in putting together these individually clear sentences. On a number of issues, from the degree of class stratification on frontiers to the labeling of the frontiersman as an innovator or as a traditionalist, the close reader emerges solidly perplexed.

This problem was evident from the first edition of *Westward Expansion*. On one hand, Billington quite sensibly modified several tenets of Turnerian thinking. "[T]he frontier seldom served as a 'safety valve' for working men," he wrote. Moreover, the "cost of moving to the West was also a barrier that few easterners could overcome." But only a page later, Billington had returned to reinforcing the standard Turnerian vision: "The history of the American frontier" was a history "of expanding opportunity for the downtrodden."[6] Each statement was, individually, clear and straightforward, but how was the reader to fit them together? How did "the downtrodden" take possession of their frontier "opportunity," if they lacked the money needed to move to where the opportunity was? Which statement represented Billington's final judgment? Or had he, in fact, reached one?

Reading his words with all the benefits of hindsight, one realizes both the precariousness of Billington's undertaking, *and* his refusal to let that precariousness cripple him. In a number of ways, Billington's conviction in the essential validity of the frontier thesis forced him into issuing judgments before the evidence had been assembled, writing verdicts before the cases had been fully presented. On the subject of frontier opportunity for the downtrodden, as on a wide variety of others, Billington had two choices: he could simply raise the question and explain that presently there was no way to answer it and, by extension, no way to write an overview of American frontier experience; *or* he could go ahead and assert, to the best of his knowledge, what seemed to him the most probable answer to these perplexing questions.

The result was, on some occasions, assertions that seemed closer to declarations of faith than to provable statements of fact. Committed to presenting a picture of the broad outlines of frontier history, Billington refused to wait, timidly avoiding risk, until a full, safe package of evidence could be assembled. Putting together a picture of a nation shaped by its pioneer origins, Billington showed a courage and a confidence that gave American frontier studies a new lease on life.

This level of confidence set Billington apart from Turner, and that permitted him to write the kind of book that Turner himself could not complete. Beginning with a restatement of the frontier thesis, *Westward Expansion* made Billington's intention to complete the Turnerian mission clear from the start. Advancing westward through "unoccupied" terrain, the American people were reshaped by "the repeated rebirth of civilization," regressing to the "primitive" and then climbing back up to the "complex." "In thought and habit men reverted toward a state of nature," in a "process that was repeated for three centuries as Americans colonized the continent." At the end of the nineteenth century, the process came to a halt: "the West itself was gone." But the traits of character and behavior spawned by pioneering lived on into the twentieth century.[7]

Turner's critics, Billington asserted, "modified, but did not refute" this model. He himself included a number of those necessary modifications in the text. The frontier was by no means the only determinant of American development; the divisions of social classes did make an appearance on the frontier; a trend toward democracy had long been "apparent in the western world" and did not require the New World's forests to give it its start. These modifications made, Billington returned to assertions of the thesis's uneroded accuracy: "Yet the most carping critic will agree that the unusual environment, and the continuous rebirth of society in the western wilderness, endowed the American people and their institutions with characteristics not shared by the rest of the world."[8]

But here was one of the central questions raised by Billington's defense of Turner. If the frontier thesis, modified and adapted and trimmed, finally came down to the assertion that the American takeover of the continent was, in some way or another, important and that the United States had emerged with some national characteristics that were not submerged into a homogeneous international norm (a norm that also failed to fit any other nation), was there then much content left in the Turner Thesis? Had it not been modified and enlarged and altered out of its former force, losing the impact of its vigorous and stimulating, if also flawed, initial claims?

Trying to avoid this risk of imprecise overgeneralization, Billington tried to pin down a modified version of Turner's definition of the term *frontier*:

> The frontier can be pictured more accurately as a series of contiguous westward-migrating zones, each representing a different stage in the development of society from elemental to complex forms. As the westward movement gained momentum, a standardized zonal pattern developed which, although varying slightly with time and place, remained largely consistent until the continent was occupied.

But this modified definition still leaned heavily on the eighteenth-century notion of the stages of civilization ("from elemental to complex") and still cast the diverse and sometimes chaotic events of western expansion in the rigid terms of a "consistent" and "standardized zonal pattern." When Billington went farther—to delineate the six zones in the pattern, frontier theory and American reality firmly parted ways. "The initial zone was the domain of the fur traders"; then "came the second group on each frontier—the cattlemen"; "wherever conditions were favorable a third zone preceded the advancing farmers—that of the miners"; the fourth frontier zone was made up of "pioneer farmers"; the "equipped farmers" created the fifth zone; and then, finally, the urban frontier closed the cycle.[9]

One could certainly not complain of a lack of precision or clear definition in this model. But this march of pioneer types, this sequence of "zones," stood in only the most remote relation to westward expansion's actual jumble of events and people. Just as important, the list got its simplicity by leaving out a whole stock of key players—Indians, women (unless they fell under the category "farmers" or town founders), Hispanics, explorers, soldiers, loggers, missionaries, federal officials, Asian immigrants, freighters, railroad builders, and European and eastern investors.

Billington, one learns from this example and many others, was a man drawn to abstractions, a man so at home with images and types, zones and processes, characteristics and traits, that they assumed a full reality for him. He built for himself and his readers a mental world that resembled a comfortably furnished room, a room where repeated patterns and persistent traits assumed substance and solidity, a room where cynicism and doubt would be ungracious gestures on the part of a guest. Stepping out of the room, the doubts set in, as one begins to question the relation between Billington's abstractions and the actual confusion and complexity of western history. But inside the room, for a guest in Billington's smoothly arranged, well-appointed mental world, the doubts are put on hold, and the abstractions carry their own reality.

Following its Turnerian introduction, *Westward Expansion* took the reader on a sweeping tour of three centuries, from Spanish exploration in the Southeast to the planting of Atlantic colonies by Englishmen; from the origins of settlement in the Midwest to the unrolling of pre–Civil War sectional conflict; from the trans-Mississippi fur trade to the agrarian disillusionment of the Granger and Populist movements. Much of the text was densely detailed, a survey of people and events and places. Holding the details together was Billington's conviction that an abstract process was at work in those details; disparate stories in different places had, as their common ground, a tie to the frontier process that was, from the beginning of American colonization, shaping a distinctive national character.

In practice, the process ran in two directions. One direction received most of Billington's attention: the sequential creation of a new frontier society, with its distinctive characteristics emerging from the pioneering process. Out of the interaction between their imported habits and their new environment, frontiersmen forged a unique society, with a unique social order. The process of change worked with remarkable speed; soon after arrival, "frontiersmen" had become "men of a different world."[10]

Another process, considerably less examined in the text, ran in the opposite direction, transforming "Wests" into "Easts." In Billington's hands, "West" and "East" were in no way fixed geographical locations; they were labels that fit particular places according to their stage of social evolution. Colonized by Anglo-Americans, a place, regardless of where it appeared on maps, became a "West." Then, in a process of maturation, the "West" became an "East." This could happen with remarkable, even mysterious speed: Englishmen had barely established themselves in colonial Virginia before colonial "frontiersmen" were pitted against colonial "easterners," as "two antagonistic societies" developed. Similarly, in Kentucky and Tennessee, for instance, Billington noted that "the transition from frontier to civilized community was accomplished almost overnight." Primitive, regressed, simple societies evolving into advanced, matured, complex societies, "Wests" evolving into "Easts"—the model stayed with Billington throughout his career, leaving him committed to the use of the phrases "successive Easts" and "successive Wests" and to the model of a process that far outweighed place. The concept could leave a reader feeling uprooted and a bit dizzy, chronically wondering "which West, which East?" and wondering as well, how a "West" that had become an "East" could still remain a distinctive, even unique society, bearing forever the marks of its pioneer origins.[11]

Here, again, Billington's firm faith in generalizations carried him past these concerns. "Wests" became "Easts" in a process so elementally clear to him that he did not feel the need to examine it. Exhibiting patterned and predictable behavior, moving through the process that always turned Wests into Easts, frontiersmen sometimes seemed to be riding a conveyor belt, a mechanism pushing them through a process set and determined by forces outside their own wills. Indeed, in some passages, Billington could make western expansion sound like the working out of an elemental law of physics: "Through the history of man's migrations population has tended to flow from regions of excessive competition and declining opportunity to newer areas where lands are cheaper, competitors fewer, and the chances for speculative gain greater." Billington was, in fact, an unapologetic user of the word *inevitable*, a habit that grew stronger over his career. He reinforced the impression of inevitability with the frequent use of deterministic figures of speech: people moved in tides, torrents, floods, and waves. In these figures of speech, the independent, freedom-seeking frontiersman became one molecule among many, his individual action only one minuscule element in a wider and deeper tide. And, to the same degree, once pioneering had fostered in the pioneers a certain set of traits, they and their children became what that process made them, inheriting characteristics and retaining traits when the circumstances for which those traits were appropriate had vanished.[12]

Billington might modify and alter some of Turner's claims, but he returned to the central claim: "the western environment did endow pioneers with unique characteristics which all shared." What were those characteristics? Here, Billington engaged in a bit of intellectual side-stepping. "The composite frontiersman who emerged from the frontier process defies accurate description," he said forthrightly. Having said that the frontiersman could not be described, Billington went on to describe him. He was "materialistic, mobile, versatile, inventive, careless of natural resources, optimistic, and nationalistic." A believer in democracy and an "individualist" within certain limits, this "product of the frontier," was, above all, "a practical opportunist."[13]

Throughout his career, Billington held to this list of characteristics. Repeating this list, Billington each time made an indirect statement that the mysteries of subjectivity did not worry him. Since most of the frontier traits he pinpointed were indeed psychological ones, insisting on their existence required him to make firm and binding statements—"the average frontiersman was a coarse materialist"; "the typical frontiersman was an incurable optimist"—that rested on a kind of omniscience, an ability to fathom fully another person's, or an entire population's, subjectivity.[14]

Given the inconsistency of human character, the exercise also required Billington to develop considerable skill in contradicting himself with tranquility. On one hand, a "strong spirit of nationalism . . . permeated each western community" as westerners involved themselves with national issues and identified with the federal government; on the other hand, "cut off" from the "stimulating thought currents of Europe or the East, frontiersmen tended to concentrate on immediate problems and grow indifferent to the society beyond their communities." On the one hand, the frontiersman was "culturally ambitious, if not for himself, at least for his children"; on the other hand, he "shrugged away responsibility for the future by asking what posterity had done for him." On one hand, the frontiersman "reshaped institutions to be workable, without regard to precedent or tradition"; on the other hand, "the West had, throughout its history, been a stronghold of political conservatism," with "periodic protests" that were "really leveled against change." On one hand, the West was a "region of poverty and discontent"; on the other hand, the West was a place where "every individual with grit, strength, and brains was assured a golden future."[15]

Was it pedantic to ask that these contradictions be reconciled or at least addressed directly? And, given the spread of Europeans all over the planet, did it betray a certain pettiness of mind, to question Billington's free-handed use of the heavily charged word *unique* to describe the American frontier experience and the resulting traits in American character?[16]

However Billington's critics and defenders might answer those questions, they would have to reckon with Billington's basic intellectual method, a method that came with both risks and rewards. When he turned to the subject of frontier character, his texts might be compared to Impressionist paintings: one misses the broad sweep of color and line if one stands too close to the canvas, examining the individual dots and strokes of the brush. Billington was, indeed, a gatherer and transmitter of impressions; he was, by his own intention, painting "the frontiersman" on a generous canvas, not trying to write a "provable" history of particular people in particular places at particular times.

Nonetheless, his focus on the "frontiersman" carried a serious risk, the risk of both occupational and racial exclusion. In various ways, the text of *Westward Expansion* made clear that Billington considered the *real* frontiersman to be the farmer. "Throughout the history of westward expansion," Billington put it explicitly, "the farmer . . . was the average frontiersman." Miners, he wrote, "differed from usual American frontiersmen," confirming the proposition that "the hardworking farmer" was "the true hero of the tale." From these clues, one has to assume that his psychological portrait of "the frontiersman" is primarily the portrait of the farming pioneer—not of the trapper, trader, prospector, miner, laundress, boarding-house keeper, cattleman, cowboy, logger, missionary, merchant, freighter, or railroader.[17]

But the problem of exclusiveness did not stop there. There was simply no question, in the content and prose of *Westward Expansion*, that the English-speaking, American white male was the star of the story. Certainly, the extended discussion of "the frontiersman's" character carried the clear assumption that "he" was white, male, and American. In other passages, the exclusion of others seems just as clear, if also less conscious: to say, for instance, that the "first pioneers on every new frontier viewed their fellow men as completely equal" was to exclude Indians, blacks, Hispanics, and Asians from the category "fellow men." And to entitle three chapters "The French Barrier," "The Spanish Barrier," and "The Indian Barrier" (and to retain those chapter titles through four more editions) was to make a clear statement that Anglo-Americans were the main characters, and the "others" got small and temporary roles as obstacles. Including the description of western Indian tribes under the chapter heading "The Natural Setting" and relying on the odd and distancing phrase "the red men," varied at times with "menacing Indians," "fleeing savages," and "lurking savages," Billington seems at first to have written the history of western expansion with almost no attention to the full human reality of those who fell outside the in-group of Anglo-Americans. His early aversion to racial exclusiveness, recorded in *The Protestant Crusade*, seemed to have been a sacrifice to the requirements of ratifying the Turner Thesis.[18]

Billington's example, however, is more complicated than that. Discussing King Philip's War in the 1670s, for instance, Billington was willing to acknowledge another point of view: "To the Indians, hostilities appeared not only justified but necessary," a logical response to relentless white expansion. But it was on the subject of Jacksonian Indian Removal that Billington's sympathies took up a surprising intensity. Acting with "brutal directness," he wrote, American officials set out to see that the Indians were "pushed from their ancestral lands." With Andrew Jackson in office, "the helpless Indians were now at the mercy of an unsympathetic president and ruthless state officers who vied with each other in making life unpleasant for the red men." The whole story was, Billington said, a "sordid drama." In the same vein, Billington frankly condemned "the blundering attempts of heartless federal officials" in responding to the "Indian barrier" in the trans-Mississippi West. Success in shattering the barrier came at "a cost of blood, wealth, and human decency which will forever stain the annals of the American frontier."[19]

Writing western history, Billington freely and directly used the word *conquest* as a synonym for expansion. He was, in other words, quite willing to admit that "the westward advance of the Anglo-American frontier was accomplished only by absorbing or pushing aside prior occupants of the continent," both natives and Dutch, French, and Spanish colonists. In his sympathy for Indians undergoing Removal and in his forthright use of "conquest," Billington was no simple cheerleader for the cause of Manifest Destiny.[20]

In many other passages, however, his judgment of the pioneers was decidedly congratulatory. In the trans-Appalachian settlements, thousands of men and women were "all engaged in . . . planting civilization in a conquered wilderness"; with the admission of all the contiguous states, "forty-eight commonwealths stood as monuments to the frontiersmen who in three centuries carried the banner of civilization from the Atlantic to the Pacific." Still, for all his susceptibility to celebrations of conquests completed and civilizations extended, Billington's tone became noticeably darker as he approached the present. He focused his concluding narrative chapter on the agrarian problems left behind by frontier expansion, and he ended the entire book with this sentence, expressing his hope that the pioneer values, now rendered inappropriate and even damaging, could be discarded:

> *. . . as [the pioneers] pass from the scene a new generation, freed*
> *from the prejudices of an outworn past where the needs of*
> *individuals transcended the needs of society, will blaze the trails*
> *into the newer world of co-operative democracy that is America's*
> *future.*

Billington was willing to celebrate the potency and usefulness of frontier values in their own time, but he was troubled to see those values lingering—and lingering with power and influence—into the times of the Depression and the Second World War. Looking at the American future, Billington seemed to hope that those all-too-persistent frontier values might, at long last, loosen their hold on the national character.[21]

Billington's second major publication in frontier history, *The Far Western Frontier, 1830–1860* (1956), stepped away from this suggestion of a triumphant past leading to a troubled present. Commissioned as part of Harper and Row's New American Nation series, this book, Billington wrote, had two purposes: to "describe" the "movement of settlers into the Far West and the national or world events which directly influenced their migration," and to "advance evidence pertaining to the generations-old conflict over the so-called 'frontier hypothesis.'" With its "checkerboard of differing environments," the Far West was "an admirable laboratory" for testing the effect of the environment in reshaping civilization: "If the record shows that each band of frontiersmen responded in its own way to the strange new world of the Far West, a fragment of evidence has been produced in support of the 'frontier hypothesis.'"[22]

These prefatory remarks, however, seemed to be aimed at another book entirely. *The Far Western Frontier* was a narrative history of various episodes in pre–Civil War American expansion: the California hide business and the Santa Fe trade, the colonization of Texas and its later independence from Mexico, the Rocky Mountain fur trade, the missionary initiative in Oregon, the overland trails, the rising political current of Manifest Destiny, the Mexican War, Mormon colonization in Utah, the far-western mining rushes, and the boom in far-western freighting. In each of these episodes, Billington used individual biography to advantage, peopling his stories with colorful and distinctive characterizations. But the development of these narratives seldom came close to the intention declared in the preface: the testing of the frontier hypothesis by an examination of pioneer behavior in different physical environments.

Instead of undergoing tests and proofs, elements of Turner's frontier thesis appeared primarily as assertions. References to "the democ-ratizing influence of the frontier," to "the corrosive effect of a wilderness environment on transplanted Easterners," to "the impact of the frontier on all who came under its influence," appear as assertions of known quantities that both author and reader could take for granted. In passages like these, frontier processes came close to carrying the status of natural law. Billington declared that "civilization must evolve at its own pace on any frontier," and "the process cannot be markedly accelerated."[23]

This sense of an unrolling, unopposable process gained particular force with Billington's repeated use of the word and concept of inevi-tability. Everything from the founding of the Santa Fe trade to friction between Mormons and eastern Gentiles carried the label "inevitable." Even without the actual word in play, Billington's phrases often sug-gested a predestined fate: the "outcome" of the clash between Spain and the United States was "never in doubt"; revolution and Texan inde-pendence "followed as naturally as day follows night"; the American people "were destined to win not only California but all the South-west." Augmented with metaphors and analogies of compulsion, fevers that took men over and compelled them into tides and floods of emi-gration, these references to inevitability made one thing clear: to Billing-ton in 1956, the frontier thesis was something closer to a natural law than a proposition or theory in need of testing.[24]

That faith permitted him to use the phrase "like all frontiersmen," certain that frontiersmen did indeed follow repeated patterns of behav-ior. In *Westward Expansion*, Billington had advanced the same model of a continuity of behavior running directly from the Atlantic colonies across the American interior. The framers of the Watauga Association in Tennessee "viewed their Association just as the Pilgrims viewed their Mayflower Compact"; "the simple democracy of the mining camps was typical of the frontier; from the days of the Mayflower Compact and the Watauga Association westerners had set up their own governments whenever they found themselves beyond the pale of law." Describing mining camp self-regulation and self-government in *The Far Western Frontier*, Billington drew the same line of continuity: the miners "fell back upon the precedents of frontier self-government that had been accumulating since the Mayflower Compact." Postulating an unbro-ken strand of behavior spanning the entire continent, Billington once again showed his faith in the transcendant reality of abstractions and characteristics. Devout Protestant dissenters in the 1620s and Califor-nia Gold Rush miners in the 1840s might seem to have little in common, but Billington had, to his satisfaction, found the shared frontier patterns in their behavior. He had, however, put aside the declared purpose of *The Far Western Frontier*, to note and analyze the pioneer response to distinctive physical environments of the Far West, and found, instead, a pattern of frontier behavior that overpowered particular places.[25]

His analytic lapses aside, Billington's gifts as a storyteller came through clearly. He was not a cautious user of adjectives, and he was willing to take leaps of imagination that, more often than not, landed him on firm ground. On some occasions, however, his pursuit of colorful re-creations of historical scenes led to doubtful propositions. While men drove wagons on the overland trail, he wrote imaginatively, "their wives and children scattered to either side to pick wild flowers or simply romp away some of the animal spirits bred by that healthy life"; trappers at the annual Rocky Mountain rendezvous "indulged in sexual orgies with passively indifferent Indian maidens." These, and a number of other declarations, went some distance beyond historical evidence, but they could certainly serve their purpose of catching the reader's attention.[26]

In *The Far Western Frontier*, Billington also encountered a familiar tension around the issue of racial diversity. He conveyed his disapproval of what he called the "completely undemocratic nativism" shown by white Californian miners toward Mexicans, Chinese, and Indians. Blaming the transformation of Americans into "heartless nativists" on "the corrosive effect of the environment" may not have been an altogether convincing assignment of causality, but the discussion nonetheless carried a clear sense that Billington found this behavior distressing. In the same vein of standing up to the claims of Anglo-American vanity, Billington was careful to begin the book with a chapter on "The Mexican Borderlands," making clear that the Spanish preceded Anglo-Americans in colonization. But having introduced them as prior residents, Billington almost immediately went on to confirm familiar stereotypes of Hispanics: the California rancheros lived in "indolence and luxury"; their food, clothes and homes were "primitive"; with life "*too* easy," they became "increasingly lazy, increasingly indolent, increasingly backward." Meanwhile, "in the other northern provinces of Mexico poverty rather than abundance bred laziness among the people"; New Mexico slipped into "apathetic indifference," with the people of "sleepy" Santa Fe enjoying "carefree lives."[27]

The "lazy" and "backward" Hispanics at least fared better than did the Indians, who received neither an initial chapter of their own nor much in the way of recognition as original inhabitants. Throughout the text, Billington stayed loyal to his term *the red men*, a phrase guaranteed to keep Indian people at an abstract distance from the reader. They remained, as well, at a distance along the ladder of civilization. When, for instance, Billington said that fur trappers came to live like Indians, he meant, according to the old model of the stages of civilization, that the mountain men thereby moved away from civilization and toward savagery.[28] Lamenting a pattern of "undemocratic nativism" in his frontiersmen, Billington himself was still partly entrapped by a kindred pattern of thought. The problem of reconciling Turner's frontier thesis with a rejection of racial exclusiveness remained unresolved.

Billington's next major book, *America's Frontier Heritage* (1966), stayed well within the tradition of considering Anglo-American men to be the significant frontiersmen, to the exclusion of all others. The book shared a number of other working assumptions familiar from *Westward Expansion* and *The Far Western Frontier*. The focus was once again on the Turner Thesis, but narrative took a backseat, this time, to a consideration of the findings of social science. Drawing on the work of political scientists, economists, psychologists, anthropologists, demographers, and sociologists, Billington undertook to record what struck him as a remarkable convergence: when travelers gave their impressions of Americans in general and American frontiersmen in particular, when Turner cataloged the characteristics of the pioneer, and when some modern social scientists described American national character, agreements considerably outweighed disagreements. All of these observers, Billington argued, converged on the familiar list of traits—a commitment to hard work, an addiction to mobility, a willingness to innovate, an enthusiasm for democracy and a conviction in human equality, a habit of wastefulness, a spirit of nationalism, a leaning toward materialism, and an inclination to optimism. Nineteenth-century visitors, especially foreign travelers, saw these traits as characteristic of Americans, and particularly characteristic of frontiersmen, or so Billington's argument ran, and now modern social scientists saw these same traits as central to the national character. Billington felt sure that this overlap of impressions indicated something closer to causality than to coincidence. Characteristics so much in evidence in frontier areas had evidently been transmitted both through time, to postfrontier generations, and over space, to easterners. The United States had a national character; the frontier was the source of many elements of that character; and thus, to Billington, many of Turner's assertions had been ratified by an unlikely coalition of tourists and social scientists.

In *America's Frontier Heritage*, Billington's major modification of Turner's thinking came in a change of adjectives. It was not, Billington now argued, so much the *physical* environment of the frontier that gave rise to new, distinctively American traits; change stemmed, instead, from the *social* environment. The "combination of land awaiting utilization and a people capable of utilizing it," he explained, "created the distinctive social environment of the American frontier." In granting the power to change human behavior to that social environment, Billington freed the Turner Thesis from the handicaps of the old-style environmental determinism, by which nature had mysteriously overpowered man.[29]

"The key feature of this environment," Billington repeatedly reminded the reader, "was the degree of opportunity offered for upward economic and social mobility." Indeed, a close reading of *America's Frontier Heritage* reveals that "opportunity" was Billington's bedrock definition of "frontier." The altered behavior of the pioneers, he wrote, was "traceable largely to the greater degree of opportunity for self-improvement that distinguished the American Wests from the Americans Easts, and from Europe." The "successive Wests" offered people from the "successive Easts" abundant land and resources; abundant land and resources meant open opportunity for individuals; open opportunity engendered the character traits of frontiersmen.[30]

How much opportunity? Here Billington's claims reached high: "there seems no question," he wrote, "that the West did offer a social environment where newcomers could sink or rise to their own natural levels"; "as long as expansion was a fact of life, improvement was certain," unleashing "a faith in the future that was justified as long as westering was the way of the present." But evaluating claims like these leads the reader back to a familiar problem posed by Billington's prose. Was he really saying, as a literal and proven fact, that success was in every deserving western emigrant's grasp? Or was he paraphrasing the faith of many of those emigrants, trying to convey how the western world looked to them, not how it was in literal fact? Billington was not, in other words, particularly concerned with clarifying the *framework* of his remarks; in all his books, though perhaps in *America's Frontier Heritage* especially, the reader circles around an unresolvable set of questions. Was Billington offering a picture of western reality that he himself believed to be accurate? Was he simply trying to capture the world view of nineteenth-century people who believed in the promise of the frontier? Or were his own views and the views of his subjects so close that no distinction had to be made between them?[31]

Time and again, discussing the "truth" of one proposition or another, Billington showed himself to be much concerned with questions of accuracy and proof, concerned enough to use the awkward (and quite uncharacteristic) verb "to validify." His declared intention was to test the validity of the frontier thesis, not to recapture the average white American or European tourist's view of the frontier. But here, Billington seemed to have landed in the midst of an incomplete transition: he had begun his career as an intellectual and cultural historian, a beginning that might well have led him in the direction of describing and analyzing American and European thoughts and beliefs about the frontier. Instead, the heavy burden of facts he had had to assemble for *Westward Expansion* sent him out of the domain of the mind, back to a more conventionally historical world of events and actions. In *America's Frontier Heritage*, he was commuting between those two worlds, between the West as it was and the frontier as people thought it should be. In some sections of the book, testing belief against fact was his declared goal; in others, deferring to the greater power of belief over fact became his operating technique. Our concern "is not with what *is*," he declared in one passage, "but with what is *thought* to be." Sometimes exploring the actual West and sometimes exploring the imagined frontier, Billington did not always make the clearest of signals when he moved from one world to the other.[32]

Inviting his readers to trust him as he steered between those worlds, Billington extended an equal trust to those he read. Fifteen years later, he would himself make a sweeping statement on the disconnection between historical actuality and the impressions of travelers: "Visitors to the United States saw not what was there," he wrote in *Land of Savagery, Land of Promise*, "but what their experiences, beliefs, prejudices, and convictions convinced them should be there."[33] But in *America's Frontier Heritage*, and in much of *Land of Savagery, Land of Promise*, no such sweeping disbelief was at work in Billington's use of his primary sources and their descriptions of frontier character. On the contrary, he was far more inclined to take travelers at their word, as they confirmed Turner's judgments, than to analyze systematically their reliability as witnesses.

Just as surprising to a reader with the benefit of hindsight was Billington's faith in that unit of wisdom known as "social science," a faith that underlay every chapter of the book. "Social scientists believe," he wrote, "that Americans stand apart" in their characteristics.[34] While it was surprising to imagine that "social scientists," with all their disciplinary, methodological, and ideological disagreement, had ever believed one thing in harmony, it was also hard to imagine that they would continue believing it. Indeed, by the 1970s many social scientists concerned with such issues saw little validity in the idea of an American character shared by blacks and whites, women and men, rich and poor. Just as much as travelers and tourists, "social scientists" would prove to be something less than rocks of interpretive reliability.

Billington, in any case, had made only a partial conversion to the means and ends of social science. One could see the limit of that conversion in his use of the word *culture*. In some sections of the book, he used the word in the anthropological sense, as the worldview and general pattern of behavior of a people. "Each group has its own patterns of behavior known as a *culture*," he wrote, "which include the shared knowledge, beliefs, customs, and habits that have been acquired by living together over the course of generations." But in most of its other appearances in the book, "culture" climbed back to its traditional level as "high culture." When, for instance, Billington said that the frontiersmen "were culturally deprived," or that they felt that with "wealth" they "could eventually buy . . . culture," he did not mean that frontiersmen lacked a worldview or a model of individual and family behavior, or that they thought money could buy such things. He had returned, instead, to a definition of "culture" as refined and sophisticated art, literature, and education. After a brief campaign, the methods and terminology of social science had surrendered ground to the old hierarchy of civilization's stages of refinement.[35]

One could see this substitution of familiar habits of thought for the empirical methods of social science most clearly on the subject of gender. Throughout his career, Billington held to the practice of using *men* as the encompassing term for all humans. While this came at the cost of a certain amount of imprecision, making it hard to tell when the population referred to was indeed all male or when it was a mixed group with both genders represented, that habit was considerably less perplexing than Billington's repeated assertions of the favored position of women on the frontier and in twentieth-century America. "We venerate our wives," Billington wrote at the very beginning of *America's Frontier Heritage*, "shower them with adulation, burden them with authority, and reduce the mere male to a henpecked nonentity." The evidence for these claims of the spoiled and pampered status of women was not easy to grasp. The claim that, to male pioneers, "women were to be sought after, venerated, and pampered" makes some sense if one takes Elizabeth Custer to be the norm, and if one dismisses the evidence of countless western women's narratives of hard work and deprivation. Otherwise, references to "the pioneer era's undue respect for women" leave the reader in double confusion—as to the evidence in support of this exalted status, and as to the standards for deciding what constitute "due" and "undue" levels in matters of respect.[36]

Passages like these seemed to rest on something closer to personal conviction than empirical research. In the belief in the universal process that transformed "Wests" into "Easts," in the concentration on agricultural enterprise as the representative frontier enterprise, in the pattern of phrasing by which traits and characteristics behaved like entities as intact and self-contained as billiard balls, and in the working assumption that universal frontier qualities overpowered particulars of place and time, Billington confidently planted assertions in disputed historiographic terrain that would have evoked timidity in a more cautious writer. Nonetheless, for all his confidence, Billington in *America's Frontier Heritage* was at his peak of tailoring and modifying, offering statements that gave every impression of contradicting each other. Consider, for instance, his assertions on the subject of class divisions and stratification in frontier communities. On the one hand, "class divisions occurred in the most primitive communities, and deepened as the social order matured"; indeed, "conditions" on the frontier "stimulated stratification." On the other hand, the frontier showed "a blurring of class distinctions," and "class lines" proved "meaningless in a land when everyone moved from one class to another—always upward—so rapidly that they could never solidify." Read closely and in relation to each other, these statements and a number of others on the same subject leave the reader in considerable confusion. Were frontier class divisions deep and significant, or were they fleeting and inconsequential? In this matter, as in many others, the evidence simply was not fully assembled and available to Billington; nonetheless, he was not going to wait for that utopian moment of full proof to come. He was certain that Turner's emphasis on an utterly egalitarian frontier society was overstated, but he could not be certain of the degree to which it was overstated, nor of the degree to which an alternate model of class stratification had to be put in its place.[37]

Various Turnerian propositions might undergo a partial modification, but Billington was standing by the basics. The frontier offered individuals opportunity; opportunity had created a different kind of social environment; that environment had encouraged the development of characteristics that persisted into our times; and those characteristics contributed to the creation of a unique American character.

At this point, however, Billington's reflections took a turn toward the solemn and sober. Originally adapted to frontier expansion, these persistent traits posed a variety of problems when the frontier ended. Life in a "closed-space" world required a different set of values, habits, and expectations. Following the closing of the frontier, the world wars, the Great Depression, and the Cold War had eroded American pride and optimism; in these changed conditions, it was time for "a philosophy of realism" to take the place of the old "philosophy of expectation." "In time," Billington wrote, "Americans may learn that men everywhere are more prisoners than masters of the era in which they live, and that no nation, no matter how powerful, can shape global society to its own image"; "three centuries of frontiering," Billington said in the book's last sentence, gave the nation its "greatest strength—and some of its most regrettable weaknesses." Created out of abundant opportunity available to all (in theory, at least), America's frontier heritage was an ambiguous legacy, a set of values poorly adapted to a world of limits.[38]

Rather than expanding on this sober theme, Billington turned next to a biography of Frederick Jackson Turner, a project that clearly engaged him at every level of both emotion and intellect. The result was Billington's best book, a full and illuminating portrait of the thinker whose ideas about American history so charmed Billington and many others.

Immersing himself in Turner's recently opened papers, Billington became "Turner's slave," an eager practitioner of an unusual but remarkably engaging literary form, "the biography of a college professor."[39] Taking the story from Turner's boyhood in Portage, Wisconsin, through to his last years in southern California, Billington gave readers open access to Turner's life and personality. Given the timing of the story, with Turner's entry into the academic world in the 1880s, the individual biography also serves as an instructive case study in the professionalization of the American university. The tiny Wisconsin history department where Turner took his undergraduate courses bore little resemblance to the sizable operation, oriented toward research and publication, that Turner left in 1910, departing for Harvard. Turner's life, this biography makes clear, carries a level of significance quite apart from his frontier thesis. He was a moving force behind, and perhaps also as a victim of, the professionalization of the professor.

In what sense victim? Much of Billington's book tracks Turner's struggles with writing. Early on, Turner fell into a pattern of procrastination and delay, waiting for the irresistible force of a nonnegotiable deadline to galvanize him into action. In a burst of professional fame after 1893, Turner went into a perfect frenzy of contract-signing, promising book after book to publisher after publisher. One determined soul, Albert B. Hart, used a combination of threats, pleas, and persistence to achieve the completion of Turner's *Rise of the New West, 1819–1829.*[40] But other publishers pled in vain, and Turner's last decades were absorbed in a chronically stymied quest to write "THE BOOK."

Why this Sisyphean struggle? Billington suggested a number of causes. Professional duties—classes, committees, graduate student supervision, public lectures, faculty recruiting—swallowed his time. But a condition so common, shared by many professors who finish books, provides an incomplete explanation. Billington suggested other causes, closer to Turner's individual temperament: his restless curiosity and wide range of interests, making it unlikely that he would devote valuable time to filling in the proof for an idea that was no longer fresh to him; his split sense of the larger generalizations appropriate to writing for public audiences, and the precise, detailed studies appropriate for professional audiences; and most important, his intractable perfectionism. "Turner's standards were so high, his sense of perfectionism so demanding," Billington summed it up, "that he never could write history as he knew it must be written."[41]

For readers less tightly tied to Turner's thinking, an additional explanation suggests itself. Both of the "big ideas" most associated with Turner—his theory of the frontier and his theory of sections—were difficult ideas to implement in extended, book-length form. To take his very abstract conception of the frontier—whether defined as physical environment or social environment, narrow line or broad zone—and to keep that concept intact while integrating it into a detailed narrative of actual events, people, and places was, as Billington was surely in the best position to know, a very difficult task. Writing *Westward Expansion* or *America's Frontier Heritage* was an intellectual enterprise modeled on the most maddening of cattle drives. In both books, Billington knew his destination; the argument had to arrive at Turnerian conclusions, partly modified but primarily reinforced. But arrival at that destination was no easy matter; pieces and parts of the evidence were always on the verge of breaking away and heading in the direction of a different conclusion entirely. The enterprise of keeping the diverse examples and case studies of Anglo-American expansion, from the Atlantic colonies to California gold mines, from Ohio homesteads to southwestern corporate farms, from pack mules to railroads, all moving in a common direction through the length of a full-size book, demanded extraordinary confidence. Turner, unlike Billington, was simply unsuited to the demands of that kind of intellectual Long Drive.

Like his other books, Billington's biography was aimed at the familiar destination of vindicating the frontier thesis. That thesis, Billington still thought, "was basically sound." In concluding chapters appraising Turner's legacy, and throughout the biography, Billington offered a variety of defenses against the familiar criticisms of the frontier thesis. Turner was no monocausationist; he was fully aware of other forces shaping American life and only stressed the frontier to make up for its previous neglect. Turner "carefully guarded himself against the cardinal sin of his profession in those days—the danger of over-generalization"; he was, in fact, a leading apostle for careful, research-tested historical inquiry. Accordingly, when he found new evidence, he revised his thinking, as he did on the efficiency of the frontier as a safety valve and on the orderly progress of civilization's stages across the continent.[42]

This was not to say that Turner was without flaws. Billington was quite willing to admit that, like a number of his disciples, Turner had been guilty of exaggeration and overstatement; failing to put enough time and effort into providing proof for the frontier thesis, he built "an increasingly shaky structure on an untested foundation," letting his convictions overpower his evidence. And Turner did show symptoms of prejudice and bigotry toward immigrants, Jews, Indians, and blacks. But, these failings aside, Turner was "basically right."[43]

On at least one count, Billington's success was complete; he had shown Turner to be a far more complex and much more sensible thinker than anyone could have imagined by simply reading the 1893 thesis. But here, and elsewhere, Billington slipped into the assumption that defending Frederick Jackson Turner was the same enterprise as defending the frontier thesis. In fact, the ideas packed together in the 1893 essay and Turner's own thinking proceeded on quite separate tracks of development. To the degree that Turner's modifications and clarifications of the original thesis appeared only in his private papers, they could not have had much effect on the public discourse on the meaning of the frontier, and one can hardly fault later critics for failing to take them into account. Turner himself may have thought, as Billington says, that he had, in 1893, "simply proposed an untested hypothesis, to be accepted or rejected after proper research," and "not an infallible formula." But the 1893 essay itself conveyed quite a different tone, a tone much closer to certainty than to tentative speculation.[44]

Considered in the full picture of his career and his private thinking, Turner did indeed "stand acquitted" and "exonerate[d]" of many of the charges brought against the thesis. But these very terms of criminal justice made Turner himself into the battleground. "Was he as grossly in error as his attackers charged," Billington put the question, "and, if so, does he deserve the fame accorded him by his contemporaries and later generations?" The question turned into one of judging Turner as a person, and the broader question—asking what relation the ideas he advanced so forcefully in 1893 might bear to the reality of western expansion—shifted into the background.[45]

Putting off publishers or balancing his strained income against his sizable debts, indulging his passion for fishing and hiking or doing everything imaginable to launch the careers of his protégés, fighting the tyranny of college football or reworking his lecture notes to reflect his changing appraisal of American history, rebelling against old models of American history or fighting back rebellion in the American Historical Association, enduring the tragic loss of his young son and daughter or struggling with his own bouts of uncertain health, the Frederick Jackson Turner that Billington captured is an enormously memorable character. Moreover, his life embodied the transformation of the American university at the turn-of-the-century, a transformation that today affects us all, from undergraduates to professors. That may, indeed, be Billington's greatest service to Turner; he wrote a biography that gave Turner's life a relevance and meaning that extend far beyond the up-and-down fortunes of a particular set of ideas focused on the frontier.

In the preface to his last study, _Land of Savagery, Land of Promise_, Billington declared that this book would be "no rehashing of the Turner theories." By this time, Turnerisms were so deeply engrained in Billington's thought that no such rehashing was necessary. The familiar list of frontier-derived traits, the development of an American character most visible and distinctive in the most recently settled regions, the origins of democracy and liberty in frontier opportunity, the insignificance of place in comparison to process—all these familiar propositions confirmed Billington's loyalty to Turner's thought, without the necessity of repeated invocations of Turner's name.[46]

In *America's Frontier Heritage*, Billington had summarized travelers' impressions of frontier life, and *Land of Savagery, Land of Promise* was a continuation of that enterprise. The focus was on European writers, and the pool this time was expanded to include writers of fiction, not just writers of travel memoirs. To assemble all the sources, Billington drew on the help of an international network of researchers and translators. *Land of Savagery, Land of Promise* thus records the extraordinary appeal that American frontier life has held for a variety of European audiences. Packing both writers of fiction and writers of nonfiction into one commodious category called "European image-makers," Billington divided their offerings into a classification of opposites: images of the frontier as a land of savagery and images of the frontier as a land of promise. In the first, the frontier was a place of violence, conflict, cruelty, and degeneracy; in the second, opportunity, progress, and upward mobility dominated the picture. As broad intellectual trends came and went in Europe, the image of the American frontier fluctuated accordingly. Romanticism inspired images of noble savages, splendid landscapes, and natural virtue; the practicality tied to industrialization swung the pendulum back to an image of wilderness as a rough and cruel place that should be bullied into giving up its resources for the greater good of progress. By the time the frontier "closed," the pendulum had come to rest on the side of savagery, with a permanently installed European image of a brutal American frontier.[47]

In sketching broad trends and categories, Billington showed his characteristic ease with enormous abstractions and generalizations. The book's working assumptions—the displacing of romanticism by industrial practicality, the strict polarity dividing the world between savagery and promise, the idea of "Europe" as a unit of study and "European image-makers" as a recognizable group engaged in a common enterprise—all showed Billington's familiar talent for finding a greater reality in abstract categories than in swirls of uncooperative facts. In fact, the most interesting sections of the book come in the moments when he broke down the unit of "Europe" into the particulars of time, place, and ideology—when writers from particular nations used their novels to showcase the virtues thought to be peculiar to their country, when Eastern Europeans jumped ahead in sympathy for Indians and even developed direct parallels between the oppression of peasants and the oppression of Indians; when Tories and Whigs used frontier images as weapons in their disputes; when nations involved in their own imperialistic expansion found the American frontier example particularly useful or even inspirational. Sometimes noting these particularities, Billington was just as often inclined to lump everyone together into one unit of "European image-makers," in sentences where they seemed to operate as a unified group.[48]

The confidence of his generalizations appeared most dramatically in his handling of the complex problems raised in the relationship between popular literature and its audiences. When, for instance, the image makers decided that Indians were noble savages, Billington wrote, "most Europeans accepted their judgment." When image makers said that "the denial of property rights was a denial of all civilization," then "their European readers agreed with them." These statements skipped lightly over a number of critical questions. How does one identify the audience for popular literature? Do we assume automatically that readers trust everything they read? Should we distinguish between the influence of fiction and the influence of nonfiction, or do we assume that trusting readers do not waste their time in calibrating different levels of credulity for different kinds of written literature? In scattered references, Billington did acknowledge these questions, trying to sort out reader response to fiction and nonfiction, but he continued to skirt the difficult problem of uncovering audience response to mass-produced literature. "So the image-makers preached, and so Europeans believed," he put it, at one peak of interpretive confidence.[49]

His habit of asserting appeared just as dramatically when Billington took up the question of the accuracy of European-authored images. He was free, one must remember, to describe and analyze the images simply as acts of the mind. "Visitors to the United States," he had written, "saw not what was there, but what their experiences, beliefs, prejudices, and convictions convinced them should be there." As accurate reporters, they were, in a word, "unreliable." In those terms, places undergoing American expansion—the "successive Wests"—served primarily as projection screens; through much of the book, the West as an actual place came close to total irrelevance. But the very word *unreliable* conveyed Billington's conviction that he himself could—and would—judge the image makers' accuracy, comparing their perceptions to the way things really were on frontiers. The "question remains: how accurate was the image projected by travelers?" he asked directly. "Which of these views was true?" Indeed, the book was peppered with remarks classifying some assertions as "true" and "accurate," and some as "false" and "distorted," sorting out what was imagined from what "really was." Repeatedly, Billington returned *Land of Savagery, Land of Promise* to the question of reliability and distortion, validity and misrepresentation. Pushing that question, he made an implicit statement that he knew when the image makers told the truth and when they did not.[50]

And yet the reader faced moments of confusion, provoked by a familiar pattern in Billington's writing. When he said that "experience showed that virtually every move" to the West "returned some profit," or when he said that "equality, liberty, and democracy were enshrined, not as distant goals, but as the accepted rules of society" along frontiers, was he simply paraphrasing the image makers, or was he agreeing with them and ratifying their accuracy? Like many western historians of his generation, Billington did not find it necessary to draw a clear and consistent line between his thinking and the thinking of the historical characters he studied. Sometimes he labeled the picture offered by the image makers as inaccurate; sometimes he offered lengthy paraphrases of their views, with clues to his cynical distance from those views; sometimes he paraphrased without any of those clues, and with, instead, a fairly clear implication that he found those writers both shrewd and accurate. The problem came in distinguishing one of those modes from the others.[51]

Consider, for instance, one of the most interesting puzzles raised by *Land of Savagery, Land of Promise.* As in his earlier work, Billington found the twentieth-century legacy of frontiering to be as distressing as it was inspirational. *Land of Savagery, Land of Promise* added a new source of distress: European writers, he thought, had settled on a distorted image of the American frontiersman's displacement of Indians as a process of brutality and cruelty. That persistent image, then, played its role in international relations, causing Europeans to see white Americans as unsavory sorts, putting coercion to use in the cause of self-interest in the late twentieth century, just as they had on the nineteenth-century frontier. The result was "the longheld belief that frontier America—and to a lesser degree the United States as a whole—was a land where might ruled over right, where brutality was the way of life, and where an Indian minority was heartlessly wiped out by white aggressors." Billington did refer briefly to the contribution that the Vietnam War and the nation's Cold War habit of "supporting any dictatorial government that promised to maintain the status quo" made to this image. Nonetheless, it remained his conviction that nineteenth-century European image makers had given the United States an unfair and distorted image as a nation that had won its territory by taking brutal advantage of Indians. This image, his implication was clear, did not reflect the reality of American expansion.[52]

But what, then, *was* that reality? Or, more accurately, what was Billington's version of it? Recall his own language from *Westward Expansion* in 1949. Indian Removal was a "sordid drama," he had written then; the "Indian barrier" had been "shattered . . . at a cost of blood, wealth, and human decency which will forever stain the annals of the American frontier." The moral critique of American expansion that he condemned as distorted and unfair in 1981 was strikingly similar to the critique he himself had offered in 1949. Evidently he had changed his thinking over the intervening three decades, but how and why? What new information had caused him to conclude that he had been too harsh in his earlier judgment of the moral costs of territorial acquisition?[53]

The question of the evidence that shaped Billington's convictions was probably most perplexing on the subject of the frontier image's impact on European life and thought. Briefly put, Billington's argument followed this course. The positive image of the frontier as a land of promise and opportunity lured many Europeans into immigrating. The departure of so many, especially farmers and workers, then became a source of concern to the upper classes. To persuade their working classes to resist the appeal of the American frontier, European elites then had to consider the possibility of democratic social and political reform. The image makers, in this chain of causality, had "forced European reformers to examine the whole structure of society there." The European image of the American frontier thus was a force behind Europe's democratic revolution and reform of the nineteenth and twentieth centuries.[54]

Appraising this argument, one encounters several substantial questions. How should we distinguish between the appeal of the image of the frontier and the image of the entire United States, with cities as well as farms acting as magnets for immigration? When immigrants made return visits to their homes and spoke of "the riches and liberty of that land of wonders beyond the seas," was this still a matter of the image of the frontier or of the nation at large? Were the "peasants who read of that golden land where all were rich and all were equal" and who "would never be the same again" responding to the image of the frontier or of the United States in general? Billington noted that "the image-makers confused the attractions of frontier life with those of life anywhere in the United States," and that confusion had its impact on his own text. Images of the nation apart from the frontier surely played their part in inspiring immigration, but when the argument of *Land of Savagery, Land of Promise* was in full swing the frontier pushed aside any other aspects of American life that were just as effective, if not more effective, in motivating immigrants.[55]

One wonders, as well, what became of Karl Marx, and the entire tribe of European radicals whose ideas and visions have seemed, at various times in American history, to be so threatening and disruptive in the eyes of American conservatives. In Billington's presentation, Europeans appeared, by and large, to be a stodgy group. "Even the most outspoken social reformers accepted" European class "divisions as irrevocable, and never dared suggest that the 'worthy poor' be moved up a notch to become the 'low paid.' " Intentionally or not, in *Land of Savagery, Land of Promise*, Billington had reversed the usual thinking about left-wing radicalism and its standing in Europe and America. Conventionally, historians have seen more consistent radicalism among European thinkers, leaving American historians to ponder the question, Why did the United States fail to develop a consistent and influential left? But Billington saw things in quite opposite terms. Europeans were caught in ruts of traditional thinking and resistance to reform; they only took up the cause of reform when forced to do so by the powerful outside force of the American frontier image. Like partners in a square dance, Europe and America under Billington's direction had switched places, with America taking a surprise position well to Europe's left.[56]

Billington, however, was aware that his ascribed chain of causality had its doubtful links. Did the image of the American frontier really reshape the political landscape of Europe? "Viewing the Old World as a whole," Billington began, "there seems little doubt that frontier liberty and opportunity as magnified by image-makers contributed to the stirrings of protest that eventually liberalized political processes." Once that forceful statement was made, Billington reversed the direction of force: "There seems little doubt, too, that their role was but small indeed; internal conditions and the inexorable course of history underlay democratic reform, not the American example." The same two-step worked in reverse order: "No sensible person could argue that the social changes that swept Europe at century's end were solely, or even primarily, a product of the frontier image"; however, "it cannot be denied that the attractions of a land where opportunity and equality awaited all stimulated a mass exodus that sent western Europe into an era of soul-searching." In those passages, the close reader ran head on into Billington's familiar habit of tailoring and modifying his statements in a way that made it difficult to know what, exactly, he had really said.[57]

In these summing-up comments, Billington's final meaning might have been hard to grasp in part because of his confessed irritability with the whole matter of precise terminology. Turner's frontier thesis, he had long felt, had been unfairly criticized by readers who bogged down in terminology, readers who claimed that the imprecision of the word *frontier* made the thesis unworkable. In *America's Frontier Heritage*, he had drawn a distinction between Turner's "statement" of the frontier thesis and the substance of that thesis. Turner might have failed to define the word *frontier*, committing a number of "semantic sins" appropriate to a man who "was by nature a poet," but "the validity of the frontier hypothesis had nothing to do with Turner's *statement* of that hypothesis." In *Frederick Jackson Turner*, Billington had repeated the same argument, insisting that "Turner wrote with exemplary clarity for those not seeking a semantic quarrel with him." Asking exactly what a word or sentence meant—whether his or Turner's—was thus a quarrel over "semantics," a waste of time and energy, a matter of willfully obtuse readers claiming that an imprecise sentence, of necessity, carried imprecise substance.[58]

Refusing to waste time in debates over precise wording, Billington similarly let conviction take over when evidence proved problematic. Especially in his earlier works, Billington had been offering final judgments of matters that were still very much under investigation. Watching that habit at work brings the reader back to a recognition of the essential mystery of causality in matters of human character and behavior. If Americans, for instance, do have a talent for squandering natural resources, as Billington said and as recent history seems to indicate, then where did that talent come from—from the frontier, as Billington thought,[59] or from the nation's early lead in industrial production? If a trait for wastefulness came from distinctive American conditions, then why is that trait so easily taught and transmitted to people of other conditions and other traditions? And what would be adequate evidence to prove—or disprove—any of the possible answers to these questions?

Whether the subject was the frontier origins of American character or the existence of a continuous process that tied Plymouth Colony and the Rocky Mountain fur trade, John Winthrop and Billy the Kid, into the same basic story, Billington was raising questions that could only be answered in degrees of uncertainty. When Billington's own high level of confidence and conviction ran into this well-entrenched uncertainty, the text that resulted would record both moods: the conviction in an orderly history where Turner's basic ideas still held, and the confusion brought into that world by the methods, concerns, and findings of mid- and late-twentieth-century professional history.

Of all those concerns, the most difficult to assimilate was the recognition of racial conflict and inequality in western expansion. From his first book on American nativism, Billington had made clear his opposition to racial and ethnic prejudice. Nonetheless, the white frontiersman was obviously the central character of Billington's version of western expansion, with only subordinate roles available to all the others. When Billington wrote, as he did repeatedly, that frontiersmen considered all men their equal, it was fairly clear that he had not thought how such a proposition would read to an Indian, Hispanic, Asian, or black reader. The paradigm of the westward-moving frontier was a white-centered paradigm, and no tinkering along the lines of an occasional reference to the undemocratic nativism of frontiersmen could change that.

In the fourth edition of *Westward Expansion*, published in 1974, shockwaves from the various movements of the 1960s evidently had reached Billington. He had, "with considerable reluctance," changed the text to identify "the heroes or villains of expansion as Negroes or Mexican-Americans when those designations applied." But he could not "resist a lingering hope that the tide will turn again, and that all men will be recognized as part of the family of mankind, all equal, all deserving of recognition for their exploits or ideas, rather than because of race, color, creed, or nationality." The hope for a common life without racial divisions and inequities testified to Billington's rejection of bigotry, but it was nonetheless a bewildering statement from a historian. Even if we should prove able to write of our future without reference to racial differences, we will never gain that license in the writing of the actual, not the imagined, past, where, as Billington himself wrote, "racial disharmony in the West rivaled that in the East."[60]

The unresolved tensions of racial exclusiveness aside, Billington spoke for all western historians when he wrote, paraphrasing Turner, that "the West had to be understood if American history was to be understood."[61] As founding president of the Western History Association, a prolific writer, and a leading encourager of younger scholars at Clark and Northwestern universities and, later, at the Huntington Library, Billington put his life behind that proposition. Following Turner's lead, Billington placed himself at the point of intersection of "Wests" and "Easts," keeping track of the waves of influence that rolled from west to east, transmitting pioneer traits to Americans in general. Tracking these persistent traits, Billington was himself a transmitter, building a bridge to connect an older set of Turnerian articles of faith to a newer, theoretically more objective set of social scientific articles of faith.

That the structure never quite spanned the distance was an indication that the gap was too great to be bridged, and in no way an indication that Billington had failed in persistence.

Everyone interested in western history could agree that the European writers, who sent ostriches into Blackfeet territory and adventurers over river routes from San Diego to Santa Fe, had the facts wrong. But beyond those easy cases, the facts of western history are very much matters of interpretation, and there is no better way to be reminded of this than to read the works of Ray Allen Billington.

NOTES

1. Ray Allen Billington, *Land of Savagery, Land of Promise* (New York: W. W. Norton, 1981), 95, 96.

2. For biographical information, see Ray Allen Billington, "The Frontier and I," *Western Historical Quarterly* 1 (January 1970):5–20; and Martin Ridge, "Ray Allen Billington (1903–1981)," *Western Historical Quarterly* 12 (July 1981): 245–50. For a general appraisal of Billington's career, see Martin Ridge, "Frederick Jackson Turner, Ray Allen Billington, and American Frontier History," *Western Historical Quarterly* 19 (January 1988):5–20.

3. Ray Allen Billington, *The Protestant Crusade, 1800–1860: A Study of the Origins of American Nativism* (New York: Macmillan, 1938), 4–5.

4. Martin Ridge, "Ray Allen Billington, Western History, and American Exceptionalism," *Pacific Historical Review* 56 (November 1987):499.

  • 5. Ray Allen Billington, *Westward Expansion: A History of the American Frontier* (New York: Macmillan, 1949), vii.

6. Ibid., 10, 11.

7. Ibid., 1, 2, 11.

8. Ibid., 3, 1, 744.

9. Ibid., 3–6.

10. Quotation from ibid., 215; see also 80, 96, 310, 328.

11. Ibid., 45, 49, 250, 11.

12. Quotation from ibid., 749; references to inevitability are on 47, 402, 654, 753; to tides, etc., on 8, 11, 246, 290, 310, 325, 615; to persistence of traits on 744. On inevitability, see also n. 24 of this text.

13. Ibid., 746, 748.

14. Ibid., 746.

15. Ibid., 745, 746, 748, 756, 744.

16. For uses of "unique," see ibid., 1, 2, 11, 308, 310, 328, 620, 743, 744, 747.

17. Ibid., 10, 616, 11.

18. Ibid., 744, 103, 422, 651, 409–13, 47, 181, 746. "Red men" appears throughout all of Billington's major books.

19. Ibid., 73, 291, 315, 651.

20. Ibid., p. 422. The word *conquest* is used freely throughout the text.

21. Ibid., 173, 721, 756.

22. Ray Allen Billington, *The Far Western Frontier, 1830–1860* (New York: Harper and Row, 1956), xvii, xviii.

23. Ibid., 30, 44, 235, 248. For the most prolonged assertion of this kind, see the discussion of mountain men, 44–50.

24. References to inevitability are on ibid., 16, 23, 65, 113, 120, 122, 144, 146, 151, 168, 181, 182, 212, 254, 270; quotations are from 1, 116, 143, 167; for metaphors of compulsion, see 91, 92, 95, 96, 98, 105, 219, 233, 243, 244, 245.

25. "Like all frontiersmen" appears on ibid., 29, 37, 129; quotations from 238, and *Westward Expansion* (1st ed.), 159, 621.

26. Ibid., 101, 47.

27. Ibid., 238, 9, 13, 4, 23.

28. Ibid., 48–53.

29. Quotation from Ray Allen Billington, *America's Frontier Heritage* (New York: Holt, Rinehart and Winston, 1966), 221; see also 49, 52–54, 90.

30. Quotations from ibid., 221, 223; see also 3, 25, 46.

31. Ibid., 113, 225, 226.

32. Ibid., 205, 139.

33. Ray Allen Billington, *Land of Savagery, Land of Promise: The European Image of the American Frontier* (New York: W. W. Norton, 1981), 74.

34. *America's Frontier Heritage*, 63.

35. Quotations from ibid., 49, 86, 164; for the use of "culture" in the "high culture" sense, see i, 3, 74–76, 79, 80, 84, 87–90, 94, 165, 200, 201, 209, 213, 230.

36. Ibid., 1, 216, 234.

37. Ibid., 97, 103, 94, 113–14.

38. Ibid., 231, 231. See also 6, 226–28.

39. Ray Allen Billington, *Frederick Jackson Turner* (New York: Oxford University Press, 1973), viii, vi.

40. Ibid., 201–5, 223.

41. Quotation from ibid., 481; for discussions of Turner's struggles with writing, see also vi–vii, 42, 160, 198–99, 208–9, 225, 233, 308–9, 382–85, 398–99, 409–15, 424.

42. Quotations from ibid., 283, 482; specific defenses of Turner appear on 149–50, 161–62, 178–79, 183, 444, 456–58, 476, 497.

43. Quotation from ibid., 199; see also 195, 198–99, 435–37, 448, 454.

44. Ibid., 447.

45. Ibid., 459, 460, 451. See also *America's Frontier Heritage*, 19–22, for the same approach of making Turner himself the target of attack, defense, and judgment.

46. *Land of Savagery*, xii.

47. See ibid., 14, 25, 79–81, 105–6, 267, 331.

48. For local and ideological particularities, see ibid., 35, 46–47, 75–76, 139, 145–46, 179–80, 317–18, 330; for broader discussions of "European image-makers" as one group, see, for instance, most of Chapter 13, "The European Reaction," 291–310.

49. Quotations from ibid., 127, 169, 208; for somewhat more careful discussions of reader response, see 38, 59–61, 222–24, 235, 275, 291–92, 331.

50. Quotations from ibid., 74, 78, 291; for references to accuracy, see 1, 2, 30, 39, 47, 71, 98, 125, 162, 171, 257, 275, 312–14, 323.

51. Ibid., 207, 241.

52. Quotation from ibid., 332; see also 129–30, 134, 144, 148, 323–24, 330–31.

53. *Westward Expansion* (1st ed.), 315, 651. The sentence remained unchanged (p. 563) in the 4th edition (New York: Macmillan, 1974), the last edition in which Billington did the textual changes; the 4th edition also refers to Removal as a "sordid drama" (p. 303).

54. Quotation from ibid., 293; see also 242, 296, 305, 307.

55. Quotations from ibid., 72, 300–302, 292; see also 29, 219, 240, 303.

56. Ibid., 242.

57. Ibid., 303, 309.

58. *America's Frontier Heritage*, 16, 22; *Frederick Jackson Turner*, 453.

59. See *America's Frontier Heritage*, 1, 3, 65, 168–70, 233.

60. *Westward Expansion*, 4th ed. vii; *Frederick Jackson Turner*, 199. For full evidence of Billington's commitment to racial inclusiveness, see Ray Allen Billington, ed., *The Journal of Charlotte Forten* (New York: Dryden Press, 1953).

61. *Frederick Jackson Turner*, 83.

BIBLIOGRAPHY

SELECTED WRITINGS OF RAY ALLEN BILLINGTON

America's Frontier Heritage. New York: Holt, Rinehart and Winston, 1966.

The Far Western Frontier, 1830–1860. New York: Harper and Row, 1956.

Frederick Jackson Turner: Historian, Scholar, Teacher. New York: Oxford University Press, 1973.

"The Frontier and I." *Western Historical Quarterly* 1 (January 1970):5–20.

Land of Savagery, Land of Promise: The European Image of the American Frontier. New York: W. W. Norton, 1981.

The Protestant Crusade, 1800–1860: A Study of the Origins of American Nativism. New York: Macmillan, 1938.

Westward Expansion: A History of the American Frontier, 1st ed. New York: Macmillan, 1949. Later editions: 1960, 1967, 1974, and, with Martin Ridge, 1982.

WORKS ABOUT RAY ALLEN BILLINGTON

Oglesby, Richard E. "Ray Allen Billington," in John Wunder, ed., *Historians of the American Frontier: A Bio-Bibliographical Sourcebook.* New York: Greenwood Press, 1988, 97–121.

Ridge, Martin. "Frederick Jackson Turner, Ray Allen Billington, and American Frontier History," *Western Historical Quarterly* 19 (January 1988):5–20.

———. "Ray Allen Billington, Western History, and American Exceptionalism." *Pacific Historical Review* 56 (November 1987):495–511.

11

Earl Pomeroy and the Reorientation of Western American History

MICHAEL P. MALONE

$\mathcal{A}$MONG ALL THE HISTORIANS of the American West during the past two generations, Earl Pomeroy has proven himself to be the most thoughtful, the most analytical, and probably the most influential. For it has been Pomeroy, more than any other scholar, who has most penetratingly and consistently confronted the long prevailing frontier hypothesis articulated by Frederick Jackson Turner and Walter Prescott Webb—emphasizing pioneering, the shaping power of the environment, and western particularism—with a markedly different interpretation. In contrast to Turner's frontier orientation and Webb's arid-lands and polemically regionalist perspectives, the West of Earl Pomeroy is a place where cities and commerce rather than countryside and agriculture set the pace, where historical imitativeness and continuity rather than innovation have been the rule. Pomeroy's West is a place that is not a land in itself but very much a part of the larger national society.

This is not to deny that Pomeroy is a westerner or a regionalist. Born in Capitola, a small town south of San Francisco, in 1915, Earl Spencer Pomeroy grew up in the West; and both as a scholar and as a resident, he has been a westerner nearly his entire life. Following undergraduate work at San Jose State College, he took his doctoral studies at the University of California at Berkeley, whose History Department, dominated in those days by Herbert Bolton, Frederic Paxson, and the great Bancroft collection, had a decidedly western orientation.[1]

The years at Berkeley clearly left lasting impressions upon him. He

took three fields of study in European history, including an exceptional
class in British constitutional history from William Alfred Morris; and
he thus emerged from graduate study with a strong bent toward institutional history and toward breadth of understanding and a comparative frame of reference. Most notably, he derived much from his major
professor, Frederic Paxson, the Pulitzer Prize–winning historian of the
frontier and successor to Turner earlier at Wisconsin. Like Paxson,
Pomeroy would combine the two fields of western American and recent
American history and would always argue that the region could only
be studied in close national context. And like Paxson, he consistently
emphasized objectivity and disciplined, methodical research. The tribute he later paid his mentor could equally well have been said of him:

> *Paxson was so complex a thinker, so little disposed to commit*
> *himself to any simple formula in the interpretation of history and*
> *of the historian's task, that no one can adequately define his*
> *position for him. . . . In his respect for larger historical truths,*
> *he often deliberately understated his conclusions, or advanced*
> *hypotheses more subtly than some others have done. Some of his*
> *colleagues have said much more of the theory of historical truth*
> *than he did. But none pursued the truth with greater keenness*
> *and devotion.*[2]

The young man who emerged from graduate school during that
frenetic time, as the world edged into war, would change remarkably
little over the years. Small and slender, with pronounced eyebrows and
a ready, kind smile, he was self-effacing to the point of shyness, and
his apparent lack of egotism was in fact genuine. He was unfailingly
polite and considerate, a likable man, a good listener and conversa-
tionalist, a voracious reader, a man of obvious intelligence, incisive with
catholic interests.

By now, he was also building a family. He met his wife Mary as a
fellow graduate student, and by all accounts they formed an especially
close bond, one of near inseparability. She too was an intellectual and
an enthusiastic reader, and they shared many interests. The Pomeroys
eventually had four children, all of whom they raised to maturity.[3]

Clearly deemed to be a promising prospect, Dr. Pomeroy began in
1940 a decade-long professional odyssey that took him to four universities. After a two-year stint at the University of Wisconsin, where Turner
and Paxson had taught before him, he moved on in 1942 to the University of North Carolina, where he contracted with the V-12 program to

teach midshipmen in the navy. He hoped to join them with a commission to serve overseas, but this did not work out; and since North Carolina could not offer him a stable position, with war's end he moved once more, this time to Ohio State. Here he remained, with recent American history still his main career focus, until 1949.[4]

During this first decade of his professional life, his scholarly productivity was truly remarkable, totaling two major books and eighteen articles.[5] His first book, *The Territories and the United States, 1861–1890: Studies in Colonial Administration*, was his dissertation, revised while at Madison and Chapel Hill and published by the American Historical Association and the University of Pennsylvania Press in 1947. It won the Albert J. Beveridge Award from the A.H.A., and it stands today as the classic work on its subject. It is one of two books by Pomeroy that will be read and lauded forever, and indeed, it must rank as one of the most influential dissertation-based monographs in the annals of American historiography.

Several features of this compact book are still striking, more than four decades after its publication. Like all of Pomeroy's renderings, it eschews the flowing narrative in favor of close analysis and an institutional and comparative focus. It is fastidiously objective, massively researched yet always with larger themes in focus, and tightly written, with few anecdotes, in fact with sentences sometimes made overly complex by being forced to carry more ideas and subtleties than they can bear. This weighty prose, which is really the natural product of its author's busily probing and weighing mind, would become more pronounced as Pomeroy matured and reached the heights of his erudition. Demanding much of the reader, it would limit his audiences, especially among the legions of "Wild West" buffs accustomed to livelier if less challenging fare.

The book is, in fact, a western study, since the territories addressed during the three decades from 1861 to 1890, from the onset of Civil War until the admission of the Northwest "Omnibus States," lay in this region. As he reflected in the preface to the 1969 edition: "I was interested in both the spectacle of administration as a phase of national politics, an index to the morals, motives, and methods of bureaucrats and of politicians in Congress, the White House, and the departments, and also what seemed to be a significant channel for the transmission of political ideas and practices from East to West." What Pomeroy found, in this book and in the articles that accompanied it,[6] was neither pronounced political innovation à la Turner nor colonial exploitation à la

Webb and other adherents of the "plundered province" school of western historians.

Rather, he delineated a territorial system that largely succeeded in transplanting national institutions into new western settings. "The distinctive quality of the American unit was that it carried not only national authority in facilitating settlement, but also American forms and ideals of self-government." This emphasis upon continuity and the success of the federal territorial system has, among other of Pomeroy's emphases, led some scholars, such as his Oregon successor Richard Maxwell Brown, to term him with admiration a "conservative consensus" historian. True enough, for he does emphasize continuity over conflict or change. But such terms can be misleading, since the picture Pomeroy paints is anything but celebratory or uncritical.

Although territorial government, in his description, did succeed as a colonial experiment, it was also wracked by complexities and problems: clashes between federally appointed executives and locally elected legislatures, political game-playing as with the "sagebrushing" appointments of uncooperative judges to remote districts, pining after federal subsidies and patronage, graft, judicial abuses, and carpetbagging. Yet, for all the carping about federal heavy-handedness, the nationalizing experiment succeeded, as Turner had said: "Through these financial ties, through the plain fact of temporary political dependency, the 'denizen of the territory involuntarily becomes a nationalist.'" The American process never evolved a "territorial service" nor a true colonial system analogous to those of the European empires. It didn't need to. By these culminating years of the process, the citizens of the western territories were thoroughly caught up in the culture of national politics. Many of them even thought, wrongly, that they could remember voting in national elections, and the transition to statehood usually came naturally and easily.[7]

Acclaimed by reviewers, *The Territories and the United States* quickly won for its author a national reputation, as a historian of the territorial system and of the West itself. Coinciding with the appearance of the early volumes of Clarence E. Carter's *The Territorial Papers of the United States*, Pomeroy's book established him as a founder of a so-called federal school of historians who interpreted the territorial system as, in Kenneth Owens's phrase, "an agency of Americanization, aiding settlement, promoting self-government, and extending American values and ideals." In the words of Howard Lamar, himself a leading analyst of the territorial system: "At least a dozen historians writing today

about government exploration or the territories acknowledge their methodological, conceptual, and intellectual debt to him [Pomeroy] in their
own publications"—among them Lamar himself, Owens, Thomas Alexander, Jack Eblen, Wallace Farnham, William Goetzmann, Lewis Gould,
John Guice, James Hendrickson, W. Turrentine Jackson, Robert Johannsen, Ronald Limbaugh, and Clark Spence.[8]

Well before the appearance of this volume, Pomeroy had begun work
on another, one that seemed conceptually detached from his first but
was not. This book, published in 1951 by Stanford University Press as
Pacific Outpost: Guam and Micronesia in American Strategy, arose out of
two natural directions in his evolving career. On the one hand, Pomeroy
has always believed that one's interests in teaching and in research
should be closely coupled, and he had been teaching courses on recent,
diplomatic, and naval topics. More to the point, as he noted in his preface, "This study began as a projection of two interests, the first being
the government of American dependencies" (that is, the "continental
territories"). The Pacific island or "insular" territories "seemed to invite
comparisons to complete the picture, and to compare populations living within other colonial arrangements."[9] In other words, he sought
to pursue his dissertation-based research in the direction of comparative territories rather than toward regional western focuses.

Like its predecessor, this volume is succinct and impressively researched, a history of U.S. strategic and defense policy in the Pacific
from the Spanish-American War territorial acquisitions until World War
II. Written in the tense atmosphere of the early Cold War years, it is,
like most books issuing from that era, somewhat nationalistic in tone
and reminiscent of the presentism of Paxson. Conversely, it is noteworthy that Pomeroy was, once again, on the cutting edge of a field
that would only later draw popular interest—the Pacific Rim. Pomeroy
straightforwardly states his "conviction that historians should take the
risks involved in exploring the parts of the past that seem to bear most
closely on present issues." Focusing upon the Mariana Islands, particularly Guam, and also upon the Marshalls and Carolines, *Pacific Outpost* presents a critical view of a vacillating American policy that veered
toward a strong defensive posture during threatening times, then lapsed
into unpreparedness as crises passed. This lack of foresight led to the
military disasters of 1941–42.[10]

Pacific Outpost is good history, although in some respects it might
be deemed dated. Although the least relevant of Pomeroy's four books
to this appraisal, it still bears witness to his manifold abilities and inter-

ests. As a diplomatic and strategic history, it is closely attuned to the "realistic" school of that time, most familiarly represented by men like Hans Morgenthau and Norman Graebner. As such, it avoids the leftist or ideological appraisal and criticism exemplified by Pomeroy's one-time Oregon colleague William Appleman Williams and instead assesses American policy as it served, or failed to serve, the national interest. Thus this venture into foreign policy and defense history seems once more to warrant the labeling of Pomeroy as a "conservative consensus" historian, in Brown's terms. But again, such labeling, if logically pursued, leads to confusion; for in this history, as in all his others, Pomeroy emerges as the objective analyst and critic, never the apologist or polemicist.

Two decades later, in his introduction to the 1969 edition of *The Territories and the United States*, Earl Pomeroy looked back upon the research pursued in *Pacific Outpost* and the articles accompanying it[11] as "false starts" in his writing career. He determined, even before the publication of *Pacific Outpost*, that comparative study of the insular territories shed relatively little light upon their earlier, continental counterparts. So he elected to shift his focus back to the continental U.S., to the West: "I turned to other relationships between East and West," as the more rewarding approach.[12]

Pomeroy's career path now shifted decisively toward western regional history, for several reasons. His home state of California had always intrigued him as the ultimate manifestation of the American spirit, and he began taking up Paxson's advice that he work on the state's history. And a major opportunity arose in the early 1950s when the distinguished historian Walter Johnson approached him about doing a far-west volume in a planned regional series. The series never came to fruition, but three volumes planned for it on the West—by Robert Athearn, Eugene Hollon, and Pomeroy—eventually appeared, each on its own. Even before Pomeroy embarked upon this ambitious project, which eventually resulted in *The Pacific Slope*, he was recruited by the University of Oregon at Eugene. Both he and his wife liked the idea of leaving Ohio for the West Coast, and in 1949 they returned to the region from which they had come.[13]

The move to Oregon was a good one. Situated in the lovely Cascade forests of what has been called "Ecotopia," the small city of Eugene proved a good place to raise a growing family. And the University of Oregon, while not on a par with Berkeley, Stanford, or Washington, was a solid and growing institution. Arriving with a considerable reputation, Pomeroy rapidly emerged as one of the university's premier faculty, a fact later recognized in 1961 when he was named Beekman Professor. This was an enhanced, not a truly endowed chair, and he could and did distribute funds from the trust to colleagues in the department. Such positions were rare and highly prestigious, however, and the appointment underscored that by then he had become a campus institution, whom many colleagues sought out for opinions and conversation. The Pomeroys developed a close and urbane circle of friends and colleagues and became true Oregonians.[14]

The History Department at Oregon during the 1950s and 1960s was relatively small but distinguished. In addition to the highly regarded southern historian Wendell H. Stephenson, it housed several who, like Pomeroy, had a strong interest in regional history, such as Edwin R. Bingham, Kenneth Wiggins Porter, and the diplomatist Paul Holbo. Pomeroy was a committed colleague with high expectations, who sometimes jarred his fellows with critical memos expressing his opinions and taking them to task, but he was a natural leader in the program and ended up serving more than one stint as department chairman.[15]

It was during his quarter-century at Oregon, of course, that Pomeroy had his greatest impact upon students. In large lecture courses, predictably, he soon gained a reputation for highly informative and meticulously organized presentations, so studiously objective that students often could not discern his own opinions. He was not a lively, popular lecturer as was his regionalist colleague "Bing" Bingham. Rather, Pomeroy had his greatest impact in graduate seminars, where his students, at first intimidated by his incredible erudition, soon became caught up in the wide-ranging flow of the dialogue and by his rewarding technique of referencing across national and disciplinary lines.

By all accounts, he was a highly dedicated and effective graduate instructor and advisor, who maintained high standards and did on occasion wash out students, but who was also a good listener and was unfailingly courteous. To his students, as well as to professional colleagues who have benefited from his critiques of their work, he has long been famous as a remarkably close reader. His painstaking critiques of their work have often been written out in great detail, to the point of suggested, specific reconstruction of sentences. During the Oregon years, he supervised twenty doctoral students and—in close collaboration with his colleagues—gave substantial direction as committee member to numerous others. Among those prominent western historians today who deem him a mentor in either role are Robert Burton, Thomas Cox,

Richard Etulain, Gene Gressley, James Hendrickson, Richard Ruetten, and Eckard Toy.[16]

During his first few years at Oregon, Earl Pomeroy began dedicating the full force of his considerable analytical energy to the larger themes of regional historiography. In a series of interpretive articles and two books dating from 1955 to 1971, he set forth his far-reaching conclusions and suggestions. Without exaggeration, the sum of these efforts warrants the characterization of Pomeroy by his distinguished student Gene Gressley as the "only man since Turner who reconceptualized western history." It is, as Howard Lamar puts it, "both as a critic of western American historiography and as an almost philosophical interpreter of the meaning of western history that Pomeroy is best known and most admired."[17]

Perhaps the most widely read piece that Pomeroy ever produced was the historiographic commentary "The Changing West," in John Higham's edited *The Reconstruction of American History* (1962), a little book that served as a bible for comprehensive-exam preparation to several generations of graduate students. In this essay, and in another that preceded it by two years—"Old Lamps for New: The Cultural Lag in Pacific Coast Historiography"—he characterized the historical writing of the Far West as "stultified" by an excessive pioneer orientation, a tendency toward antiquarianism, and an increasingly debilitating isolation from the mainstream of national historiography.[18]

He stated his critique more fully and forcefully in his 1955 *Mississippi Valley Historical Review* article "Toward a Reorientation of Western History: Continuity and Environment," which Richard Etulain rightly characterizes as "perhaps the most widely cited recent essay on western history." In this major revisionist statement, the most far reaching he ever penned, Pomeroy severely indicted historians of the West for not reexamining the philosophical premises upon which they were basing their craft. In so doing, he clearly bruised some egos and caused those of a more traditionalist persuasion to view him as in the field but not really of it. As he began the essay:

> *The books we write about the West, a literary critic remarked*
> *recently, no longer explain our national history, no longer*
> *represent the historical possibilities of the West itself as they once*
> *seemed to do in the generation of Theodore Roosevelt and*
> *Frederick Jackson Turner. They may explain less because many*
> *historians of the West do not write well, and because many have*
> *narrowed the limits within which they write, even while*

investigators in other fields have broadened their inquiries and the West itself has greatly grown and changed. More fundamentally, most of those who write western history seem to assume that physical environment has dominated western life and has made the West rough and radical. Although he may scorn the popular appeal of the "Western" novel and motion picture, the historian has himself often operated within a formula, neglecting the spread and continuity of "Eastern" institutions and ideas. . . . Today the environmental-radical theme in western history has lost much of its appeal. To Turner the frontier was a cause that acted ultimately on the East; but now the effects that he thought he saw seem to have other causes, if they exist at all. . . . Though the old environmental-radical theme no longer seems relevant to the present as it once did, it tends to govern the limits of western history-writing.[19]

Pomeroy, it might seem, was announcing himself to be a thorough-going anti-Turnerian. Indeed, he did take Turnerians and neo-Turnerians to task for their "fixation on pioneer experiences and on the early stages of rural settlement," their depiction of the moving frontier as a re-birthing proto-civilization that in and of itself spawned the new values of a rising civilization. And like his contemporary Henry Nash Smith, he criticized Turner himself on some occasions as a propagator of myths: "Turner never wholly cut himself off from the romantic tradition. In his best-known essays he wrote as a poet no less than as a social scientist, using language that must have appealed to the emotions of Americans who were in a mood to indulge themselves in nostalgic glances backward even as they moved from farm to city."[20]

In truth, however, Pomeroy did not deprecate Turner the scholar; in fact, he admired him, particularly for his social science, broad-gauged approach to issues and institutions. What he did not like was how the fields of western and state and local history during the years after Turner's demise were drifting into isolation from the broad field of United States history and from the other social sciences, which, in turn, were turning their backs on history as well. In fact, he believed that western historiography suffered a "cultural lag," which could only be redressed by bringing it back into the linkage it had had with national scholarship as long ago as the 1880s.

Rather the trouble with western history may be that we are not enough like Turner in his larger qualities: his concern for both analysis and synthesis, his effective English style, and the

keenness of his mind. Turner advocated a radical-environmental
approach, but it is clear enough from what he said about other
forces in the West, including eastern forces, that he did not hold
to that approach alone. The prophet was less orthodox than the
priesthood. He was a good salesman, and he had other errors to
combat in his time, by overemphasis if necessary.[21]

Pomeroy found fewer redeeming features in that other founding
father of western historiography, Walter Prescott Webb. Although he
wrote little about Webb, what he did write and say clearly indicate that
he considered the Texas historian, "who carried geographical determinism further than Turner had," to be simplistic, even a bit provincial in his approach.

Pomeroy strongly advocated the comparative approach in history,
and in fact routinely practiced it. But in one of his most impressive
essays, "The West and New Nations in Other Continents" (1967), he
cautioned against overly facile comparisons and seemed unimpressed
by Webb's sweeping "Great Frontier" thesis. Predictably, he criticized
those scholars who, like Webb, deftly compare different societies while
ignoring the subtle distinctions imposed by history and geography. And
he concluded that the pioneering territories of the American West were
not particularly comparable to the "new nations" of the evolving "Third
World," since the former sought mainly continuity while the latter
sought liberation from their pasts. Neither did Webb's brand of regional
advocacy and polemicism, representing the so-called plundered province school of the 1930s and 1940s, set well with a scholar of Pomeroy's
objective and dispassionate persuasion.[22]

Actually, it has never been Pomeroy's style to engage in dispute,
and he spent less time attacking the Turner–Webb environmental–
deterministic paradigm than he did in setting forth his own contrary
interpretation. That interpretation, again, was most directly stated in
his 1955 article, "Toward a Reorientation of Western History: Continuity and Environment":

If we refuse to let another generation, in effect, force its
interpretations on us by excluding such data as do not fit them,
we may see that conservatism, inheritance, and continuity
bulked at least as large in the history of the West as radicalism
and environment. The Westerner has been fundamentally
imitator rather than innovator, and not merely in the obvious
though important sense that his culture was Western European

*rather than aboriginal. . . . The colonial everywhere, by virtue
of his colonial status, tends to chafe against economic and
political bonds, but he remains a colonial, which is to say a
cultural transplant, often more traditionalist in attitude than his
cousins in the older settlements. . . . American culture often
was diluted on the frontier, but often loyalty to it was
strengthened. . . . The raw frontier, which the settlers changed
as they enveloped it, usually had been more in flux than the
larger West behind it; and the disposition of the settlers was
basically to conserve and transport what they had known before.
Institutions and values changed less than geography, individual
fortunes, and techniques. . . . In fact most attempts to illustrate
the western spirit by referring to large and purposeful
institutional innovations are likely to break down. . . . In part
the conservative West of the nineteenth century was the copy of
the East that it tried to be. It contained hierarchies of culture,
wealth, and influence in which the upper classes were small but
influential beyond their size; it clung to traditional institutional
forms and social practices; and it hungered after intellectual and
social contact and parity with the East.*[23]

The historical perspective of Earl Pomeroy thus stood in stark contrast to those of both Turner and Webb. Contrary to Turner's innovating, nation-building frontiersmen, Pomeroy's frontier societies were stratified and hierarchical. In this depiction, his cosmopolitan and sophisticated view of the far-western frontier closely matched the visions of world frontiers that would be delineated brilliantly thirty years later by William H. McNeill and Bernard Bailyn. Again, in contrast to Turner and Webb, who emphasized the baleful effects of closing frontiers, Pomeroy stressed the continuity of history and particularly the unfailing instinct of frontier folk not to innovate, but rather to imitate and re-create the eastern culture and society from which they had sprung. He especially admired the work of American colonial historians and believed that their successful methods of institutional analysis should be applied to western history.[24]

All of this naturally led him to stress the role of western cities, over those of the countryside and agriculture, as the real pace-setters in the building of the West. In one of his major articles, "The Urban Frontier of the Far West" (1971), he commented that "probably in 1961 the Pacific states became the most urban in the country, passing the Middle Atlantic group. By the test of the census, they had been more urban than the nation as a whole since the 1860s." In Pomeroy's Far West, cities did not grow up to serve agrarian hinterlands, but rather vice versa. Urban historians of the region, such as Lawrence Larsen and Bradford Luckingham, are quick to recognize him as a pioneer in the field of regional urban history.[25]

The theme of western imitativeness is one of the most prevalent in Pomeroy's writing, particularly in his 1960 *American Quarterly* article "Rediscovering the West," and in his 1957 book *In Search of the Golden West: The Tourist in Western America.* This handsomely printed and illustrated book was, like its two predecessors, compact and succinct; unlike them, it was published by a major commercial house, Alfred A. Knopf, an indication of its author's rising reputation. It arose, he explained, as a "byproduct" of his ongoing work on a major regional history. "I read, for background, all the travelers' accounts of the West within reach, and in them I found a theme." That theme did not involve a history of western tourism, but rather a focus upon westerners' promotion of tourism and upon what the tourists themselves perceived. "My purpose," he wrote in introducing the volume, "is chiefly to consider what the West has meant to tourists and to those who set out to attract tourists. . . . I have not attempted to give a complete picture of that important phase of western economic development. This is about people and their ideas rather than about their money."[26]

In Search of the Golden West did in fact trace many aspects of the rise of regional tourism—how, for instance, the first comers tended to be rail born and upper class and how the discovery of the great outdoors and the rise of the car expanded and democratized tourism. But true to his word, Pomeroy stuck mainly to cultural themes; and in doing so, he demonstrated how the pioneer western promoters of tourism were almost slavishly imitative in approach.

At first, the western promoters largely ignored their own heritage and environmental attractions. Instead, eager to show potential immigrants and investors from the East and from Europe that they were not rustics, they tried simply to re-create that which was fashionable in the older region and the Old World. For example, they erected new Saratogas or Newports in the forms of palatial tourist hotels like the Del Monte at Monterey or the Raymond at Pasadena. Only in time did they realize the appeal of the environment and of the heritages of the Indians, the Hispanics, and, of course, the American pioneers. "The Spaniard, the American pioneer, and the Indian joined hands posthumously," frequently in mawkish pagaeantry, he wrote, to score the themes of western tourism. Meanwhile, as the industry grew enormously in size and monetary importance, the tourists themselves mostly rushed through the region, oblivious to its natural and historical realities.[27]

In Search of the Golden West received good reviews, and over the past three decades it has stood as the leading work on the subject, recently joined by a more broadly gauged book by John Jakle. Of Pomeroy's three books on the West, it is the least imposing, in part because it is the least ambitious, and in part probably because it seems that any such study—such as Ray Allen Billington's *Land of Savagery, Land of Promise*—that rests so heavily upon travel accounts seems inevitably to become somewhat tedious aand repetitious.[28] The book is, however, still widely read and rewarding to the reader, and it is a testament to its author's research skills and forebearance and to his abilities as a historian of cultural topics.

Eight years later, in 1965, appeared Earl Pomeroy's major work to date, the culmination of the project from which the preceding volume had derived. *The Pacific Slope: A History of California, Oregon, Washington, Idaho, Utah, and Nevada* was, once again, published by Alfred A. Knopf, again beautifully bound and illustrated, with copious footnotes at the bottoms of the pages. Unlike its three predecessors, this book was lengthy, 404 pages to be exact. Ever since the date of its appearance, it has been regarded as a masterwork. Among numerous favorable reviewers, Dorothy Johansen termed it "a remarkably successful synthesis of complex backgrounds, institutions, and characteristics of the area . . . a landmark in western historiography." Two decades later, Howard Lamar, himself a peer of Pomeroy at the forefront of the field, called it "easily the most complex and sophisticated history of the American West ever written."[29]

To characterize this weighty volume is to reiterate the traits and conclusions of its author as summarized above. It is neither a flowing narrative nor for many easy to read, and complex sentences have to be read and re-read. It is thoroughly, impressively researched in primary and secondary sources; and it musters statistics in a manner most enlightening, in a style that refreshingly predates the self-conscious "quantification" of recent years. Amid the heavy prose, however, are gems of Pomeroy's wry humor, such as: "Soon the immigrants of 1841–8 settled down to deplore the manners and morals of those who came in 1849, and then the pioneer societies incorporated both groups, to criticize those who came later still." And always, there are his remarkable breadth, which allows him to range deftly from social and cultural to economic and political topics with authority, and his statesmanlike objectivity.

Witness this characterization that could both warrant again the "conservative consensus" tag and serve as a model to historians of all persuasions:

> *The rule of the railroads was undemocratic and in some respects*
> *both economically and politically oppressive. But in the long run*
> *the companies' interests were in the country's favor much more*
> *than against it, and materially the railroads built more than they*
> *smothered or destroyed. Westerners sometimes complained that*
> *the railroads stifled Western industry by making westbound rates*
> *too low and oppressed Western agriculture by making eastbound*
> *rates too high. Yet it was in large part because of the*
> *railroads—because of their existence and their policies—that the*
> *Far West emerged from a colonial to a mature and more balanced*
> *economy.*[30]

This reference to the "Far West" calls to mind yet another consistent feature of Pomeroy the regionalist. Throughout his career, he has always been most interested in the region west of the continental divide, rather than in the West broadly defined as the entire expanse beyond the 98th meridian (the Dakota–Texas tier westward). Such a focus perhaps offers some context for his emphasis upon cities and commerce and consequent lesser emphasis upon the formative role of agriculture and rural life, which is more prevalent east of the divide than west of it.

In *The Pacific Slope*, Pomeroy addresses the six states of the Far West, with Arizona excluded. This state he omits with the rather unconvincing comment that, at least in early times, it "looked more to New Mexico than to the coast, and in becoming more like southern California it has found no great need for fellowship and traffic with it," and added that Eugene Hollon could handle Arizona better in his regional history than Pomeroy could in this one. In fact, the allocation of states between the volumes written by Athearn, Hollon, and himself left Pomeroy, against his protests, with this rather awkward configuration.[31]

One of the most revolutionary aspects of this book, again characteristic of Pomeroy, is its emphasis not upon pioneering but upon the evolution of institutions and society and upon the modern period. As he comments in the preface:

> *I have tried to focus on men and events that explain the West as*
> *a developing community, emphasizing traits and institutions.*
> *The early years need not lose meaning if we traverse them at*
> *more than the speed of an immigrant's oxcart, the later years at*

> *less than the speed of a jet-propelled aircraft. . . . When one*
> *approaches Western history from the point of view of the*
> *development of communities, traits, and institutions, farms,*
> *cities, political parties, and social ideas loom larger than trouble*
> *with Indians, who were never the barrier to settlement west of*
> *the Rockies that they were to the east. This is not to disparage*
> *romantic history, but merely to note that I have not written it.*[32]

The text of *The Pacific Slope* moves rapidly past the early period of Spanish–Mexican origins and the fur trade. Indeed, by page 54 it is past the Gold Rush. Its main focus is upon the subsequent building and development of agricultural, financial, commercial, transportation, and industrial institutions and upon the stages of political development, such as Progressivism and the "political fundamentalism" of the 1920s. Each of the six states is examined in considerable detail, and regional trends emerge quite clearly, usually with California depicted as the pace-setter.

Throughout, Pomeroy reiterates again and again the overarching themes of cities as the primary agencies of regional civilization-building and of the direct transplanting of eastern culture on the West Coast. "The Pacific Slope is both the most Western and, after the East itself, the most Eastern part of America. . . . The Far West was more distinctively urban in its own way. San Francisco and Portland grew earlier, in comparison with their hinterlands, than Chicago and Detroit; they were the bridgeheads from which the East conquered the wilderness." And again: "As the rural West emptied its population into the cities from mine, farm, and forest, it almost seemed to be reverting to that degree of detachment from urban ways that had obtained when pioneer San Francisco was a piece of the East in exile, having no more in common with the Mexican cattle ranches to the south than a clipper ship had with a school of whales that crossed its wake."[33]

Perhaps the most salient fact about this book is that Pomeroy did indeed write the kind of history he had been calling for in his essays. Rather than the pioneer-oriented, neo-Turnerian narrative long typical of the field, this book was a sharp departure toward an analytical history that conceptualized regional development in national context. Thus we see less of the founding of the Southern Pacific Railroad than of its subsequent growth and policies, its roles in societal context. The sophistication of Pomeroy's economic and political chapters in this book have never been equalled in a general western history. In the longer perspective, *The Pacific Slope* will surely be seen as the harbinger of a new kind of regional history, less romantic than the state of the art that preceded it, but more rigorous, more insightful, more nationally main-streamed, and more focused upon the modern period.

By the time this book appeared, Earl Pomeroy was well recognized in many quarters as the most thoughtful contemporary historian of the American West. His own doctoral students were, by now, along with others who considered him something of a mentor, carrying for-ward his ideas and practices. Increasing honors came his way, includ-ing an invited lectureship at the Bologna Center of Johns Hopkins University in 1963–64, the Coe Visiting Professorship at Stanford in 1967–68, and a senior fellowship from the National Endowment for the Humanities in 1968.

In 1970 he rose to the presidency of an organization in which he has long been active, the Pacific Coast Branch of the American Histor-ical Association. His presidential address, "Josiah Royce, Historian in Quest of Community," focused appropriately upon the philosopher and erstwhile historian of California who had penetratingly described "the tension of individualism and social responsibility" that so char-acterized the settling of the Far West. Pomeroy obviously saw some-thing of himself in this philosopher–historian and student of community and social atomism on the frontier, and he thought of extending his study to a full book. As he wrote of Royce:

> He pictured frontiersmen in naturalistic rather than epic
> proportions, more given to looting than to conquest, though
> sometimes also to grotesque self glorification; he described social
> disintegration in pioneer settlement when the frontier was
> becoming the seat of virtue in national tradition, and
> apostrophes to frontiersmen as commonwealth-builders were
> standard in Fourth-of-July oratory.[34]

One honor that did not come his way seemed then, and still seems now, perplexing—the presidency of the Western History Association (WHA),* that largest of his peer groupings, which was founded just prior to the publication of *The Pacific Slope*. This glaring omission, which was underscored when Pomeroy's own student Gene Gressley won the honor in 1985, seemed to stem from the fact that Pomeroy has always

---

*After this book was in-press, Professor Pomeroy was named vice-president of the WHA and succeeds to the presidency in 1993.

been something of an outsider among traditional historians of the West. However politely, he always frowned upon the romantic, "wagon-wheels" genre so prevalent in the W.H.A. and never fit into the jovially buffish atmosphere characteristic of that organization, especially in its early years.[35] It is an omission which, with each passing year, becomes more embarrassing, not to Pomeroy but to the W.H.A. itself.

If Pomeroy seemed an outsider among traditional western historians, he also experienced the stigma that attaches to this subdiscipline of United States history. As his reputation grew, he received employment queries from prominent universities outside the Pacific Slope. But neither his doctoral alma mater, Berkeley, nor Stanford, which did invite him to a visiting lectureship, seemed interested in emphasizing in this way the history of their own region, which still bore the onus of the "cowboys and Indians" stereotype that he had done so much to dispel. Had they chosen to pursue this logical interest, he would likely have been their choice for a senior or endowed professorship; but they elected instead to stress the histories of other regions than the one in which they existed, thereby demonstrating perhaps their cosmopolitanism but also forfeiting the cultural leadership that their fellow citizens had the right to expect from them and distancing themselves from much of the literate public around them.

After more than a quarter-century at the University of Oregon, Pomeroy did make a professional move, not to an old, established doctoral program in western history, but rather to a major new research department in the region. Following a visiting appointment in 1976, he accepted a permanent appointment in history at the University of California at San Diego a year later. Here he remained for a decade, until his retirement in 1984. The San Diego years were rewarding in many ways. He enjoyed the collegial stimulation of some of America's most able and eminent historians, among them H. Stuart Hughes, Ramón Ruiz, Harry Scheiber, and Leften Stavrianos; and they recognized his abilities by prevailing upon him to accept the department chairmanship for a time. However, tragedy struck when his wife and constant companion of many years, Mary, died of a brain tumor in 1977. When he retired, he decided to move back to Eugene, the place that had never, in many ways, ceased to be home, and continued to work diligently at his office in the History Department at the University of Oregon, now as an emeritus professor.[36]

Meanwhile, he continued his lifelong pursuit of scholarship, which included a regimen of reading both in-depth on the West and on a

broad range of other interests. By the early 1970s the pace of his publication rate lessened, but by now he was at work on his most ambitious
undertaking thus far. This is a volume on the twentieth-century West
in the long-standing New American Nation series, edited by Henry
Steele Commager and Richard B. Morris for Harper and Row, a most
prestigious assignment that clearly signifies his status in the field. The
New American Nation series features two earlier volumes on the frontier by Francis Philbrick and Ray Allen Billington, a recently published
volume on the late-nineteenth-century West by Rodman Paul, and the
forthcoming Pomeroy contribution. He continues to be active in other
ways as well, for example as a coeditor of a new series on the modern
West by the University of Nebraska Press.

In one sense, this is an even more ambitious project than was *The
Pacific Slope*, because it embraces the entire "West," including the Plains
states (sans Texas), a considerably larger and more diverse expanse than
the Far West alone. To those who have read any of the completed chapters, including this writer, it is readily apparent that this book, like its
predecessors, will be exceptionally well researched and highly analytical and interpretive.[37]

As he passed the fiftieth anniversary of his entry into the profession of history, Earl Pomeroy could look both backward and forward
with considerable satisfaction. Following his retirement from San Diego,
several dozen of his friends, students, and admirers gathered for a sup-
per in his honor at Sacramento during the course of the annual conference of the Western History Association. It was a genuine tribute, made
somewhat ironic in that it coincided with the gathering of the chief
organization in the field, which had yet to come to terms either with
his own contribution or with the reorientation that he had led in its
scholarly direction. The dimensions of that contribution are considerable. Unlike scientists, historians seldom consider frequency of cita-
tion as an evidence of influence; but it is worth noting that, in my edited
volume of 1983, *Historians and the American West*, Pomeroy is cited approx-
imately as many times as either Turner or Webb.[38]

It is safe to predict that, still exceptionally vigorous and insightful
in his mid-seventies, he will have considerably more to say about western regional history. But even from the perspective of today, it is clear
that Earl Pomeroy will always be recognized as the key figure in the post-
Turnerian reconceptualization and reorientation of western United States
history that began at midcentury. This is not to term him a self-conscious
revisionist, for narrow argumentation is not his style. As he put it in a

1955 letter to Merle Curti: "What I'm most concerned with is not a conservative interpretation of the West or an emphasis on conservative factors to the exclusion of others, but rather with a more interpretative, thoughtful approach and with not ruling out any interpretations or factors arbitrarily."[39]

His writings bear out that prospectus. Facing a conventional wisdom in the field that sometimes unquestioningly dwelt upon the shaping environment, the central importance and innovation of the frontier experience, and the romantic narrative, he argued instead for avoidance of particularism and for the crucial importance of the national perspective, for close analysis of evolving institutions, society, and culture. If his style of history has not reshaped the field, it certainly has afforded it intellectual depth. His style and scholarship do command an ever-growing loyalty among practitioners of the craft, and offer the best hope for a true comprehension of the past in the years to come.

NOTES

1. Interview with Earl Pomeroy, October 13, 1988; Gerald D. Nash, "Pomeroy, Earl S.," in Howard R. Lamar, ed., *The Reader's Encyclopedia of the American West* (New York: Thomas Y. Crowell, 1977), 947; Howard R. Lamar, "Earl Pomeroy: Historian's Historian," *Pacific Historical Review* 56 (November 1987):550–51.

2. Pomeroy interview; letter, Earl Pomeroy to the author, February 7, 1989; Lamar, "Earl Pomeroy," 550–52; Earl Pomeroy, "Frederic L. Paxson and His Approach to History," *Mississippi Valley Historical Review* 39 (March 1953):673–92, quote from 691–92.

3. Pomeroy interview; interviews with Gene M. Gressley, October 15, 1988; Paul S. Holbo, November 11, 1988; and Richard T. Ruetten, December 28, 1988.

4. Pomeroy interview; Nash, "Pomeroy, Earl S.," 947; Lamar, "Earl Pomeroy," 557.

5. These early articles, in addition to those cited below, include "Election of the Governor of Puerto Rico," *Southwestern Social Science Quarterly* 23 (March 1943):355–60; "The Atlantic Charter in Puerto Rico," *The South and World Affairs* 5 (April 1943):10, 21; "Mercantile Aims and British Expansion in the Lesser Antilles, 1713–1730," *Historian* 5 (Spring 1943):119–23; "Colonial Government by United States Naval Officers," U.S. Naval Institute, *Proceedings* 69 (October 1943):1320–23; "The Visit of the Russian Fleet in 1863," *New York History* 24 (October 1943):512–17; "French Substitutes of American Cotton, 1861, 1865," *Journal of Southern History* 9 (November 1943):555–60; "The Lebanon Blues in the Baltimore Campaign, 1814: Extracts from a Company Orderly Book," *Military Affairs* 12 (Fall 1948):168–74; "Wisconsin in 1847," *Wisconsin Magazine of*

History 33 (December 1949):216–20; and "The Myth after the Russian Fleet, 1863," *New York History* 31 (April 1950):169–76.

6. Earl S. Pomeroy, *The Territories and the United States: 1861–1890: Studies in Colonial Administration* (Philadelphia: University of Pennsylvania Press, American Historical Association, 1947; Americana Library edition, Seattle: University of Washington Press, 1969), xiii ("Introduction to the 1969 Edition"); see the related articles, "Carpetbaggers in the Territories," *Historian* 2 (Winter 1939):53–64; and "Lincoln, the Thirteenth Amendment, and the Admission of Nevada," *Pacific Historical Review* 12 (December 1943):362–68.

7. "The distinctive quality" quote is from Pomeroy, "The Territory as a Frontier Institution," *Historian* 7 (Autumn 1944):41; Richard Maxwell Brown quote is from his "Historiography of Violence in the American West," in Michael P. Malone, *Historians and the American West* (Lincoln: University of Nebraska Press, 1983), 258; "Through these financial ties" quote is from *The Territories and the United States*, 100.

8. Kenneth N. Owens, "Government and Politics in the Nineteenth-Century West," in Malone, *Historians and the American West*, 154; cf. Jo Tice Bloom, "Territorial Government," in Roger L. Nichols, ed., *American Frontier and Western Issues: A Historiographical Review* (New York: Greenwood Press, 1986), 237; Lamar, "Earl Pomeroy," 547; for a sampling of reviews, see Herman J. Deutsch in *Pacific Northwest Quarterly* 38 (April 1947):172–73; and George L. Anderson in *American Historical Review* 52 (July 1947):751–52.

9. Pomeroy interview; Earl S. Pomeroy, *Pacific Outpost: American Strategy in Guam and Micronesia* (Stanford, Calif.: Stanford University Press, 1951), xiii–xiv.

10. Pomeroy, *Pacific Outpost*, vii; see reviews by George H. Blakeslee in *American Historical Review* 58 (April 1953):633–34; and Julius W. Pratt in *Mississippi Valley Historical Review* 39 (June 1952):153–54.

11. These articles include Earl Pomeroy, "The American Colonial Office," *Mississippi Valley Historical Review* 30 (March 1944):521–32; "Sentiment for a Strong Peace," *South Atlantic Quarterly* 43 (October 1944):325–37; "The Navy and Colonial Government," U.S. Naval Institute, *Proceedings* 71 (March 1945):291–97; "The Problem of American Overseas Bases: Some Reflections on Naval History," U.S. Naval Institute, *Proceedings* 73 (June 1947):689–700; and "American Policy Respecting the Marshalls, Carolines, and Marianas, 1898–1941," *Pacific Historical Review* 17 (February 1948):43–53.

12. "Introduction to the 1969 Edition," *The Territories and the United States*, xiii–xiv, and fn. 11.

13. Pomeroy interview; Lamar, "Earl Pomeroy," 555. The other planned series volumes mentioned are Robert G. Athearn, *High Country Empire: The High Plains and Rockies* (New York: McGraw-Hill, 1960); and W. Eugene Hollon, *The Southwest: Old and New* (New York: Alfred A. Knopf, 1961). Pomeroy's California studies include "The Trial of the Hounds, 1849," *California Historical Society Quarterly* 29 (June 1950):216–20; "California, 1846–1860: Politics of a Representative Frontier State," *California Historical Society Quarterly* 32 (December 1953):

291–302; and "California's Legacies from the Pioneers," in George H. Knoles, ed., *Essays and Assays: California History Reappraised* (Sacramento: California Historical Society, 1973), 79–90.

14. Pomeroy, Gressley, and Holbo interviews; interview with Richard Maxwell Brown, October 12, 1988.

15. Pomeroy, Holbo, Gressley, and Brown interviews; Lamar, "Earl Pomeroy," 558; letter, Gene M. Gressley to the author, February 16, 1989.

16. Gressley and Ruetten interviews; interview with Richard W. Etulain, December 28, 1988; Lamar, "Earl Pomeroy," 557.

17. Gressley interview; Lamar, "Earl Pomeroy," 552.

18. Earl Pomeroy, "The Changing West," in John Higham, ed, *The Reconstruction of American History* (New York: Harper and Row, 1962), 71; Pomeroy, "Old Lamps for New: The Cultural Lag in Pacific Coast Historiography," *Arizona and the West* 2 (Summer 1960):108–11.

19. Etulain interview; Earl Pomeroy, "Toward a Reorientation of Western History: Continuity and Environment," *Mississippi Valley Historical Review* 41 (March 1955):579–83, 596–97.

20. The first quote is from "The Changing West," 71; the second is from Pomeroy, "Josiah Royce, Historian in Quest of Community," *Pacific Historical Review* 40 (February 1971):18–19; cf. Henry Nash Smith, *Virgin Land: The American West as Symbol and Myth*, Vintage ed. (1950; New York: Random House, 1957), chap. 12; letters, Earl Pomeroy to the author, February 7, 1989; Gene M. Gressley to the author, February 16, 1989.

21. Quote is from "Toward a Reorientation of Western History," 599; "The Changing West," 71–75; "Old Lamps for New," 108–11; Pomeroy and Gressley interviews.

22. Webb quote is from Earl Pomeroy, "What Remains of the West?" *Utah Historical Quarterly* 35 (Winter 1967):50; "The West and New Nations in Other Continents," in J. A. Carroll, ed., *Reflections of Western Historians* (Tucson: University of Arizona Press, 1967), 241–45; Pomeroy, "The Urban Frontier of the Far West," in John G. Clark, ed., *The Frontier Challenge: Responses to the Trans-Mississippi West* (Lawrence: University Press of Kansas, 1971), 7–29; Gressley interview; "The Changing West," 75; cf. William G. Robbins, "The 'Plundered Province' Thesis and the Recent Historiography of the American West," *Pacific Historical Review* 55 (November 1986):577–97.

23. "Toward a Reorientation of Western History," 581–83, 596–97; Richard W. Etulain, "Visions and Revisions of the American West: Recent Trends in Western Historiography," paper presented to the annual convention of the Organization of American Historians, St. Louis, April 9, 1989, 22–23.

24. The best essay statements of these themes, in addition to ibid., are "What Remains of the West?"; and "Old Lamps for New"; cf. William H. McNeill, *The Great Frontier: Freedom and Hierarchy in Modern Times* (Princeton, N.J.: Princeton University Press, 1983); and Bernard Bailyn, *The Peopling of British North America: An Introduction* (New York: Alfred A. Knopf, 1986). The influ-

ence of early American historians such as Carl Becker and Charles M. Andrews was stressed in Pomeroy and Etulain interviews; in a letter from Pomeroy to the author, February 7, 1989; and in "Toward a Reorientation of Western History," 598.

25. "The Urban Frontier of the Far West," quote on 7–8; Lawrence H. Larsen, "Frontier Urbanization," in Nichols, *American Frontier and Western Issues*, 80; Bradford Luckinham, "The Urban Dimension in Western History," in Malone, *Historians and the American West*, 331–32.

26. Pomeroy, "Rediscovering the West," *American Quarterly* 12 (Spring 1960):20–30; Pomeroy, "Law and Government Policy for Agriculture: Comment," *Agricultural History* 49 (January 1975):152; first quote is from Pomeroy, *The Pacific Slope: A History of California, Oregon, Washington, Idaho, Utah, and Nevada* (New York: Alfred A. Knopf, 1965), vii; the second quote is from Pomeroy, *In Search of the Golden West: The Tourist in Western America* (New York: Alfred A. Knopf, 1957), viii.

27. *In Search of the Golden West*, quote on 44.

28. See the reviews by Walker D. Wyman in *American Historical Review* 63 (October 1957):144–45; Emmett A. Greenwalt in *Pacific Historical Review* 26 (November 1957):411; and Edwin H. Carpenter, Jr., in *Utah Historical Quarterly* 26 (January 1958):87–88; cf. John A. Jakle, *The Tourist: Travel in Twentieth-Century America* (Lincoln: University of Nebraska Press, 1985); and Ray Allen Billington, *Land of Savagery, Land of Promise: The European Image of the American Frontier* (New York: W. W. Norton, 1981).

29. Review by Dorothy O. Johansen in *Oregon Historical Quarterly* 67 (March 1966):78–79; Lamar, "Earl Pomeroy," 549; see other reviews by Paul G. Hubbard, in *Journal of American History* 52 (December 1965):643–44; Andrew Rolle, in *American Historical Review* 71 (January 1966):685; D. E. Livingston-Little, in *California Historical Society Quarterly* 45 (June 1966):162–73; and William S. Greever, in *Arizona and the West* 8 (Autumn 1966):274–75.

30. *The Pacific Slope*, first quote on 35; second quote on 101–2.

31. *The Pacific Slope*, vi; cf. Hollon, *The Southwest: Old and New*.

32. *The Pacific Slope*, v, vii.

33. *The Pacific Slope*, quotes on 3, 6, 314.

34. Nash, "Pomeroy, Earl S.," 947; Pomeroy, "Josiah Royce," 7, 13.

35. Gressley, Etulain, Ruetten, and Brown interviews.

36. Pomeroy and Gressley interviews.

37. Cf. Francis S. Philbrick, *The Rise of the West: 1754–1830* (New York: Harper and Row, 1965); Ray Allen Billington, *The Far Western Frontier: 1830–1860* (New York: Harper and Row, 1956); Rodman W. Paul, *The Far West and the Great Plains in Transition, 1859–1900* (New York: Harper and Row, 1988); Ruetten interview.

38. Lamar, "Earl Pomeroy," 558; *Historians and the American West*, 446–48.

39. Pomeroy to Merle Curti, April 17, 1955, Curti Papers, State Historical Society of Wisconsin, Madison (copy furnished by Richard Etulain).

BIBLIOGRAPHY

WESTERN AND TERRITORIAL WRITINGS OF EARL POMEROY

"The American Colonial Office." *Mississippi Valley Historical Review* 30 (March 1944):521–32.

"American Policy Respecting the Marshalls, Carolines, and Marianas, 1898–1941." *Pacific Historical Review* 17 (February 1948):43–53.

"The Atlantic Charter in Puerto Rico." *The South and World Affairs* 5 (April 1943): 10, 21.

"California, 1846–1860: Politics of a Representative Frontier State." *California Historical Society Quarterly* 32 (December 1953):291–302.

"California's Legacies from the Pioneers." In George H. Knoles, ed., *Essays and Assays: California History Reappraised*. Sacramento: California Historical Society, 1973, 79–90.

"Carpet-baggers in the Territories." *Historian* 2 (Winter 1939):53–64.

"The Changing West." In John Higham, ed., *The Reconstruction of American History*. London: Hutchinson and Co., 1962, 64–81.

"Colonial Government by United States Naval Officers." U.S. Naval Institute *Proceedings* 69 (October 1943):1320–23.

"Comments on Space, Time, Culture and the New Frontier." *Agricultural History* 37 (October 1963):31–33.

"Election of the Governor of Puerto Rico." *Southwestern Social Science Quarterly* 23 (March 1943):355–60.

"Frederic L. Paxson and His Approach to History." *Mississippi Valley Historical Review* 39 (March 1953):673–92.

In Search of the Golden West: The Tourist in Western America. New York: Alfred A. Knopf, 1957.

"Josiah Royce, Historian in Quest of Community." *Pacific Historical Review* 40 (February 1971):1–20.

"Lincoln, the Thirteenth Amendment, and the Admission of Nevada." *Pacific Historical Review* 12 (December 1943):362–68.

"The Navy and Colonial Government." U.S. Naval Institute *Proceedings* 71 (March 1945):291–97.

"Old Lamps for New: The Cultural Lag in Pacific Coast Historiography." *Arizona and the West* 2 (Summer 19600):707–26.

Pacific Outpost: Guam and Micronesia in American Strategy. Stanford, Calif.: Stanford University Press, 1951. New edition, 1970.

The Pacific Slope: A History of California, Oregon, Washington, Idaho, Utah, and Nevada. New York: Alfred A. Knopf, 1965. Paperbound edition, Seattle: University of Washington Press, 1974.

"The Problem of American Overseas Bases: Some Reflections on Naval History." U.S. Naval Institute *Proceedings* 73 (June 1947):689–700.

"Rediscovering the West." *American Quarterly* 12 (Spring 1960):20–30.

The Territories and the United States, 1861–1890: Studies in Colonial Administration. Philadelphia: University of Pennsylvania Press, American Historical Association, 1947. Paperbound edition, Seattle: University of Washington Press, 1969.

"The Territory as a Frontier Institution." *Historian* 7 (Autumn 1944):29–41.

"Toward a Reorientation of Western History: Continuity and Environment." *Mississippi Valley Historical Review* 41 (March 1955):579–600.

"The Trial of the Hounds, 1849." *California Historical Society Quarterly* 29 (June 1950):161–65.

"The Urban Frontier of the Far West." In John G. Clark, ed., *The Frontier Challenge: Responses to the Trans-Mississippi West*. Lawrence: University Press of Kansas, 1970, 7–29.

"The West and New Nations in Other Continents." In John A. Carroll, ed., *Reflections of Western Historians*. Tucson: University of Arizona Press, 1969, 237–61.

"What Remains of the West?" *Utah Historical Quarterly* 35 (Winter 1967):37–55.

"Wisconsin in 1847." *Wisconsin Magazine of History* 33 (December 1949):216–20.

WORKS ABOUT EARL POMEROY

Lamar, Howard R. "Earl Pomeroy, Historian's Historian." *Pacific Historical Review* 56 (November 1987):546–60.

Nash, Gerald D. "Pomeroy, Earl S." In Howard R. Lamar, ed., *The Reader's Encyclopedia of the American West*. New York: Thomas Y. Crowell, 1977, 947.

Conclusion

Visions and Revisions: Recent Interpretations of the American West

RICHARD W. ETULAIN

$\mathcal{S}$IXTY YEARS AGO WHEN THE
first national conference convened to study the history of the trans-
Mississippi West, its participants illustrated the variety of contemporary approaches to western history. Although ill health kept the titan
in the field, Frederick Jackson Turner, from attending, his presence
seemed to shadow nearly every session. Indeed, several of his former
students, including Herbert Eugene Bolton, Colin B. Goodykoontz,
Archer B. Hulbert and Joseph Schafer, were present, as were others
like Frederic Logan Paxson and Percy Boynton who closely followed
some of Turner's frontier interpretations.

Conversely, other participants represented important changes taking place in western historiography. Walter Prescott Webb presented
an overview of his regionalistic approach, which appeared in expanded
form in *The Great Plains* two years later; geographer Carl Sauer argued
for a cultural-landscape perspective on western history; and Bolton urged
listeners to follow a Borderlands schema in writing about the West. In
addition, Schafer outlined an exhaustive study of Wisconsin rural life,
similar to the probing examinations new social historians would call
for much later. Still other presenters championed new or more searching research on Indians, religion, and literature, topics that many western historians had previously overlooked. In brief, the roundup at
Boulder brought together several leading historians of the West who
either emphasized traditional frontier perspectives, called for new methodological approaches, or noted topics previously overlooked in historical writings about the West.[1]

If a similar conference were convened six decades later, it too would reflect a field of historical studies in flux. Some western historical writings of the last half-century bear the unmistakable marks of Frederick Jackson Turner, Frederic Logan Paxson, Walter Prescott Webb, and Herbert Eugene Bolton as well as the telltale influences of such later scholars as James Malin, Ray Billington, Earl Pomeroy, and Henry Nash Smith. As the illuminating essays in this collection make clear, many of the themes, approaches, and conclusions of these earlier historians remain at the center of western historical writing since 1970. That is, western historians continue to debate the frontier, sectional, and regional themes of Turner and Webb, while those treating border relationships between the United States and Mexico often begin with the ideas of Bolton. If the overview syntheses that Paxson and Billington first published in 1924 and 1949, respectively, are now less influential, these notable summaries still provide narratives useful to historians and general readers, especially those interested in the nineteenth-century frontier. Meanwhile, Smith's pathbreaking study of the mythic West, *Virgin Land: The American West as Symbol and Myth* (1950), remains one of the most provocative works ever written about the West, continuing to influence dozens of historians four decades after its publication. Concurrently, Earl Pomeroy's challenges to western historians to reconsider continuities from east to west and to study legacies from the pioneer past into the twentieth-century West persisted well into the 1970s and 1980s. Finally, the rising influence of environmental history brought about a rediscovery of James Malin, who called for larger emphases on ecology and human environments while employing varying kinds of statistical formulations. Clearly, in the two decades following 1970, these historians and their major writings continued to have large influences on students and scholars specializing in western history.

RE-VISIONING THE AMERICAN WEST

At the same time, new currents are pulsing through the field. Western historians have discovered the twentieth century, and fresh emphases on urban, ethnic, and family history have added new vistas to western historical writing, often in the work of nonwestern historians working on regional topics. Others are applying the novel methodologies of the new social historians to western subjects, and still others are attempting to provide western history with all-encompassing perspectives. This marriage of earlier interpretations and new topical and

methodological emphases has enriched and broadened the field of western historiography. In fact, despite this new diversity—and some
resulting fragmentation—western historical writing may have arrived
at an important juncture, poised for a new generation of overviews based
on a synthesis of earlier visions and later revisions.[2]

THE TWENTIETH-CENTURY WEST:
A NEW FRONTIER

The twentieth-century West is a newly discovered and rapidly
expanding field of western historiography. Although Turner and Webb
and other writers such as James Malin and Bernard DeVoto supplied
brief pioneering studies of the modern West in the first half of the present century, not until Earl Pomeroy and Gerald Nash published their
pathbreaking volumes in the 1960s and 1970s did the field seem a viable
one for research and publication. During those two decades several western historians repeatedly urged their colleagues to explore the modern
West; in the last fifteen years they have begun to accept this challenge.
In fact, so promising has the topic become that it threatens to become
the new frontier of western historical scholarship in the 1990s.[3]

If historians and journalists like Neil Morgan, Neal R. Peirce, and
Peter Wiley and Robert Gottlieb published early partial portraits and
later impressionistic overviews, Pomeroy and Nash provided bench-
mark interpretations influencing much of what is being currently written about the twentieth-century West. In his most significant book to
date, *The Pacific Slope* (1965), Pomeroy skips over much of the romantic
and narrative frontier history that filled previous accounts of the Far
West and emphasizes instead eastern and international influences on
the Pacific Slope, continuities between the nineteenth and twentieth
centuries, and the expanding hegemony of western urban areas. In
emphasizing the twentieth century, he draws no fault line across the
1890s, separating the pioneer era and the later urbanizing and indus-
trializing Far West. For Pomeroy, the Pacific Slope has been surprisingly urban from its English-speaking beginnings, and the region owes
as much or more to eastern legacies as to unique western circumstances.
In two ways Pomeroy broke fellowship with the close-knit fraternity of
earlier western historians: he downplayed the molding power of a new,
unique frontier environment, and he stressed the recent rather than
the pioneer West.[4]

Whereas Pomeroy limited his notably interpretive volume to the

Pacific Slope territories and states, Gerald Nash treated the full range of western states west of the 95th meridian in his *American West in the Twentieth Century* (1973), the first full-scale history of the modern West. Nash asserts that the recent West is best understood when divided into colonial (1898–1941) and pacesetting (1941–1971) eras. Although westerners were victims of a colonial economy and culture until the outbreak of World War II, that event did more than any other to point the West in another direction. Largely because of spiraling government expenditures, mushrooming urban-industrial complexes (particularly in California), and burgeoning populations in many areas of the West, the region threw off much of its earlier colonialism and, in some ways, became an economic and sociocultural pacesetter for the rest of the nation. Like Pomeroy, Nash devotes lengthy sections to economic and political developments and demonstrates how these regional developments are frequently closely tied to national and worldwide happenings. For nearly two decades, Nash's overview synthesis has served as a model introduction to the modern West.[5]

Other historians have begun to deal with more specific facets of the twentieth-century West. Richard Lowitt's well-researched *The New Deal and the West* (1984) supplies a much-needed study of the impact of governmental policies on the West during the 1930s, and Gerald Nash's *The American West Transformed* (1985) and *World War II and the West* (1990), building on the conclusions of his extensive research and earlier publications, demonstrates the transforming power of World War II on the West, particularly on its cities and ethnic groups. On the other hand, Robert G. Athearn treats primarily the social and cultural history of the northern Rockies and Great Plains in his lively volume *The Mythic West in Twentieth-Century America* (1986). And in a recently published collection of original essays, *The Twentieth-Century West: Historical Interpretations* (1989) edited by Nash and Richard W. Etulain, a dozen or so authorities treat various aspects of the social, cultural, political, economic, and environmental history of the new West.[6]

Finally, in the newest overview of the West since 1900, Michael P. Malone and Richard Etulain, although clearly indebted to the earlier writings of Webb, Pomeroy, and Nash and drawing on scholarship published in the last decade, nonetheless add emphases missing from earlier studies. Placing more stress than previous writers, for example, on the roles of women and family, historiography, and religion, Malone and Etulain also emphasize the plains and interior West, in addition to pointing out the burgeoning power of the West's two behemoths—California and Texas. At the same time, they follow earlier scholars in stressing economic and political forces more than social or cultural trends.[7]

As the twentieth-century draws to a close, many other historians will undoubtedly discover dozens of subjects in the modern West needing further research, and still others will construct overview summaries based on these new waves of research. Indeed, since three university presses have recently announced series on the modern West, a new surge of research and writing on the topic is likely to occur in the next decade or so.[8]

THE WEST AS NEW HISTORIOGRAPHICAL FRONTIER: URBAN, ETHNIC, AND FAMILY HISTORY

The most widely voiced criticism of western historical writing is its alleged failure to use the innovative approaches of recent historiography. Even western historians have joined in this chorus. For example, Michael P. Malone concludes that "historians of the West have been noticeably slow in taking up the newer methodologies that became popular during the 1970s." In the same book, Rodman W. Paul provides a similar criticism: "we in western history have as yet ventured only cautiously and partially into the ferment of new thinking that has characterized the profession nationally.[9] The conclusions of these two western specialists are but light jabs compared to the knockout blows other critics have aimed at western historians, particularly by doubters who dismiss western historical writing as provincial, out of date, and essentially insignificant.

How valid are these conclusions? Have western historians been slower, for instance, than historians of the South and New England during the last two decades in utilizing newer approaches to American history? No systematic study has addressed this question, even if a satisfying answer were possible. Still, if one uses articles appearing in the *Western Historical Quarterly*, the *Pacific Historical Review*, the *Journal of Southern History*, and the *New England Quarterly* as means for comparison, one cannot conclude from essays published in the two non-western journals that historians in the South and New England have embraced the new methodologies more readily than their western brethren. Since such inexact comparisons are not likely to be fruitful, however, one ought instead to survey what western historians have been doing in applying the new approaches of the last generation of historiography to their field.

Generally, palpable evidence exists that western historians are addressing new topics and frequently utilizing some of the new-fashioned historiographical approaches in several fields but especially in studies of urban, ethnic, and family history. Limited space forbids more than a severely selective listing.

The pathbreaking urban studies of Earl Pomeroy, Richard C. Wade, and Robert R. Dykstra published before 1970 and the rising interest of Americans in cities in the 1960s and 1970s helped to spark new interest in urban studies among western historians of the last two deccdes.[10] The most prolific of these recent students of western urbanism is Carl Abbott. In his urban biography of Portland, in his essays on the Sunbelt, and in his work on twentieth-century urbanization, Abbott utilizes statistics, demography, community studies, investigations of core–periphery relationships, and research materials on ethnic and gender experiences.[11] Similar kinds of wide-reaching research characterize the writings of Roger W. Lotchin, William Issel, and Robert W. Cherny, whose works on California urbanization of the nineteenth and twentieth centuries help scholars and students to understand cities that have dominated the Far West since the first English-speaking immigrants arrived in substantial numbers.[12] In the Southwest, Bradford Luckingham supplies thorough, factual surveys of Phoenix and other southwestern cities while Howard N. Rabinowitz provides a brief overview of modern Albuquerque. Their findings and those of several other urban historians are included in the useful volume *Sunbelt Cities*. In larger perspective, Gunther Barth's in-depth study of San Francisco and Denver as instant cities reveals how much those urban areas differed from other western cities of the nineteenth century.[13]

Still other western historians contribute revealing monographs on social change or conflict in less-populated areas of the frontier. Utilizing a variety of graphs and charts to demonstrate change over time, Ralph E. Mann studies social, economic, and political mobility in the early mining towns of Grass Valley and Nevada City, whereas Roger McGrath employs two trans-Sierra communities to study patterns of violence in the pioneer West.[14] Two other leading western historians, Richard Maxwell Brown and Carlos Schwantes, have written numerous provocative studies of violence and labor conflict. Both employ traditional historical methods as well as interdisciplinary social science techniques to analyze and explain their topics.[15]

The emphases of these historians of urbanization and community remind western specialists that their region was surprisingly urban early on. And, as we shall see, the additional insights of scholars trained primarily in urban history have markedly influenced not only the conclusions historians have reached but also the research methods they are using to study the American West.

Even more numerous are those scholars dealing with ethnic groups in the West. Earlier, Carey McWilliams, Moses Rischin, and Andrew Rolle, among others, wrote pioneering books and essays about diverse ethnic and immigrant experiences in the West at the same time that ethnologists like John Ewers and Edward H. Spicer directed their attention to western Indians. But this trickle of publications turned to a stream and then to a flood in the late 1960s and then on into the 1970s and 1980s. If American historians in the 1960s and 1970s, perhaps stimulated by the heightened interest in American ethnicity in those decades, treated ethnic groups in eastern metropolitan areas, blacks in eastern cities and the South, and immigrants throughout the country, western historians have been busily engaged with tracing Indian, Hispanic, and European groups in the West.

A majority of the recent studies treating the ethnic West center on Indians and Chicanos. Francis Paul Prucha's numerous publications dominate the scene of those working on American Indian policy, but several other historians cover new topics or utilize innovative techniques in addressing Indian policy or the history of western Indians. Arrell M. Gibson and William T. Hagan have produced a series of solid studies— some studying policy, others reflecting the newer research methods popular in the social sciences.[16] And James P. Ronda, Lawrence C. Kelly, Donald L. Parman, and Kenneth R. Philp open up new topics and owe debts to anthropologists in their very useful books on Lewis and Clark and Indians and on John Collier and Indian policies of the 1920s and the New Deal. In another area, Margaret Connell Szasz draws upon ethnographic work in two installments of her planned three-volume history of Indian education.[17] Most daring conceptually are the writings of Robert Berkhofer, Jr., and Richard White. Berkhofer employs insights from literary and art critics, anthropologists, and other social scientists to show how shifting images of Indians have been more the products of the popular desires and fears of non-Indians than the outcomes of thorough research by scholars. Meanwhile, White, invoking theories of dependency and hegemony, demonstrates how often the history of American Indians has been a conflict between outside influences and tribal desires for independence.[18] Several of these writers, as well as other scholars like Herbert T. Hoover and Wilcomb E. Washburn, urge western historians to move away from contact and policy history to place more stress on "Indian-Indian" history, or accounts of the internal affairs of tribal history.[19] In using ethnology, psychology, and other social sciences, western historians are gradually beginning to see Indian societies and cultures with different eyes.

Few areas of western historical writing have been as alive with activity and controversy as the field of Chicano historiography. This activity has followed two routes. First, such writers as Albert Camarillo, Mario T. García, Ricardo Romo, and Richard Griswold del Castillo have provided admirable monographs on Chicano communities in California and the Southwest.[20] Each of these authors makes abundant use of statistics, demography, and other disciplines and focuses on notable changes and continuities over time within these ethnic communities. Those following the second route, such as Rodolfo Acuña, Oscar J. Martínez, and Robert J. Rosenbaum, frequently building on this spate of recent monographs but sometimes working through fresh primary and secondary sources, have furnished overviews of Hispanic experiences in the nineteenth and twentieth centuries.[21] And still others like Juan Gómez-Quiñones and Sarah Deutsch have examined general themes in Chicano historiography or specific questions of race, class, and gender.[22] Nearly all of these studies employ theoretical frameworks foreign to traditionally trained western historians and thus are suggestive of broader perspectives useful for studying ethnicity in the American West.

Concurrently, the work of Frederick C. Luebke surpasses that of all other scholars treating European ethnic experiences in the West. In a series of provocative essays and books, Luebke has not only laid out interpretive frameworks drawing upon the research of geographers, folklorists, linguists, anthropologists, and demographers; he has himself written pioneering works on European ethnic groups, especially those about Germans on the Great Plains.[23] Other writings about European immigrants appearing since 1970 have been briefer, less innovative, and more closely tied to earlier interpretations of the West. Still, the useful essays in Stephan Thernstrom's indispensable *Harvard Encyclopedia of American Ethnic Groups* and in other collections fill in large gaps and represent fresh approaches to European immigrant groups.[24] And, as will become clear, nonhistorians have made notable contributions on these topics from alternative viewpoints.

In another area, extraordinary stress on masculinity as the central ingredient of the western code retarded studies of western women and families before 1970. On the other hand, earlier historians of the West were no more reluctant than writers in other regions to deal with these topics. At much the same time that American scholars began addressing topics of gender and family, western historians also initiated work on these new subjects.

Nearly a decade ago, Joan M. Jensen and Darlis A. Miller, in their superb historiographical overview of western women, called for more attention to cross-cultural topics, the twentieth century, and new approaches to women's history.[25] In the last ten years—and in the previous decade—western historians have addressed several of these needs. For example, Sandra Myres and Glenda Riley supply recent overviews of nineteenth-century women, and in doing so, they open up an important new field, even while following traditional perspectives in western historical writing. Less thorough but more revisionist are the writings of Lillian Schlissel and John Mack Faragher, who emphasize women reluctant to move west and those unwilling to be passive pawns of patriarchal fathers, husbands, and brothers. Meanwhile, Julie Roy Jeffrey, beginning with feminist assumptions of female assertiveness on the frontier, discovered instead that women replicated eastern experiences more often than they lived novel, pathbreaking lives in the West. Of these writers, only Faragher and Jeffrey employ methods and conclusions from the new social history, while Myres and Riley supply cross-cultural perspectives.[26]

Several historians previously cited have dealt with multicultural influences in their studies of ethnic groups, but others have focused on minority women and families. For instance, utilizing social science approaches, Richard Griswold del Castillo furnishes a useful study of Chicano families, while Alfredo Mirandé and Evangelina Enríquez, drawing on their backgrounds in sociology and comparative literature, have produced a helpful overview of Chicanas.[27] Meanwhile, the techniques of oral history and literary criticism inform the works of Gretchen M. Bataille, Kathleen Miller Sands, and Rayna Green on Native American women.[28] One should also note the impressive research on Japanese families by John Modell and Black women by Lawrence B. de Graaf and Glenda Riley.[29] In addition, in the past two decades several historians have treated the unique circumstances of Mormon women in the American West.[30]

Nor should one overlook the recent work on women in the twentieth-century West. Karen Anderson's brief overview of ethnic, urban, and occupational experiences and the new overview of California women by Joan M. Jensen and Gloria Ricci Lothrop are convenient beginning places. Other specialists focus on women as cultural figures, especially as writers and artists making use of landscape in their works. The paucity of these preliminary investigations remind one again that the twentieth-century West remains the most fertile era of western history for future scholarship.[31]

Finally, a growing number of historians have filled notable gaps in the history of western women and families while sometimes simultaneously calling for innovative approaches to the history of the West. For example, Sylvia Van Kirk, Jennifer S. H. Brown, Jacqueline Peterson, and John Mack Faragher point out ways by which historians may reexamine and evaluate women's roles in the Canadian and American fur trade, while Albert L. Hurtado breaks new ground in his studies of Indian households on the California frontier. And of major importance is Elliott West's new study of childhood in the pioneer West, a book that provides an overview synthesis even while it demonstrates how interdisciplinary research may inform without muddling a model and pathbreaking work.[32]

So impressive have been the numbers of these recent works by western historians on urban, ethnic, and family experiences in the West that one might conclude that these studies dominate contemporary western historiography. They do not, but when their influence is reckoned in conjunction with the large impact of nonhistorians and nonwesterners working on the same topics, one realizes how much these recent developments are enriching, challenging, and even redirecting trends in historical writing about the West.

TOTAL WESTERN HISTORY: BRAUDEL OUT WEST

For nearly two decades or more, historians, chiefly those specializing in early modern or more recent European history, have been influenced by Fernand Braudel's concept of total history. Advocating the far-reaching study of all classes and segments of society and numerous aspects of elite and popular cultures, Braudel and likeminded historians have called for nothing less than the study of a total society or culture. No historian has been as equally ambitious in his or her prospectus for studying the American West. None has aimed at, for example, the comprehensiveness of Braudel's *The Mediterranean and the Mediterranean World in the Age of Philip II*. For that matter, neither have historians dealing with other aspects of American history. But a handful of western specialists have essayed broader-based thematic studies of the West, ones intended as overviews or as total histories of the region.

A particularly provocative example of this ambitious new kind of western history is Patricia Nelson Limerick's *The Legacy of Conquest* (1987).[33] Limerick strives for a sweeping study of continuities of the nineteenth-century "legacies" that have helped shape the modern West. Utilizing a host of pertinent secondary sources as well as numerous newspaper articles, Limerick especially traces economic and social patterns of the frontier West continuing to hold sway in the contemporary West. Poignantly aware of pioneer mistreatment of land, other natural resources, and Indians and Hispanics, Limerick provocatively notes the persistence of these attitudes and actions well into the twentieth century. In her narrative, studded with lively turns of phrase and attractive pen portraits, Limerick persuades one of the necessity of seeing the West whole rather than mistakenly divided into two segments by the 1890s. In attempting an overview of the nineteenth- and twentieth-century Wests with major focus on a half-dozen notable themes, Limerick essays the most ambitious study of the trans-Mississippi West thus far published.

Equally ambitious in its scope and even more pointed in its conclusions, Donald Worster's vividly written *Rivers of Empire* (1985) draws upon the earlier environmental emphases of Webb, DeVoto, and James Malin to provide a searching critical analysis of the power that aridity and the control of water have had in shaping the West.[34] Convinced that developers and irrigation moguls have always dominated the West, Worster boldly traces the patterns of this dominance through the nineteenth and twentieth centuries and up to the present. Influenced markedly by the ideas of Karl Wittfogel and Karl Marx, especially their conclusions about power and the hegemonic command of resources, Worster discovers a similar blueprint among planners and corporations controlling western waters throughout the region's history. In regulating water in the West, these wielders of power have created "rivers of empire."

Worster's emphases are not entirely new. Webb and Malin had called for more attention to ecological conditions in the West, and DeVoto, echoing their perspectives, also castigated easterners and westerners alike who invaded the West or sold their resource birthrights like modern-day Esaus oblivious of their tomorrows. Worster preaches from DeVoto's earlier sermons, updating the message and joining writers like Wallace Stegner, William L. Kahrl, and Marc Reisner in calling for

a revisioned West, one in which "freedom and democracy rather than
. . . wealth and empire" (p. 335) determine the region's future.[35] But
in the scope of his coverage, in his conviction that water and its control will shape the West, and in his determination that the West of the
future must follow different paths, Worster supplies an encompassing—
and passionate—vision missing from most recent treatments of the
West. He too has a decided Braudelian view of total history in interpreting the American West.

Now that the uncrossable 1890s have been bridged and paths marked
through the previously uncharted wilderness of the modern West, other
scholars seemed poised to follow the trails Limerick and Worster have
blazed. Indeed, several such endeavors are underway. One of the major
challenges for western historians in the next generation will be to explore
and chart other courses between the pioneer and modern Wests. As
they do so, one hopes these writers utilize previous signposts without
overlooking the new surveys more recent scholars have just completed.

EXPANDING THE WEST:
NONWESTERNERS AS WESTERN HISTORIANS

Many of the major contributions to historical writing about the West
have come from scholars trained in fields distinct from western history. Using their backgrounds in other disciplines or in competing fields
of history, these scholars have added new insights and conceptions as
well as broader perspectives to the study of the American West. Indeed,
these nonwesterners, as much as western specialists, are the reinvigo-
rating agents of western historiography during the past two decades.

In the area of western cultural history, for example, the writings of
literary scholars John R. Milton, Annette Kolodny, Don D. Walker, and
Max Westbrook illustrate how much the careful application of literary
criticism and myth studies add to an understanding of frontier and
western literature.[36] Moreover, American Studies scholars and art historians John G. Cawelti, Richard Slotkin, Brian W. Dippie, and William H. Goetzmann expand our comprehension of western popular
culture and western art in their analytical studies,[37] and cultural historians David B. Tyack, Ferenc M. Szasz, John H. Lenihan, and Reyner
Banham supply the best recent analyses of western education, religion,
film, and architecture.[38]

No less significant are the signal studies of geographers dealing
with the American West. Building on the earlier insights of geogra-

pher Carl Sauer, D. W. Meinig has produced a string of compelling essays and monographs on several physical and cultural subregions of the West, and in doing so, he illustrates what other scholars might do in analyzing varied cultural landscapes of the West.[39] Geographer Terry G. Jordan's studies of southwestern ethnic groups, regional material culture, and frontier cattle raising provide additional paradigms for western historians,[40] as do William A. Bowen's analysis of early settlement in the Pacific Northwest, John L. Allen's revealing treatment of the Lewis and Clark expedition, and David J. Wishart's innovative discussion of the western fur trade.[41]

Scholars trained in urban and ethnic studies have likewise contributed pioneering volumes in these fields since 1970. In addition to those writers mentioned previously, one must list John W. Reps's notable works on urban planning in the frontier West; the important findings of Peter R. Decker and Howard P. Chudacoff on economic, social, and physical mobility in San Francisco and Omaha; and the useful urban biographies of Seattle and Tucson by literary scholars Roger Sale and C.L. Sonnichsen.[42] Urban historians Lawrence H. Larsen and Lyle W. Dorsett have also furnished solid studies of several western cities. As urban historian Gunther Barth has recently asserted, traditional approaches to the West have so emphasized rural and agricultural life that the development of western towns and cities was previously overlooked.[43] But in the last generation, urban historians, laboring alongside western specialists, have so leavened western historiography that new examinations of the region usually include segments on the impact of western urbanization.

Still other authorities investigating western ethnicity have focused on varied ethnic groups living in western cities and rural areas. Although several scholars, as we have seen, have centered on Chicano urban experiences, other groups such as the Irish, Basques, or Blacks are just beginning to find their interpreters—for example in the recent works of R. A. Burchell, William A. Douglass, Norman Crockett, Thomas C. Cox, and Douglas H. Daniels.[44] These investigations are forcing western historians to rethink ethnic complexities of the pioneer and modern Wests.

In this regard, few recent monographs offer more provocative fare than David Montejano's *Anglos and Mexicans*, which analyzes and evaluates a century and a half of rural and urban experience along the Rio Grande in south Texas.[45] Utilizing a variety of social science techniques and drawing on equally diverse source materials, Montejano supplies the most stimulating study of ethnicity in the West in the last few years. His keen observations about the interplay between the shifting influences of capitalism, ethnicity, and family and community organizations, combined with the author's skillful use of analytical and narrative modes of presentation, make this a premier study by a nonhistorian. Equally provocative are the monographs and overviews of Richard Griswold del Castillo and Arnoldo De Leon.[46] Specialists in ethnic history, these two writers focus on Chicano urban and family patterns as well as on Hispanic–Anglo conflicts and in doing so encourage western specialists to enlarge their visions of the varied peoples of the West.

Nonwesterners have also concentrated on additional notable aspects of western social history. For example, Joan M. Jensen, Julia Kirk Blackwelder, and Vicki L. Ruiz, centering on class, ethnic, and other cross-cultural differences, have explained varied women's experience in the twentieth-century Southwest and California.[47] In addition, Robert L. Griswold, in dealing with marriage and divorce in rural northern California, illuminates a topic that most western historians have overlooked. And historian D'Ann Campbell and sociologist Marion S. Goldman, appropriating techniques from several social sciences, disclose much about women of the 1940s and prostitution in the Gold Rush era.[48]

Finally, historians of political culture and political scientists have turned to the West as a region upon which to focus their revealing overviews and case studies. For example, Daniel J. Elazar and Ira Sharkansky identify varieties of political culture characterizing the West and the nation, and Richard Jensen urges western historians to modernize Turner's sectional theory through more attention to political ideologies and culture.[49] Robert W. Cherny and especially Paul Kleppner, in a clutch of computer-aided studies of western and national politics, furnish new interpretations of political trends and parties in the nineteenth and twentieth centuries.[50]

Clearly, these nonwesterners and nonhistorians have made major contributions to western historiography. As literary critics, as cultural historians and social scientists, as historians of urbanization and ethnicity, and as specialists in competing fields of American history, these scholars have enriched historical writing about the West during the last two decades, supplying novel analytical tools for historians, providing unusual perspectives on western topics, and adding information on new subjects or expanding knowledge on older topics. If western specialists remain open to these new concepts and additional findings, their historical writings in the next decade or two are likely to be more alive conceptually as well as more wide-reaching in the subjects and periods covered.

RECENT WESTERN HISTORIOGRAPHY—
TOWARD SYNTHESIS

Two broad trends, then, characterize historical writing about the American West during the last two decades. A majority of those inter-preting the West follow at least one of the visions that inspired Turner, Webb, Bolton, Billington, Pomeroy, or Smith. But other writers have revisioned the West, emphasizing twentieth century, urban, ethnic or family topics, thematic developments, or the perspectives of non-westerners.

Now, a single question seems paramount: will these visions and revisions remain separate trends, or are there possibilities for synthe-sis? Is there, to use terms Bernard Bailyn employs in a different con-text, the possibility of marrying the *manifest* and *latent*?[51] In this case, the juxtaposing of the earlier, well-accepted visions of the West with the more recent (and sometimes pathbreaking) reinterpretations of the region? Answers to these questions not only help to explain writings about the West published since 1970 but also suggest an agenda for western historians through the end of the century.

As the handful of following examples indicate, the synthesis is under-way and at several stages of development. The most recent editions of the widely adopted western history texts by Ray Allen Billington, Mar-tin Ridge, and Robert Hine illustrate an early phase of synthesis. These writers incorporate limited amounts of the new research on the twen-tieth century, ethnic groups, and women into their bibliographies and texts. And the cited works of Francis Paul Prucha, Rudolfo Acuña, Carl Abbott, and Kevin Starr illustrate parallel synthetic overviews of eth-nic, urban, and cultural topics.[52]

Rodman W. Paul's new volume treating the West from the Civil War to 1900 in the New American Nation series exemplifies the next stage of synthesis. Although built primarily on the author's solid work on frontier economic developments, the study also draws extensively on recent studies of mining, social and economic mobility, urbanization, and ethnicity.[53] The same is true of Malone and Etulain's general study of the twentieth-century West, which uses the ideas of Turner and Webb and follows Pomeroy's call for attention to continuities between East and West, even while the volume discusses western cities, ethnic groups, families, and major political and economic groups of the modern West.[54] A third example of this middle stage of synthesis is Gerald Nash's *The West Transformed*, a volume based on his notable work on the recent West but also strengthened considerably through his judicious empha-ses on urbanization and minority groups.

If these writers epitomize two stages of synthesis showing how historians have combined traditional narratives with new topical or innovative methodological emphases, other interpreters have pushed on to a third stage of synthesis. The best examples of this third phase are the provocative volumes by Patricia Nelson Limerick and Donald Worster. Both writers see the West more holistically than do most western historians, both utilize well the new subjects and methods of recent western historiography, and both essay analytical volumes without forgetting the power and attractiveness of gracefully written narrative. In addition, Limerick and Worster provide new opportunities of rediscovering the web of associations that entangle as well as direct the West: legacies from the pioneer past, ties to other regions and the nation, and links between the region and the larger world. And judging from the excellence of their previous performances, the forthcoming volumes by Howard Lamar, William Cronon, and Richard White threaten to add further notable examples to these newer synthetic studies of the West.[55]

Not all western specialists admire these stuttering steps toward synthesis, however. Indeed, like many other American historians, some westerners view these strivings toward wholeness as out of place and coercive—like a sheepherder trying to lead a remuda of recalcitrant cowboys. But these hesitations are like so much muttering among historiographical graybeards. What cannot be accepted or stopped can only be criticized. Clearly, the winds of change are blowing toward wholeness after a generation or more spent in scrutinizing parts.[56] And the search for synthesis will continue to move ahead as surely as the West remains a notable and influential region.

Nearly two generations ago Earl Pomeroy closed his classic essay calling for a reorientation of western history by stating: "Good books on western history still do appear, and few fields present so many subjects for other good books still to be written."[57] What Pomeroy asserted almost four decades in the past remains true—with one major difference. Good books about the West will continue to appear, but the time is ripe for a season of new synthetic treatments. The earlier visions of Turner, Webb, Bolton, Billington, Pomeroy, and Smith and the more recent revisions of the last two decades should pollinate one another; from their union will come a new crop of synthetic offspring. If so, we shall enjoy in the next generation the fruits of a New Western Historiography.

NOTES

1. The proceedings of the Boulder conference were published in James F. Willard and Colin B. Goodykoontz, eds., *The Trans-Mississippi West* (Boulder: University of Colorado, 1930). Turner made several suggestions about the most appropriate participants for the conference in his correspondence with Willard, December 20, 1928, February 4, March 11, 1929, Frederick Jackson Turner Papers, Boxes 40, 41, Henry E. Huntington Library, San Marino, California.

2. The most useful discussions of recent trends in historical writing about the West are contained in two collections of historiographical essays: Michael P. Malone, ed., *Historians and the American West* (Lincoln: University of Nebraska Press, 1983), and Roger L. Nichols, ed., *American Frontier and Western Issues: A Historiographical Review* (Westport, Conn.: Greenwood Press, 1986). A useful brief survey appears in Rodman W. Paul and Michael P. Malone, "Tradition and Challenge in Western Historiography," *Western Historical Quarterly* 16 (January 1985):27–53. A very good earlier overview remains unpublished: Howard R. Lamar, "Trends in Western Historiography," a paper presented at the annual meeting of the American Historical Association, San Francisco, December 1975. More recently, Gene M. Gressley has published two abbreviated introductions: "Whither Western History? Speculations on a Direction," *Pacific Historical Review* 53 (November 1984):493–501; and "The West: Past, Present, and Future," *Western Historical Quarterly* 17 (January 1986):5–23. Gerald D. Nash has forthcoming an extensive overview of western historiography in his *Creating the West: Historical Interpretations, 1890–1990* (Albuquerque: University of New Mexico Press, 1991). To keep a tight rein on citations that threaten to expand an essay into a book, textual commentaries will be limited primarily to book-length studies, and footnotes will include pertinent historiographical essays listing numerous other sources.

3. This section summarizes the longer discussion in Etulain, "The Twentieth-Century West: A New Historiographical Frontier," in Gerald D. Nash and Richard W. Etulain, eds., *The Twentieth-Century West: Historical Interpretations* (Albuquerque: University of New Mexico Press, 1989), 1–31.

4. Pomeroy, *The Pacific Slope: A History of California, Oregon, Washington, Idaho, Utah, and Nevada* (New York: Alfred A. Knopf, 1965); Morgan, *Westward Tilt: The American West Today* (New York: Random House, 1961, 1963); Wiley and Gottlieb, *Empires in the Sun: The Rise of the New American West* (New York: G.P. Putnam's, 1982).

5. Nash, *The American West in the Twentieth Century: A Short History of an Urban Oasis* (Englewood Cliffs, N.J.: Prentice-Hall, 1973); also see Nash's "The Twentieth-Century West," *Western Historical Quarterly* 12 (April 1982):179–81.

6. Lowitt, *The New Deal and the West* (Bloomington: Indiana University Press, 1984); Nash, *The American West Transformed: The Impact of the Second World War* (Bloomington: Indiana University Press, 1985); Nash, *World War II and the West:*

Reshaping the Economy (Lincoln: University of Nebraska Press, 1990); Athearn, *The Mythic West in Twentieth-Century America* (Lawrence: University Press of Kansas, 1986); Nash and Etulain, *The Twentieth-Century West: Historical Interpretations*.

7. Malone and Etulain, *The American West: A Twentieth-Century History* (Lincoln: University of Nebraska Press, 1989).

8. Martin Ridge and Walter Nugent edit a twentieth-century West series for Indiana University Press; Gerald D. Nash edits a similar series for the University of Arizona Press; and Earl Pomeroy, Howard R. Lamar, and Michael P. Malone edit a third series on the modern West for the University of Nebraska Press.

9. Malone, "Introduction," and Paul, "Preface," in Malone, *Historians and the American West*, 10, viii.

10. Pomeroy, "The Power of the Metropolis," *The Pacific Slope*, 120–64; Wade, *The Urban Frontier: Pioneer Life in Early Pittsburgh, Cincinnati, Lexington, Louisville, and St. Louis* (Chicago: University of Chicago Press, 1959, 1964); Dykstra, *The Cattle Towns* (New York: Alfred A. Knopf, 1968).

11. Abbott, *Portland: Politics, Planning, and Growth in a Twentieth-Century City* (Lincoln: University of Nebraska Press, 1983); *The New Urban America: Growth and Politics in Sunbelt Cities* (Chapel Hill: University of North Carolina Press, 1981); "The Metropolitan Region: Western Cities in the New Urban Era," in Nash and Etulain, *Twentieth-Century West*, 71–98.

12. Lotchin, *San Francisco, 1846–1856: From Hamlet to City* (New York: Oxford University Press, 1974); Issel and Cherny, *San Francisco, 1865–1932: Politics, Power, and Urban Development* (Berkeley: University of California Press, 1986); see, too, the extensive listings in Lawrence H. Larsen, "Frontier Urbanization," in Nichols, *American Frontier and Western Issues*, 69–88.

13. Luckingham, *Phoenix: The History of a Southwestern Metropolis* (Tucson: University of Arizona Press, 1989); *The Urban Southwest: A Profile History of Albuquerque, El Paso, Phoenix, and Tucson* (El Paso: Texas Western Press, 1982); "The Urban Dimension of Western History," in Malone, *Historians and the American West*, 323–43; Rabinowitz, "Growth Trends in the Albuquerque, SMSA, 1940–1978," *Journal of the West* 18 (July 1979):62–74; Richard M. Bernard and Bradley R. Rice, eds., *Sunbelt Cities: Politics and Growth since World War II* (Austin: University of Texas Press, 1983); Barth, *Instant Cities: Urbanization and the Rise of San Francisco and Denver* (New York: Oxford University Press, 1978); and Luckingham, "The American Southwest: An Urban View," *Western Historical Quarterly* 15 (July 1984):261–80.

14. Mann, *After the Gold Rush: Society in Grass Valley and Nevada City, California, 1849–1870.* (Stanford: Stanford University Press, 1982); Mann, "Frontier Opportunity and the New Social History," *Pacific Historical Review* 53 (November 1984):463–91; McGrath, *Gunfighters, Highwaymen and Vigilantes: Violence on the Frontier* (Berkeley: University of California Press, 1985); also see Elliott West, "Five Idaho Mining Towns: A Computer Profile," *Pacific Northwest Quarterly* 58 (July 1982):108–20.

15. Brown, *Strain of Violence: Historical Studies of American Violence and Vigi-*

lantism (New York: Oxford University Press, 1975); "Historiography of Violence in the American West," in Malone, *Historians and the American West*, 234–69; Schwantes, *Radical Heritage: Labor, Socialism, and Reform in Washington and British Columbia, 1885–1917* (Seattle: University of Washington Press, 1979); "The Concept of the Wageworkers' Frontier: A Framework for Future Research," *Western Historical Quarterly* 18 (January 1987):39–55.

16. Gibson, *The American Indian: Prehistory to the Present* (Lexington, Mass.: D. C. Heath, 1980); Hagan, *American Indians*, rev ed. (Chicago: University of Chicago Press, 1979); Roger L. Nichols, "Historians and Indians," in Nichols, *American Frontier and Western Issues*, 149–77; also see Brian W. Dippie, *The Vanishing American: White Attitudes and U.S. Indian Policy* (Middletown, Conn.: Wesleyan University Press, 1982).

17. Ronda, *Lewis and Clark among the Indians* (Lincoln: University of Nebraska Press, 1984); Kelly, *The Navajo Indians and Federal Indian Policy, 1900–1935* (Tucson: University of Arizona Press, 1968); *The Assault on Assimilation: John Collier and the Origins of Indian Policy Reform* (Albuquerque: University of New Mexico Press, 1983); Parman, *The Navajos and the New Deal* (New Haven: Yale University Press, 1976); Philp, *John Collier's Crusade for Indian Reform 1920–1954* (Tucson: University of Arizona Press, 1977); Szasz, *Education and the American Indian: The Road to Self-Determination since 1928* (Albuquerque: University of New Mexico Press, 1974, 1977); *Indian Education in the American Colonies, 1607–1783* (Albuquerque: University of New Mexico Press, 1988).

18. Berkhofer, *The White Man's Indian: Images of the American Indian from Columbus to the Present* (New York: Alfred A. Knopf, 1978); "The Political Context of a New Indian History," *Pacific Historical Review* 40 (August 1971):357–82; White, *The Roots of Dependency: Subsistence, Environment and Social Change among the Choctaws, Pawnees, and Navajos* (Lincoln: University of Nebraska Press, 1983).

19. Hoover, "American Indians from Prehistoric Times to the Civil War," and Robert C. Carriker, "The American Indian from the Civil War to the Present," in Malone, *Historians and the American West*, 15–38, 177–208; Washburn, "The Writing of American Indian History: A Status Report," *Pacific Historical Review* 40 (August 1971):261–81.

20. Camarillo, *Chicanos in a Changing Society: From Mexican Pueblos to American Barrios in Santa Barbara and Southern California, 1848–1930* (Cambridge, Mass.: Harvard University Press, 1979); García, *Desert Immigrants: The Mexicans of El Paso, 1880–1920* (New Haven: Yale University Press, 1981); Romo, *East Los Angeles: History of a Barrio* (Austin: University of Texas Press, 1983); Griswold del Castillo, *The Los Angeles Barrio, 1850–1890: A Social History* (Berkeley: University of California Press, 1979).

21. Acuña, *Occupied America: A History of Chicanos*, 3d ed. (New York: Harper and Row, 1988); Martínez, *Troublesome Border* (Tucson: University of Arizona Press, 1988); Rosenbaum, *Mexicano Resistance in the Southwest: "The Sacred Right of Self-Preservation"* (Austin: University of Texas Press, 1981).

22. Gómez-Quiñones and Luis Leobardo Arroyo, "On the State of Chicano

History . . . ," *Western Historical Quarterly* 7 (April 1976):269–308; Deutsch, *No Separate Refuge: Culture, Class, and Gender on an Anglo-Hispanic Frontier in the American Southwest, 1880–1940* (New York: Oxford University Press, 1987).

23. Luebke, *Immigrants and Politics: The Germans of Nebraska, 1880–1900* (Lincoln: University of Nebraska Press, 1969); "Ethnic Group Settlement on the Great Plains," *Western Historical Review* 8 (October 1977):405–30; "Ethnic Minority Groups in the American West," in Malone, *Historians and the American West*, 387–413.

24. Thernstrom, ed., *Harvard Encyclopedia of American Ethnic Groups* (Cambridge: Harvard University Press, 1980); Gordon Hendrickson, ed., *Peopling the High Plains: Wyoming's European Heritage* (Cheyenne: Wyoming State Archives and Historical Department, 1977); Helen Z. Papanikolas, ed., *The Peoples of Utah* (Salt Lake City: Utah State Historical Society, 1976).

25. Jensen and Miller, "The Gentle Tamers Revisited: New Approaches to the History of Women in the American West," *Pacific Historical Review* 49 (May 1980):173–213. Also see Susan Armitage, "Women and Men in Western History: A Stereoptical Vision," *Western Historical Quarterly* 16 (October 1985):381–91, and the collected essays in Armitage and Elizabeth Jameson, eds., *The Women's West* (Norman: University of Oklahoma Press, 1987).

26. Myres, *Westering Women and the Frontier Experience 1800–1915* (Albuquerque: University of New Mexico Press, 1982); Riley, *The Female Frontier: A Comparative View of Women on the Prairie and the Plains* (Lawrence: University Press of Kansas, 1988); Schlissel, *Women's Diaries of the Westward Journey* (New York: Schocken Books, 1982); Faragher, *Women and Men on the Overland Trail* (New Haven: Yale University Press, 1979); Jeffrey, *Frontier Women: The Trans-Mississippi West 1840–1880* (New York: Hill and Wang, 1979). For a helpful essay demonstrating the new ways in which women's history might be taught in western courses, see William Cronon, et al., "Women and the West: Rethinking the Western History Survey Course," *Western Historical Quarterly* 17 (July 1986):269–81.

27. Griswold del Castillo, *La Familia: Chicano Families in the Urban Southwest, 1848 to the Present* (Notre Dame, Ind.: University of Notre Dame Press, 1984); Mirandé and Enríquez, *La Chicana: The Mexican-American Woman* (Chicago: University of Chicago Press, 1979).

28. Batille and Sands, *American Indian Women: Telling Their Lives* (Lincoln: University of Nebraska Press, 1984); Green, *Native American Women: A Contextual Bibliography* (Bloomington: Indiana University Press, 1983).

29. Modell, *The Economics and Politics of Racial Accommodation: The Japanese of Los Angeles 1900–1942* (Urbana: University of Illinois Press, 1977); De Graaf, "Race, Sex, and Region: Black Women in the American West, 1850–1920," *Pacific Historical Review* 49 (May 1980):285–313; Riley, "American Daughters: Black Women in the West," *Montana: The Magazine of Western History* 38 (Spring 1988):14–27.

30. Claudia L. Bushman, ed., *Mormon Sisters: Women in Early Utah* (Cambridge, Mass.: Emmeline Press, 1976); Vicky Burgess-Olson, ed., *Sister Saints*

(Provo: Brigham Young University Press, 1978); Kenneth W. Godfrey, et al., *Women's Voices: An Untold History of the Latter-day Saints, 1830–1900* (Salt Lake City: Deseret Book Company, 1982).

31. Anderson, "Western Women: The Twentieth-Century Experience," in Nash and Etulain, *The Twentieth-Century West*, 99–122; Jensen and Lothrop, *California Women: A History* (San Francisco: Boyd and Fraser Publishing Company, 1987); Vera Norwood and Janice Monk, eds. *The Desert Is No Lady: Southwestern Landscapes in Women's Writing and Art* (New Haven: Yale University Press, 1987); for extensive listings of women involved in western literature and culture, see Jensen and Miller, "The Gentle Tamers," 179–80, and Richard W. Etulain, *A Bibliographical Guide to the Study of Western American Literature* (Lincoln: University of Nebraska Press, 1982). For a convenient listing of research on women in the modern West, see Pat Devejian and Jacqueline J. Etulain, comps., *Women and Family in the Twentieth-Century American West: A Bibliography.* Occasional Paper, no. 1, Center for the American West (Albuquerque: University of New Mexico, 1990).

32. Van Kirk, *Many Tender Ties: Women in Fur Trade Society, 1670–1870* (Norman: University of Oklahoma Press, 1983); Brown, *Strangers in Blood: Fur Trade Company Families in Indian Country* (Vancouver: University of British Columbia Press, 1980); Peterson and Brown, eds., *The New Peoples: Being and Becoming Metis in North America* (Lincoln: University of Nebraska Press, 1985); also see the essays and comments by Van Kirk, Peterson, Faragher, and many others in Lillian Schlissel, et al., eds., *Western Women: Their Land, Their Lives* (Albuquerque: University of New Mexico Press, 1988); Hurtado, *Indian Survival on the California Frontier* (New Haven: Yale University Press, 1988); West, *Growing Up with the Country: Childhood on the Far-Western Frontier* (Albuquerque: University of New Mexico Press, 1989).

If more space were available, strong recent work on other topics should be mentioned here. For example, in addition to the items listed in footnotes 34 and 35, the notable books and essays on western water and land by Norris Hundley, Jr., Donald J. Pisani, and John Opie should be underscored, as well as those on environmental topics by Opie, William G. Robbins, Richard White, William Cronon, Patricia Nelson Limerick, and Stephen J. Pyne. Of note, too, are the recent works by Leonard J. Arrington, Thomas G. Alexander, and Jan Shipps on the Mormons and the comparative perspectives of Howard R. Lamar, Jerome O. Steffen, and W. Turrentine Jackson.

33. Limerick, *The Legacy of Conquest: The Unbroken Past of the American West* (New York: W. W. Norton, 1987).

34. Worster, *Rivers of Empire: Water, Aridity, and the Growth of the American West* (New York: Pantheon Books, 1985); *Dust Bowl: The Southern Plains in the 1930s* (New York: Oxford University Press, 1979); "History as Natural History: An Essay on Theory and Method," *Pacific Historical Review* 53 (February 1984): 1–19; Richard White, "American Environmental History: The Development of a New Historical Field," *Pacific Historical Review* 54 (August 1985):297–335.

35. Stegner, *The Sound of Mountain Water* (Garden City, N.Y.: Doubleday, 1969); Kahrl, *Water and Power: The Conflict over Los Angeles' Water Supply in the Owens Valley* (Berkeley: University of California Press, 1982); Reisner, *Cadillac Desert: The American West and its Disappearing Water* (New York: Viking Penguin, 1986).

36. Milton, *The Novel of the American West* (Lincoln: University of Nebraska Press, 1980); Kolodny, *The Land before Her: Fantasy and Experience of the American Frontiers, 1630–1860* (Chapel Hill: University of North Carolina Press, 1984); Walker, *Clio's Cowboys: Studies in the Historiography of the Cattle Trade* (Lincoln: University Press, 1981); for a full listing of Westbrook's many essays on western literature, see Etulain, *A Bibliographical Guide*, 46, 201.

37. Cawelti, *The Six-Gun Mystique* (Bowling Green, Ohio: Bowling Green University Popular Press, 1971, 1984), and *Adventure, Mystery, and Romance: Formula Stories as Art and Popular Culture* (Chicago: University of Chicago Press, 1976); Slotkin, *Regeneration Through Violence: The Mythology of the American Frontier, 1600–1860* (Middletown, Conn.: Wesleyan University Press, 1973); Dippie, *Looking at Russell* (Fort Worth: Amon Carter Museum, 1987); William H. Goetzmann and William N. Goetzmann, *The West of the Imagination* New York: W. W. Norton, 1986).

38. See the comments on western culture in Tyack's *The One Best System: A History of American Urban Education* (Cambridge: Harvard University Press, 1974); Szasz, *The Protestant Clergy in the Great Plains and Mountain West, 1865–1915* (Albuquerque: University of New Mexico Press, 1988); Lenihan, *Showdown: Confronting Modern America in the Western Film* (Urbana: University of Illinois Press, 1980); Banham, *Los Angeles: The Architecture of Four Ecologies* (London: Allen Lane the Penguin Press, 1971).

39. In addition to Meinig's books—*The Great Columbia Plain: A Historical Georgraphy 1805–1910* (Seattle: University of Washington Press, 1968); *Imperial Texas: An Interpretive Essay in Cultural Geography* (Austin: University of Texas Press, 1969); *Southwest: Three Peoples in Geographical Change, 1600–1970* (New York: Oxford University Press, 1971)—see his "American Wests: Preface to a Geographical Interpretation," *Annals of the Association of American Geographers* 62 (June 1972):159–84; "The Continuous Shaping of America: A Prospectus for Geographers and Historians," *American Historical Review* 83 (December 1978): 1186–1205, and comments, 1206–17.

40. Jordan, "A Century and a Half of Ethnic Change in Texas, 1836–1986," *Southwestern Historical Quarterly* 89 (April 1986):385–422; *Trails to Texas: Southern Roots of Western Cattle Ranching* (Lincoln: University of Nebraska Press, 1981).

41. Bowen, *The Willamette Valley: Migration and Settlement on the Oregon Frontier* (Seattle: University of Washington Press, 1978); Allen, *Passage through the Garden: Lewis and Clark and the Image of the American Northwest* (Urbana: University of Illinois Press, 1975); Wishart, *The Fur Trade of the American West, 1807–1840: A Geographical Synthesis* (Lincoln: University of Nebraska Press, 1979).

42. Reps, *Cities of the American West: A History of Frontier Urban Planning* (Princeton, N.J.: Princeton University Press, 1979); *The Forgotten Frontier: Urban*

Planning in the American West before 1890 (Columbia: University of Missouri Press, 1981); Decker, *Fortunes and Failures: White Collar Mobility in Nineteenth-Century San Francisco* (Cambridge: Harvard University Press, 1978); Chudacoff, *Mobile Americans: Residential and Social Mobility in Omaha, 1880–1920* (New York: Oxford University Press, 1972); Sale, *Seattle: Past to Present* (Seattle: University of Washington Press, 1976); Sonnichsen, *Tucson: The Life and Times of an American City* (Norman: University of Oklahoma Press, 1982).

43. Larsen, *The Urban West at the End of the Frontier* (Lawrence: Regents Press of Kansas, 1978); Dorsett, *The Queen City: A History of Denver* (Boulder: Pruett Publishing Company, 1977); Dorsett and A. Theodore Brown, *K. C.: A History of Kansas City, Missouri* (Boulder: Pruett, 1979); Barth, *Instant Cities*.

44. Burchell, *The San Francisco Irish, 1848–1880* (Berkeley: University of California Press, 1980); Douglass and Jon Bilbao, *Amerikanuak: Basques in the New World* (Reno: University of Nevada Press, 1975); Crockett, *The Black Towns* (Lawrence: Regents Press of Kansas, 1979); Cox, *Blacks in Topeka, 1865–1915: A Social History* (Baton Rouge: Louisiana State University Press, 1982); Daniels, *Pioneer Urbanites: A Social and Cultural History of Black San Francisco* (Philadelphia: Temple University Press, 1980).

45. Montejano, *Anglos and Mexicans in the Making of Texas, 1836–1986* (Austin: University of Texas Press, 1987).

46. Griswold del Castillo, *La Familia*; De León, *The Tejano Community, 1836–1900* (Albuquerque: University of New Mexico Press, 1982); *They Called Them Greasers: Anglo Attitudes toward Mexicans in Texas, 1821–1900* (Austin: University of Texas Press, 1983).

47. Several of Jensen's essays are published or listed in Jensen and Darlis A. Miller, eds., *New Mexico Women: Intercultural Perspectives* (Albuquerque: University of New Mexico Press, 1986); Blackwelder, *Women of the Depression: Caste and Culture in San Antonio, 1929–1939* (College Station: Texas A&M University Press, 1984); Ruiz, *Cannery Women, Cannery Lives: Mexican Women, Unionization, and the California Food Processing Industry, 1930–1950* (Albuquerque: University of New Mexico Press, 1987).

48. Griswold, *Family and Divorce in California, 1850–1890: Victorian Illusions and Everyday Realities* (Albany: State University of New York Press, 1982); Campbell, "Was the West Different?: Values and Attitudes of Young Women in 1943," *Pacific Historical Review* 47 (August 1978):453–64; Goldman, *Gold Diggers and Silver Miners: Prostitution and Social Life on the Comstock Lode* (Ann Arbor: University of Michigan Press, 1981).

49. Elazar, *Cities of the Prairie: The Metropolitan Frontier and American Politics* (New York: Basic Books, 1970); "Political Culture on the Plains," *Western Historical Quarterly* 11 (July 1980):261–83; Sharkansky, *Regionalism in American Politics* (Indianapolis: Bobbs-Merrill, 1970); Jensen, "On Modernizing Frederick Jackson Turner: The Historiography of Regionalism," *Western Historical Quarterly* 11 (July 1980):307–22.

50. Cherny, *Populism, Progressivism, and the Transformation of Nebraska Poli-*

tics, 1885–1915 (Lincoln: University of Nebraska Press for the Center for Great Plains Studies, 1981); Kleppner, "Voters and Parties in the Western States, 1876–1900," *Western Historical Quarterly* 14 (January 1983):49–68; "Politics without Parties: The Western States 1900–1984," in Nash and Etulain, *The Twentieth-Century West*, 295–338.

51. Bailyn, "The Challenge of Modern Historiography," *American Historical Review* 87 (February 1982):1–24.

52. Billington and Ridge, *Westward Expansion: A History of the American West*, 5th ed. (New York: Macmillan Company, 1982); Hine, *The American West: An Interpretive History*, 2d ed. (Boston: Little, Brown and Company, 1984).

53. Paul, *The Far West and the Great Plains in Transition 1859–1900* (New York: Harper and Row, 1988).

54. Other examples of this stage of synthesis include Michael P. Malone and Richard B. Roeder, *Montana: A History of Two Centuries* (Seattle: University of Washington Press, 1976), and Carlos Schwantes, *The Pacific Northwest: An Interpretive History* (Lincoln: University of Nebraska Press, 1989).

55. Lamar and Cronon are beginning a general overview of the West for W. W. Norton, and White's long synthesis will be published by the University of Oklahoma Press in 1991.

56. Major statements on the ongoing controversy among historians over narrative, synthesis, and recent trends in social history include Lawrence Stone, "The Revival of Narrative: Reflections on a New Old History," *Past and Present* 85 (November 1979):3–24; Thomas Bender, "Wholes and Parts: The Need for Synthesis in American History," *Journal of American History* 73 (June 1986):120–36; Eric Monkkonen, "The Dangers of Synthesis," *American Historical Review* 91 (December 1986):1146–57; and responses to Bender's essay and his rejoinder in "A Round Table: Synthesis in American History," *Journal of American History* 74 (June 1987):107–30. Suggestions for synthesizing western history are presented in two new provocative essays: Michael P. Malone, "Beyond the Last Frontier: Toward a New Approach to Western American History," *Western Historical Quarterly* 20 (November 1989):409–27; and William G. Robbins, "Western History: A Dialectic on the Modern Condition," *Western Historical Quarterly* 20 (November 1989):429–49.

57. Pomeroy, "Toward a Reorientation of Western History: Continuity and Environment," *Mississippi Valley Historical Review* 41 (March 1955):600. Two other essays that deal with recent trends in western historiography are Walter Nugent, "Western History: Stocktakings and New Crops," *Reviews in American History* 13 (September 1985):319–29; and Elliott West, "Cowboys and Indians and Artists and Liars and Schoolmarms and Tom Mix: New Ways to Teach the American West," in Dennis Reinhartz and Stephen W. Maizlish, eds., *Essays on Walter Prescott Webb and the Teaching of History* (College Station: Texas A&M University Press, 1985), 36–60. Also see Howard R. Lamar's splendid essay, "Much to Celebrate: The Western History Association's Twenty-Fifth Birthday," *Western Historical Quarterly* 17 (October 1986):397–416.

Contributors

ALLAN G. BOGUE is Frederick Jackson Turner Professor of History at the University of Wisconsin in Madison. He is the author of *Money at Interest: The Farm Mortgage on the Middle Border* (1955), *From Prairie to Corn Belt: Farming on the Illinois and Iowa Prairies in the Nineteenth Century* (1963), *The West of the American People* (coauthored and edited with James E. Wright and Thomas D. Phillips, 1970), and numerous other publications in western, agricultural, and political history. His most recent book is *The Congressman's Civil War* (1989). He has been president of the Organization of American Historians, the Economic History Association, the Agricultural History Society, and the Social Science History Association. Currently he is doing research on western agricultural development during the nineteenth and twentieth centuries.

WILLIAM CRONON is Associate Professor of History at Yale University, where he teaches courses in the history of the American West and North American environmental history. He is the author of *Changes in the Land: Indians, Colonists, and the Ecology of New England* (1983), and has a forthcoming book on the history of Chicago's relationship to its western hinterland in the second half of the nineteenth century, entitled *Nature's Metropolis: Chicago and the West, 1848–1893*. He is currently president of the American Society for Environmental History.

RICHARD W. ETULAIN is Professor of History and director of the Center for the American West at the University of New Mexico, where he teaches courses in western and cultural history and historiography. His most recent books are *Conversations with Wallace Stegner on Western History and Literature* (1983, 1990), *Faith and Imagination* (1985), *Ernest Haycox* (1988), *The Twentieth-Century West: Historical Interpretations* (coedited with Gerald D. Nash, 1989), and *The American West: A Twentieth-Century History* (coauthored with Michael P. Malone, 1989). He edits the Oklahoma Western Biographies series, coedits (with Gerald D. Nash) the series Contemporary America: The U.S. Since 1945, and is currently at work on a cultural history of the modern American West.

ROBERT V. HINE is Professor of History at the University of California, Riverside. He has taught western American history there since the campus opened. His most recent books are *The American West: An Interpretive History* (1984), *California's Utopian Colonies* (1983), *In the Shadow of Frémont: Edward Kern and the Art of American Exploration, 1845–1860* (1982), and *Community on the American Frontier: Separate but Not Alone* (1980). His biography of Josiah Royce is forthcoming.

PATRICIA NELSON LIMERICK is Professor of History at the University of Colorado, Boulder. Born and raised in Banning, California, she is the author of *Desert Passages: Encounters with the American Deserts* (1985) and *The Legacy of Conquest: The Unbroken Past of the American West* (1987). She is preparing a new book entitled *Troubled Land: Failure and Defeat in Western Expansion.*

MICHAEL P. MALONE is Professor of History and President of Montana State University. His major books include *Montana: A History of Two Centuries* (with Richard B. Roeder, 1976), *The Battle for Butte: Mining and Politics on the Northern Frontier, 1864–1906* (1981), *Historians and the American West* (edited, 1983), and *The American West: A Twentieth Century History* (coauthored with Richard W. Etulain, 1989). He is co-editor of the University of Nebraska Press series on the twentieth-century West, and he is currently at work on a biography of James J. Hill.

LEE CLARK MITCHELL is Professor of English and director of the program in American Studies at Princeton University, where he teaches courses in American literature and intellectual history. He has written *Determined Fictions: American Literary Naturalism* (1989) and *Witnesses to a Vanishing America: The Nineteenth-Century Response* (1981), and has published widely on Stephen Crane, Henry James, and Mark Twain. His present project is "Writing Westward: Imagining America beyond the Frontier," a book-length study of the formula Western from Cooper to Peckinpah.

CHARLES S. PETERSON is a Professor of History at Southern Utah State College and Professor Emeritus at Utah State University. He is a former editor of the *Western Historical Quarterly* and a former director/editor of the Utah Historical Society and *Utah Historical Quarterly*. He is author of *"Take Up Your Mission": Mormon Colonizing along the Little Colorado River* (1972); *Look to the Mountains: Southeastern Utah and the La Sal National Forest* (1975); and *Utah: A Bicentennial History* (1977). He is currently working on a history of Utah from statehood to the end of World War II (1896 to 1945).

MICHAEL C. STEINER is Professor of American Studies at California State University, Fullerton, where he teaches courses in American cultural history, regionalism, folk studies, and the built environment. He has published in the fields of western history and cultural geography, has recently coauthored with Clarence Mondale *Region and Regionalism in the United States* (1988), and is currently completing a book on American regional theory during the 1920s and 1930s.

ELLIOTT WEST is Professor of History at the University of Arkansas, where he teaches courses in western and American Indian history. He is the author or editor of four books, including *Growing Up With the Country: Childhood on the Far-Western Frontier* (1989) and *The Saloon on the Rocky Mountain Mining Frontier* (1979). He is currently at work on two books on the social history of the plains frontier.

DONALD E. WORCESTER is Ida and Cecil Green Distinguished Emeritus Tutor at Texas Christian University, where he teaches courses on historiography and writing and editing. His most recent books are *The Texas Cowboy* (1986), *The Spanish Mustang: From the Plains of Andalusia to the Prairies of Texas* (1986), *The Texas Longhorn: Relic of the Past, Asset of the Future* (1987), *The War in the Nueces Strip* (fiction, 1989) and *A Visit from Father and Other Tales of the Mojave* (1990). He has served as president of the Western Writers of America, the Western History Association, and Westerners International. He has received two Spurs for nonfiction and the 1988 Saddleman award from Western Writers of America and is currently writing historical fiction.

Index